Continental and Mediterranean imports to Atlantic Britain and Ireland, AD 400–800

Continental and Mediterranean imports to Atlantic Britain and Ireland, AD 400–800

by Ewan Campbell

CBA Research Report 157
Council for British Archaeology
2007

Published 2007 by the Council for British Archaeology
St Mary's House, 66 Bootham, York YO30 7BZ

Copyright © 2007 Author and Council for British Archaeology

ISBN 978 1 902771 73 1

British Library Cataloguing in Publication Data
A catalogue for this book is available from the British Library

Cover designed by BP Design, York

Typeset by Archetype IT Ltd, www.archetype-it.com

Printed and bound in the UK by The Alden Press

Front cover illustrations: (clockwise from top left) E1 jar, Loch Glashan E140; polychrome plaque, Mote of Mark M4; St Menas flask, Meols M1; Glass Group A, with wheel-engraved letters, Whithorn G294; Glass Group B, complete phial, Mullaroe G219

Back cover illustration: Iona Abbey, looking east from Torr an Aba

Contents

List of figures viii
List of plates x
List of tables xii
Acknowledgements xiii
Summary xiv
List of sites xvii

1 Introduction. 1
   1.1 Research aims 1
   1.2 Scope and terminology 3
   1.3 Previous research 4
   1.4 Approaches to the data 7
   1.5 Methodology and structure 11

2 Mediterranean pottery 14
   2.1 Phocaean Red Slipware 14
   2.2 African Red Slipware 16
   2.3 Late Roman Amphorae 18
   2.4 Mediterranean coarsewares 24
   2.5 Mediterranean 'packages' 25

3 Continental pottery 27
   3.1 *Dérivées sigillées paléochrétiennes*, Atlantic Group 27
   3.2 Class E ware 32
   3.3 Miscellaneous wares 52

4 Imported glass 54
   4.1 Introduction 54
   4.2 Group A: Late Roman/Mediterranean tradition 56
   4.3 Group B: Germanic tradition 60
   4.4 Group C: decorated Atlantic tradition 64
   4.5 Group D: undecorated Atlantic tradition 69
   4.6 Group E: Whithorn tradition 69
   4.7 Form and function 72
   4.8 Conclusions 73

5 Miscellaneous material 74
   5.1 St Menas flask 74
   5.2 Coins 74
   5.3 Unclassified pottery 76
   5.4 Other Byzantine finds 78
   5.5 Other Continental finds 78

5.6 Miscellaneous material 79
5.7 Conclusions. 82

6 Patterns of consumption: taphonomic studies at Dinas Powys 83
6.1 Techniques of analysis 83
6.2 Pottery distributions. 87
6.3 Glass distributions. 92
6.4 Reinterpretation of the phasing of Dinas Powys 96
6.5 Social interpretation of distributions 97
6.6 Conclusions. 101

7 Patterns of consumption: taphonomic studies at other sites 102
7.1 Tintagel. 102
7.2 Cadbury Castle. 103
7.3 Longbury Bank. 103
7.4 Trethurgy. 104
7.5 Loch Glashan. 105
7.6 Whithorn 106
7.7 Conclusions. 108

8 Patterns of distribution: import site characteristics 109
8.1 Ireland 109
8.2 Scotland 116
8.3 Wales and the Marches 117
8.4 Somerset 118
8.5 Cornwall and Devon 119
8.6 Summary of Welsh and English sites 122
8.7 Summary of import site characteristics. 123

9 Mechanisms of distribution. 125
9.1 The Late Roman background 125
9.2 The Mediterranean trading system. 126
9.3 The Continental trading system 132
9.4 Conclusions: changing distribution systems 138

10 Conclusions 140

Bibliography 142
Index 155

Electronic media deposited with ADS

Relational database with detailed catalogue of sites and import groups
GIS allowing display and querying of data

Appendices
Appendix 1 Fabrics of import wares
Appendix 2 Full description of E ware
Appendix 3 Origin of Group C cone beakers with 'merrythought' chevrons
Appendix 4 Dyestuffs on E ware
Appendix 5 Charter of St-Denis
Appendix 6 Catalogue and reassessment of unpublished metalwork and other finds from Dinas Powys
Appendix 7 Contexts and sizes of pottery from Dinas Powys
Appendix 8 Distributions of miscellaneous material from Dinas Powys
Appendix 9 Reinterpretation of the phasing of Dinas Powys

List of Figures

1	Major kingdoms and regions in early medieval Britain and Ireland	1
2	Location of all sites with imported material in the Atlantic West	2
3	Import routeways c 600, after Hodges 1982 and Campbell 1991	10
4	Phocaean Red Slipware from Insular sites	15
5	Distribution of Insular PRS	16
6	PRS distribution in the western Mediterranean	16
7	African Red Slipware from Insular sites	17
8	Distribution of Insular ARS	18
9	Chronology of Insular ARS	18
10	Distinctive features of Insular LRA	20
11	Forms of Late Roman amphorae found in Insular contexts	21
12	Reconstruction of unidentified LRA (B34) from Dinas Powys	22
13	Distribution of LRA	22
14	Relative proportions of LRA types in Insular and western Mediterranean contexts	23
15	Reconstruction of LR2 amphora (B38) from Dinas Powys	23
16	Distribution of the eastern Mediterranean and north African 'packages' of wares	25
17	Distribution of Insular DSPA	27
18	Comparison of relative proportions of DSPA forms in France and Insular sites	28
19	DSPA from Insular sites	29
20	DSPA from Insular sites	30
21	Forms of E ware	33
22	Relative proportions of different E ware forms	34
23	Volume of E ware forms	35
24	Rim and body diameter ratios of E ware forms	35
25	E ware from Insular sites. Form E_{1B}, large jars	36
26	E ware from Insular sites. Form E_{1C}, small jars	37
27	Continental white gritty wares from Frankish cemeteries	38
28	E ware from Insular sites. Form E_1, jars	40
29	E ware from Insular sites. Form E_2, beakers	41
30	E ware from Insular sites. Form E_3, bowls	42
31	E ware from Insular sites. Form E_4, jugs	43
32	E ware from Insular sites. Form E_{4B}, tubular-spouted jugs	44
33	E ware from Insular sites. Form E_5, lids; Form E_6, bottle; Form E_7, carinated jar	45
34	Distribution of E ware	46
35	Continental E ware	47
36	Rim forms of E_1 jars	50
37	Late white gritty wares	53
38	Reconstructions of Group Cb cone beaker from Dinas Powys and Group E cone beaker from Whithorn	54
39	Distribution of glass imports	55
40	Imported glass from Insular sites. Group A, Mediterranean tradition	57
41	Imported glass from Insular sites. Group B, Germanic tradition	59
42	Imported glass from Insular sites. Group Ca, decorated Atlantic tradition	66
43	Imported glass from Insular sites. Group Cb, decorated Atlantic tradition	67
44	Imported glass from Insular sites. Group Cc, decorated Atlantic tradition	68
45	Distribution of Group C glass	69
46	Imported glass from Insular sites. Group D, undecorated Atlantic tradition	70
47	Imported glass from Insular sites. Group E, Whithorn tradition	71
48	Distribution of Group B glass and possible supply routes from Anglo-Saxon England	73
49	Distribution of miscellaneous imported material	74
50	Miscellaneous imported pottery	77
51	Theoretical sherd size curves for low-fired prehistoric ware, small well-fired vessels and large well-fired vessels	84
52	Maximum sherd size curves for all E ware from Dinas Powys and a single trampled vessel (E27) from Dalkey Island	84
53	Maximum sherd size curves for E ware from sites with different depositional histories	85

54	Theoretical sherd size curves for a single assemblage through successive phases of degradation	86
55	Two possible sherd size curves for different parts of the same vessel	86
56	Main features of Dinas Powys	88
57	Distribution of individual PRS vessels at Dinas Powys	88
58	Distribution of sherds from three LRA vessels at Dinas Powys	89
59	Distribution of DSPA vessels at Dinas Powys	90
60	Distribution of E ware vessels at Dinas Powys	90
61	Distribution of vessels found in building drip gullies, showing fanning out from Building 2 to the midden areas	91
62	Dinas Powys distribution of pottery vessels by function	91
63	Distribution of glass vessel sherds at Dinas Powys	93
64	Distribution of individual Group C glass vessels with chevron trails	94
65	Distribution of fused glass at Dinas Powys	95
66	Cut 17 at Dinas Powys	97
67	Alcock's original phasing of Dinas Powys	98
68	Rephasing of Dinas Powys	98
69	Suggested activity areas at Dinas Powys	99
70	Maximum sherd size curves for ARS and PRS from Radford's excavations at Tintagel	102
71	Maximum sherd size curves of LRA from Cadbury Castle	103
72	Whithorn stratigraphy, showing actual position of E ware vessel sherds	106
73	Whithorn stratigraphy, with individual E ware vessels and processes of dispersal upwards and downwards	106
74	Whithorn stratigraphy, with first occurrence of E ware vessels	106
75	Whithorn stratigraphy, showing first occurrence of Mediterranean vessels	107
76	Whithorn stratigraphy, showing first occurrence of glass vessels	107
77	Suggested trading routes for E ware	112
78	Political map of Ulster in the Early Historic period, with E ware sites	113
79	Ulster sites with souterrain ware and E ware, showng political boundaries	113
80	Changing distribution systems for imported pottery	125
81	Late Roman material from Ireland	126
82	Association of Mediterranean imports with tin and lead production	130
83	Comparison of distribution of all Mediterranean and Continental imports	133
84	Contoured distribution map of E ware	134
85	Suggested date ranges of imports	139

List of Plates

(between pages 108 and 109)

1 Phocaean Red Slipware with stamped hares, Dinas Powys P13
2 African Red Slipware, Whithorn A29–32
3 LR1 complete vessel, Turkey
4 LR1 amphora with red-painted graffito, Whithorn B245
5 LR2 amphora with graffito, Whithorn B242
6 LR3 amphora, Whithorn B246
7 DSPA, Dinas Powys
8 DSPA mortarium showing crudely formed pouring spout, Dunadd D11 (© Trustees of the National Museums of Scotland)
9 E ware fabric in thin section, Dunadd E79
10 E ware showing string cut-off on base, Buiston E12 (© Trustees of the National Museums of Scotland)
11 E ware handle showing wheel-thrown profile, Dunadd E74 (© Trustees of the National Museums of Scotland)
12 E ware spout showing finger-smearing and attachment method, Buiston E13 (© Trustees of the National Museums of Scotland)
13 E ware handle, showing finger-smearing attachment, Dunadd E76 (© Trustees of the National Museums of Scotland)
14 E ware showing orange oxidised firing marks on exterior, and grey reduction patch on interior, Iona E108 (© Trustees of the National Museums of Scotland)
15 E_1 jar, Dunadd E56 (© Trustees of the National Museums of Scotland)
16 E_2 beaker, with sooting showing secondary reuse, Buiston E12 (© Trustees of the National Museums of Scotland)
17 E_3 bowl, Dunadd E69 (© Trustees of the National Museums of Scotland)
18 E_4 jug, Dunadd E76 (© Trustees of the National Museums of Scotland)
19 E_{4B} spouted pitcher, Buiston E13 (© Trustees of the National Museums of Scotland)
20 Late form of E_1 jar, Loch Glashan E140
21 Glass Group A, with wheel-engraved letters, Whithorn G294, 296
22 Glass Group B, claw beaker, Dinas Powys G93
23 Glass Group B, squat jar, Dinas Powys G83
24 Glass Group B, complete phial, Mullaroe G219 (National Museum of Ireland)
25 Glass Group B, claw beaker, Dunnyneill Island G370
26 Glass Group B, reticella vessel, Birsay G7 (© Trustees of the National Museums of Scotland)
27 Glass Group B, opaque red/brown streaky glass, Birsay G13 (© Trustees of the National Museums of Scotland)
28 Glass Group B, bichrome green/yellow vessel, Birsay G6 (© Trustees of the National Museums of Scotland)
29 Glass Group B, turquoise vessel, Dunadd G137 (© Trustees of the National Museums of Scotland)
30 Glass Group B, moulded ribs of palm cup, Whithorn G300
31 Glass Group Cb, reconstructed cone beaker rims, Dinas Powys G98, 101
32 Glass Group Ca, rim of cone beaker with opaque white trails, Mote of Mark G274 (© Trustees of the National Museums of Scotland)
33 Glass Group C, bichrome vessel with blue rim, Whithorn G326
34 Glass Group C, vessel with white rim, G305 Whithorn
35 Glass Group Cc, Mote of Mark, decoration of festoons (© Trustees of the National Museums of Scotland)
36 Glass Group C, Whithorn, pink/amber diachroic G276
37 Glass Group E, Whithorn, G342, showing unmarvered white trails dragged alternately up and down
38 St Menas flask, Meols M1 (D Griffiths)
39 Gold-leaf glass tessera, Dunadd G140 (© Trustees of the National Museums of Scotland)
40 Silver-in-glass bead, Loch Glashan M13

41	Polychrome plaque, Mote of Mark M4 (© Trustees of the National Museums of Scotland)
42	Polychrome plaque, Mote of Mark M4, showing original edge with iron staining (© Trustees of the National Museums of Scotland)
43	Dinas Powys, drip gully of Building 2 which acted as an artefact trap (L Alcock)
44	Dunadd, looking west (Crown copyright: RCAHMS)
45	Ardifuir, looking south down the Sound of Jura from the interior of the dun (Crown copyright: RCAHMS)
46	Loch Glashan from the west (Crown copyright: RCAHMS, Horace Fairhurst collection)
47	Dunollie, looking north (Crown copyright: RCAHMS)
48	Dumbarton Rock from the Clyde, looking north (Crown copyright: RCAHMS)
49	Iona Abbey, looking east from Torr an Aba
50	Little Dunagoil, Bute, looking west
51	Mote of Mark, looking north (reproduced by courtesy of David Longley)
52	Whithorn Priory, site of main excavations
53	Deganwy, looking west along the north Wales coast
54	Hen Gastell during excavation
55	Tintagel, general view looking north
56	Tintagel, the harbour

List of Tables

1	Relative ranking of top ten sites in each import group (MNV)	31
2	Sites with unusual forms of E ware	45
3	Sooting on E ware bases	51
4	Distribution of colours amongst imported glass groups	55
5	Types of decoration in imported glass groups	56
6	Forms of imported glass vessels	72
7	Vessel-to-sherd ratios for pottery at Dinas Powys, Cadbury Congresbury and Cadbury Castle	87
8	Vessel-to-sherd ratios for E ware from different sites	87
9	Weight (g) of fused and unfused glass at Dinas Powys	95
10	Percentage recovery of imported vessels at Trethurgy	105
11	Pottery on early medieval sites in Ulster	115

In Appendices

12	Summary of imported Mediterranean pottery and glass vessels (MNV)
13	Summary of imported Continental pottery and glass vessels (MNV)
14	Summary of imported glass vessels, Groups A–E (MNV)
15	Summary of E ware vessel forms (MNV)
16	Import site characteristics: Cornwall and Devon
17	Import site characteristics: Wales and Somerset
18	Import site characteristics: Ireland
19	Import site characteristics: Scotland and Isle of Man
20	Heavy mineral analyses of E ware and other wares
21	Neutron activation analyses of E ware
22	Results of dye analysis on E ware vessels

Acknowledgements

An artefact-based study such as this relies on the help of numerous individuals and institutions, not all of whom can be named personally. However I would like to thank the staff of the following museums for their help in allowing access to their collections: National Museum of Wales (Mark Redknap, Yolanda Stanton and Liz Walker); National Museum of Ireland (Michael Ryan, Raghnall Ó Floinn and Pat Wallace); Ulster Museum (Richard Warner); National Museum of Scotland (David Clarke, Trevor Cowie, Mike Spearman, Fraser Hunter, Andy Heald, Craig Angus and Ian Scott); British Museum (Sue Youngs); Stranraer Museum (John Pickin); Newport Museum (Bob Trett); Tenby Museum (John Tipton); Glasgow Museum and Art Gallery (Helen Adamson and Colleen Batey); Hunterian Museum (Euan MacKie); Museum of Islay Life (Irene Miller), Isle of Man Museum; Royal Institute of Cornwall, Truro; Bute Museum, Rothesay; Torquay Museum; Exeter Museum (John Allan); Winchester Museums Service; University College, Cork; and Tours depôt (Bernard Randoin).

I would also like to extend particular thanks to all those individuals who have allowed me access to unpublished artefacts and/or stratigraphic details from their excavations: Leslie Alcock (Dinas Powys, Dumbarton Rock, Dundurn, Cadbury Castle); Paul Ashbee (Bar Point); W F L Bigwood (Kildalloig Dun); Paul Blinkhorn (Athelney); John Bradley (Moynagh Lough); BUFAU (Cefn Cwmwd); David Caldwell (Dundonald); Brigitte Camus (Chadenac); Sheila Cregeen (Poltalloch); Anne Crone (Buiston); Barry Cunliffe (Le Yaudet); Ian Doyle (Cabinteely); Sandy Gerrard (Carew Castle); Margaret Gowen (Marshes Upper); Peter Hill (Whithorn); Charles and Nancy Hollinrake (Carhampton); Jeremy Huggett and Chris Arnold (New Pieces); Heather King (Clonmacnoise); Lloyd Laing and David Longley (Mote of Mark); Con Manning (Killederdardrum); Chris Morris and Colleen Batey (Tintagel); David Neal (Samson); Mary O'Donnell (Kedrah); Pendragon Society (Llanellen); Henrietta Quinnell (Trethurgy); Philip Rahtz (Cadbury Congresbury); Richard Reece (Iona); Chris Saunders (Grambla); Charles Thomas (Gwithian, Tean, Tintagel); Sam Turner (Mothecombe); and Paul Wilkinson (Hen Gastell). I am particularly indebted to Leslie Alcock, David Caldwell, Ian Doyle, John Lewis, Philip MacDonald, Kevin Martin, Cathy O'Mahony, Jenny Price, Cliona Papazian, Richard Warner and Jonathan Wooding for bringing new finds of imports to my attention. Special mention must be made of the help given to me by the late Professor Leslie Alcock, who generously provided me with access to the original site records and plans of his excavations at Dinas Powys, as well as discussion of the stratigraphy.

A number of specialists have helped with particular parts of this monograph: Penny Walton Rogers with the analyses of dyestuffs and information on madder; John Percival with a translation and comments on a Carolingian charter; and Stephen Driscoll with NAA analysis of E ware. The staff, students and postgraduates of the department of Archaeology, UWCC (now University of Cardiff), provided a supportive environment during the writing of my PhD thesis, but I would like to mention in particular Viola Diaz, Bob Jones, J P Brown, Howard Mason and John Morgan for technical support. At the University of Glasgow, staff have similarly provided much support, and I would particularly like to thank Jeremy Huggett for much patient advice with the computing aspects of the data. The line illustrations were prepared for publication by Lorraine McEwan from originals by the author. Photographs not by the author are acknowledged separately, but I would particularly like to thank Duncan Anderson for taking the photographs of material in the National Museums of Scotland's collections and the Trustees for permission to reproduce them.

This monograph has benefited from numerous discussions with colleagues, particularly James Graham-Campbell, Ken Dark, Wendy Davies, Leslie Alcock, Nancy Edwards, Michael Fulford, Jeremy Knight, David Longley, Margaret Nieke, Keiran O'Conor, Stephen Driscoll, Peter Hill, Paul Williams, Jonathan Wooding, and other members of the Early Medieval Wales Research Group. The original postgraduate research was funded by a grant from the Board of Celtic Studies, and the University of Glasgow's Hunter Marshall Fund made a substantial contribution to publication costs. Most of all I would like to thank my supervisor Alan Lane, who gave constant encouragement to finish the original thesis, and my partner Ronni Richards for sharing me with this project over too many years.

Summary

Imported pottery and glass is of fundamental importance in assessing the chronology and function of sites in Atlantic Britain and Ireland in the period AD 400–800, but these have not previously received detailed publication. This monograph gives an integrated discussion of the finds, covering not just their provenance, typology, dating and distribution, but also their function in society. The text is supplemented by an interactive Web-based database giving full details of all finds, including their stratigraphic context, which will be updated as new finds occur.

The study shows that two successive trading systems brought this material to Insular sites. The first of these brought Late Roman amphorae (LR1–4) and fine red-slipped tablewares from the eastern Mediterranean and north Africa in a restricted period from the late 5th to mid-6th centuries. The second system brought glass vessels, finewares and coarsewares from western France in the later 6th and 7th centuries. Both trading systems were sustained rather than haphazard, but neither seems to have been fully commercial market trading. The Mediterranean trading system shows direct links with Byzantium, and it is suggested that there was Imperial involvement, perhaps centred on the acquisition of tin, lead and silver from mines in south-west England. The later Continental system also has peculiarities which suggests the involvement of Merovingian elites, though the motives are less clear.

Material from almost 150 sites is listed, including around 370 Mediterranean and 600 Continental pottery or glass vessels. A new classification of the glass is presented, Groups A–E, which will enable more accurate dating of sites. Scientific analysis suggests that the Continental coarsewares (Class E) were used as transport containers for luxury goods such as purple dyes.

Novel methods of analysing small assemblages are introduced (most sites produce only a few vessels), based on taphonomic study of the finds from key sites such as Dinas Powys, Glamorgan, Wales, and Whithorn Priory, Galloway, Scotland. An analysis of the characteristics of all the sites on which imports are found suggests that the main sites were royal, and that the elites on these sites controlled redistribution of exotic luxury goods to their client sites in order to bolster their social position. The nature of the return trade is unclear, but metals and slaves are likely to have been the major goods traded.

This book is intended for both British and Continental specialists who wish for full details of the pottery and glass, but also for anyone with an interest in how trade and exchange influenced the development of Insular society at a time of transition from the late Roman/late Iron Age period to the emerging kingdoms of the Middle Ages.

Résumé

Le verre et la céramique importés sont d'une importance fondamentale quand il est question d'évaluer la chronologie et la fonction des sites en Irlande ainsi que sur la côte atlantique de la Grande-Bretagne durant les années 400 à 800 mais, précédemment, ces importations n'avaient pas fait l'objet d'une publication détaillée. Cette monographie présente une discussion structurée des découvertes car elle couvre non seulement leur provenance, leur typologie, leur datation et leur répartition, mais également leur fonction dans le contexte social. Une base de données interactive sur la Toile s'ajoute à ce texte, fournissant des détails complets sur toutes les découvertes, y compris leur contexte stratigraphique, et ces détails seront mis à jour au fur et à mesure de l'apparition de nouvelles découvertes.

L'étude montre que deux systèmes successifs d'échanges commerciaux avaient apporté ce matériel aux sites insulaires. Le premier de ces systèmes avait apporté des amphores de la fin de la période romaine (LR1–4) ainsi que de belles sigillées rouges en provenance de la Méditerranée orientale et d'Afrique du Nord pendant une période allant de la fin du 5ème siècle au milieu du 6ème siècle. Le deuxième système avait apporté des vaisseaux en verre, des céramiques de pâte fine et des céramiques de pâte grossière en provenance de l'Ouest de la France à la fin du 6ème siècle et au 7ème siècle. Les deux systèmes d'échanges commerciaux étaient soutenus plutôt que pratiqués n'importe comment, mais ni l'un ni l'autre ne semble avoir été un négoce à base entièrement commerciale. Le système des échanges commerciaux méditerranéens indique l'existence de liens directs avec Byzance et on a suggéré que l'empire y participait, participation peut-être axée sur l'achat d'étain, de plomb et d'argent provenant des mines du sud-ouest de l'Angleterre. Vers la fin, le système continental témoignait également de certaines particularités qui suggèrent que des membres de l'élite mérovingienne y participaient, bien que les motifs soient moins clairs.

Du matériel provenant de près de 150 sites est porté sur la liste, y compris environ 370 vaisseaux en verre ou en céramique provenant de la Méditerranée et 600 provenant du continent européen. Une nouvelle classification du verre est présentée, les groupes A-E, ce qui permettra d'effectuer une datation plus précise des sites. L'analyse scientifique suggère que les céramiques de pâte grossière provenant du continent européen (Classe E) étaient utilisées en tant que récipients pour le transport d'articles de luxe tels que les teintures pourpres.

De nouvelles méthodes d'analyse de petits ensembles sont introduites (la plupart des sites n'ont fourni que quelques vaisseaux), sur la basé de l'étude taphonomique des découvertes provenant de sites clés tels que Dinas Powys, au Glamorgan, dans le pays de Galles, et le Prieuré de Whithorn, au Galloway, en Ecosse. Une analyse des caractéristiques de tous les sites sur lesquels ont découvertes des importations suggère que les principaux sites étaient royaux, et que les élites implantées dans ces sites contrôlaient la redistribution des articles de luxe exotiques à leurs sites clients dans le but d'étayer leur propre position sociale. La nature de l'échange commercial en retour n'est pas claire, mais il est probable que les métaux et les esclaves étaient les principaux articles du commerce.

Ce livre est conçu à la fois pour les spécialistes et britanniques et continentaux qui désirent obtenir des détails plus amples concernant la céramique et le verre, et également pour tous ceux qui s'intéressent à l'influence exercée par le négoce et les échanges sur le développement de la société insulaire pendant une période de transition entre la fin de l'ère romaine/la fin de l'âge du fer et l'apparition des royaumes du moyen-âge.

Zusammenfassung

Importierte Keramik und Glas sind von fundamentaler Bedeutung, wenn es darum geht, die Chronologie und Funktion von Fundstätten entlang der Atlantikküste von Großbritannien und Irland in der Zeit von 400–800 AD zu beurteilen. Diese Abhandlung beinhaltet eine vollständige Diskussion der Funde, sie umfaßt nicht nur deren Herkunft, Typologie, Datierung und Verteilung, sonder auch deren Funktion innerhalb der Gesellschaft. Der Text wird durch eine interaktive Webseite ergänzt, in der alle Details und der stratigraphische Zusammenhang aller Funde aufgelistet wird, und die mit neuen Funden laufend aktualisiert wird.

Diese Studie zeigt, daß durch zwei, zeitlich abgegrenzte Handelssysteme Materialien in entlegene Siedlungen gebracht wurden. Die erste Handelsperiode brachte spätrömische Amphoren (LR1–4) und Tafelgeschirr aus *terra sigillata* aus dem östlichen Mittelmeer und Nordafrika. Diese Periode war nur von kurzer Dauer und reichte vom späten 5. bis in die Mitte des 6. Jahrhunderts. In der zweiten Handelsperiode, vom späten 6. bis 7. Jahrhundert, wurden Grasgefäße, Feinkeramik und Grobkeramik aus Westfrankreich importiert. Beide Handelssysteme waren nicht willkürlich, sondern von dauerhafter Natur, sie können aber nicht nur als reine kommerzielle Marktwirtschaft angesehen werden. Das mediterrane Handelssystem hatte eine direkte Verbindung mit Byzantinum, und es wird vorgeschlagen, daß Königshäuser beteiligt waren, vor allem beim Erwerb von Zinn, Blei und Silber von Minen aus südwest England. Das spätere kontinentale Handelssystem wies ebenfalls Besonderheiten auf, die auf den Einfluß der Merowinger deuten könnten, die Motive sind aber weniger offensichtlich.

Material aus fast 150 Fundstellen wird aufgelistet, und besteht aus Keramiken und Glasgefäßen von denen 370 aus dem Mittelmeerraum und 600 aus dem Europäischen Festland stammen. Eine neue Klassifikation der Glasgefäße wird beschrieben, Gruppen A-E, die es ermöglicht die Fundstellen noch präziser zu datieren. Wissenschaftliche Analysen haben gezeigt, daß die Rohkeramiken aus dem Europäischen Festland (Klasse E) als Transportgefäße für Luxusgüter benutzt wurden, wie zum Beispiel Farbstoff aus Purpur.

Neue Methoden um kleine Fundgruppen zu untersuchen, werden vorgestellt (von den meisten Fundstellen wurden nur wenige Gefäße geborgen), sie basierten auf taphonomische Studien von typischen Fundgruppen, wie die aus Dinas Powis, Glamorgan, Wales, und das Priorat von Whithorn aus Galloway, Schottland. Eine Analyse der Charakteristiken von Fundstellen, bei denen importierte Waren gefunden wurden, hat gezeigt, daß die wichtigsten Fundstellen von Herrscherklassen geprägt wurden, und daß diese Eliten die Weiterverteilung von Luxusgütern an andere Empfänger kontrollierten, um ihre soziale Position zu verbessern. Mit welcher Art Gegenware gehandelt wurde, ist unklar, es wird angenommen, daß sie hauptsächlich aus Metallen und Sklaven bestand.

Dieses Buch richtet sich an Spezialisten aus Großbritannien und dem europäischen Festland, die an einer vollständigen Inventur von Keramik und Glas interessiert sind, aber auch an alle, die sich dafür interessieren, wie Handelsaustausch die Entwicklung von isolierten Gesellschaften beeinflußt hat, in einer Zeit, die vom Übergang aus der spätrömischen/späten Eisenzeit zu den aufsteigenden Königreichen des Mittelalters geprägt war.

List of sites

Sites referred to in the text. Site names in capitals are those with accepted material; those in upper and lower case have rejected or uncertain material.

Old counties have been used, with new ones given in brackets. British sites have OS grid references; Irish sites have Irish grid references

Site name	Other identifier	County	Country	Grid reference
Abercorn		West Lothian (Lothians)	Scotland	NT 082 792
ARDIFUIR		Argyll (Strathclyde)	Scotland	NR 788 969
ARMAGH, CASTLE ST.		Armagh	Ireland	2876 3453
ATHELNEY		Somerset	England	ST 34 28
BALLINDERRY No. 2		Offaly	Ireland	2215 2391
BALLYCATTEEN		Cork	Ireland	1582 0459
BALLYFOUNDER		Down	Ireland	3621 3496
BANTHAM		Devon	England	SX 663 437
BAR POINT	St Mary's, Scilly	Cornwall	England	SV 918 129
BORDEAUX	St Seurin	Gironde	France	
BROUGH OF BIRSAY	Mainland	Orkney	Scotland	HY 24 29
BRUACH AN DRUIMEIN	Poltalloch	Argyll	Scotland	NR 820 972
BRYHER	Scilly	Cornwall	England	SV 87 14
BUISTON	Buston crannog	Ayrshire (Strathclyde)	Scotland	NS 415 435
CABINTEELY	Mount Offaly, Dalkey	Dublin	Ireland	3233 2242
CADBURY CASTLE	South Cadbury, Cadbury Camelot	Somerset	England	ST 628 252
CADBURY CONGRESBURY		Somerset (Avon)	England	ST 440 650
CAHERLIHILLAN	Cathair Leithuilleann, Iveragh	Kerry	Ireland	0572 0835
CALDEY ISLAND		Pembroke (Dyfed)	Wales	SS 143 968
CANNINGTON CEMETERY		Somerset	England	ST 255 405
CAREW CASTLE		Pembroke (Dyfed)	Wales	SN 045 037
CARHAMPTON	Eastbury farm	Somerset	England	ST 012 427
CASHEL	Cormac's Chapel	Tipperary	Ireland	20750 14100
CASTLE HILL, DALRY	Howrat	Ayr (Strathclyde)	Scotland	NS 286 538
CATHAIR FIONNURACH	Cathair a Bhoghas Bally-navenooragh, Dingle	Kerry	Ireland	0429 1107
CEFN CWMWD	Rhostrehwfa, Anglesey	(Gwynydd)	Wales	SH 45 74
CHADENAC		Charente-Maritime	France	
CHUN CASTLE		Cornwall	England	SW 405 339
CLATCHARD CRAIG		Fife	Scotland	NO 243 178
CLOGHER		Tyrone	Ireland	2540 3514
CLONMACNOISE		Offaly	Ireland	2011 2308
COLP WEST		Meath	Ireland	3122 2746
COYGAN CAMP		Carmarthen (Dyfed)	Wales	SN 284 092
CRAIG PHADRAIG		Inverness (Highland)	Scotland	NH 640 453

xvii

Site name	Other identifier	County	Country	Grid reference
Craigs Quarry		East Lothian (Lothians)	Scotland	NT 508 836
CRUACH MHOR	Islay	Argyll (Strathclye)	Scotland	NR 30 54
DALKEY ISLAND		Dublin	Ireland	3279 2262
DEGANWY		Caernarfon (Gwynedd)	Wales	SH 783 795
DERRYNAFLAN		Tipperary	Ireland	2180 1495
DIAL ROCKS	Tresco, Scilly	Cornwall	England	SV 8890 1556
DINAS EMRYS		Caernarfon (Gwynedd)	Wales	SH 606 492
DINAS POWYS		Glamorgan (South Glamorgan)	Wales	ST 148 722
DOLPHIN TOWN	Tresco, Scilly	Cornwall	England	SV 8936 1537
DOOEY	Cloghastucken	Donegal	Ireland	1758 4016
DOWNPATRICK	Cathedral Hill	Down	Ireland	3482 3445
DRUMACRITTEN No.1		Fermanagh	Ireland	2549 3327
DUMBARTON ROCK	Alt Clut	Dunbarton (Strathclyde)	Scotland	NS 400 744
DUN ARDTRECK	Skye	Inverness (Highland)	Scotland	NG 335 358
DUNADD		Argyll (Strathclyde)	Scotland	NR 837 935
DUNDONALD CASTLE		Ayr (Strathclyde)	Scotland	NS 364 345
DUNDURN		Perth (Tayside)	Scotland	NN 707 232
DUNGARVAN CASTLE		Waterford	Ireland	2262 0930
DUNNYNEILL ISLAND	Strangford Lough	Down	Ireland	35474 35384
DUNOLLIE		Argyll (Strathclyde)	Scotland	NM 852 315
EDERLINE	Loch Awe,	Argyll	Scotland	NM 8821 0394
Elie	Elie Links	Fife	Scotland	NO 470 020
GARRANES	Lisnacaheragh	Cork	Ireland	1473 0641
GARRYDUFF No. 1		Cork	Ireland	1925 0862
GLASTONBURY MOUND	Beckery	Somerset	England	ST 488 388
GLASTONBURY TOR		Somerset	England	ST 512 387
Gloucester	St Oswald's Priory	Gloucestershire	England	SO 83 18
Goodrich Castle		Hereford	England	SO 575 196
GRACEDIEU		Dublin	Ireland	3170 2526
GRAMBLA		Cornwall	England	SW 693 283
GRANSHA		Down	Ireland	3531 3769
GUISSENY		Finisterre	France	
GWITHIAN		Cornwall	England	SW 585 422
HALLIGGYE		Cornwall	England	SW 714 239
HAM HILL		Somerset	England	ST 478 170
HELLESVEAN		Cornwall	England	SW 505 400
HEN GASTELL	Briton Ferry	Glamorgan	Wales	SS 73 94
HERPES	Courbillac, Rouillac	Charente	France	
HIGH PEAK		Devon	England	SY 103 859
INISCEALTRA		Clare	Ireland	1698 1850
IONA		Argyll (Strathclyde)	Scotland	NM 286 245
KEDRAH		Tipperary	Ireland	2062 1227
KELSIES		Cornwall	England	SW 772 604
KILBRIDE	Corraneary	Cavan	Ireland	26340 33560
KILDALLOIG DUN		Argyll (Strathclyde)	Scotland	NR 745 190

Continental and Mediterranean imports to Atlantic Britain and Ireland, AD 400–800 xix

Site name	Other identifier	County	Country	Grid reference
KILLEDERDADRUM		Tipperary	Ireland	1950 1721
KILLIBURY		Cornwall	England	SX 008 737
KILLUCAN		Westmeath	Ireland	2575 2558
KIONDROGHAD			Isle of Man	NX 396 002
KNOWTH		Meath	Ireland	2999 2738
LAGORE		Meath	Ireland	2986 2528
LANGFORD LODGE		Antrim	Ireland	3096 3750
LAVRET	Ile de Brehat	Cotes-du-Nord	France	
LE YAUDET	Ploulec'h, Lannion	Cotes-d'Armor	France	
LES CLEONS	near Haute-Goulaine	Loire-Atlantique	France	
LESSER GARTH		Mid-Glamorgan	Wales	ST 126 822
LINNEY BURROWS	Brownslade	Pembroke (Dyfed)	Wales	SR 896 976
LISDOO		Fermanagh	Ireland	2363 3332
LISDUGGAN NORTH No.1		Cork	Ireland	1433 1039
LISLEAGH 1		Cork	Ireland	1786 1065
LITTLE DUNAGOIL		Bute (Strathclyde)	Scotland	NS 086 532
LLANDOUGH		Glamorgan	Wales	ST 1679 7325
LLANELEN		(West) Glamorgan	Wales	SS 511 933
LOCH GLASHAN		Argyll (Strathclyde)	Scotland	NR 916 925
LOCHLEE		Ayr (Strathclyde)	Scotland	NS 455298
LONGBURY BANK		Pembroke (Dyfed)	Wales	SS 112 999
LOOE ISLAND	St George's Island	Cornwall	England	SX 257 515
LOUGH FAUGHAN		Down	Ireland	3446 3411
LOUGHSHINNY	Drumanagh	Dublin	Ireland	3270 2560
Luce Sands	Mid Torrs	Kirkcudbright (Dumfries & Galloway)	Scotland	NX 135 559
LUSK		Dublin	Ireland	3220 2540
LYDFORD		Devon	England	SX 510 847
MARGAM		(West) Glamorgam	Wales	SS 819 867
MARSHES UPPER No. 3		Louth	Ireland	3080 3060
MAWGAN PORTH		Cornwall	England	SW 854 672
MAY'S HILL	St Martin's, Scilly	Cornwall	England	SV 936 155
MEOLS	Wirral	Cheshire	England	SJ 21 89
MOTE OF MARK		Dumfries & Galloway	Scotland	NX 845 540
MOTHECOMBE		Devon	England	SX 610 474
MOYNAGH LOUGH		Meath	Ireland	2819 2860
MULLAROE		Sligo	Ireland	1533 3318
Nendrum		Down	Ireland	3524 3636
NEW PIECES		Montgomery (Powys)	Wales	SJ 298 140
NEWTONLOW CRANNOG		Westmeath	Ireland	2379 2369
PADSTOW	Harbour Cove	Cornwall	England	SW 912 768
PAGANS HILL	Chew Stoke	Avon (Somerset)	England	ST 556 626
PERRAN SANDS		Cornwall	England	SW 770 560
PHILLACK		Cornwall	England	SW 565 385
PORT Y CANDAS			Isle of Man	SC 285 816
Portlaoise			Ireland	198 247

Site name	Other identifier	County	Country	Grid reference
RANDALSTOWN	St Anne's Chapel	Meath	Ireland	2846 2712
RATHGUREEN	Cottage townland, Dunkellin barony	Galway	Ireland	13877 22002
RATHINTAUN (CRANNOG No. 61)	Lough Gara	Sligo	Ireland	1727 3004
RATHMULLAN		Down	Ireland	3478 3373
REASK		Kerry	Ireland	0365 1043
REAWLA		Cornwall	England	SW 605 363
SAINT-LAURENT-DES-COMBES	Gueyrot	Gironde	France	
SAMSON	Scilly	Cornwall	England	SV 878 128
SCRABO HILL		Down	Ireland	3477 3726
Slievegrane Lower	Saul	Down	Ireland	35157 34543
SMITHSTOWN		Meath	Ireland	3130 2704
SPITTAL BALLEE		Down	Ireland	3526 3415
ST MERRYN		Cornwall	England	SW 865 749
ST MICHAEL CAERHAYS		Cornwall	England	SW 976 414
ST MICHAEL'S MOUNT		Cornwall	England	SW 52 30
Swords		Dublin	Ireland	3180 2470
TARBAT	Portmahomack	Easter Ross	Scotland	NH 914 839
Taunton		Somerset	England	ST 23 24
TEAN	Scilly	Cornwall	England	SV 908 165
TEESHAN		Antrim	Ireland	3080 4065
TINTAGEL		Cornwall	England	SX 05 89
TOURS		Indre-et-Loire	France	
TRETHURGY	St Austell	Cornwall	England	SX 034 556
Trim		Meath	Ireland	257 281
VILLEBOIS-LAVALETTE	Grotte	Charente	France	
WENLOCK PRIORY	Much Wenlock	Shropshire	England	SJ 625 001
WHITHORN		Wigtown (Dumfries & Galloway)	Scotland	NX 440 403

1 Introduction

1.1 Research aims

The imported goods of the title of this corpus consist mainly of pottery from the Mediterranean as well as both pottery and glass from north-western Europe. The study incorporates the results of nearly twenty years' specialist work by the author on this material. These imports are of importance for the study of Atlantic Britain and Ireland in the early medieval period for a number of reasons. Firstly, some at least of the pottery is closely datable in its production area, meaning that it can be used for independent dating on sites which often have no other means of being accurately dated. The second major area of importance of the imported pottery is as an indicator of trade and exchange, which in turn gives some insight into the economic development and social status of sites where the imports are found, with implications for the nature of society as a whole. This is of use in supplementing the extremely meagre historical documentation for trade in this period, as well as enabling comparisons to be made with other areas such as Anglo-Saxon England and Continental Europe. Finally, the stratigraphic and taphonomic context of the material gives us detailed information both on stratigraphic sequences, and on patterns of usage and consumption, which can give insights into the complex interaction between material culture and personal and social identity.

These chronological, economic and cognitive fields of enquiry do not exist in a vacuum, of course. The period AD 400–800 is one of the major transitional periods of British history, lying between the period of Roman colonisation and the development of the early medieval states from a mosaic of small polities (Fig 1). Discussion of the imports has become tied up in a number of academic debates which revolve around this transitional period. These include the nature and speed of the end of *Romanitas* in Britain, with some arguing for catastrophic change in the early 5th century, others a period of Late Antiquity lasting until the 7th century, and others at points between these two poles (see for example the papers in Collins and Gerrard 2004; Wilmott and Wilson 2000). Related to this is the question of identity: were the Britons of the Atlantic West an unchanged Romano-British population, a resurfacing Iron Age indigenous populace, or a new hybrid post-Roman people developing their own unique identity (see for example Dark 1994, 255–7; cf Hines 2000)? In terms of economics, were the imports the result of personal travel, mercantile trade, prestige good exchange, or diplomatic initiatives from Byzantium (see papers in Dark 1996; Harris 2003; Kingsley and Decker 2001; Wooding 1996b)? Finally, the imports have been related to the question of post-Roman urbanism in north-western Europe: can the import sites be viewed as 'proto-urban' (for background see Hodges and Hobley 1988; Carver 1993; 2000; Doherty 1980)? Many of these issues are inter-related, but there is very little good-quality archaeological data from the Atlantic region which can be utilised in discussion. The importance of the imports as indicators of social and economic development has been recognised in regional studies, for example in south-west England (Pearce 2004, 235–9; Turner 2006, 54–6), as well as in works of Europe-wide synthesis (Wickham 2005, 814–16).

The larger assemblages of imports are found on sites which have a played a key role in the interpretation of Early Historic society. These sites include Tintagel in Cornwall (Radford 1935; Thomas 1993); Cadbury Castle (Alcock 1995) and Cadbury Congresbury (Rahtz *et al* 1992) in Somerset; Dinas Powys in south Wales (Alcock 1963a; 1987); Whithorn Priory (Hill 1997) and the Mote of Mark (Laing and Longley 2006) in south-western Scotland; Dunadd in western Scotland (Lane and Campbell 2000); Clogher in Ulster (Warner 1979); and Lagore in Meath (Hencken 1950). These sites have been significant in the development of our understanding

Fig 1 Major kingdoms and regions in early medieval Britain and Ireland

of the period due to, for example: the early use of scientific excavation and production of a contextualised report (Dinas Powys); the quantities of finds (Tintagel); the range of material recovered (Lagore, Dunadd); or the well-stratified deposits (Clogher, Whithorn). The import assemblages on these sites have in turn influenced the excavators' interpretations of the sites: Radford (1956, 69) related the imports to a monastic interpretation of Tintagel; Alcock (1963a, 55) saw them as signs that Dinas Powys was a princely court or *llys* settlement; Hill (1997, 28) viewed them as an indication of monastic immigrants from Gaul; and Lane and Campbell (2000, 253) used them to support the view that Dunadd was a royal inauguration site.

Because of their chronological sensitivity, the imports are a key, perhaps *the* key, factor in any discussion of these complex issues. The imports therefore deserve to be published fully in order that any claims based on this evidence can be properly assessed. Accordingly, this monograph sets out to provide those core data, along with a reasoned interpretation of the significance of the material based on the archaeological evidence they provide. Unlike many pottery and glass assemblages, the quantities involved are very small (most sites produce only one or two sherds). This had two consequences for this study. Firstly, as it was important to extract as much information as possible from this sparse material, all aspects of the production/distribution/consumption/discard cycle were considered in detail, with chapters here on typology, distribution and taphonomy. Secondly, techniques of analysis had to be developed to deal specifically with small assemblages and assess their importance (Chapter 6.1).

There are many practical difficulties in the study of the imported material, which has been found on almost 150 sites in Ireland, Scotland, England and Wales (Fig 2). Several of the important sites are unpublished or were unpublished when this work was commenced in the early 1980s (many of the major sites have only been published in the last ten years), and much of the material is scattered widely over western England, Wales, Scotland and Ireland, making it difficult for any one person to examine every sherd. Although some of the material is in museums, much is still in private (mainly excavators') hands, contributing to the difficulty of study. Hand-lists of some of the material have been published at various times, but these contain neither full descriptions, comprehensive illustrations nor contextual information (Radford 1956; Harden 1956; Thomas 1959; 1981; Peacock and Thomas 1967; Wooding 1996b; Campbell 1988b; 2000a). Despite this preliminary work almost all the major aspects of the imported pottery are or have been controversial, with arguments over the date, provenance, function and significance of the material, and even the identification of many of the sherds. A full publication of the material is therefore necessary, and the opportunity has been taken to make the underlying data available by Internet dissemination through

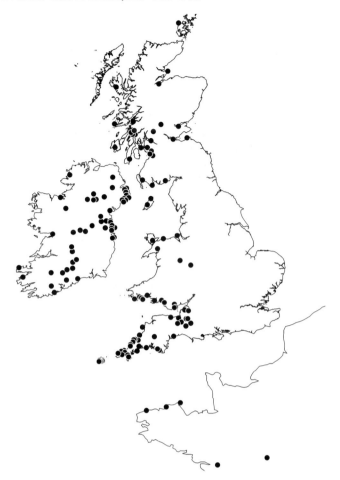

Fig 2 Location of all sites with imported material in the Atlantic West

the Archaeology Data Service. These data consist of a relational database (see below Chapter 1.5), with site co-ordinates which allow for incorporation of the data in a GIS, and a series of additional appendices and tables giving more detailed information on aspects of the imports.

The basis of this corpus is my unpublished PhD thesis (Campbell 1991), work mainly undertaken in the mid-1980s. Since the mid-1980s, I have published a large number of specialist reports on imported material from individual sites and areas (Campbell 1986a; 1986b; 1988b; 1989a; 1989b; 1995b; 1997; 2000a; 2000b; 2000c; 2004; forthcoming a; Campbell and Lane 1993a; Crone and Campbell 2005), but also a number of generic papers summarising my conclusions (Campbell 1996a; 1996b, Campbell and Bowles forthcoming). The report on the Whithorn material also had an extended discussion on the nature of the imports (Campbell 1997). A wide-ranging review of glass imports resulted in a new classification in 'traditions' as Groups A–E, in a paper of proceedings from a 1986 conference (Campbell 2000a). Group A were vessels in the Late Antique Mediterranean tradition, often with wheel abraded decoration. Group B vessels belong to the 'Germanic' tradition of Anglo-Saxon England and the adjacent parts of the Continent. Groups C and

D formed the main bulk of the Atlantic area imports from western Gaul, while Group E vessels were confined to Whithorn.

Although the study covers both Mediterranean and Continental imports, it concentrates the detailed descriptions on the Continental wares (E ware pottery and Groups B–E glass), as these were more widely distributed, and least known in terms of chronology and provenance, when I started this work. Inevitably, over the twenty years during which this study has been undertaken, my ideas and techniques have developed and changed. This has caused some problems in the variability of recording, as it has proved impossible to revisit all the material for this publication (see Chapter 1.5). Despite some minor inconsistencies, I believe the corpus will be a valuable tool for understanding a major transitional period, the development of the medieval state from its Roman and Iron Age predecessors, as well as providing data for a variety of educational purposes.

1.2 Scope and terminology

The *chronological range* of the corpus is the post-Roman, pre-Viking period, roughly AD 400–800. There is no generally accepted term for this period in the geographic areas covered. The period has been referred to as the Dark Ages, the Migration Period, the Age of Invasions, the Age of Saints, sub-Roman, Early Christian, early medieval, Early Historic, Anglo-Saxon, post-Roman, pre-Norman, Late Antique, Late Celtic and Late Iron Age depending on the background, date, area of study or theoretical stance of the author. At present in Britain, the terms Early Historic, early medieval and Early Christian are in general use, with Late Iron Age in some northern Atlantic coastal areas where continuity of Iron Age communities is clear. All of these terms have problems, and it is difficult to promote one over another. In the context of this publication, which will be of interest to readers on the Continent as well as in Britain, I have used terms with generic European significance. I have chosen to use **early medieval** as the commonly accepted term for the period from the 5th to 11th centuries (Hines 2003, 199). Although my own personal preference is for Dark Age for the period of the 5th to 9th centuries, I will here use **Early Historic**, following Prof Leslie Alcock's influential definition (Alcock 1981, 150), as the period when indigenous documentary sources begin to appear (as opposed to writings of outsiders from the Mediterranean world). When I use **Roman** it refers to the period of Roman imperial occupation of Britain, ending by AD 410; **post-Roman** refers to the immediately succeeding period.

The *geographic scope* of the study is the whole of Ireland and of Britain west of the areas of Anglo-Saxon influence (Fig 1). This area is sometimes referred to as the 'Celtic West', as the peoples inhabiting it spoke languages of the Celtic group (Welsh, Manx, Cornish, Cumbric, Pictish and Gaelic). However, the problems associated with the label 'Celtic' (for a review see James 1999) make it preferable to use the neutral geographic identifier the '**Atlantic façade**' (eg Cunliffe 2001, 18, fig 1.9) or '**Atlantic West**' for this area. Similarly, the term 'British Isles', while geographically correct, has unfortunate political overtones for post-colonial Ireland. Usually I will use '**Insular**' in opposition to 'Continental', as a descriptor for the whole of Britain and Ireland, and '**Britain**' for island of Britain (ie England, Wales and Scotland).

A further problem relates to the use of the term 'Irish' to translate the '*Scotti*' of early medieval Latin sources. It is well known that the word *Scotti* mutated in meaning during this period, initially describing people from Ireland, then all Gaelic speakers, whether in Ireland or Scotland, before being applied to the peoples of Scotland, whether or not Gaelic speakers, and now used as a term for English speakers in Scotland (see Ferguson 1998 for a summary). To translate *Scotti* as 'Irish' runs the risk of confusion between people from Ireland and Irish (ie Gaelic) speakers. Given the considerable debate over the origins of Scottish Gaelic speakers (Campbell 2001), it is more neutral to translate the term as '**Gaelic**'. Indeed some historians and linguists are now using the term 'Old Gaelic' instead of 'Old Irish' for the same reasons.

There seems to be a clear distinction in both the types and provenances of imports to Britain in the Early Historic period, Anglo-Saxon areas receiving material from the Mediterranean via the Rhone/Rhine overland route (Huggett 1988; Harris 2003), and the Atlantic areas receiving a different set of material by the western sea-route. It could be argued that this distinction is a self-fulfilling one, the product of archaeologists only examining assemblages in their respective areas. While there may be a small element of this at work here, as I did not search many collections outside my chosen geographical area, I do not believe it is significant. At Whithorn, which was a major Atlantic import site in the 6th and 7th centuries, importation ceased when the Anglo-Saxons gained control of the site in the early 8th century. Other import sites which came under the area of control of Anglo-Saxons in the 7th century in Somerset seem to cease receiving Atlantic imports at this time. At other sites in Anglo-Saxon areas which might be expected to have the Atlantic type of imports because of links with western areas (eg Jarrow, Poundbury), careful searching has not produced any material. Specialists in Anglo-Saxon glass have not recognised the distinctive Group C–E material on a single Anglo-Saxon site, and it is improbable that Phocaean Red Slipware and Late Roman amphorae could lie unrecognised in Anglo-Saxon pottery assemblages. While some Anglo-Saxon material is found on western sites, particularly in Somerset and south-eastern Scotland, I know of no instance where Atlantic imports are found on an Anglo-Saxon site. The pottery from the one site claimed to have such material, Abercorn (West Lothian), turned out to be later medieval.

The *terminology* of the pottery and glass has been undergoing a process of development over the last 50 years. Radford (1956) originally defined four groups of pottery, labelled Class A–D wares, later expanded with Classes E–G by Thomas (1959). As sources have been identified it has become normal to apply names used in the production area rather than these alphabetical group names. This process has not been consistent, and in particular British authors have tended to keep the labels for amphora sub-types (B*i*, B*ii*, B*iv* etc). As these types are well known in the Mediterranean under their own terminology (most usefully as Riley's Late Roman Amphora 1–8), this will be used here to allow easier comparison with publications dealing with the production areas. Similarly D ware is now referred to, using the Rigoirs' terminology, as DSPA (Rigoir 1968; Rigoir *et al* 1973). Only Thomas's E ware has not had its production area discovered, and so remains in use, both here and on the Continent. Although it would be possible to propose a name such as Atlantic White Gritty Ware for E ware, it seems better to await discovery of kiln sites and name it from these as is normal practice in medieval pottery studies.

1.3 Previous research

An imported pottery vessel, an E ware beaker from Buiston crannog, was illustrated as long ago as 1882 (Munro 1882, fig 250), and the pottery now known as E ware was recognised as being of early medieval date certainly by 1929 (Craw 1930), and possibly even earlier (Curle 1914, 164). However, it was not until Ralegh Radford's excavation of Tintagel in the 1930s that it was suggested (on advice from Mortimer Wheeler) that some of this pottery was imported (Radford 1935, 415). The work of the Harvard expeditions to Ireland also in the 1930s produced many vessels which Hencken (1950, 125) believed, probably on the advice of Gerhard Bersu, might be of Merovingian origin, but the Second World War interrupted the search for a source.

It was Radford's publication of the Tintagel pottery in 1956 which marked the start of the proper study of imported pottery in what was then called Dark Age Britain and Ireland. In his paper he classified the wares at Tintagel into four classes, labelled A to D, and provided a catalogue of sites with similar wares which he believed to be imports (Radford 1956). Radford recognised the Mediterranean origin of his Classes A and B ware, and that his Class A (fine redslipped bowls) had two distinct fabrics, A*i* and A*ii*. His Class C was suggested to be of French origin, but he could give no suggestion as to the provenance of Class D, except to notice a general resemblance to late Romano-British vessels. He dated the Class A wares to the mid-5th to 6th centuries, possibly lasting into the 7th (*ibid*, 69). Radford viewed the presence of the Mediterranean pottery as evidence of trade bringing wine, oil and tableware 'for the service of the Church or the luxury of the rulers' (*ibid*, 69). The return trade he suggested, on the evidence of Strabo and Patrick's *Confessio*, to be slaves, hunting dogs and possibly leather, along with Cornish tin, Irish gold and copper. The dating and provenance of these Mediterranean wares did not advance further until modern excavations in the Mediterranean produced well-dated sequences. Indeed as late as 1963 Alcock could argue for the possibility of a Roman (pre-AD 400) date for the Classes A, B and D (Alcock 1963b, 285–90).

Meanwhile, in the early 1950s Charles Thomas was excavating another Cornish site, Gwithian, which produced some of the Tintagel groups of pottery along with further types. In a series of short papers (Thomas 1954; 1956; 1957) he added to and refined Radford's classification, leading eventually to a wide-ranging review of all the wares (Thomas 1959). In this paper he gave better descriptions of Radford's Classes A and B, dividing Class B into four sub-groups B*i*, B*ii*, B*iii* and B*iv*. For the first time it was recognised that some of the Class A vessels were of eastern Mediterranean origin, the Late Roman B or C of this area. The B*i*, B*ii* and B*iv* amphorae were also attributed to the east Mediterranean, possibly the Greek Islands or Byzantium. Thomas also suggested that B*i* held wine and B*ii* olive oil, and concurred with Radford's suggestion that these contexts were 'to fulfil the liturgical needs of the Celtic Church, or to indulge the nostalgic tastes of local chieftains' (*ibid*, 91). Class C was pointed out to be of medieval local manufacture, and since 1959 the term has not been used. Class D remained problematic: while noting Alcock's view of a possible origin in the Bristol Channel area, Thomas noted that similar wares were found in France (*ibid*, 95).

Thomas also extended Radford's classification, creating Classes E, F and G. Class E included both the Gwithian coarse gritty pottery and that which had been found on Irish sites by Hencken in the 1930s, and on Scottish sites such as Dunadd and Mote of Mark at various earlier times. E ware was divided into five forms, E*i*–E*v*. Thomas's Classes F and G were later abandoned, being found to be mainly Romano-British in origin (Thomas 1981), though one example of Class F from Dunadd has been reinstated as an unclassified Continental import (Lane and Campbell 2000, 102–3, Fabric A2). As for Class E ware, Thomas proposed a Rhenish origin and a date of the 5th to 8th centuries (*ibid*, 105), suggested a function as 'a coarse kitchen ware', and mentioned the close association of E ware and imported glass, which at that time was also believed to be of Rhenish origin (*ibid*, 106). In the absence of documentary evidence for trade with this area he suggested Frisian merchants were trading with Cornwall, a point he later developed in relation to the bar-lug pottery of Cornwall (Thomas 1968). A much fuller catalogue than Radford's of all the import wares was appended to this classic paper. The realisation that glass was also imported at this period also came in the 1950s with Harden's publication in the Leeds' *Festschrift* of a summary of the material from Celtic sites along with that from Anglo-Saxon graves (Harden 1956a, 149–52). Harden suggested a Merovingian origin for the glass from Celtic sites and introduced the speculation that some of it was being brought in and used as scrap to make inlay for jewellery.

In the late 1950s Bernard Wailes undertook a thesis on the imported pottery of Britain (Wailes 1963). Wailes studied the northern French pottery in detail and it is his work that Thomas drew on in his 1959 paper when suggesting a Rhenish origin for E ware. Wailes made his drawings of northern French vessels from cemetery assemblages available to me (Fig 27) and these generally show that this material is similar to, but not identical with, E ware.

Thus by the end of the 1950s the main outlines of the study of imported pottery and glass had been defined and a period of consolidation ensued. The publication of *Dinas Powys* in 1963 presented a new assemblage of imported pottery and glass (Alcock 1963a). Alcock's discussion of the imported pottery followed the same line as his other 1963 paper in the Cyril Fox *Festschrift* already mentioned, in being sceptical of an entirely post-Roman date for Classes A and B (*ibid*, 126–31). However it was Harden's analysis of the Dinas Powys glass fragments that was to have a lasting impact (Harden 1963). Harden dated this glass to the 5th and 6th centuries, and suggested that this date applied to the glass from other sites in Celtic areas (*ibid*, 179). He also suggested that the distinctive white-trailed glass which predominates at Dinas Powys and other western sites was specially chosen as broken sherds to bring to the west. Alcock took up this point in the main discussion, suggesting that the glass was imported as cullet for jewellery and bead making (Alcock 1963a, 52–3). The date and function of the glass found on Celtic sites had, since the Dinas Powys report, been interpreted in these terms, until my own re-evaluation of the Dinas Powys material reached different conclusions (first published in Campbell 1993).

The later 1960s and the 1970s saw little new research in this area. The excavations at South Cadbury (Cadbury Castle), Cadbury Congresbury and Glastonbury Tor provided many new examples of the wares but most of these were not fully published for another twenty years. In 1967 Thomas, along with David Peacock, put forward a new theory of the provenance of E ware, based on petrological work (Peacock and Thomas 1967), suggesting an origin in the Paris basin or Aquitaine (probably the latter), rather than the Rhineland. The petrological basis of this work was questioned by myself in 1984, when I showed that the heavy mineral analysis of the E ware was not distinctive of the Aquitaine, though it did not rule out this area (Campbell 1984). Meanwhile, in France, the work of the Rigoirs had established a typology and chronology for Radford's D ware (Rigoir 1968; Rigoir *et al* 1973). Their work showed that D ware was one regional group (hereafter DSPA) of a tradition of Late Roman stamped fine slipwares, named by them *dérivées des sigillées paléochrétiennes*. They recognised three separate groups of these wares, one in the Languedoc, one in Provence and one in western France. This last group (*groupe Atlantique*) contained exact parallels to the reduced greywares found at Dinas Powys, the other two groups tending to be earlier in date and consisting mainly of oxidised redwares.

The next major advance came in 1979 when Richard Warner gave a brief outline of the results of his excavations on the Irish royal site of Clogher, Co. Tyrone (Warner 1979). Warner showed that there was a clear stratigraphic differentiation between the Mediterranean wares (B*i*, B*ii*), which occurred in the ditch of the earlier enclosure, and E ware, which was found at a higher level in the ditch of the ringfort, the two ditches being separated by a sterile layer of yellow clay. Warner dated the yellow layer to the late 6th century by a combination of historical documentation, radiocarbon dates and typological methods, and suggested that E ware was not common in the west until the 7th century. This view was supported by Alcock as a result of his Scottish excavations, particularly at Dunollie, and he expressed his view that E ware may have continued into the 8th century (1983b, 49). However, throughout the 1970s and most of the 1980s Charles Thomas continued to suggest a much earlier starting date for E ware, based on the supposed evidence from Gwithian which he suggested showed contemporaneity of E ware and the Mediterranean wares (Thomas 1976b; 1981; 1982).

While the controversy over the date of the Continental imports was simmering in Britain much work was being carried out in the Mediterranean which led to an elucidation of the dating, provenance and typology of the Mediterranean wares found in Britain. John Hayes, in his *Late Roman Pottery* (1972) and *A Supplement to Late Roman Pottery* (1980), established the typology and chronology of 'Late Roman C' and 'Late Roman B' as well as other red slipwares of the Mediterranean. Late Roman C was renamed Phocaean Red Slipware (PRS) as evidence for its production in ancient Phocaea (western Turkey) became clear (Langlotz 1969; Mayet and Picon 1986). Hayes' work showed that the British examples of PRS belonged to his Form 3, as did most other western Mediterranean examples, which he dated to the period AD 450–*c* 600. Hayes divided Form 3 into eight sub-types (3A–H), based on the rim form, shape of vessel and decoration, giving very precise dates to each type, based largely on the evidence from the Athenian Agora excavations. Hayes dated the British examples known to him using this system: for example the well-known stamped dish from Dinas Powys, which adorns the dust jacket of the report, was dated by him to *c* 460–490 (Hayes 1972, 337). The precision of Hayes' dates can be criticised, as can his over-reliance on rim forms, but a general sequence of Form 3 can be discerned from early to late forms which enable fairly precise dates to be given to the Insular finds.

Hayes' work also resolved the confusion between 'Late Roman B' and 'Late Roman C' (roughly equivalent to Radford's Ai and Aii), identifying African Red Slipware (ARS) made in the Carthage area as the other major production centre of the 5th- to 7th-century Mediterranean fine wares. His dating of ARS, however, undertaken before the major Carthage excavations, was later subject to revision (Hayes 1977), causing some confusion amongst British workers (see Burrow 1979, 227, postscript). The dating and typology of ARS was finally clarified with the publication of the British expedition's excavations at Carthage (Fulford and Peacock 1984). Michael Fulford's section on the fine wares enabled me to date the British examples by comparing the Carthage groups with the whole British assemblage (Chapter 2.2), but the work had more wide-ranging implications as Fulford and Peacock attempted to give a history of trading relationships in the Mediterranean based on a quantitative study of the Carthage amphorae. They were able to show, contrary to previous opinion, that the Vandal invasions of north Africa in the mid-5th century did not disrupt trade or pottery production. They suggested that trade with the eastern Mediterranean was mainly confined to the late 5th to mid-6th centuries, being ended by the reimposition of imperial control in the west by Justinian (*ibid*, 258–62).

While the chronology of the fine wares (ARS and PRS) was being refined, there was also a great deal of work being carried out on the amphorae. John Riley published a series of papers outlining the sequence of forms found on Late Roman sites in Palestine (1975), Benghazi (1979) and Carthage (1981). In the Benghazi report Riley identified a 'package' of Late Roman Amphora types which were commonly exported around the Mediterranean. These eight forms have become the standard nomenclature, as LR1–8, here adopted for the British examples. Another major work was that of Simon Keay (1984) on Spanish amphorae which provided a detailed study of many, mainly north African, amphorae from dated contexts in Catalonia. Keay's work confirmed that of Fulford and Peacock in terms of the date of the eastern Mediterranean trade to the west. This work on amphorae showed that most forms were long-lived, and therefore difficult to date accurately, though the ebb and flow of trade in different wares graphically illustrated the economic rise and fall of various regions.

Another aspect of the amphorae which came under increasing scrutiny was the question of provenances. The pioneering work on the petrology of amphorae was undertaken by David Peacock (1977a; 1977b; 1982), who contributed the amphorae report to the Carthage volume discussed above. This work culminated in *Amphorae and the Roman Economy: an introductory guide* (1986), published jointly with David Williams, which summarised the known typologies, provenances, dates and contents of Roman amphorae. This work, along with Keay's and Riley's, has brought order into what was a rather chaotic series of classification systems. Although Peacock and Williams specifically stated that their numbering system was not intended to replace other well-known systems (such as those of Robinson, Kuzmanov, Keay, Riley and Panella) it has been used as such by some authors. One other major publication at this time was Bass and Van Doornick's *Yassi Ada, a 7th-century Byzantine Shipwreck* (1982). This site gave valuable details of a trading vessel sunk *c* AD 625, which carried an amphora cargo consisting of LR1 and LR2, precisely those amphorae commonly found in Britain. Alcock, noting the large quantity of amphorae in this wreck's cargo, has argued against a substantial Insular trade with the Mediterranean in the 6th century, given the relatively small numbers of imported amphorae found on Insular sites (Alcock 1987, 90, fig 4.1).

More recently, there has been an upsurge of synthetic publications on Late Antique trade in the Mediterranean, with important publications by Parker (1992), Reynolds (1995), Vroom (2003) and Kingsley (2004) looking at patterns of trade in the Mediterranean of Late Antiquity. The proceedings of an Oxford conference on *Economy and Exchange in the East Mediterranean during Late Antiquity* (Kingsley and Decker 2001b) looked at a number of aspects of this trade. These publications have both refined typological and quantification studies, and also clarified issues of trade, shipping and social economy. Some papers from the Oxford conference have direct significance to the Atlantic trade routes, for example Mango's discussion of the information to be derived from the Life of St John the Almsgiver (Mango 2001), or Karagiorgou's on the possible function of LR2 as a container for the military *annona* (Karagiorgou 2001). A broader chronological and thematic view is provided by Barry Cunliffe's recent volume on the Atlantic seaboards, *Facing the Ocean: The Atlantic and its peoples* (Cunliffe 2001).

Returning to the Continental wares, a number of authors have discussed the trading system involved in its importation to Britain, starting with the Thomas (1959) paper mentioned above. Lloyd Laing in his *Archaeology of Late Celtic Britain and Ireland c 400–1200 AD* followed Thomas in believing E ware to be a cooking ware and coarse tableware (1975, 237). Richard Hodges, in a series of papers and books (1977; 1978; 1981; 1982; 1988; 1989) outlined a new theory of trade in the early medieval period based on an eclectic mix of theoretical stances including that of the economic anthropologist Polanyi, the new archaeology of Colin Renfrew, the new geography of Carol Smith and others, and historians such as Braudel. The resulting approach is a stimulating overview of the development of towns and the state in north-western Europe perhaps best summarised in *The Anglo-Saxon Achievement* (1989).

Hodges' thesis, in so far as it affects western Britain, can be summarised as follows. After the breakdown of the Late Roman marketing system, exchange of luxury goods was confined to the courts of local rulers. The growth of this trade by merchants between courts began to threaten the rulers' exclusive control over luxuries (and therefore power), leading the rulers to confine exchange within specific *emporia* where trade was under royal regulation. Hodges speculated that Charlemagne attempted to revive the economy of the markets by increasing this long-distance trade. Hodges divided early exchange places into two types: Type A, which consist of peripheral exchange centres or fairs; and Type B, which were true *emporia*. Dalkey Island is quoted as an example of Type A, and *Hamwic* as Type B (Hodges 1982, 51–2).

Hodges' theories will be discussed further, but as far as E ware is concerned he made little attempt to discuss the trade, and in fact did not show the Atlantic trading routes at all on his maps. He has suggested that wine was the key to this trade, and that 'adventurous Irish monks' were the traders involved: '[d]oubtless, the church led the way' in the importation of Continental pottery (Hodges 1977, 241). In this paper he suggested the trade permeated all levels of society, but in his 1982 book he saw the E ware trade as a 'directional trade, perhaps parallel with those preferring the Anglo-Saxon courts' (Hodges 1982, 37), though now the trade operated 'in both directions, though on a most inconclusive scale' (*ibid*, 38). He further suggested that the lack of Aquitanian gold coins in the Celtic West suggests that this trade did not commence before the early 7th century.

Chris Arnold, in his survey of the sub-Roman to Anglo-Saxon transition, also concentrated mainly on the English 'Saxon' area, but notes an apparent cultural divide between the Celtic and Anglo-Saxon areas in terms of the imported pottery (Arnold 1984, 116). He suggests that the concentration of Mediterranean pottery in south-west England could be because 'Cornish sailors loaded their boats with the metals and travelled to the Mediterranean returning with luxury commodities and religious inspiration', rather than Mediterranean traders coming to Britain (*ibid*). As we have seen, and as will be discussed in more detail, this is most unlikely given the evidence for Byzantine trade with the western Mediterranean and Spain at this period.

The authors quoted above have tended to discuss the imported pottery as a minor digression in the history of the trade and economic development of Saxon England, though Arnold does note that the concentration of power implied by the pottery occurs earlier in the Celtic West than in Anglo-Saxon England (*ibid*, 119).

A number of student theses have been undertaken on the imports from Ireland. In the early 1980s Mary O'Donnell undertook a survey of Irish E ware, though this thesis was unavailable to me (O'Donnell 1984). At the same time Edward Bourke was conducting a survey of imported glass in Ireland (Bourke 1987), later published in detail (Bourke 1994). In the 1990s Ian Doyle studied the Late Roman amphorae (Doyle 1996), and later produced a number of papers on specific items or sites (Doyle 1998; 1999). Jonathan Wooding wrote an undergraduate thesis on E ware, which was an admirable survey of the historical and published evidence (Wooding 1983). Wooding followed this up with a number of short papers derived from his PhD thesis on trade (Wooding 1987; 1988; 1996a), and finally with a major survey of the evidence for trade in the Atlantic areas (Wooding 1996b). Wooding's approach is discussed in the next section, but he also discussed the function of the imports, and classified the glass imports into three groups, as well as giving a valuable and incisive discussion of all the possible historical sources for trade in the period. He discusses the evidence for a wine trade with Bordeaux associated with E ware, showing that this is based on the outdated theories of Zimmer (1909), which can now be seen to be based on a false and biased view of certain historical sources (Wooding 1983, 54–63; 1987; 1996a). He concludes that E ware was part of the general cargoes of small tramp vessels, along with nuts, salt and wine traded in return for clothing and leather goods. He localises this trade in the mouth of the Loire on historical grounds and with Gaulish merchants. As will be seen I come to somewhat similar conclusions in this study, though with important differences on the organisation of the trade.

Wooding originally suggested that the function of E ware was in preparing porridge, which he claimed could not be made in wooden or metal cooking-pots (Wooding 1988). In his later work he is more circumspect, while still suggesting its use mainly as cooking ware (Wooding 1996b, 82), but also saying that 'Identifying a universal usage pattern for E ware may prove difficult, as any consumer may have found their own use for it' (*ibid*, 81). At the same time he dismisses my own arguments that it was mainly used as a transport container for luxury goods. These points will be discussed in detail later in Chapter 3.2.

1.4 Approaches to the data

Given the problem which this publication addresses, namely the nature and function of imported goods in the Atlantic façade, there are immediate constraints on any investigation imposed by the limitations of the evidence outlined in the opening sections of this chapter. This makes it necessary to try to maximise the use of the data which are available. The methodological approaches and problems which are involved in this study can be divided into three areas of increasing levels of generalisation.

At the most fundamental level is the cataloguing and typological classifying of the imported pottery and glass (Chapters 2–5). The only issues of theoretical approach involved in this part of the study relate to the problems of defining what is meant by a 'type' of pottery or a 'form', in this case relating to E ware and its forms. The Mediterranean wares have been classified in their area of production and that classification is adopted here as the Insular material is not sufficient for an independent analysis. The definition of types is a general problem which affects all natural sciences and has led to the development of attempts to apply objective criteria to the problem (numerical taxonomy) in the biological and geological fields (see Adams and Adams 1991 for a review).

A numerical, 'objective', approach to the classification of E ware did not seem appropriate to this study for a number of reasons which are fully discussed by Shephard (1956, 306–22). Firstly, the number of vessels involved is not large, and complete profiles can be obtained for only a handful of vessels of each apparent form. This would make any statistical results meaningless. Secondly, E ware is undecorated, meaning that very few characteristics are available to be analysed. Almost all the research on differentiating types of ceramics has been concerned with decorated wares (Plog 1980; Arnold 1985; Nelson 1985). Therefore in defining E ware it seemed more appropriate to adopt an all-inclusive definition when looking at the general analysis of its occurrence, while noting those examples which seemed to fall near the boundaries of the defined ware in order to see whether their inclusion would affect the overall results. In fact, this approach led to problems only in a tiny minority of cases (eg the Dun Ardtreck sherd E81), where it proved difficult to decide whether a sherd belonged to the E ware type or not. Such occasional outliers and anomalies are to be expected in any archaeological data-set. The few examples of imported wares generally similar to E ware, but outside the normal range of form or fabric, have been given the generic term 'late white gritty wares' (Chapter 3.3).

The second level of analysis involved on-site patterning of finds, particularly ceramics and glass, their relationship to rubbish disposal processes, and the implications of this in trying to reconstruct some aspects of social behaviour. The analysis of rubbish disposal patterns is a surprisingly recent development in archaeology, given that rubbish (in its broadest sense) is the primary data of all archaeology. Ülrike Sommer has suggested that the reasons for this may be in western industrialised society's cultural attitudes to dirt, which is equated with manual rather than mental labour: as she puts it, 'a career in ruins might be acceptable, but a career in rubbish certainly is not' (Sommer 1990, 50–2). Most of the work in this field has been carried out by American archaeologists of the processual school, based originally on the definitions of Schiffer (1972; 1976). Schiffer divided rubbish into two major categories: *primary refuse*, which has been deposited at its place of use; and *secondary refuse*, which has been redeposited elsewhere, by human, animal or soil processes. Refuse, in this widest sense, includes all artefacts, waste products and structures which have been left on a site to be discovered by archaeologists and which are therefore in some sense unwanted goods (rubbish). Primary refuse includes *de facto* refuse, items which were too large or heavy to be removed. In the early medieval period this category usually includes only earthworks and crannog substructures, though these too can be reused, removed or reincorporated in other structures.

It is obviously of prime importance for archaeologists to be able to distinguish between these two categories of rubbish, as primary refuse is material contemporary with its context while secondary refuse is often not. The principles behind attempts to distinguish modes of rubbish disposal are derived from the biological sciences, particularly palaeontology, and involve the study of taphonomy, the processes of decay and burial of an organism or, in the case of archaeology, an artefact. In this system the assemblage of artefacts in use on a site is equivalent to a biologist's 'living community' (*biocoenosis*), and those artefacts which are buried and survive to the present are a 'burial assemblage' (*taphocoenosis*). In archaeology. taphonomy in its widest sense describes the processes which occur after the discard of an artefact or ecofact and before its retrieval. These processes are mainly determined by the cultural attitudes of the inhabitants of a site to the artefacts or waste products concerned, and therefore give some hope of reconstructing at least some part of the belief system of these inhabitants (eg Moore 1982). 'Rubbish' and 'refuse' are clearly culturally determined categories, and a more neutral term such as discard might be preferable. Some discard, such as goods in grave deposits, was certainly intentional, and there is increasing evidence of structured deposition in early medieval as well as prehistoric contexts (Hamerow 2006). In addition to the well-known examples from Cadbury Congresbury and Cadbury Castle, other possible instances are discussed from Trethurgy and Dinas Powys.

Until fairly recently most taphonomic studies in archaeology have been concerned with biological taphonomy in prehistoric contexts (for instance to distinguish between scavenged and hunted bone assemblages) or flintwork debitage studies. Ceramic and glass studies are fewer and have only been adopted in Britain since the 1980s (for early examples see Bradley and Fulford 1980; Fischer 1985). In a study of Peruvian modern-day ceramics, DeBeor and Lathrop (1979, 127–34) examined the discard and reuse of ceramics (and all other rubbish) within a village compound. Several interesting results emerged from this study including the fact that the main house and the living area around it were kept virtually free of all rubbish. Primary refuse was concentrated in work areas which had not been swept up while secondary refuse collected around the margins of the site (*ibid*, fig 4.6). More minor concentrations occur near storage areas (where pots are often broken) and in eaves-drip gullies. As we shall see, this distribution is remarkably similar to that at Dinas Powys, despite the differences in culture, chronology and climate between the two sites. A further important innovation of this paper was the production of a sherd size graph to illustrate that sherds in trampled areas (pathways) were smaller than those in other areas (*ibid*, fig 4.8). This was the basis of the techniques which I developed to help to distinguish primary and secondary refuse on early medieval sites (Chapters 6–7).

It had been hoped that these studies would reveal regional or other patterns of refuse disposal, but the lack of building plans and well-recorded assemblages, meant that only a few case studies could be undertaken. No overall conclusions about cultural attitudes to rubbish disposal resulted (cf Moore 1982), but insight was gained into the processes of discard on particular sites.

Related to taphonomic studies is the concept of cultural biographies of objects (Kopytoft 1986) and structures (Gerritson 1999). These studies look at the changing patterns of use and symbolic meaning of artefacts over their lifetime of use. A specific example of this kind of analysis is my study of the sooting patterns on E ware, which shows that the vessels were often reused for a variety of purposes, changing their original function (Chapter 3.2).

At the third, and larger-scale, inter-site level of analysis of the imports, theoretical approaches are concerned with how patterns of distribution may relate to a society's economy and organisation. Colin Renfrew has put forward a series of models for types of distribution in pre-market economies which he suggested could be identified by differing fall-off curves (Renfrew 1977; Hodges 1982, 19). This type of distance-decay model does produce a pattern for E ware which is strikingly similar to Renfrew's model for directional trade and redistribution (Campbell 1991, illus 185). However, there are problems in relating the fall-off curves to particular systems of exchange (Hodder 1978a, 158–64) even before relating them to a particular type of social organisation, such as a central place of power under the control of a chieftain or ruler. The idea that the social organisation can be 'read off' the archaeological record, has, of course, been widely criticised but, nevertheless, if patterns exist in the archaeological data then these have to be explained. Rather than focusing on individual traits or models of exchange (for some of the dangers see Samson 1999), this thesis attempts to integrate the evidence of the imports with the structural, material and historical evidence of the import sites in order to put the imports in a meaningful context.

An important early attempt to consider the function of trade and exchange in the Atlantic West was Charles Doherty's 1980 paper *Exchange and Trade in Early Medieval Ireland*. Doherty attempted to integrate the documentary and archaeological evidence for exchange and trade with the anthropological work of Mauss, Polanyi and Sahlins. He was primarily concerned to try to show that Irish society was economically developed before the Viking impact, and that 'we can detect the emergence of a primitive medieval state' (*ibid*, 85). Doherty presented evidence from the Irish Law tracts in order to show how gifts were used to bind clients to lords and sub-kings to over-kings. The gifts of kings include prestige military equipment such as horses and swords as well as luxury items, while tribute to kings consisted mainly of agricultural render. The church had a similar system of exchange though as the return was usually a spiritual benefit, the wealth of the churches could increase through time. Doherty was at some pains to point out the role of monastic centres (some of which are termed *civitas* in contemporary sources) as places of internal exchange, though the evidence for this applies to the 9th century or later (*ibid*, 81). Perhaps this viewpoint led him to give undue prominence to the role of the church in the Early Historic pottery trade (*ibid*, 77), suggesting that wine for the Mass was the prime motive behind the trade. E ware is described as a 'luxury item' and at the same time 'kitchen ware', with no further explanation. Much of Doherty's evidence concerns a later period than our study, but is used in an attempt to show that Irish society was undergoing changes towards a market economy and urban development before the Viking trading stations such as Dublin were founded. Critiques of Doherty's approach have been articulated in papers by Mary Valante (1998) and Cathy Swift (1998). This debate impinges on general discussions of the concept of urbanism in the early medieval period, itself a major area of controversy since a resurgence of interest in the 1970s (Biddle 1976; Hodges and Hobley 1988; Carver 1993; 2000; Brogiolo and Wade-Perkins 1999). This debate is too broad to be considered in detail here, though the implications of the non-development of towns throughout the Atlantic West is addressed in the final chapter.

There is no doubt that changes were taking place in Irish society from the 7th century onwards, and this may explain the surge of collecting and writing down of secular laws, canon laws, annals and genealogies between 660 and 760, but there is little or no documentary evidence to show monastic or other church involvement in the trade in imported goods. As we shall see the archaeological evidence also does not support the idea of a church-based trade. However, if Doherty was right that by the 8th, or at the latest the 10th, century the monastic *oenach* or fair was the principal place of exchange in Ireland, it might help to explain why royal-controlled trading centres or towns did not develop in Ireland until Ireland fell under Norse domination. Despite the documentary evidence that kings were involved in law making in the field of trade (Doherty 1980, 79), Doherty presented little evidence to show royal involvement or direct control over it until the 10th century. Doherty's paper is useful in that it chronicles the gradual transformation of Irish society towards a market economy from a tribal redistributive economy and he showed the prime role of religious institutions in this process, but the chronology of the early part of this transformation and

Fig 3 Import routeways c 600: right, after Hodges 1982, fig 5; left, after Campbell 1991, illus 198

the means by which it occurred are not discussed in detail.

The major writings on trade in the early medieval period have been those of Richard Hodges (1982; 1988; 1989; 2000; Hodges and Whitehouse 1983). As already mentioned Hodges' work is based on a number of theoretical positions which seem to change in successive publications, making it difficult to criticise his theoretical stance coherently. Trade in the Atlantic façade is hardly considered by Hodges to be of any importance in a European context. For instance, his maps of trade routes in north-west Europe consistently ignore the Continental and Mediterranean trade discussed in this corpus (Fig 3). It may be that the rise of the English state and the development there of a market economy are regarded by Hodges as of more importance than the corresponding lack of these developments in the west, but his failure to note the evidence for the existence of similar trade in the 6th and 7th centuries in both areas undermines his thesis that trade was the crucial factor in the English (and French) developments. Critiques of Hodges' work have been given by Chris Arnold (1983) and at length by Grenville Astill (1985) and John Naylor (2004), and will not be repeated here.

The most recent publication on trade has been that of Wooding (1996b), *Communication and Commerce along the Western Sealanes AD 400–800*. Wooding gives a robust critique of previous approaches, including those of Zimmer at the beginning of the 20th century, the 'western seaways' theorists such as Crawford (1936) and Bowen (1969; 1972), and the work of archaeologists such as Hodges (1982) employing 'substantive' economic approaches. Wooding (1996b, 5) argues that archaeologists have been overly influenced by these earlier models in interpretations of the types of interaction indicated by the imports. Wooding also provides a thorough discussion of shipping and the sea-lanes from a sailing perspective, while integrating the documentary evidence. His main conclusions are that specific local political and social conditions led to different patterns of exchange which varied widely and intermittently even within the short early medieval period. As will be seen, I come to very similar conclusions. Where we differ is on the importance attached to the imports within each of the episodes, with Wooding being in favour of a more 'minimalist' interpretation on the 'tramp steamer' model (*ibid*, 96), while I argue for short periods of sustained semi-commercial trading driven by elites in Byzantium and Gaul.

1.5 Methodology and structure

In order to catalogue the pottery I established a recording form to ensure uniformity of data recording, and looked in detail at every sherd in order to resolve the following specific questions:

- how many vessels were represented on each site?;
- what was the context of the sherds and their relationship to other artefacts?;
- what evidence was there of function in terms of sooting, staining, residues or wear marks?

More general questions relating to the whole assemblage were: was all E ware from a single production area or were there variations in fabric which would suggest several centres of production?; what could be inferred about the ceramic technology of the ware?; what was the range of forms and how did they compare with known Merovingian forms?

The detailed discussion of the typology, chronology and function of the imports is given in Chapter 2 for the Mediterranean wares, Chapter 3 for the Continental pottery, in Chapter 4 for the glass, and in Chapter 5 for other miscellaneous material. Detailed catalogues of the Continental wares in the database are supplemented by briefer listings of the Mediterranean wares. A full discussion and analysis of E ware is given in Appendix 2, with a summary in Chapter 3.2. Summaries of the numbers and types of vessels of all the imports are given in Tables 12–15. The database is organised by category, with separate tables for each class of material, and one for the sites. The basic unit of recording is the vessel, with vessel numbers being assigned to most material: for ARS, A1, A2...; for LRA, B1...; for PRS, P1...; for DSPA, D1...; for E ware, E1...; for glass, G1...; for unclassified pottery, U1...; and for miscellaneous material, M1... Individual sherds are given sub-numbers where necessary; for example, E67.1 is a rim sherd of vessel E67 from Dunadd. These are the numbers quoted in the text.

I have already mentioned that various authorities have disagreed in the past about the attribution of sherds to the various import classes, leading, for example, to the publication of a table giving a variety of expert opinion on each sherd (Fowler *et al* 1970, 30–5). Part of the reason for this is the wide variety of preservation conditions which occur on Atlantic sites, often highly acidic. Most of the imported pottery has varying amounts of calcareous inclusions such as limestone, or is made from a calcareous clay, which tends to decay to varying extents in these environments. These post-depositional processes can produce sherds which superficially look very different from each other, and from standard unweathered examples from Mediterranean or Continental contexts. Even sherds which can be shown to be from the same vessel can exhibit this variety of appearance. For example the DSPA sherds from Hen Gastell look very different in colour and texture from sherds of the same ware from Dinas Powys, and at first glance could appear to be an entirely different ware. My own geological training meant that I was able to identify many inclusions in the pottery by means of a hand-lens or high-powered microscope without resort to thin-sectioning, and gave me insight into taphonomic and post-depositional processes. I am therefore satisfied that my identifications are more reliable and consistent than those given in previous lists, and in fact I have noted several examples of wrong attribution. In particular the supposed examples of E ware from Dinas Emrys, Craigs Quarry, Abercorn, Luce Sands and some from Bantham had to be rejected. Sherds which I have personally examined are distinguished in the database. Some scientific analyses of E ware were undertaken to try to provenance the ware, but for a variety of reasons these were not particularly fruitful (Appendix 2, Tables 20 and 21; Campbell 1984).

As far as overall distributions were concerned I recorded all sherds and vessel numbers from each import site as far as I was able. Given the scattered and inaccessible nature of some material, I am pleased to have been able to have examined around three-quarters of all the Continental material personally. The scope of this enquiry was mainly limited to sites suggested as import sites in the catalogues of Thomas (1959; 1981). A number of other likely Welsh sites were checked for undiscovered imports, including Gateholm (Campbell 1985), Llantwit Major, Sudbrook and Llancarfan, but the large amount of time spent searching unsorted medieval and Roman assemblages did not repay the effort involved as all of these proved to be negative. A number of new sites were discovered, such as Carew Castle, Margam and Caldey Island, but these were found either by chance or where a pottery specialist had isolated unknown fabrics for further study.

A crucial factor in the quantification studies was the decision to attribute as many sherds as possible to individual vessels. This was done not just to establish the minimum number of vessels represented on each site, but to enable distribution plans of individual vessels to be plotted. This information provided crucial clues to site stratigraphy, chronology and taphonomic processes. It became clear in this study that the use of sherd numbers or sherd weights, both standard recording methods, is often entirely misleading in assessing the relative significance of import sites due to vagaries of the taphonomic processes at work (cf Orton *et al* 1993, 21–2). The work by Clive Orton and others has shown that the most statistically reliable method of quantification for this purpose is the estimated vessel equivalent (EVE), usually based on rim percentages (*ibid*, 168–71). However, the measure used in this study, the minimum number of vessels (MNV), termed estimate of vessels represented (EVREP) by Orton (*ibid*), has shown its worth in distinguishing between different grades of site, and can be demonstrated to be a useful measure (see

Chapter 7). The reason is that the small size of the Atlantic assemblages studied here do enable attribution of sherds to individual vessels on the basis of vessel size, form, fabric variations, colour and other minor differences. The attribution of sherds to individual vessels is of course a much more subjective measure than that of rim percentages, but work at Whithorn suggested that some confidence can be placed in the attributions. At that site, the imports were studied 'blind' (ie without knowledge of their stratigraphic or horizontal context), but the suggested vessels formed coherent groups of sherds when plotted on site plans (Hill 1997, illus 10.21–10.42). If EVE, or the more abstract pottery information equivalent (PIE) (Orton and Tyers 1990), had been used as a measure, almost all the sites would have appeared to produce no more than a single vessel, and others none at all, though in fact many have significant numbers of vessels. For example, over 80 E ware vessels are represented by only one or two bodysherds. The mathematical procedures for overcoming this sparseness of data would not work due to the lack of assemblages to merge (cf Orton *et al* 1993, 174–5). In larger assemblages, EVE is a more accurate representation of the relative numbers of vessels, because it becomes impossible to attribute sherds to vessels with certainty in these large assemblages and the objective measure of rim percentages provides a standard measure to compare assemblages. However, because sherds are not assigned to individual vessels in this system, it cannot be used for distributional studies on individual vessels such as those carried out in this study.

The imported glass was recorded and analysed in much the same way as the pottery, though the sherds are often tiny and therefore difficult to study. Colour is often the best means of differentiating individual vessels of the same form, but many vessels can only be identified by the decorative patterns which are only present on a small proportion of the vessel sherds, so the minimum vessel numbers here may be an underestimate in comparison to those of pottery. There is a far greater variety of forms amongst the glass vessel imports, and because of the extreme fragmentation it is more difficult to establish the typology of vessels. One of the unexpected revelations of this study was the abundance and variety of the imported glass, making it at least as significant an import as the pottery.

Once the basic data on the identification and recording methodology were established, it was necessary to look at the on-site distributions of the imports, both horizontally and vertically, in order to ascertain stratigraphical relationships (with their chronological implications), possible indications of the function of the wares, and associations both between the different imports and with other materials. In order to carry out this detailed analysis the site of Dinas Powys in South Glamorgan was chosen as a trial site in the 1980s (Chapter 6). The reasons for this choice were that this was the only Early Historic British site which had all the classes of known import wares present, the excavation records allowed the detailed plotting of all the finds, and the material was easily accessible in the National Museum of Wales. In addition Dinas Powys was the only major British site of the period to have been scientifically excavated and published at that time (Alcock 1987, v). This study necessitated a reappraisal of the finds from Dinas Powys and the mapping and analysis of the distributions of all the finds (Campbell 1991, chapters 2–3, appendix 8). Following on from this analysis it became clear that the stratigraphy of the site needed a radical reinterpretation (Appendix 9).

In order to answer some of the questions posed above it was necessary to develop certain techniques of analysis of the pottery and glass. To assess the questions of residuality and association it was necessary to measure every sherd in order to plot sherd-size graphs, and try to assign every sherd to a particular vessel in order to determine sherd-to-vessel ratios (Chapter 6.1). These techniques followed on from the pioneering work of Ian Burrow at Cadbury Congresbury (Burrow 1979), and the studies by anthropologists and prehistorians mentioned in the previous section. All the finds from Dinas Powys were recorded and plotted on distributions plans (Campbell 1991, illus 88–124). A certain amount of material was found not to have been published by Alcock and was catalogued (Appendix 6). The work at Dinas Powys led to a number of spin-off studies which have been published elsewhere. To try to assess the significance of Dinas Powys in a Welsh context a more detailed study of the evidence for early medieval settlement in Wales was undertaken (Campbell 1991, 111–27). Part of this research was incorporated in *Early Medieval Settlements in Wales AD 400–1100* (Edwards and Lane 1988; Campbell 1988b), and also resulted in the excavation of Longbury Bank in 1988–89 as a site for comparison with Dinas Powys (Campbell and Lane 1993a). Other publications which resulted from this initial research were papers on the new discoveries from Caldey and Margam (Campbell 1989a), on a Kentish squat jar from the Dinas Powys glass assemblage (Campbell 1989b), and the discovery of the 10th-century royal crannog at Llangorse (Campbell and Lane 1989).

Apart from Dinas Powys, some other sites had sufficient information on horizontal and vertical distributions to provide insights into chronology or taphonomic processes. These included Tintagel, Cadbury Castle, Longbury Bank, Trethurgy, Loch Glashan, and Whithorn (Chapter 7). Whithorn provided the best stratigraphic sequence of any Atlantic site, with up to eighteen sub-phases distinguishable within the two hundred years of pre-Saxon occupation deposits. The analysis of the Whithorn imports presented here builds on the published report by developing graphic techniques for displaying aspects of residuality and intrusion. Having discovered which sites had imports, I analysed the characteristics of these sites (Chapter 8). As it was clearly impossible to list all the attributes of all these sites indiscriminately, the analysis concentrated on items which might be of significance in relation to questions of trade, status and economy. The basis on which the characteristics were chosen is discussed in detail in Chapter 8, but they relate in the main to topographic location; size and type of enclosure; evidence of weapons, precious metals, jewellery manufacture and craft specialisation; and documentary evidence. This body of material forms the second major dataset of this study, and is summarised in Tables 16–19.

All these different analyses are brought together in a discussion of the distribution mechanisms of the successive Early Historic trading systems (Chapter 9). It is suggested that the Mediterranean trade was not a purely commercial venture, but had an Imperial source, related to the official procurement of metals, and that this trade lasted for a considerable period in the first half of the 6th century. The succeeding Continental trade of the later 6th and 7th century also had peculiarities which suggest the involvement of Aquitanian elites. The motivation is less clear, but may have involved trade in slaves. This contact between the Atlantic West and Gaul was precocious in British terms, but seems not to have developed into the early market economies seen in the later mid-Saxon trading settlements of southern and eastern England. In summary, while the import trade was a small part of the Early Historic Atlantic economies, it had a significant impact in the transformation of small, tribal-based polities to the larger regional entities which were the predecessors of the later nations of Wales, Scotland and Ireland (Chapter 10).

2 Mediterranean pottery: Late Roman Amphorae, Phocaean Red Slipware, African Red Slipware

As described in the preceding chapter, there have been significant advances in our understanding of the imported pottery and glass in the Atlantic West in the last twenty years or so. This chapter, and the following two, will deal with 'traditional' questions of typology, chronology and provenance of the imports.

2.1 Phocaean Red Slipware (PRS) (Pl 1; Fig 4)

This red-slipped pottery was formerly known as 'Late Roman C' in the Mediterranean and as Radford's Class A ware in this country. Radford's original division of the A wares into two groups, Ai and Aii, does not correspond exactly to the division between PRS ware and African Red Slipware, but PRS ware is mainly his Ai group. The major advance in our knowledge of this ware came with the work of Hayes (1972; 1980) on the Mediterranean fine wares. PRS is now known to have been made in western Turkey, ancient Phocaea, from the 4th to the 7th centuries. Kiln sites have been discovered there (Langlotz 1969) and confirmed by chemical analysis (Mayet and Picon 1986).

PRS consists of a series of fine tablewares in the long tradition of red *terra sigillata* wares of the Mediterranean. As its name suggests, it has a red-slipped surface, burnished to a gloss, though not as highly as in samian ware. It occurs in a restricted variety of forms, all deep plates or shallow dishes, often with rouletted decoration on the rim and stamped patterns in the interior. The fabric is distinctive: the colour is generally orange/red, but can vary, with some burnt sherds being grey, and the slip is generally a darker, browner red. The paste is fine and smooth with very distinctive abundant minute yellow limestone inclusions which give a mottled appearance (Appendix 1). There is no quartz visible. The outer surface is characteristically minutely rilled, presumably by burnishing on a wheel. The wall tends to be very thin (2–3mm).

Hayes (1972, 464, map 33) has shown that it was only during the period of production of his Form 3 that the ware was traded outside the eastern Mediterranean, and it is this form that is found in Insular contexts. Form 3 consists of shallow, thin-walled bowls or dishes, often with rouletting around the exterior of the rim. The fine red-slipped fabric is distinctive in the presence of abundant yellow limestone flecks. The typology established by Hayes enables the British examples to be closely dated, though it should be noted that dates given by Hayes are his estimates based on a small number of coin-dated groups rather than hard and fast limits. It is also difficult to use Hayes' over-elaborate subdivisions of Form 3 as these were based on complete vessels whereas the Insular material is fragmentary and rim forms are not a totally adequate guide. Hayes also never actually defined the differences between his form variants, merely illustrating examples which he has attributed to each form.

The varieties of Form 3 found in Insular contexts are 3C, 3D, 3E and 3F, which appear to be a chronologically related group of forms (Fig 4). In terms of specific attributions of vessels these number: 12 Form 3C; 1 Form 3D; 9 Form 3C/E/F; 11 Form 3E; 4 Form 3F; and 4 Form 3E/F. Notably missing are Forms 3A and 3B which date to the mid- to late 5th century, and the 3G and 3H varieties of the mid- to late 6th century. Definite examples of Form 3F, dated by Hayes to the second quarter of the 6th century, are also rare. In terms of the stamped motifs, few can be assigned to certain types. The earliest is the series of stamped hares from Dinas Powys (Hayes Motif 35, Group II), a motif which does not continue past AD 500 (Pl 1). The Cadbury Castle cross belongs to Motif 79, or less likely 68, dating to the late 5th to mid-6th century. There are two crosses from Tintagel of Motif 71 or 72, Group III, dating to the late 5th to early 6th century. The Insular forms therefore appear to date to the period of AD 500 ± 25 years. If the group of PRS from Dinas Powys (Fig 4) is a contemporary group then it would seem to date to the period around AD 500 or the last quarter of the 5th century. The PRS thus seems to be slightly earlier than the African Red Slipware. A similar typological range is seen in the western Mediterranean (Reynolds 1995, 35), though there are a few examples of later 6th-century forms at sites such as Marseille. It should be noted that the claimed late 6th-/7th-century Form 10 vessels from Tintagel (Thomas 1981, 6) appear to me to be Form 3E/F (P29, P51, P52). Similarly, the vessel claimed by Thomas (1981, 7) as early Form 2 PRS from Garryduff is not accepted as PRS by myself or Doyle (1999, 71). Unfortunately, these have entered the literature as facts in previous discussions of the trade between Britain and the Mediterranean (eg Reynolds 1995, 35), obscuring the tight chronological grouping of the eastern Mediterranean imports revealed in this study.

Although it has been claimed that the presence of stamped crosses on some PRS dishes indicates a religious function for the vessels (Radford 1956, 69), and even church organisation of trade (Hodges 1977), this can be dismissed as almost all the British examples come from secular sites. Only two sites, the churchyard at Phillack, Cornwall, and the cemetery at Cabinteely, Dublin, could be considered

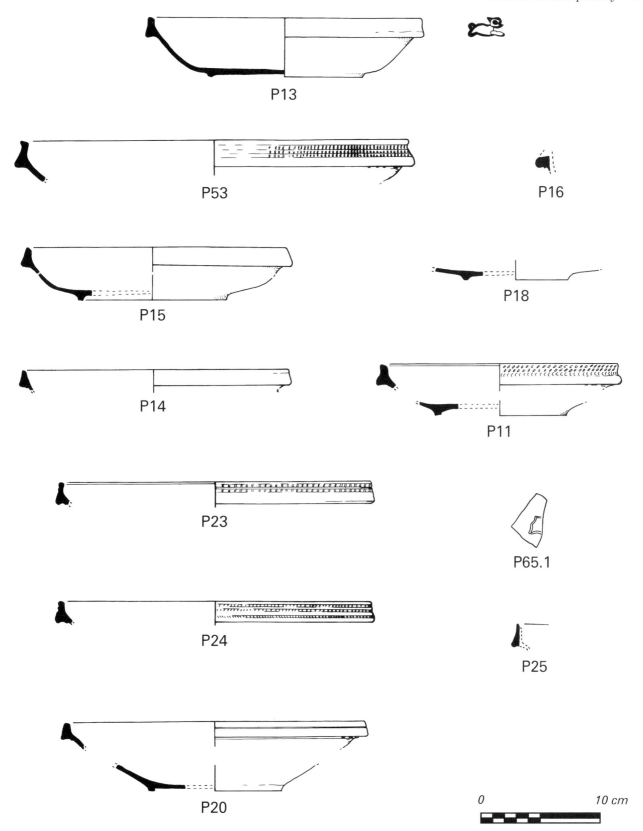

Fig 4 Phocaean Red Slipware from Insular sites. Hayes Form 3C/E: P13 Dinas Powys; P53 Tintagel. Form 3D: P16 Dinas Powys. Form 3E: P14, P15 Dinas Powys; P20 Longbury Bank; P23–4 Cadbury Castle. Form 3C/F: P25 Cadbury Castle. Form 3F: P11 Coygan Camp. Form 3: P18 Grambla. Peacock stamp: P65.1 Tintagel

to be religious sites, with Caldey Island another possibility. More cogently, the work of Hayes shows that the stamps on the pottery were the result of changing fashions within the production area, with an early fashion for animal stamps such as lions, hares and stags, and that this gave way in the early

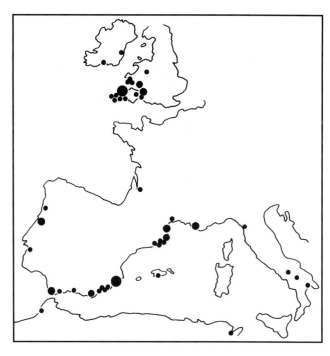

Fig 5 Distribution of Insular PRS

Fig 6 PRS distribution in the western Mediterranean. Size of symbols proportional to numbers of vessels (MNV)

6th century to stamps of human figures and particularly crosses. Thus the Dinas Powys bowl, as one of the earliest of these imports, is stamped with the currently fashionable animals, while the later examples mainly have crosses. The presence of the crosses is thus entirely incidental to the function of the vessels. However, this does not negate the possibility of direct influence of these Christian motifs on the religious art of the period (Haseloff 1987, 45; Thomas 1987).

There are seventeen sites with PRS, producing a minimum of 62 vessels, though almost half of these come from one site, Tintagel (Fig 5). The number of vessels in Insular contexts may appear small, but this number must be seen in relation to the equally small numbers reported from western Mediterranean sites (Fig 6). In this context, the Insular numbers are surprisingly large, given the greater distance from the source of production. The most recent summary shows 26 PRS sites in the western Mediterranean (France, Spain, Portugal and north Africa), mostly producing a few vessels each, with only three sites (Conimbriga, Benalúa and Belo) reaching double figures (Reynolds 1995, app B.2; Delgado *et al* 1975; Prieto 1984). These three sites lie on southern coasts, on the sea-route to Britain. There is a significant gap in the distribution along the north-eastern coast of Spain and the Balearics (Reynolds 1995, 35) and in Carthage, suggesting a direct route from the eastern Mediterranean via southern Spain and Portugal (*ibid*, 135).

The small numbers of vessels found at all these western sites suggests that these fine wares were never more than space fillers in a larger bulk cargo, and not intended to form a major source of supply for fine tablewares in the western Mediterranean, where African Red Slipware was much more commonly imported. Reynolds (1995, 128) classifies these finewares as secondary cargoes, and Parker (1984) has stressed the varied and multi-source nature of known shipwreck cargoes. Of course in Insular contexts, where no comparable finewares were available, they may have acquired a *cachet* beyond their normal importance. We should remember, however, that pottery vessels, even fine decorated slipwares in antiquity, were always seen as being of lower status and value than metal vessels, which were probably imported alongside the pottery (eg Mango 2001). However, it is also the case that the PRS vessels were unlikely to have been merely for use by the crew of the Byzantine cargo vessels. Although some slipware dishes have been found in galley quarters in well-preserved wrecks, for example at Yassi Ada (Bass and van Doornick 1982, 167), the widespread occurrence of PRS would seem to indicate deliberate trade rather than casual exchange of personal items by crew members. Almost all the Insular PRS is found on sites which have also produced amphorae (LR1–8) of the east Mediterranean 'package' (Chapter 2.5), further confirmation of the integrated nature of the imported assemblages.

2.2 African Red Slipware (ARS) (Pl 2; Fig 7)

These red-slipped vessels correspond partly to Radford's original definition of Aii ware (1956, 61, fig 14), though some of the examples illustrated are PRS. ARS forms have been fully studied by Fulford and Peacock (1984) on the British excavations at Carthage, and the dating of the forms found there can be applied to the Insular examples. This work supersedes the pioneering work of Hayes (1972). ARS was produced in the Carthage region from the 2nd to the 7th centuries, and was widely exported around the western Mediterranean, but it is very rare in post-Roman contexts in Britain and Ireland. Small amounts were imported throughout the Roman period (Bird 1977), but these probably represent personal possessions rather than an organised trade. A much wider variety of forms were produced than with PRS, but the forms found in Insular contexts are almost all dishes and bowls. As

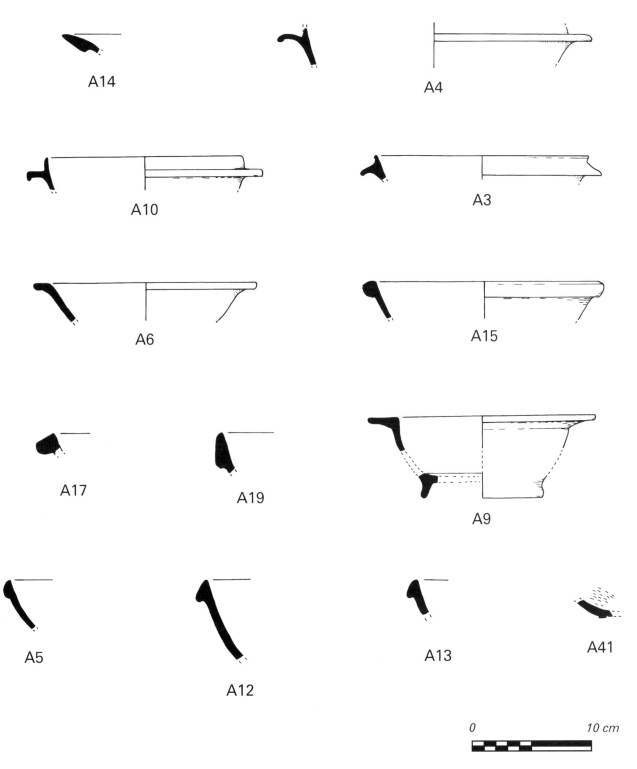

Fig 7 African Red Slipware from Insular sites. Fulford and Peacock Form 44: A14 Tintagel. Form 47.2: A3, A4 Dinas Powys; A10 Tintagel. Form 50: A6 Dinas Powys. Form 50/52: A17 Tintagel. Form 52: A15 Tintagel. Form 55: A9 Tintagel. Form 58: A5 Dinas Powys; ? A19 Tintagel. Form 64: A12, A13 Tintagel. Form ?: A41 Tintagel

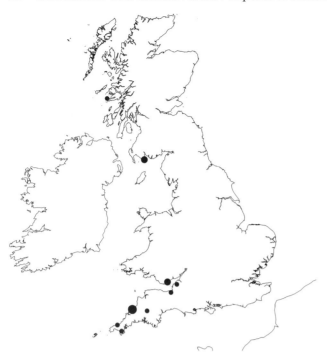

Fig 8 Distribution of Insular ARS

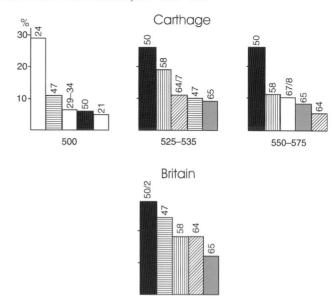

Fig 9 Chronology of Insular ARS. Comparison of Insular forms with those from three successive dated groups from Carthage (data from Fulford and Peacock 1984)

with PRS, stamped internal decoration is common, but rouletting is rarer.

ARS lacks the distinctive fabric of PRS, having a quartz sand-tempered fabric which is difficult to distinguish from that of some Romano-British late red slipwares. This distinction is particularly difficult in the case of those vessels which have similar forms to late Romano-British wares, for example Fulford's Form 47 which is very similar to Young's (1977) form 51 of Oxford ware. The fabric is described by Fulford and Peacock (1984, 16–18) from a study in the production area around Carthage. Normally it is a hard, brick-red fabric with quartz and limestone inclusions. The limestone is abundant, of small (up to 0.5mm) yellow grains. The quartz is generally small, with occasional larger grains, some of which are very rounded (wind-blown desert sand), but it is enough to give the ware a rougher feel than PRS. The slip is variable in colour and texture, but is generally of a paler colour than PRS. In this country (as at Dinas Powys) the fabric is often degraded, being soft and with no visible slip.

ARS is found on ten Insular sites, all in Britain (Fig 8). Apart from the four vessels from Dinas Powys and Whithorn (Pl 2), the only substantial amount of ARS in Britain is from Tintagel, which accounts for half the known total. The forms identifiable amongst the minimum of 32 vessels include 1 Fulford Form 44; 4 Form 47; 4 Form 50; 2 Form 52; 1 Form 55; 4 Form 58; 3 Form 64; and 6 Form 65. The date of the British examples can be accurately determined using the sequence worked out at Carthage (Fulford and Peacock 1984). The forms found in Britain are fairly long-lived, though confined to the 6th century. A more precise estimate of the date of this phase of importation can be gained by looking at the range of forms taking all the British examples as a group and comparing the proportions of the various forms with dated groups from Carthage (Fig 9). The composition of the British group is quite different from that from the pit-group dated to around 500 at Carthage, but is similar to those from c 525–535 and 550–575. A closer comparison of the graphs shows that the British group should date to the second quarter of the 6th century because of the absence of Forms 67 and 68 and the presence of Form 47. In fact, all the of the Form 47 vessels belong to the sub-group 47.2, dated by Fulford to a short period c 525–550. This analysis assumes that the most popular vessel forms at Carthage were the ones exported, but this does appear to be the case. There is no guarantee that any particular ARS vessel belongs to this narrow date-range, but the overall pattern seems clear. The only example of an identifiable stamp on ARS comes from Cadbury Congresbury and belongs to Hayes style E(ii), dated by him to c 530–600, supporting an attribution to the second third of the 6th century for the Insular ARS. The north African imports therefore seem to be slightly later in date than the eastern Mediterranean ones (Fig 9).

The same arguments about the nature of the ARS imports apply as with PRS, and these can be seen as secondary cargoes in shiploads of bulk materials represented by the north African amphorae found on the same sites.

2.3 Late Roman Amphorae (Pls 3–6; Fig 10)

The work of Fulford and Peacock (1984) at Carthage, Keay (1984) in Spain and Riley (1975; 1979; 1981;

Riley *et al* 1989) in the south-eastern Mediterranean has greatly improved our knowledge of the Mediterranean amphorae which were imported into Britain in the Roman and post-Roman periods. Despite these advances, a major difficulty remains in that all of these amphorae were long-lived types. The small fragments found in this country rarely allow any distinctive details of the form to be ascertained, so that they can only be dated by the fine wares (PRS and ARS) which accompany them. The analysis of the Insular ARS and PRS given above suggests that Mediterranean wares only reached Britain during the period *c* 475–550, a conclusion supported by Fulford (1989, 4). In the Mediterranean, however, stratified urban sequences have enabled a fuller picture of the fluctuations in east Mediterranean trade to be built up (Reynolds 1995, 70–83), showing a longer period of importation, for the entire 5th and 6th centuries and into the 7th. The implications for the nature of the British trade are considered later in Chapter 9.2.

Radford's original definition of Class B clearly referred to LR2 amphorae, though he recognised there were a variety of other types present. The main varieties of amphorae in Insular contexts were originally subdivided into four types, B*i*–B*iv*, by Charles Thomas, with B*v* and B*vi* added subsequently and the unidentified B*iii* relabelled B*misc* (Thomas 1959; 1981). While this terminology has become embedded in the literature, as explained above, I here use the Mediterranean system of numbering eastern Mediterranean Late Roman Amphorae (LR1–7) according to the system of Riley (1981) from the Carthage excavations, to enable easy comparison with Mediterranean sources, as this has become the standard nomenclature in Mediterranean publications (Fig 11). As an excellent summary of amphorae, including correspondences between the numerous typologies and fabric descriptions, has been published (Peacock and Williams 1986), it is not necessary to repeat this information in full here. Riley *et al* (1989, 151) identified six of these types (LR1–5 and north African forms) as part of a 'standard package' of amphorae types found throughout the Mediterranean in the 5th and 6th centuries as the product of large-scale trade. These are indeed the types found in Britain and Ireland. Recently, Karagiorgou (2001) has argued that variations in the fabric of these standard vessel forms require qualification of the classification system, on the lines of 'Form LR1, Fabric 3'. This has not proved possible in this study, but it can be stated that the fabric of LR2 from Insular sources is remarkably consistent, while that of LR1 shows wide variation, reflecting the number of known production areas.

LR2 amphorae (British B*i*) are now known to have been produced in the Argolid region of the Peloponnese (Megaw and Jones 1983; Munn 1985), and possibly on Chios and Kos (Vroom 2003, 143). Sub-varieties of form identified in the Yassi Ada assemblage are believed to be chronologically earlier forms (Karagiorgou 2001, 139). The origin of LR1 (British B*ii*) has been more controversial, with Peacock and Williams suggesting the Antioch region on the basis of increased olive oil production in this area. However, Fulford (1978, 69–70) has illustrated the fallacy of associating amphorae forms with food-producing areas, given a complex picture of cabotage trade in the Mediterranean which effectively masks any such links. The most recent work suggests one source in Cilicia, south-eastern Turkey, and others in Cyprus and Rhodes (Empereur and Picon 1989). It is clear that the form of LR1 was copied extensively, probably because it was a standard transport form (Pl 3). LR3 (British B*iv*) was probably produced in the Sardis area of western Turkey (ancient Phocaea), not far from the source of PRS (Pl 6). British B*v* is a general term for late north African cylindrical amphorae of the 'Africana Grande' type, as Riley did not include these in his numbering system. Keay has distinguished many forms of these, particularly his Type VII, but the Insular examples are so fragmentary that they cannot be assigned to any of these forms. LR4 (British B*vi*) refers to amphorae of Gazan Palestinian origin, while LR5, also from Palestine, has not so far been identified in Insular contexts. One possible instance of LR7, produced in Egypt, has been noted (B181). In this study, LRA is used as a general term for amphorae from unidentified sources (superseding Thomas's B*iii* and later B*misc*). Most of these consist only of undiagnostic sherds in a wide variety of fabrics, but one of these can be partly reconstructed (Fig 12).

I have already noted that all of these types of amphorae are long-lived and cannot in themselves usually be accurately dated to the post-Roman period. The exception is LR3, which undergoes a change from a single-handled form to one with two handles around AD 400 (Robinson 1959, 17). Where the two-handled form can be identified, as at Dinas Emrys (Fig 10, B33), the vessel can be confidently assigned to the period of post-Roman importation. It is also become clear that LR2 undergoes typological change around the second half of the 6th century (Karagiorgou 2001, 131, fig 7.1). Although it is very difficult to reconstruct the complete form of any British LR2 vessels, some characteristics of the early form are present in the Tintagel material. These include the flaring, cup-shaped mouth and the projecting basal toe (Fig 10, B100). This supports the dating of the Mediterranean imports, derived from the associated finewares, as not continuing after the mid-6th century. As neither LR2 nor LR1 have so far been found in Insular Roman contexts, and were not exported to the western Mediterranean before the 5th century (Reynolds 1995, 71), it is likely that all Insular examples of these types can be assigned to the later system of importation. LR4 and B*v*, however, *are* found in Late Roman contexts in Britain, for example at York, London and many other sites (Tyers 1996; Tomber and Williams 1986),

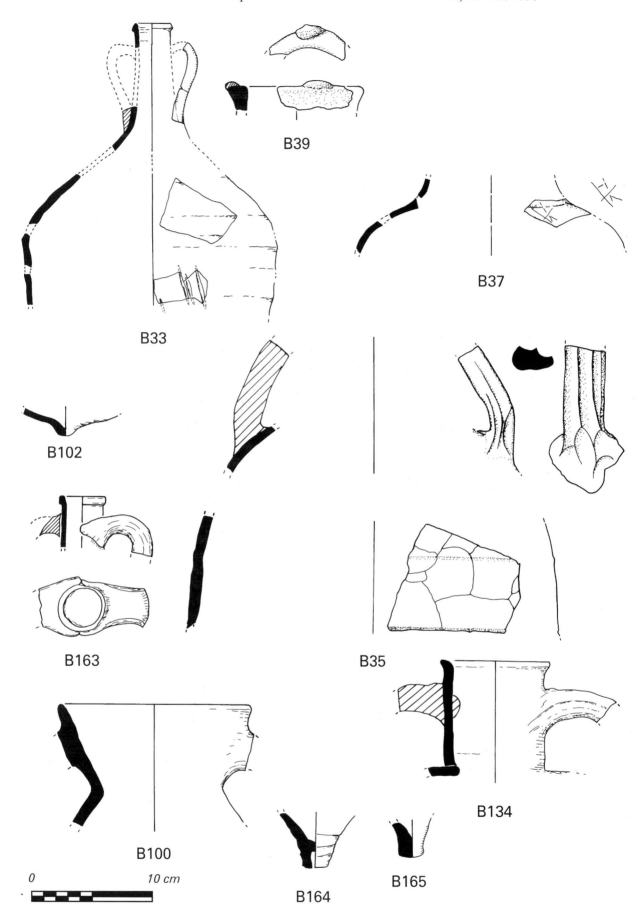

Fig 10 Distinctive features of Insular LRA. LR1: B35, B37 Dinas Powys; B134 Tintagel. LR2: B100, B102 Tintagel. LR3: B33 Dinas Emrys; B163, B164, B165 Tintagel; LR4: B39 Dinas Powys

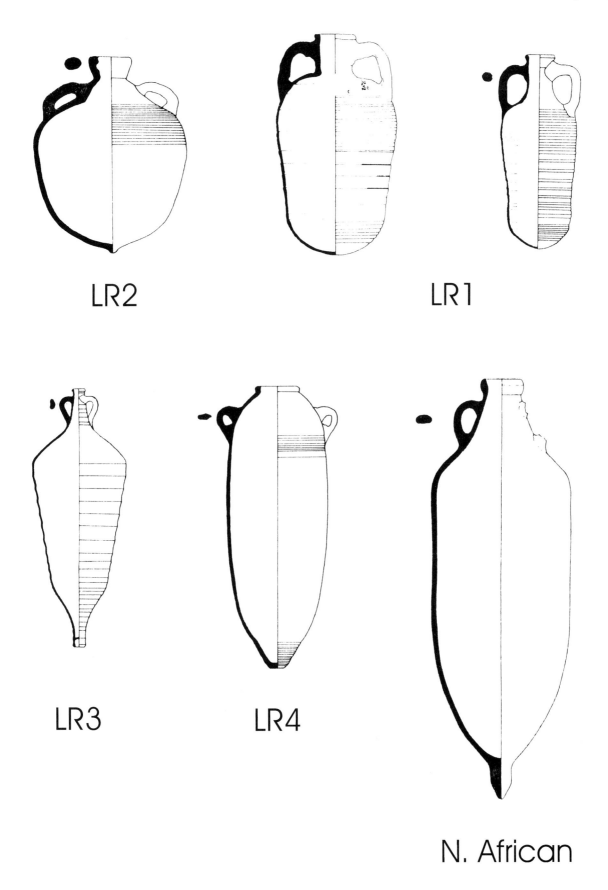

Fig 11 Forms of Late Roman amphorae found in Insular contexts

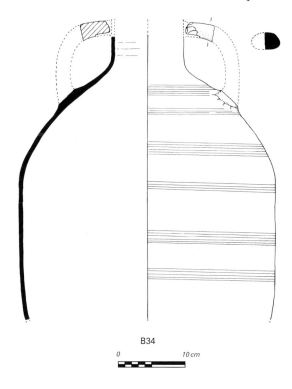

Fig 12 Reconstruction of unidentified LRA (B34) from Dinas Powys

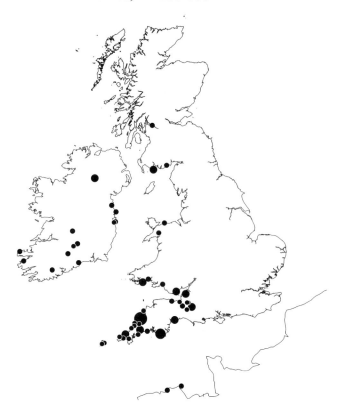

Fig 13 Distribution of LRA

and their occurrence cannot be taken by themselves as an indication of post-Roman activity without good supporting evidence. Consequently, Figure 13 only plots those found in secure post-Roman contexts or areas outside of Roman control.

Only a small proportion of the total number of amphorae are unidentified LRA forms (Fig 14). This is unlike the situation in the Mediterranean where a large proportion of types are often unidentified (Arthur 1986; Reynolds 1995, app B.6). This may be due to difficulties in assigning undistinctive sherds to the LRA group, but it could also be an indication of the very specifically directed nature of the Mediterranean trade to Britain (see Chapter 9.2). The total number of amphorae is not large, at just 250 vessels, with LR2 and LR1 being the most abundant, with only small quantities of LR3 and LR4. B*v* is abundant only at Tintagel. These are spread over nearly 50 sites, but almost 30 have only produced a single vessel (Fig 13). However, as with the PRS, these quantities are very similar to those in the western Mediterranean, where a total of 360 vessels has been recorded from around seventeen sites (Reynolds 1995, app B.3).

The relative proportions of LRA types (Fig 14) is thus markedly different from most western Mediterranean assemblages where LR2 is rare and LR4 is common (Reynolds 1995, 81). LR2 in the western Mediterranean usually accounts for only a few percent of quantified assemblages, compared with the 28% in Atlantic contexts (*ibid*, app B.5). Although the quantification methods differ in these two areas (MNV as opposed to sherd weight), this cannot seriously affect the overall differences. The almost complete absence of LR4 is also striking given that it is widespread and abundant on western Mediterranean sites.

Certain new details of the amphorae have been discovered on the material. For instance at Dinas Powys there is a possible *graffito* on the neck of an LR1 amphora (Fig 10, B37), which is very similar to some from the 7th-century Yassi Ada wreck (Bass and van Doornick 1982, fig 8.8). A very abraded rim fragment has clay accretions round the top which seem to be typical of Gaza LR4 amphorae (Fig 10, B39). The form has a rather more upright rim than is usual, but it is matched by a few examples from Spain (Keay 1984, fig 122, 3; Type LIV D, E). The traces of a red/brown exterior slip are also matched on the Spanish examples. A similar sherd was found at Tintagel (Ti 34.04). However, the fabric is unlike the 'Palestinian' amphorae from the latest Roman contexts at Exeter and Trethurgy. It also proved possible partially to reconstruct an LR2 amphora, showing that it has the typical globular shape of this type before the mid-6th century (Fig 15; see also Rahtz *et al* 1992, fig 124). Amongst the unidentified Tintagel material is a hollow twisted spiked foot of an amphora similar to LR7 (B181), which if correctly identified would be the only example from an Insular context. As with the coarsewares

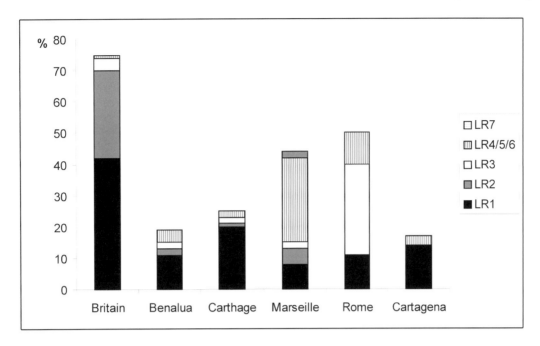

Fig 14 Relative proportions of LRA types in Insular and western Mediterranean contexts

discussed below, this needs to be confirmed by a specialist familiar with this material. At Whithorn, an LR1 amphora has a *graffito* cross infilled with red paint (Pl 4; Campbell 1997, illus 10.16, 3e,d), while one LR2 amphora had part of a red-painted *dipinto*, and another had a *graffito* (Pl 5; *ibid*, illus 10.15, 2b, 3b). These complement previously reported examples from Tintagel (Thomas and Thorpe 1993, figs 57, 58).

One further type of ceramic has to be discussed here. During the period of the Mediterranean import

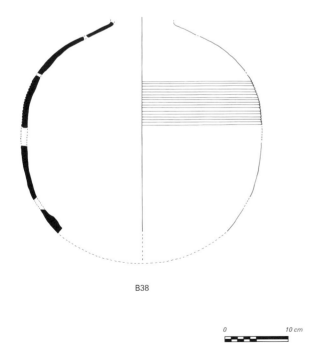

Fig 15 Reconstruction of LR2 amphora (B38) from Dinas Powys

phase, amphorae began to have stoppers made not of cork, but of ceramics sealed with plaster or other material (Kingsley 2004, 47, lower illus). Sometimes these were specially manufactured in the same fabric as the amphora (Karagiorgou 2001, fig 7.1, 3), but more commonly they were manufactured by cutting crude discs from abandoned sherds. Discs of appropriate size and shape to act as stoppers have been found at Tintagel (Thomas and Thorpe 1993, fig 56), and one from Cadbury Congresbury (Rahtz *et al* 1992, 172, fig 128, G 0201), which, though in the report described as a pot-lid, is too small for such a function. Other claimed examples are less convincing (Batey *et al* 1993, fig 8b). At least one example from Tintagel retains traces of pitch or resin used to seal the mouth, confirming that at least some of these are not of local manufacture. Presumably such discs would have been made on an ad hoc basis each time the amphora was filled, and thus the stopper could be of a completely different provenance to the amphora. This might account for some of the sherds of unidentified fabrics found on Atlantic sites (Wooding 1996b, 49).

Having discussed the typology and chronology of the LRA, we should enquire into the contents of the amphorae, the actual goods transported for trade. From documentary sources it is well known that wine and olive oil were the major liquid goods traded in antiquity, but also mentioned are fish sauces (*garum*), other oils, unguents and delicacies. Although most amphorae were designed to hold liquids, not all goods carried in amphorae were liquid: olives, nuts, fruits, sweetmeats, fish, seeds and other goods have been found, as well as more mundane materials such as nails. Before the advent of scientific archaeology the only way to tie these commodities to particular forms of amphorae was through rare inscriptions scratched (*graffiti*) or painted (*dipinti*) on the exteriors, or through tying general areas of production of commodities to amphorae produced in these areas. Thus B*v* was associated with north African olive oil, and LR4–5 with Gaza wine. Resin linings found in many amphorae were taken to indicate that these held wine. Chemical analysis was expected to yield better results, but for a number of reasons it is difficult to interpret the results. Organic residues break down under burial conditions, making it difficult to reconstruct the original molecular structure with confidence. Chemical analysis has been carried out on some sherds from Tintagel, but the results were inconclusive (Hartgroves and Walker 1988, 26–7; Batey *et al* 1993, 61). Other commodities, like wine, do not have a characteristic organic 'signature' that can be easily read. In some cases, the results of scientific analysis has been rejected by archaeologists. For example, analysis of LR3 amphorae resulted in the discovery of lipids and olive oil, suggesting an unguent was carried (Rothschild-Boros 1981, 83–4). However, the large quantities of this amphora type found on western Mediterranean sites make this an implausible commodity, and wine has been suggested as the normal contents (Reynolds 1995, 71). Thomas's suggestion that LR3 were water-jars of the ship's crew (1982, 24), and not used to transport commodities is untenable given the large quantities traded in the Mediterranean. The holes punched in the shoulder reported by him seem likely to have had the same function as those in Gaza amphorae, as a means of satisfying Jewish customers that the wine was ritually pure (Kingsley 2004, 46). I have not been able to confirm the presence of any such holes in the British material.

It is only with the rise of scientific excavation of shipwreck sites that our understanding of amphorae contents has been put on a secure footing. At the 7th-century Yassi Ada A wreck, 680 of the 900 LR1 and LR2 amphorae in the cargo were lifted and the organic contents examined, including those from sealed vessels. Surprisingly, many of the LR1 amphorae, traditionally associated with olive oil, produced grape pips, showing they held wine, at least in this cargo, as did many of the LR2 amphorae. However, eroded olive pips were also found in many amphorae, some of them pitch-lined (Karagiorgou 2001, 146). Resin linings have been found in some examples of LR1 (Reynolds 1995, 71), supporting the hypothesis of multiple uses. Again, although B*v* north African amphorae were traditionally associated with the massive olive oil production of the region, wreck sites have produced sealed amphorae containing fish bones and scales (Kingsley 2004, 47). What seems to have been happening is a recycling of old amphorae to accommodate whatever commodity was being shipped. The Yassi Ada wreck contained a wide variety of sub-types, some of which were believed to be decades old at the time of deposition (Karagiorgou 2001, 139–40). One wreck from Palestine, Dor D, contained a cargo of empty amphorae from a variety of sources (Kingsley 2004, 70–1). While some documentary sources quote merchants as specifying new amphorae (Kingsley 2004, 34), it is clear that there was a great deal of reuse of empty amphorae for a wide variety of purposes. Without an appreciation of the evidence for recycling and reuse of amphorae from shipwreck sites in the Mediterranean, interpretation of the British evidence, based on ideas of what is a 'normal' variety of wares, is suspect (cf Wooding 1996b, 48–9). Coupled with the signs that standard forms of amphora, such LR1, were copied at a number of different sources, and that the change in neck shape of LR2 may indicate a change in type of contents over time, it is very difficult to be sure which commodities were reaching Britain in the 6th century in the specific amphorae found here, but probably wine and olive oil were involved, and possibly other exotic foodstuffs. Whether olive oil was a commodity which would have been appreciated is another matter. Wooding notes that wine and other exotics are noted in the commentaries on the Irish sea-laws, but not oil (Woooding 1996b, 51), perhaps suggesting it was not seen as an important commodity.

2.4 Mediterranean coarsewares

In their unpublished survey and catalogue of the Tintagel pottery carried out in 1988, Thomas and Thorpe identified a series of Mediterranean coarsewares, alongside the fine tablewares and amphorae discussed above (Thorpe 1988). Some details have been published since then (Thomas and Thorpe in Batey *et al* 1993, 56, 58–60; Thorpe 1997), though full details await a forthcoming work. There is nothing inherently implausible in such a suggestion, as shipwreck investigations have shown that the galleys of merchant vessels were well stocked with such items as casseroles, jugs, amphorettas, plates, lamps and water jars (eg Kingsley 2004, illus p 53). There is also growing evidence for trade in coarsewares around the western Mediterranean (Reynolds 1995, fig 166–70). While the majority of such wares are of western Mediterranean origin (eg Pantellerian and Lipari wares), eastern coarsewares are found, though with restricted distributions. There is therefore no reason why such wares should not have reached Britain, if there was a market for such low-value items.

In my own examination of Radford's Tintagel material, I was not convinced that any other than a handful of the claimed coarsewares were other than sherds from small amphorae, though I have not examined Mediterranean coarsewares myself. The many distinctive morphological features of these wares (Reynolds 1995, figs 124–36) seemed to be lacking in the Insular material. If coarsewares were being traded to Britain, one might expect them to belong to these identifiable classes of ware which were known to have been exported. Thorpe describes a number of these coarseware fabrics (in Batey *et al* 1993, 56), and gives them names such as East Mediterranean Sandy Cream Ware, but these cannot be matched to known exported wares. One fabric (Fabric 21) has undergone petrological analysis which suggests an eastern Mediterranean source, and another (Fabric 22) has been matched with Almagro 51 amphora fabric (Keay XIX). The question is not whether there are so far unidentified wares amongst the extensive collections at Tintagel, as there clearly are, but whether these belong to coarseware forms used as kitchenware rather than tablewares of ARS and PRS manufacture, or to unknown types of amphorae used for transporting goods. Of the published and unpublished material, very little seems likely to fall into that category. Given that a certain amount of Romano-British pottery is present on the site, there is scope for confusion, and at least some of the claimed coarseware belongs in that group. However this leaves a residue of material which could indeed be Mediterranean coarseware. Two published sherds of Fabric 1 are convincing as non-amphorae (Batey *et al* 1993, fig 9, 302, 83), though the fabric description sounds much like ARS. Clearly further work on these wares is needed by those familiar with the Mediterranean coarsewares before any definite statements can be made. Small amounts of unidentified fabrics exist at other major import sites, and occasional matches can be seen, for example between the Dinas Powys and Tintagel fabrics, but again this needs further work by specialists familiar with the Mediterranean material.

2.5 Mediterranean 'packages'

The Atlantic trade with the Mediterranean can be seen, from the analyses in Chapter 2.1–2.4, to have had characteristics which distinguish it from the general trade patterns in the western Mediterranean. Firstly, the Atlantic imports came from two restricted areas of the Mediterranean, which for convenience I have labelled the 'Aegean', covering the Aegean and north-eastern Mediterranean (PRS, LR1, LR2, LR3), and the 'African', from modern Tunisia (ARS, B*v*). Markedly absent are wares from the south-eastern Mediterranean, Palestine, Gaza and Egypt (LR4–7) which are normally found alongside the Aegean wares in the Mediterranean. Secondly, the date range of the wares is much more restricted than is usual in the western Mediterranean, being confined to the period *c* 475–550.

Turning to the British distribution, we find the same grouping of LR1–3 and PRS on the 47 known sites (Fig 16). Although all four types are not always found on the same sites, the geographical clustering is very strong. The small numbers of vessels found on most sites statistically reduce the chances of all four types being recovered together even if all were originally present, as three-quarters of all sites produced fewer than four vessels. If this concept of a package of wares is accepted, the PRS vessels which formed part of it enable us to date the period of importation. As was discussed previously, the forms of PRS found in Britain are all Hayes Form 3 and can be dated to a restricted period within this range, possibly from the late 5th to the first third of the 6th century. The

Fig 16 Distribution of the eastern Mediterranean 'package' of wares (left) and north African 'package' (right)

accompanying LR1 and LR2 amphorae cannot be precisely dated in themselves, as they are long-lived forms, though evidence has been presented that some of the LR2 was of a form pre-dating the mid-6th century. Thus while any particular LR amphora in an Insular context could have been produced at any date from the 5th to the 7th century, the date of importation is likely to be in the late 5th or early 6th century. The date of individual examples of LR3 is more of a problem, as early (one-handled) varieties of this form are found in 4th-century Roman contexts. Some of the western examples of LR3 can be shown to be of the later, 5th- to 6th-century form with two handles (Fig 10, B33), but otherwise it can only be assumed that sherds of LR3 found on Atlantic sites are of this later date. One site which is unusual in that the assemblage appears to be dominated by LR1 amphorae, with few LR2, is Bantham. Whether this represents a possible chronologically early phase of importation, or is due to patchy horizontal distribution within the site (as is apparent at Dinas Powys and other sites), or is due a specific supply mechanism, remains to be seen.

If the number of 'Aegean' vessels per site is plotted the concentration in south-west Britain is marked (Fig 16). The outliers to this distribution are almost all single vessels. Only Garranes in southern Ireland is an exception to this, having three types of ware and quantities of each. Vessels on the other sites in Ireland and Scotland probably represent redistribution from contacts with the south-west. It is much less likely that they are the result of sporadic visits by pilgrims and other travellers to the Mediterranean as has sometimes been suggested. Apart from the objection that amphorae are bulky and awkward to transport (tableware is another matter), one would expect a greater variety of Mediterranean amphora types if this was the mechanism of importation. The Yassi Ada wreck shows that LR1 and LR2 amphorae formed complementary cargoes on board vessels of the period, alongside small amounts of LR3 and PRS (Bass and van Doornick 1982). There seems no doubt that this association of wares represents a package of goods traded directly from the eastern Byzantine Empire, rather than the result of tramping and cabotage by general-purpose cargo vessels, moving from port to port in a random course dictated by the availability of goods or markets. The implications of this are discussed later in Chapter 9.2.

The 'African' package of wares is much rarer than the Aegean, and the full association of amphorae and finewares is seen only at Tintagel. At the other fifteen sites with this material, finewares and amphorae are found separately (Fig 16). In some cases this may be due to the statistical factors outlined above, and redistribution from key import sites in the south-west, but there remains the possibility that a few sherds could be the result of individuals bringing mementos or complete vessels back from trips to the Mediterranean, probably as pilgrims. For example, the sherd of ARS from Iona lies far outside the normal distribution of the African wares, but the recent discovery of a number of ARS vessels at Whithorn, alongside other imports, suggests caution in dismissing the trading model of exchange even for these outliers. Other examples of Bv could be the product of the Late Roman phase of importation, for example at Dalkey Island and Loughshinney, where other Romano-British material is present. The lack of well-stratified sequences on these sites, and the possibility of residuality, makes it difficult to assess which system brought the amphorae to the sites. However, at Trethurgy, the Bv sherds were stratified in the entrance passageway in a 6th-century or later context (Quinnell 2004, 104, though wrongly stated to be east Mediterranean ware), showing that Tintagel was not the only site receiving north African amphorae in the 6th-century phase of importation.

As was discussed in the previous section, the African system of imports can be fairly precisely dated to the middle third, or even second quarter, of the 6th century, probably taking over from the Aegean system of the previous half-century. Its association mainly with one site, Tintagel, also suggests a brief period of importation. Why there should have been a change in the origin of the Atlantic imports is discussed under the heading of models of exchange in Chapter 9.2, but it remains possible that this later phase of the Mediterranean import system included Aegean amphorae as well as African ones, rather than representing cargoes made up exclusively of African wares. However, the lack of later forms of PRS would then have to be explained. Otherwise, the African phase seems to share the characteristics of the Aegean one, and they are discussed together in subsequent chapters.

In summary then, this review of the evidence has shown that the Mediterranean system of imports consists of two sub-phases, an earlier Aegean phase bringing wares from the north-eastern Mediterranean, and a later African phase bringing wares from the Carthage area. These phases can be fairly precisely dated to c 475–525 and c 525–550 respectively, thus providing a welcome chronological fixed point in dating many Atlantic sites where other methods of dating are absent. The quantities of vessels imported and the number of sites on which they are found are broadly comparable to the situation in the western Mediterranean of Late Antiquity, despite the much greater distance from the source of supply. The variety of wares, however, is much less than in the western Mediterranean, which has significant impact on any discussion of possible models of exchange involved.

3 Continental pottery: DSPA, Class E Ware

3.1 *Dérivées sigillées paléochrétiennes, Atlantic group (DSPA)* (Pls 7–8; Figs 19–20)

Typology

Two important papers, published after the Dinas Powys report, have established beyond doubt that Radford's Class D was in fact made in France and is the last in a long line of stamped fine tablewares of the Roman and post-Roman periods, perhaps ultimately derived from African Red Slipware (Rigoir 1968; Rigoir *et al* 1973). It can be securely identified with the 'Atlantic' group of the *dérivées sigillées paléochrétiennes* (DSP) of the Rigoirs, the other two groups being the 'Provençal' and the 'Languedoc'. These wares have been referred to previously as Visigothic wares or *paléochrétienne grise*. Unlike most other fine slipwares, those of the Atlantic group were fired in a reducing atmosphere, producing grey wares with a black slip, rather than the normal orange/red wares. The other two groups contain a mixed assemblage of orange and grey wares, and there seems to be a chronological development from oxidised to reduced wares. While almost all the Insular examples of DSPA are grey wares (Pl 7), some sherds when burnt revert to a buff colour, for example at Hen Gastell, causing possible confusion with other wares. The roundel from Dinas Emrys (Fig 19, D1), cut from the base of a DSP plate stamped with a Christian motif, is from a rare oxidised example of DSPA or one of the other DSP groups. It is not from a lamp of PRS ware as Thomas suggested (1981, 8). The types of vessels found include plates, bowls, cups and mortaria, often decorated with stamped and rouletted designs.

DSPA is rare in Atlantic contexts, being found on only fourteen sites, producing a minimum of only 27 vessels (Fig 17). The forms represented on Insular consumption sites are not a true reflection of the overall proportion of forms produced in France (Fig 18), where Forms 1 and 4 (plates) and 6 (bowls) are the commonest (Rigoir *et al* 1973, fig 7). In contrast, at Dinas Powys there are two Form 4, four Form 16 and three Form 29 vessels. Indeed the occurrence of three Form 29 mortaria is very surprising as there are only six mortaria out of a total of 375 vessels (1.6%) recorded from western France (*ibid*), and at Bordeaux a quantitative study showed they comprised only 9% of the assemblage (Soulas 1996, 247). The same concentration of mortaria is seen in the overall figures for identifiable vessels in the Insular material: nine Form 4 plates; seven Form 16 or 14 bowls; and nine Form 29 mortaria (35%). Such a complete difference in proportions needs to be explained. It presumably indicates selection of forms, either by the importer or the exporter, for a particular market. Mortaria were used for preparing purées of fruit and vegetables in a distinctive Roman tradition of food production. The presence of so many of these vessels at Dinas Powys and in other Insular sites would appear to indicate the presence of people there with memories of, or aspirations to, a Roman type of lifestyle. There may be chronological factors at work in the absence of Forms 1 and 18, which are common in the French assemblages, but which may have been replaced by Forms 4 and 16 (Rigoir *et al* 1973, 223–5), but until we have better dated urban assemblages from France it will be difficult to judge whether this is the case.

Chronology

The Rigoirs' studies have elucidated the typology and distribution of the ware. Unfortunately, the absolute chronology of the ware was still obscure when they were writing due to a lack of material from modern, well-recorded excavations. Hayes

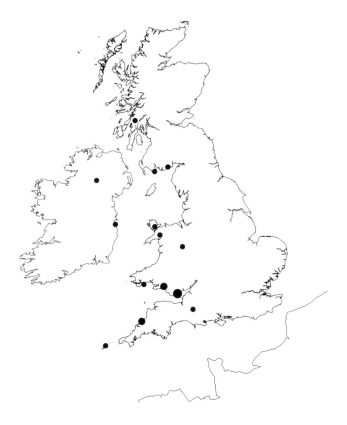

Fig 17 Distribution of Insular DSPA

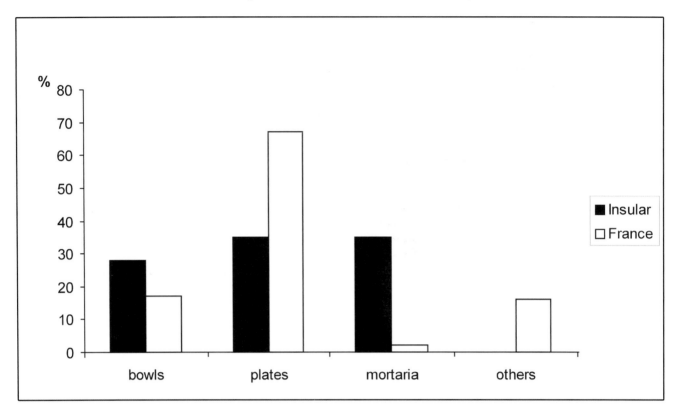

Fig 18 Comparison of relative proportions of DSPA forms in France and Insular sites

(1972, 404) suggested on purely typological grounds that the Atlantic group did not start until the 6th century, and de Maillé (1960, 229) had earlier suggested a *floruit* in the 6th century. James (1977, 241) quoted one source which suggests production continuing into the 7th century. More recently, urban excavations have supported a mainly 6th-century date. In Tours, DSPA starts around the beginning of the 6th century and is found throughout 6th-century deposits (Randoin 1981, 105). In Bordeaux, some forms are found from the early 5th century, but others such as the mortaria become abundant in 6th-century levels (états 12 and 13), suggesting production at that date (S Soulas pers comm; 1996, 247). At both sites they also occur in later, 7th-century, deposits, but there are substantial problems of residuality, as in all major urban assemblages (Foy and Hochuli-Gysel 1995, 160). However, one kiln dated to the 7th century has been reported at Lezoux (Wickham 2005, 747).

Provenance

The Rigoirs suggested that DSPA was produced in the Bordeaux area, and this claim has been strengthened by petrological studies (Soulas 1996, 252). There is no doubt that there was a major production centre around Bordeaux, and the evidence of the die-linked stamps shows that its products were widely traded (Rigoir *et al* 1973, f14). However, it seems likely that there was more than one production centre. The Rigoirs' distribution map shows a second concentration of sites centred on the Loire between Orléans and Tours. Work at Poitiers has shown that imitations of DSPA in a local fabric were being produced there (B Camus pers comm) and other production centres are possible, for example Tours (Wooding 1996b, 56) and other sites in south-western France (Soulas 1996, 252).

Examination of the few British examples of DSPA which do not come from Dinas Powys shows that they have variable fabrics, and some do not match any of the Rigoirs' forms. The Dunadd bowl for instance (Fig 20, D11) seems to be a copy of an E ware bowl form, but executed in a DSPA fabric and made into a mortarium by the addition of a pouring spout (Pl 8). A similar instance of this copying can be seen in a small beaker in Dieppe Museum. This has the form of an E$_2$ beaker but again is in a grey DSPA fabric (J Knight pers comm). A sherd from May's Hill, Scilly (Thomas 1985, fig 86, 1), while in a DSPA fabric, has a latticed scheme of decoration not matched in any published French material. It seems likely then that DSPA type of wares were produced at a number of places in France, but until the different sources are characterised, it is best to retain one overall label for this general type of ware.

The group of nine DSPA vessels from Dinas Powys is unique in Insular contexts as other sites have only a handful of sherds each. The Dinas Powys vessels have a uniform, very fine fabric,

Continental pottery: DSPA, Class E Ware 29

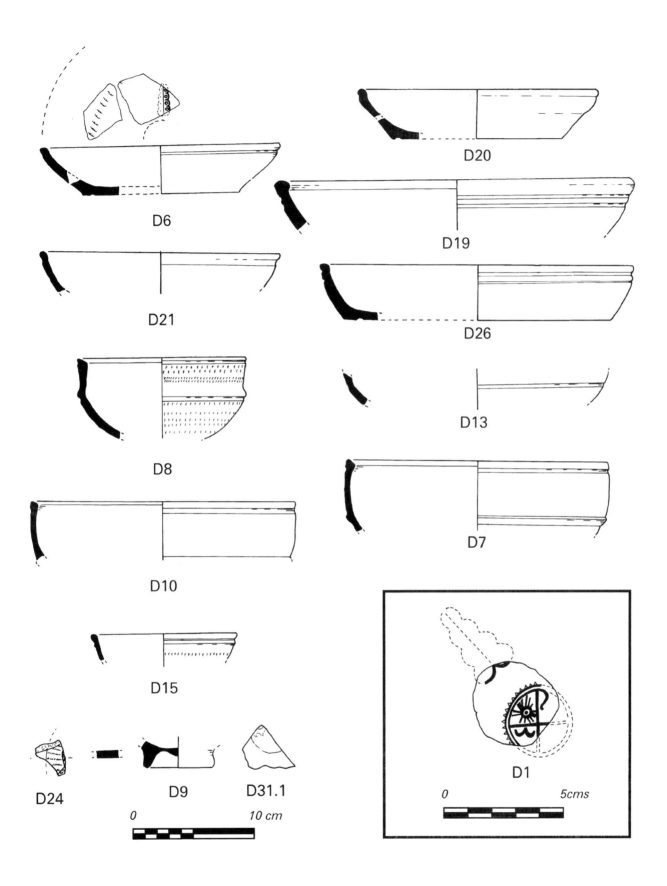

Fig 19 DSPA from Insular sites. Rigoir Form 4: D6 Dinas Powys; D19 Whithorn; D20, D21 Hen Gastell; D26 New Pieces. Form 14: D13 Longbury Bank. Form 16: D7, D8, D9, D10 Dinas Powys. Form 16/30: D15 Cadbury Castle. Decorated Form 4 basal sherds: D1 Dinas Emrys; D24 Cefn Cwmwd; D31.1 Tintagel

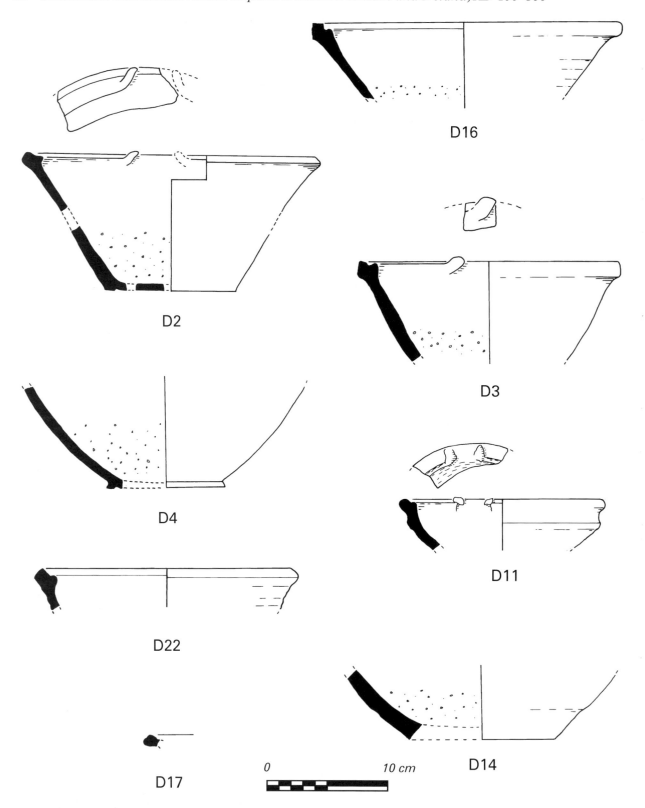

Fig 20 DSPA from Insular sites. Mortaria, Rigoir Form 29: D2, D3, D4 Dinas Powys; D11 Dunadd; D14 Mote of Mark; D16, D17 Tintagel; D22 Hen Gastell

and some of the forms can be matched exactly to vessels from the Bordeaux area. For example D2 matches no 4371, D3 matches no 2770 and D8 matches no 2802 in the Rigoirs' list of forms (Rigoir *et al* 1973). On the other hand, not all the

parallels are with vessels from the Bordeaux area. D7 matches a vessel from Nantes (no 2923) and the stamp on D6 is matched by one from Orléans (no 2291), as well as several from around Bordeaux. Although on the whole it is likely that the Dinas

Table 1 Relative ranking of top ten sites in each import group (MNV)

Site	E ware	Glass	DSPA	Aegean
Dunadd	1st	–	5th=	–
Whithorn	2nd	1st	5th=	6th
Dinas Powys	3rd=	3rd	1st	5th
Mote of Mark	3rd=	4th	5th=	–
Samson	3rd=	–	–	–
Garryduff No. 1	6th=	–	–	–
Tean	6th=	–	–	–
Dalkey Island	8th	–	–	–
Gwithian	9th	–	–	7th
Longbury Bank	10th=	6th	4th	10th
Clogher	10th=	–	5th=	–
Lagore	10th=	–	–	–
Bantham	10th=	–	–	2nd
Loch Glashan	10th=	–	–	–

Powys vessels were produced around Bordeaux, this does not necessarily mean that there was direct contact between the two areas. Complicated chains of sale and resale of goods are documented in the post-medieval period and are suspected for earlier periods (Allan 1983, 39). An exchange centre near the mouth of the Loire (?Noirmoutier or Nantes) would make sense both in terms of the parallels to the Dinas Powys vessels and in navigational terms. As noted above, the vessels from other sites whose fabric or decoration differs from those of Dinas Powys may be from as yet unidentified sources in this area of France.

Distribution

The overall distribution of these vessels throws some light on the date of importation (Fig 17). The problem with DSPA is that its believed period of production, in the 6th century, could overlap with the date of importation of either the Mediterranean wares or with the later E ware, and thus be part of either system. In the north, at Dunadd, Whithorn and the Mote of Mark, the DSPA is found in association only with E ware (Table 1). In south Wales, at Longbury Bank and Dinas Powys, DSPA is found in association with both E ware and Mediterranean wares. However in the south-west, at Tintagel and Cadbury Castle, DSPA is found on sites which only have the earlier Mediterranean wares. This suggests that some importation of DSPA may have taken place in the earlier part of the 6th century, but that importation continued into the later 6th or even 7th century along with E ware. It is also possible that the DSPA filled a gap, though on a very small scale, between the cessation of the Mediterranean trade around AD 550 and the commencement of the E ware trade in the late 6th century. This might explain the distribution of DSPA at Dinas Powys where the sherds are spatially distinct (Fig 59) from both other sets of imports. In this sense then, DSPA could be seen as the precursor to the E ware trade. The DSPA from Dunadd found in association with E ware is an imitation of an E ware form. This may have been produced in the same area as E ware and imported along with E ware vessels. As discussed above, there were local varieties of DSPA-type wares produced in various parts of northern and western France. The relative lack of DSPA from Ireland (found on only two sites) suggests that it ceased to be imported before E ware became available over much of the interior of Ireland, but so few vessels have been found outside the south-west of Britain that this absence may not be significant.

It is difficult to reach any conclusion on this issue from the data available. It is unfortunate that only two sherds of DSPA have been found in good stratified contexts which enable a judgement to be made on the contemporaneity or otherwise of other imported wares. At Tintagel, one sherd of a mortarium was found in Trench C15, Phase U, along with substantial quantities of LRA, and just below a sherd of ARS (Barrowman et al forthcoming). This confirms that DSPA was being imported by at least the mid-6th century. At Whithorn, the single sherd of DSPA was found in the same deposit as most of the E ware and Group C glass (Period 1.10), though the excavator considered it might have been displaced from an earlier 6th-century context (Hill 1997, 319). At Dinas Powys, the only site with a quantity of DSPA and a fairly good stratigraphy, there is only one sherd of DSPA under Bank 1, though there are quantities of PRS, ARS and LRA in these deposits. However, there are also a few early sherds of glass and E ware under Bank 1, which can be dated to the later 6th century. On this evidence one might be inclined to associate DSPA with the Mediterranean phase import system, but the evidence is shaky given the very small numbers of stratified sherds. There is a difference in the degree of association between DSPA and other imports on the fourteen DSPA sites. It is associated with Mediterranean imports on 12 sites, glass on 10 sites, and E ware on 8 sites, which might suggest that it was part of a late phase of the Mediterranean system (Table 13). Whatever the case, it seems that DSPA is a transitional phase between the two main systems. Because of the origin of DSPA in the same region as the glass and E ware, I will classify it as part of an early phase of that system, though it is probably transitional between the two systems. As we do not know how late DSPA continued to be produced in France, we can only say that it seems to have been imported for a period in the middle part of the 6th century, but possibly over most of the century.

Except at Dinas Powys the number of vessels of DSPA is small and could not in itself be taken as an indication of trade rather than casual contact, but the association of DSPA with sites which were major centres for the Mediterranean or Continental trades makes it probable that it was also a traded item. The small numbers found indicate that, like the E ware, it was only a minor 'space-filler' in a cargo of bulkier, more perishable goods. Thomas has suggested that DSPA vessels were contemporaneous with E ware and that DSPA was the tableware part of a package of household wares (Thomas 1976b). This is unlikely for the simple reason that only eight out of 74 sites with E ware have also produced D ware, and the spatial distributions are distinct, so they cannot be seen as a 'package' in the same way as the Aegean package of wares. It seems much more likely that E ware was a successor to DSPA, but what this means in terms of the type of trade involved is discussed later. The small quantity of DSPA makes it difficult to draw any substantial conclusions from its distribution in Britain, but it does seem to show a continuing interest in exotic goods at certain important sites of the 6th century, as the concentrations of D ware occur on sites which have concentrations of other imports. In this sense there is some continuity of consumption patterns, even if the trading systems were distinct.

3.2 Class E ware (Pls 9–20; Figs 25–33, 35–6)

Introduction

The label 'E ware' was proposed by Thomas (1954, 68) to supplement Radford's subdivision of the Tintagel imported pottery into classes A, B, C and D wares (Radford 1956). The ware comprises a variety of jars, bowls and jugs in a distinctive white gritty fabric with a 'pimply' surface. The vessels have no decoration, other than an occasional incised groove. It was first fully described by Thomas (1959), who proposed a Rhenish origin and a 5th- to 8th-century date. At this time Bernard Wailes was examining French Merovingian pottery to look for parallels to E ware (Wailes 1963). Wailes's thesis was unpublished, but he believed that he had found parallels to E ware, particularly amongst the Frankish cemeteries of the Rouen region. Some of these Merovingian forms which are closest to E ware are illustrated (Fig 27) but comparison of these forms with the Insular E ware forms makes it clear that there are very few close parallels, and none with the commonest E ware form, the E$_1$ jar. The next major paper on E ware was by Peacock and Thomas (1967), who proposed an origin in Aquitaine or the Paris basin on the basis of Peacock's heavy mineral analysis. The attribution to Aquitaine and particularly the Bordeaux region has become generally accepted, though the petrological basis for this has been criticised (Campbell 1984). Thomas has also published a series of updates of the distribution of the ware (1959; 1976b; 1981) without any more fundamental analysis being undertaken. More recently both Wooding (1996a; 1996b) and Thomas (1990) have discussed the mechanism of exchange involved in the E ware distributions. A fuller discussion of E ware than the other import wares (ie the typology, fabric and technical production aspects) is given in Appendix 2 because the production area is unknown, and because it is such a widespread and critical element of the material culture of Insular Atlantic sites. A summary of this discussion is given below.

Production

The fabric of E ware is basically a white gritty ware, with a distinctive pimply surface where the large angular quartz grits protrude through the surface which has been wet-wiped on the wheel. Although the white colour immediately distinguishes it from most medieval red (oxidised) and grey (reduced) wares, it can be confused with some Roman coarsewares, medieval Scottish White Gritty Wares, unglazed Saintonge ware, and northern French wares such as Normandy Gritty Ware. Unfortunately, the mineralogy of the inclusions is not very distinctive, causing problems both for identification and provenance (Chapter 1.5). The commonest fabric (Fabric E1) is very uniform (Pl 9), varying only in the proportion of earthy iron ore present, which can impart a reddish colour. A few vessels have rounded rather than sub-angular quartz inclusions (Fabric E2).

The ware is well fired, and a variety of lines of evidence suggest a kiln temperature of around 1000°C and well-controlled firing conditions. Although generally a white ware, occasionally

Continental pottery: DSPA, Class E Ware

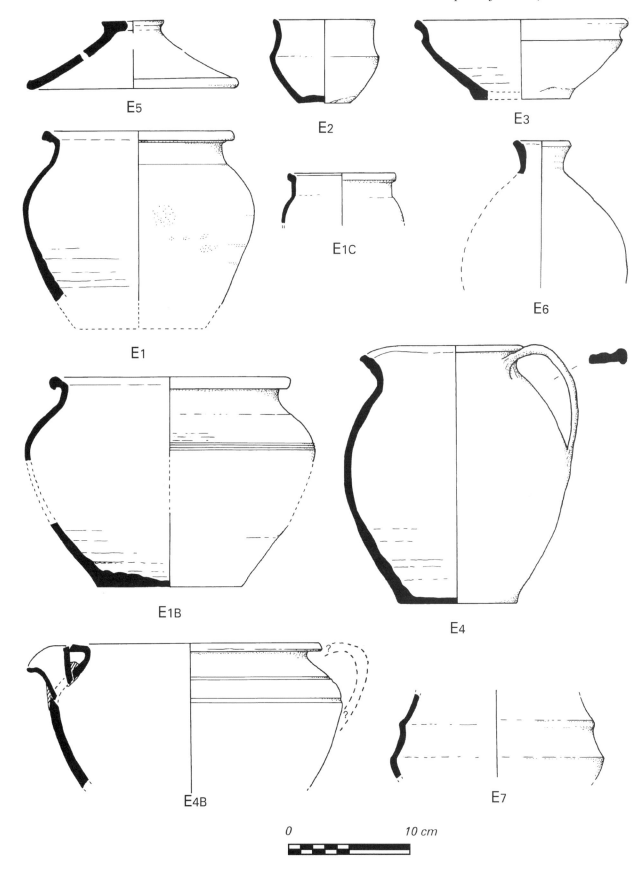

Fig 21 Forms of E ware

orange or grey firing marks are present (Pl 14). Vessels appear to have been produced to a series of standardised forms, with a restricted range of sizes and shapes. Techniques of throwing include the use of jigs or formers for the body shape, and throwing small vessels 'off the lump' (Pl 10).

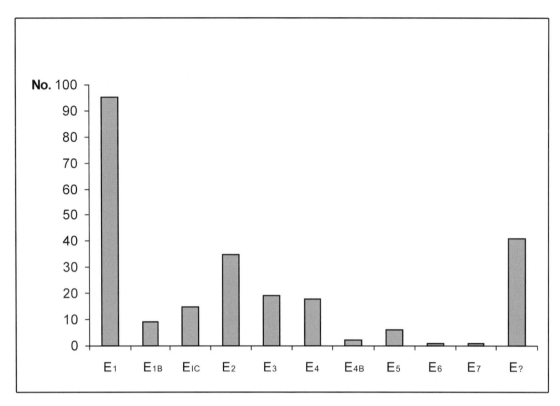

Fig 22 *Relative proportions of different E ware forms*

Although E ware is basically a plain ware, there are a few distinctive features. Handles are always wheel-thrown, having a distinctive section which distinguishes them from most British medieval pottery which has rolled or pulled handles (Pl 11). This feature is characteristic of all French medieval wares. A distinctive feature of handles and tubular spouts is that they are luted to the vessel body with a smeared fingermark (Pls 12–13; Figs 31–2). Decoration, consisting only of single incised horizontal lines, occasionally in groups, is very rare, being found on only 5% of vessels. This contrasts with many other Merovingian and Carolingian wares which have stamped and rouletted decoration.

These details of production enable a number of conclusions to be drawn about the organisation of the E ware production process. The standardised sizes and shapes of the main forms (E1, E2, E3), the use of formers to throw the vessels, throwing 'off the lump', the lack of decoration, and the similarity of fabric and finish amongst the assemblage, all point to a non-domestic scale of production. The kiln temperature and control of oxygen supply show the continuing use of kilns of a type standard in the Roman world. This in turn suggests there was no great disruption of the pottery production industry between the end of the Roman period and the date of production of E ware, and that it may have been produced in an existing area of production in Late Roman times. There seems to be much more variation in the Merovingian 5th-/6th-century wares found in Frankish cemeteries, and these may have been produced on a more local scale. The Insular assemblage as a whole is a highly coherent group, both in terms of fabric and form, suggesting that the vast majority of the vessels came from a single area of production. The very minor occurrences of E2 fabric (4% of the assemblage) shows that some vessels were produced in a different area, though it could be close by; otherwise, there is little to distinguish these vessels from those with E1 fabric.

Typology

Thomas originally (1956, 14) classified E ware into three forms: Ei jars, Eii beakers and Eiii spouts and handles. In his 1959 paper he amended and extended this classification to five forms: Ei jars, Eii beakers, Eiii bowls, Eiv pitchers and Ev lids (later relabelled E1–E5) (Thomas 1959; 1981). This classification is still broadly useful. So few complete profiles of vessels are available that it would be unproductive to introduce a completely new classification, but a few subtypes and new forms are here adopted (Fig 21). All the common E ware forms are directly descended from Frankish forms with very little alteration, as can be seen by comparison with these wares (Böhner 1958, abb 1b), and not from Late Roman western French wares as Thomas has claimed (Thomas 1990, 7). Studies of Late Roman pottery in northern and western France all show that E ware forms are not present in the Late Roman period, except for

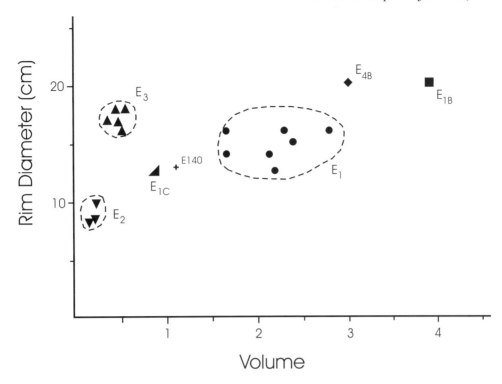

Fig 23 Volume (in litres) of E ware forms, showing restricted fields

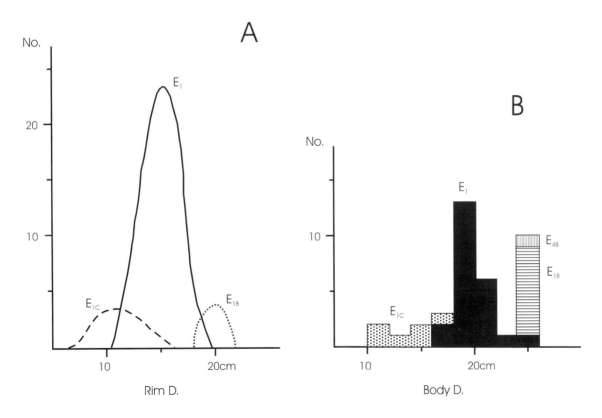

Fig 24 Rim and body diameter ratios of E ware forms

the generic *olla*, and possibly the E3 bowl (Gabet 1969; Galliou and Ménez 1986; Tuffreau-Libre 1980). Of course, it is of interest that Frankish forms are being made in western France at this period, given the relative lack of evidence for Frankish settlement here (James 1977), but these forms seem to have replaced Romano-Gallic forms widely in the early medieval period, certainly by Carolingian times.

By far the commonest form of E ware is the E1

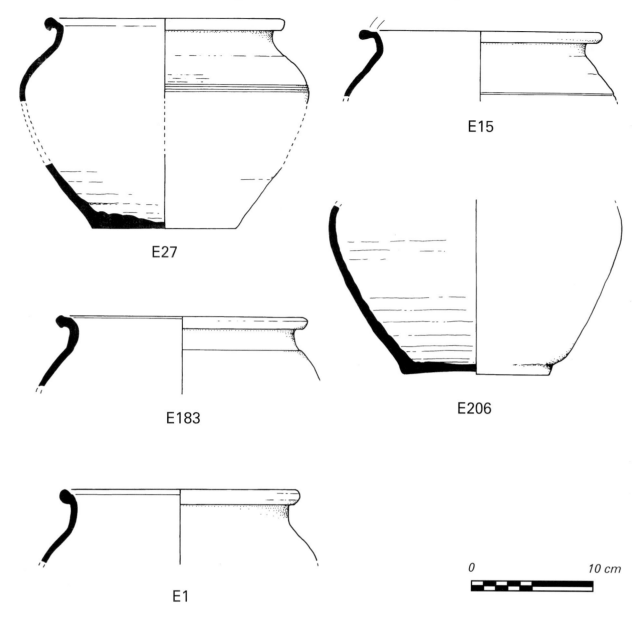

Fig 25 E ware from Insular sites. Form E1B, large jars: E1 Ardifuir; E15 Carew Castle; E27 Dalkey Island; E183 Samson; E206 Teeshan

jar with around 115 vessels, about 60% of the total number of identified E ware vessels (Fig 22; Table 15). Although often referred to as a 'cooking-pot', this form is more likely to be a multi-purpose storage jar (Pl 15; Fig 28). The neutral term jar, or *olla*, is to be preferred. While generally similar forms of jar are common throughout the Roman period, and into the early Middle Ages, exact matches to the E ware form and rim details are difficult to find (see below). Although the form of the E ware jar is fairly standardised, there are some clear subdivisions of the form, with larger (E1B), and smaller (E1C), versions being distinguishable not just by size, but also by variations in the proportions of the vessels. This is best seen on a graph of volume of vessels, though there are very few of these measurements (Fig 23). Measurement of the rim diameters of the E ware jars

shows that most of the vessels have a diameter of 14–18cm with the mode at 16cm, and that while each sub-form overlaps in size range, each has a normal distribution curve, suggesting that these subjective groups have some reality (Fig 24).

At the larger end of the E1 range there is a group of distinctive vessels, here termed E1B (Fig 25). These larger vessels have a relatively wider mouth than the normal E1 form, giving them a squatter appearance, shown by their different height to width ratio. The two known E4B vessels with tubular spouts (Fig 32, E13, E192) seem to be basically of this form, but made into pitchers by the addition of spouts and, presumably, handles.

At the smaller end of the scale the vessels appear to be rather different, though no complete profile is available. These 'small E1', as Wailes (1963) termed the equivalent Merovingian forms, approach the

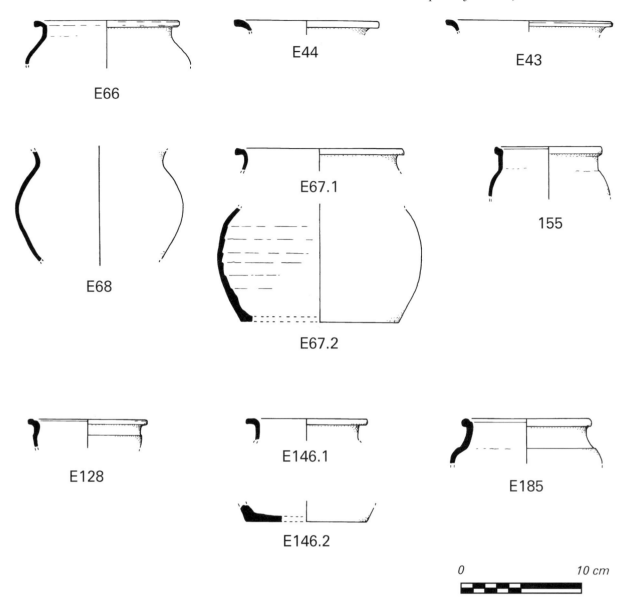

Fig 26 E ware from Insular sites. Form E₁C, small jars: E43, E44 Dinas Powys; E66, E67, E68 Dunadd; E128 Lesser Garth; E146 Longbury Bank; E155 May's Hill; E185 Samson

size of E2 carinated beakers but differ in having sharply everted rims. The form of the body is different from the normal E1 in having thinner walls and a more upright neck. I have termed these E1C forms (Fig 26). It can be difficult to distinguish between E1C and E2 forms when only the base is present. Although these E1C vessels must have had a volume similar to that of E2 beakers, the everted rim shows they could not have functioned as drinking vessels, but must have been containers of some kind. It is not entirely clear whether this form is a small version of the E1 jar, or a form of E2 beaker with an everted rim. Wailes's analysis of the forms from Merovingian sites suggests that there the E1C form is more closely related to the E2 form than the E1 form. Various stages of transition between E2 and E1C forms can be seen in this material (Fig 27). For this reason in my thesis I originally classed these forms as E2B, but the clearly different function of the E2 and E1C vessels, and the similarity of E1C to E1 forms has led me to label them E1C. The vessels of E1C form which are closest to the British examples are found mainly in the lower Seine area, particularly from near Evreux, Eure, at Muids, Bueil, Merey and St Pierre-du-Vauvray. The similarity of this little group of wares to the E1C vessels might suggest that this is the region of production of E ware, but the lack of E1 forms from these cemeteries suggests otherwise. Hodges notes the similarity of the fabric of these vessels to his Class 11 and Normandy Gritty Ware, suggesting a long-standing production centre in this area (Hodges 1981, 75). Although this fabric is similar to E ware, it is not identical, and for reasons discussed below it is unlikely that this is the production area of E ware.

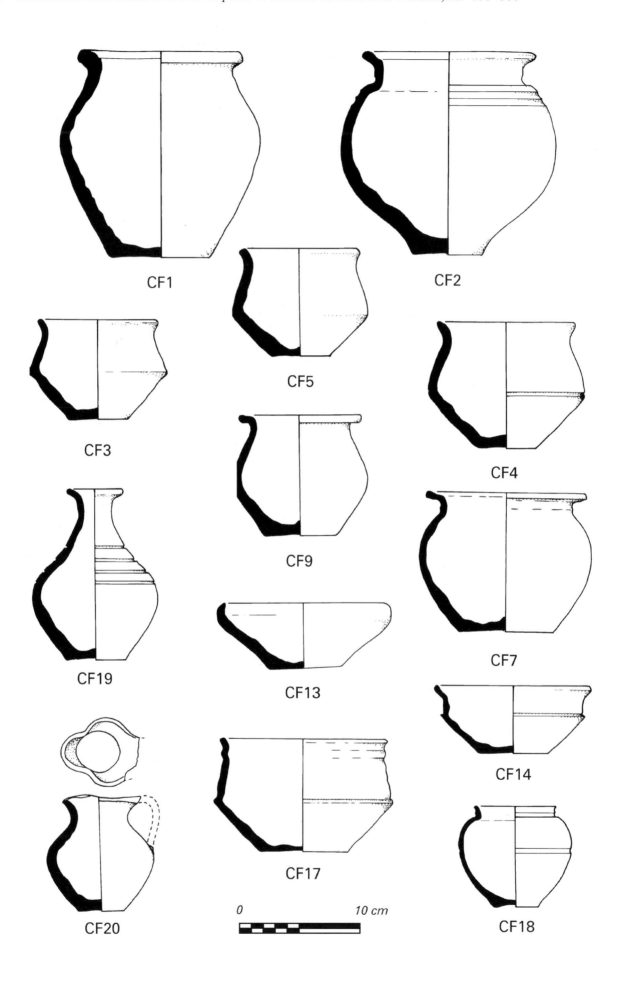

Although the E1 jar form contains a remarkably homogeneous assemblage of vessels, which give the impression of being of uniform form and of having been produced over a relatively short period of time, there are some indications of typological development. Most notable is the almost complete vessel from Loch Glashan (Pl 20; Fig 28, E140; Crone and Campbell 2005, fig 32, vessel 5). The body shape of this vessel is more angular and higher shouldered than normal, with almost no neck and a triangular rim. The form seems to be a late version of the E ware jar, tending in form towards Carolingian jar profiles such as one from Corbeilles (Loiret) (Hodges 1981, fig 7.8, 4) and a *Hamwic* Fabric 128 import (Timby 1988, fig 11, 220). It has, however, not reached the globular body form of these 9th-/10th-century jars. It is most unfortunate that this vessel, unlike the other E ware from the site, had no organic residues to be dated, but it appears to be stratigraphically later than them (Crone and Campbell 2005, 56–7). All these factors point to a later date than most E ware, perhaps in the 8th century. One of the few vessels with a similar rim form was found at Whithorn (E271) in a context later than the bulk of E ware, possibly dating to the late 7th century (Campbell 1997, 322, vessel 9). Another vessel from Whithorn, E278 (Campbell 1997, 322, fig 10.19, no 16) has characteristics of fabric which relate it to a group of white gritty wares discussed below (Chapter 3.3), suggesting a late date in the E ware range, but unfortunately its stratigraphic position was not clear.

The small carinated beakers of Thomas's Class E2 are the next most numerous form (Pl 16), with about 33 examples known (Figs 22 and 29). This is a standard Merovingian form and the E ware examples are a coherent group of vessels with the height and rim diameter falling in a restricted field of values (Fig 23). This form of vessel, along with the small E1C jars, seems to be a feature of funerary deposits in Frankish cemeteries, as they occur more frequently there than in settlement assemblages.

The E3 bowls (Pl 17) are a similarly coherent group on the height/diameter graph but only nineteen examples are known (Figs 22 and 30). Although carinated bowls are found in the Rhenish assemblages (Böhner 1958, taf 1 and 6) it is not entirely clear whether this was a purely Frankish form. In her study of Roman wares Tuffreau-Libre illustrates a progression of bowl forms which ends with a form very similar to the E3 bowl in the 4th century (Tuffreau-Libre 1980, fig 93). The bowls from Frankish cemeteries illustrated by Wailes (Fig 27) generally have a much smaller diameter than E3 vessels, though they are of similar height. They seem to be more like wide versions of E2 beakers, and none can be said to be like an E3 bowl, but they may well be precursors. The E3 form did not survive into the 8th century, as most bowls from that period onwards have flanged rims (Hodges 1981; Timby 1988). In this sense then it is the most characteristic E ware form, apparently restricted to the period of production of E ware.

The E4 jugs with pinched (trefoil) spouts (Pl 18) are less easy to define as there is no complete profile known (Fig 31). Indeed, no base can certainly be associated with any upper body. Although there are many jug rims at Dunadd, none of the bases can be definitely associated with any of these, though one possible example provided the basis for Figure 21. The E ware vessels with tubular spouts (Pl 19) are here classed as E4B (Fig 32), though as noted above they are obviously related to the E1B form rather than the E4. A characteristic feature of these vessels is the form of construction of the handle. All the handles were wheelthrown, as can be seen from the sections, the throwing grooves and folds at one edge of the handles (Pl 11). This technique (sometimes referred to as a 'French roll') was a continuing tradition in France from the Roman period to modern times, unlike the pulled or rolled handles found in most British medieval vessels. They were luted onto the surface of the vessels rather than being inserted through a hole. The upper end was attached to the lip or underside of the rim (Fig 31, E75, E76), luted underneath and with a thumb smear from the upper surface of the rim across the handle (Pl 13). This last feature is not seen on the Merovingian material which I have examined, and may be specific to the E ware production area.

Spouts were formed in two ways. The commoner pinched spout of the E4 vessels was simply formed by pulling part of the rim out and down, while pinching it slightly. The shape is not as markedly spouted as with most jugs with trefoil spouts in other wares. The tubular spouts of the E4B vessels were inserted through a hole in the shoulder of the vessel, and luted on with applied clay on the exterior and interior. One edge of the spout was attached to the rim in the same manner as the strap handles, by smearing the rim over the spout (Pl 12). Both the known spouts were further adapted by pinching them into a trefoil spout. These E4B vessels seem to be based on an unusual DSPA pitcher (Rigoir form 36) which has three small handles, an identical method of spout formation, and the same body profile as E4B. These pitchers

Fig 27 (opposite) Continental white gritty wares from Frankish cemeteries (after Wailes 1963). CF1 Rijnsburg, Zuid Holland; CF2 Tourville-la-Rivière, Seine-Maritime; CF3 Corbie, Somme; CF4 Merey, Eure; CF5 Barille-la-Rivière, Seine-Maritime; CF7 ?Pas-de-Calais; CF9 St Pierre-du-Vauvray, Eure; CF13 Eprave, Namur; CF14 Rhenen, Utrecht; CF17 Sommery, Seine-Maritime; CF18 Therouanne, Pas-de-Calais; CF19 Soissons area, Ainse; CF20 Compiegne area, Oise

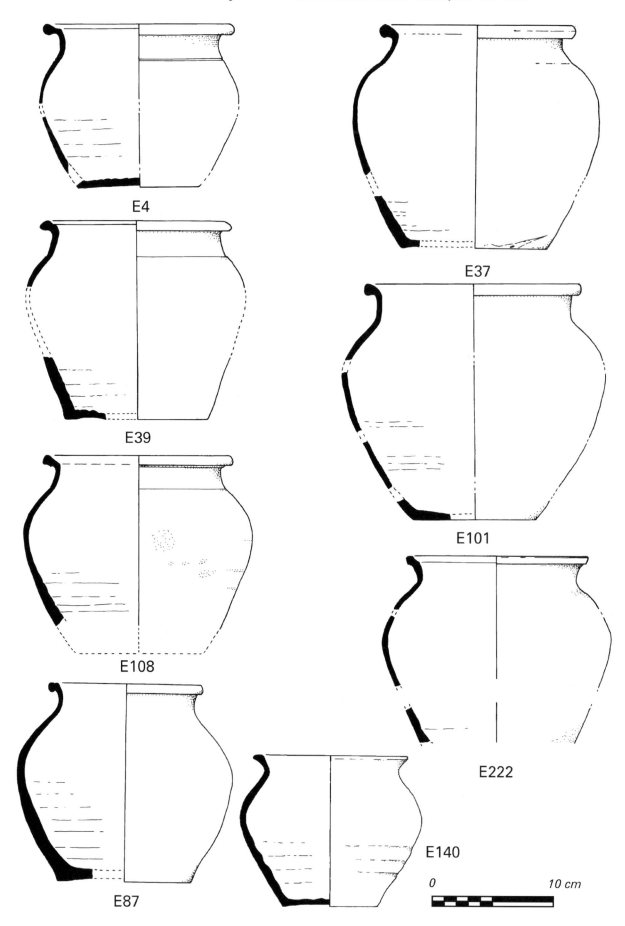

Fig 28 E ware from Insular sites. Form E1, jars: E4 Ballinderry no. 2; E37, E39 Dinas Powys; E87 Garranes (after Warner); E101 Gwithian; E108 Iona; E140 Loch Glashan; E222 Dundonald Castle

Continental pottery: DSPA, Class E Ware 41

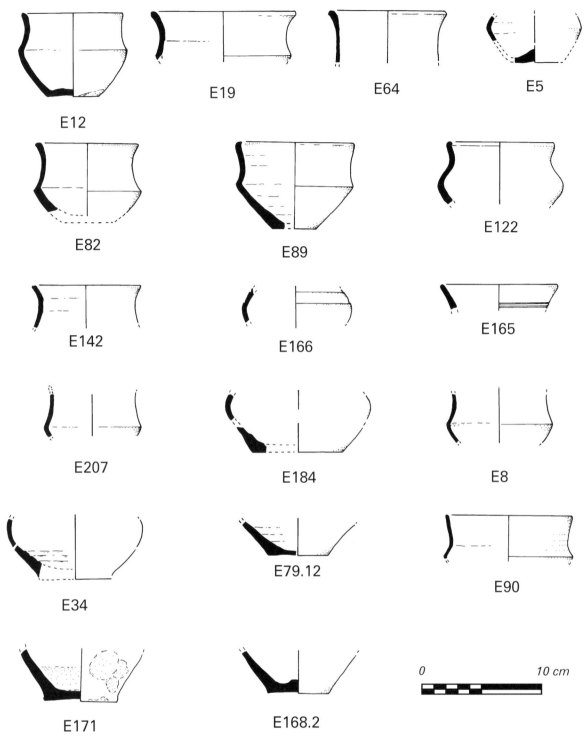

Fig 29 E ware from Insular sites. Form E2, beakers: E5 Ballycatteen; E8 Ballyfounder; E12 Buiston; E19 Clogher; E34 Dalkey Island; E64, E79.12 Dunadd; E82 Dunollie; E89, E90 Garryduff; E122 Lagore; E142 Lochlee; E165, E166, E168.2 Mote of Mark; E171 Port y Candas; E184 Samson; E207 Trethurgy

do not occur until 6th-century levels (*états* 12–13) at Bordeaux (Soulas 1996, 247).

Not all handles are from large vessels. One handle of much smaller size than usual is known from the Mote of Mark (E167). This probably belongs to a small jug similar to some known from Merovingian cemeteries, for example one from Compiegne (Fig 27, CF20). It is no doubt signifi-cant that the only other known small jug came from Whithorn (E213), and that was one of only two E ware vessels in an earlier context than the main group of E ware vessels, probably dating to Hill's import stage 2 of the mid- to later 6th century (Campbell 1997, 321, illus 10.19, vessel 6). Jugs are as rare as bowls in the E ware assemblage, with only eighteen examples known.

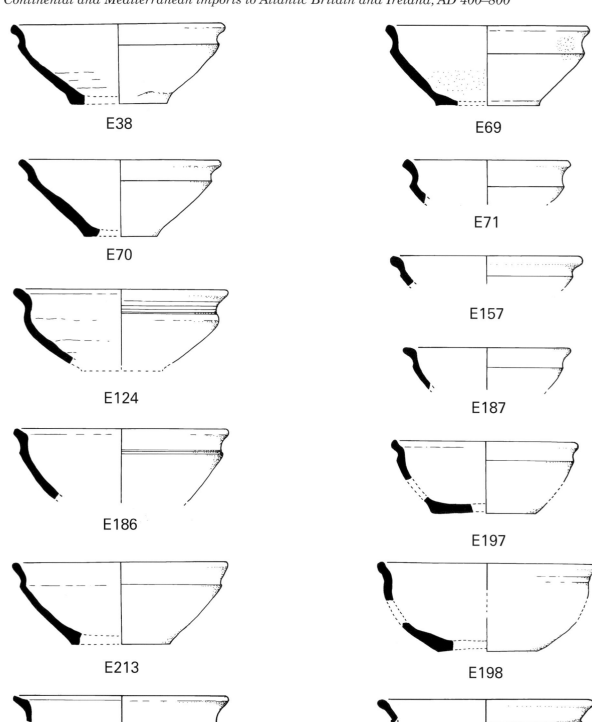

Fig 30 E ware from Insular sites. Form E3, bowls: E38 Dinas Powys; E69, E70, E71 Dunadd; E124 Lagore; E157 Mote of Mark; E186, E187 Samson; E197, E198 Tean (after Thomas 1985); E213 Whithorn; E240, E241 Clonmacnoise

Thomas's last form, the E5 lid, is not technically a separate form as these lids were used on E1 jars (Fig 33). The example from Bar Point St Mary's (E11) fits the accompanying E1 jar (E10) and is pierced, perhaps to allow steam to escape when used as a cooking-pot. The form is very rare, though several have been found recently in Ireland (I Doyle pers comm).

There are a few other rare vessels which do not fall into this classification (Fig 33). From Dumbarton

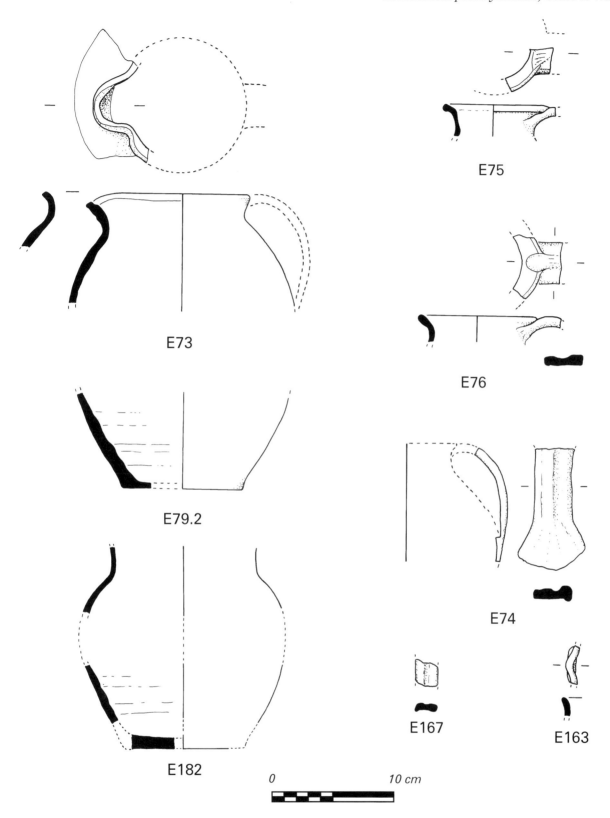

Fig 31 E ware from Insular sites. Form E4, jugs: E73 / 79.2, E74, E75, E76 Dunadd; E167, E163 Mote of Mark; E182 Samson

Rock comes what appears to be the neck of a bottle (E52), here classed as E6. Presumably this is related to the series of 'Frankish' bottles imported extensively into south-eastern Britain in the 7th century (Evison 1979), none of which are found in the Atlantic area. From Samson, Scilly, comes part of the upper body of a double-carinated biconical vessel (E190) of a form found in 5th-/6th-century Merovingian grave assemblages, here classed as E7. The vessel classed as an E6 unguent jar by

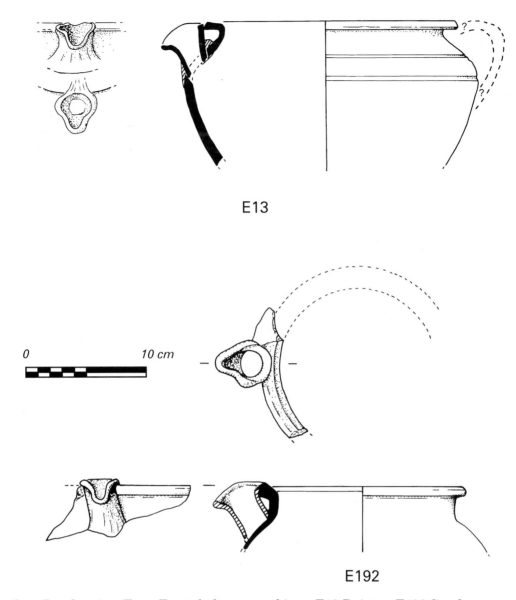

Fig 32 E ware from Insular sites. Form E4B, tubular-spouted jugs: E13 Buiston; E192 Scrabo

Thomas (1990, fig 1, 6), after O'Donnell, in fact falls within the normal range of variation of E2 beakers. Finally, Earwood (1992) has claimed that some turned wooden vessels are skeuomorphs of E ware and other imported vessels, but this has been refuted as the parallels are not close (Crone and Campbell 2005, 61).

Having reviewed the classification of the E ware vessels it is now possible to look briefly at the distribution (Fig 34), though this will be done in more detail in Chapter 8. Not surprisingly, in view of the preponderance of the form, E1 jars have the same distribution as E ware generally. E2 vessels share this widespread distribution, but the less common forms are noticeably confined to a number of major coastal sites which will be defined as centres of importation. It can be shown that this situation is not a result of the larger number of vessels found on the major sites. A comparison of the proportion of the various forms found on major and minor sites show a strong disparity between the groups (Table 2). The E3 bowls, E4 jugs and the other unusual forms are concentrated on the major sites. It seems as if the E2 beakers were preferentially distributed to the smaller sites, while the uncommon forms were kept on the major sites. This will be discussed in more detail in Chapter 9.

Chronology

The chronology of E ware is a matter of considerable controversy (Thomas 1959, 1981; Warner 1979; Campbell 1996b) and importance. The importance lies in the fact that E ware is generally the only material found on Atlantic sites of this period which is theoretically capable of independent, external dating. Many of the common artefacts remain unchanged throughout the second half of

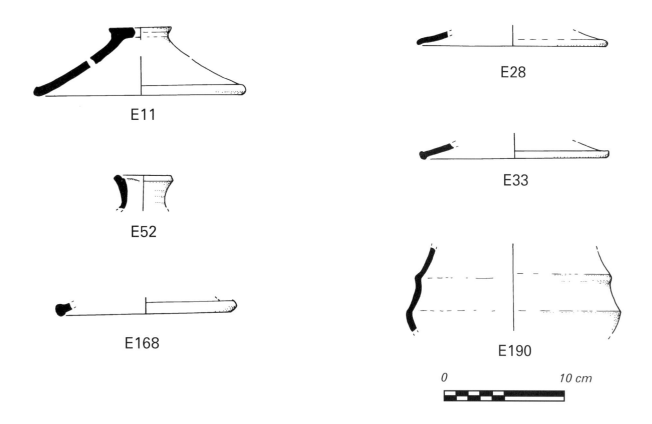

Fig 33 E ware from Insular sites. Form E5, lids: E11 Bar Point (after Ashbee); E28, E33 Dalkey Island; E168 Mote of Mark. Form E6, bottle: E52 Dumbarton Rock. Form E7, carinated jar: E190 Samson

Table 2 Sites with unusual forms of E ware

SITE	E3	E4	E4B	E5	E6	E7	DSPA	Glass	Other import	royal	fort/ crannog
Buiston	–	–	1	–	–	–	–	+	+	–	+
Cabinteely	–	–	–	1	–	–	+	–	+	–	–
Clatchard	–	1	–	–	–	–	–	+	–	–	+
Clonmacnoise	2	–	–	–	–	–	–	–	–	–	–
Dalkey Island	–	–	–	2	–	–	–	+	+	–	–
Dinas Powys	1	1	–	–	–	–	+	+	+	?	+
Dumbarton	–	1	–	–	1	–	–	+	+	+	+
Dunadd	4	6	–	–	–	–	+	+	+	+	+
Killucan	–	1	–	–	–	–	–	–	–	–	–
Lagore	1	–	–	–	–	–	–	+	–	+	+
Mote of Mark	1	2	–	1	–	–	+	+	+	–	+
Scrabo	–	1	1	–	–	–	–	–	–	–	+
Whithorn	4	1	–	–	–	–	+	+	+	–	–
SCILLY											
Bar Point	–	–	–	1	–	–	–	–	–	–	–
Samson	3	2	–	–	–	1	–	–	+	–	–
Tean	2	1	–	–	–	–	–	–	+	–	–

Fig 34 Distribution of E ware

the first millennium, while the dating of the finer decorative metalwork of the period is highly contentious. It would appear then that E ware with its widespread distribution is well placed to provide a framework for the chronology of the period.

Before considering the evidence for the date of E ware, however, a few comments should be made. Firstly, E ware is unsuited to close typological dating, as it is an undecorated coarse ware. Medieval coarse pottery has been shown to be a poor chronological indicator, with forms remaining conservative for many generations and it is likely that the same situation applied in the early medieval period. Secondly, Continental evidence for the date of manufacture is almost entirely lacking. Even if this evidence were available, it does not follow that the dates of importation covered the same period as the dates of manufacture.

A more general problem, however, is the question of stratigraphic association and residuality. The difficulties of assessing the degree of residuality of pottery will be illustrated in the following chapters in the case of Dinas Powys. Even where it is fairly certain that the E ware itself is in a contemporary context, as at Gransha or Dalkey Island (Chapter 8.1), the problem of the reliability of the association with other artefacts remains. On most sites the only potentially datable objects found with E ware are decorated metalwork and fine beads. In many cases it is difficult to be sure if such objects represent *in situ* contemporary losses. For example, the very fine zoomorphic brooch from Ballinderry No. 2 crannog was found beneath the floor-planking but the excavator considered that it had been hidden there after the building of the house, though this interpretation has now been disputed (Newman 1989, 14). The hiding of fine brooches is reported elsewhere: the silver brooch at Cahercommaun was hidden in a souterrain (Hencken 1938), and at Pant-y-Saer the tinned penannular was found lying against the inside wall of structure A where it could have been placed for safe-keeping (Phillips 1934). In other cases the association of E ware and metalwork is stratigraphically unsound, as at Loch Glashan, where the brooch lies in an unsealed deposit of mud outside the crannog building (Crone and Campbell 2005).

These objections have been spelled out in detail because there has been a tendency, particularly where Irish sites are concerned, to ignore stratigraphical considerations in the dating of metalwork. Irish sites in the past have often been given a 'date' which is then transferred to all the objects from that site. Chris Lynn has shown that this 'date' is usually that quoted by the excavator even when this is totally out of date or based on specious or circular arguments (Lynn 1986, 69).

The evidence for the date of E ware, as with any type of pottery, rests on a variety of evidence, none of which is conclusive but which taken together points to a restricted period of time. The wide distribution of E ware, occurring in a wide variety of small and large political and cultural units, shows that its importation cannot be regarded as due to the random activity of travellers, but must be part of some organised trading activity (Chapter 9.3). This provides the justification for looking at the evidence for the date of importation *in toto*, and not only on individual sites. We are thus trying to date the period of activity of a trading system rather than a series of individual finds.

In summary (see Appendix 2 for full details), this trading system can be broadly dated after the period of Mediterranean imports in the mid-6th century, and before the Anglian occupation of Whithorn in the early 8th century. The Whithorn excavations are a key to the detailed chronology (Chapter 7.6), but a variety of other evidence supports this dating. The *floruit* of E ware seems to be in the earlier 7th century, but the range goes from the later 6th to the late 7th century.

Provenance

Ideas on the provenance of E ware have shifted from the Rhineland (O Ríordáin 1947; Hencken 1950), to north-western France (Thomas 1957), back to the Rhineland (Thomas 1959), to Aquitaine (Peacock and Thomas 1967; Hodges 1977) and north to the Loire (Wooding 1996b, 78; Thomas 1990). Only the evidence of kilns is capable

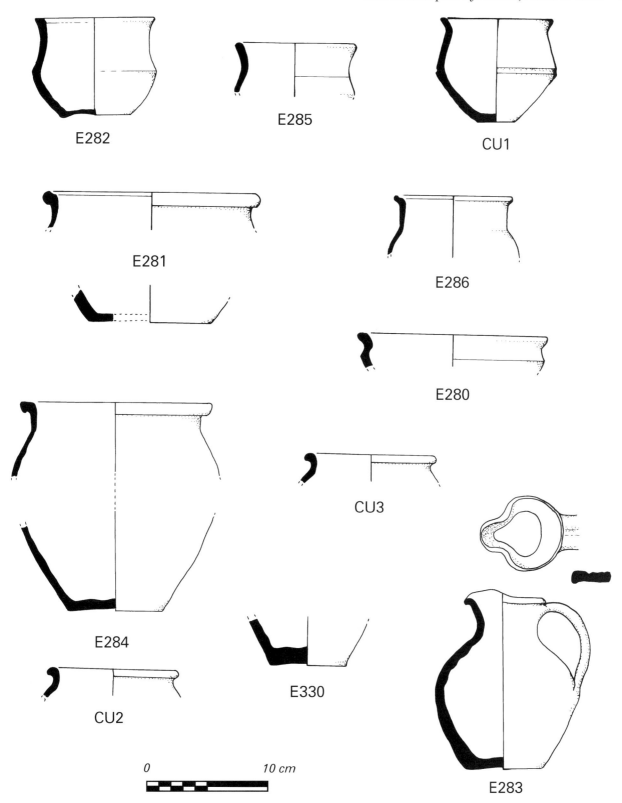

Fig 35 Continental E ware: E280 Chadenac; E281 Guissény; E282, E283 Herpes; E284 Les Cléons (after Wailes); E285, E286 Tours. Rejected or uncertain E ware: CU1 Dieppe (after Knight), CU2 Les Cléons (after Wailes), CU3 Mane-Geren (after Wailes)

of finally resolving this question, though the discovery of large numbers of vessels in a single area of France would be a pointer to the production source. In the absence of such information a number of clues can be gained from a study of the fabric and form of E ware, scattered finds on the Continent and historical sources. Analysis of the typology and fabric of the ware makes it clear that the pottery comes from a single coherent source, and that this lies within the area of Merovingian France.

Typological analysis of the forms shows that the E ware vessels are a late form of Frankish wares which developed in the Rhineland in the 4th to 5th centuries, and that the production source must lie in an area of Frankish settlement, or Frankish influence (*contra* Thomas 1990, 22). Carolingian successor forms to E ware are widely scattered over northern and western France, giving little clue as to any single source for the forms. Recent excavations of settlement sites in northern France have not produced any E ware (eg de Saint Jores and Hincher 2001). Material in Frankish cemeteries studied by Wailes (1963) shows only general similarities except for vessels of form E1C which cluster around the Rouen area. Conventional interpretations of the cemetery evidence show Frankish influence as common north of the River Loir (*sic*), and with a smaller concentration in the Vendée and Poitou (Zeiss 1941). On the other hand James (1977; 1988, 113) sees no evidence for Frankish settlement south of the Loire in western France, except for the area around Herpes, which has produced E ware vessels, as well as many Anglo-Saxon objects.

The mineralogy of the fabric suggests an origin in an area of red, haematite-cemented sandstone which was ultimately derived from the degradation of granitic material. Although this is likely to be in an area of Tertiary rocks (Peacock and Thomas 1967), Mesozoic rocks cannot be ruled out (Campbell 1984). The geological map of France therefore suggests the Charente or lower Seine, though small pockets of younger rocks are found in the Armorican massif and lower Loire. Red sandstones are rare in these areas and this fact may enable a source to be found despite the unpromising nature of the mineral assemblage. The fabric is similar to that of Normandy Gritty Ware and Merovingian wares from the lower Seine valley (Hodges 1981, 74–5), where there were extensive production sources in the medieval period and whose chemical analysis is similar to that of E ware (Dufournier 1981). A general similarity to medieval Saintonge ware has been claimed, though this is not so coarsely gritted, but much fieldwork in the area of production has failed to locate any possible source (Chapelot 1983, 51).

Certain Continental finds of E ware are few, scattered between Brittany and Charente (Fig 35). The finds on the northern coast of Brittany (Guisseny and Le Yaudet) would appear to be offshoots of the Insular distribution. The sherd from Le Yaudet is in a post-Roman context with only residual Roman pottery. The finds at Tours are within large assemblages of local ceramics, and must be imports there. The E ware reported from a Roman villa at Les Cléons, near Nantes, are missing but look reliable in terms of form. Here a late building overlay the villa, and a 7th-century gold coin was recorded from the site. Both Les Cléons and Tours are sites easily accessible via the Loire, and do not indicate production areas. There is a group of sites in the Poitou-Charentes region which geologically may be in production areas. The most interesting is the cemetery at Herpes, a site which has produced material from a wide variety of sources. There is at least one E2 beaker from here, and Wooding (1996b, 77, fig 8) reports two others. At the churchyard of a chapel at Chadenac, Brigitte Camus showed me a stray surface find of an E3 bowl. P-R Giot reported an E ware rim from the Grotte de Villebois-Lavalette, which although unusual, is matched by some Insular examples (Wooding 1995, fig 9, ew13). These sites are all in the Saintes region, the major medieval production centre for Saintonge wares which were widely exported to Britain from the 13th century onwards.

Turning to historical sources, the evidence for trade contacts has been evaluated by several authors recently, with Wooding providing the most detailed account (Doherty 1980; James 1982; Wooding 1983, 1987, 1996a, 1996b). The only places mentioned in contemporary sources in connection with trade with Atlantic Insular sites are Noirmoutier, in the *Vita Filiberti*; Nantes and the mouth of the Loire, in the *Vita Columbani*; and Poitiers in the story of the exile of Dagobert II. The 9th-century charter of St-Denis, Paris, mentioned in connection with the export of madder (Chapter 5.6; Appendix 5), if it does refers to E ware trade in the 7th century, points to possible links with the lower Seine (merchants from Rouen are mentioned as trading with foreigners). Finally, the mint spots of the only two Merovingian coins from the Atlantic West are in Sarthe, on a tributary of the Loire, perhaps pointing to a north-western French source, if the finds are genuine ancient losses. James (1977, 223) in his study of the coinage of western France showed that Aquitaine was an economic backwater at this period with little contact with the rest of Gaul, but the Loire valley was more open to trade with northern areas.

In total this evidence helps to clarify the picture, with three areas, around Rouen, the lower Loire, and in the Saintonge, all being possible candidates for a production centre based on geological background and parallels to the E ware fabric. The apparent lack of E ware in Merovingian cemeteries, museum collections and 6th- to 8th-century settlement sites in northern France rules out this area as a source. This leaves the lower Loire, or more likely, Poitou-Charentes (rather than modern Aquitaine) as likely production areas. Very little pottery has been published from Merovingian cemeteries in western France, but a study of all the sites listed by James (1977) shows that, with the exception of the area around Herpes, pottery grave-goods from the area between the Loire and Gironde seem to be continuations of Late Roman forms. Zeiss (1941, Taf. 1, 2) illustrates an E2 form of beaker from Rouillé, Vienne, not far from Poitiers. Examination of pottery from excavations on the site of the Poitiers baptistery (kindly made possible by the excavator, B Camus), did not produce any E ware, though there were some thin-walled vessels very similar to later vessels from sites around the Firth of Clyde (see below Chapter 3.3). Whatever the case, the export route for E ware would seem to have passed the Loire estuary at some point.

Function

Thomas's description of the E ware vessels as 'a robust kitchenware' (Thomas 1981, 20) is often quoted as an indication of the function of these vessels, but no detailed study of the form and function of these vessels has been attempted previously. By far the commonest form of E ware is the E1 jar. This form is often referred to as a 'cooking-pot' by analogy with later medieval 'cooking-pots', but the shape is quite different. The relatively narrow base, high shoulder and flat base create an unstable profile unsuitable for placing in the ashes of a hearth. In addition, these are relatively small vessels with a low volume (1.5–2.5 litres) compared to later cooking-pots. The E1 form is directly descended from the later Roman storage jar or *olla*. Although this form, like the medieval cooking-pot, could be used for a variety of purposes, it seems that it was basically a storage container. The sharply everted rim (Fig 36) seems to be designed to enable a cover of cloth or leather to be placed over the mouth of the vessel and tied beneath the rim. The large E1B and small E1C forms are generally similar, and probably had the same function. The fabric supports this conclusion. The very hard proto-stoneware fabric with quartz tempering is quite unsuitable for the repeated heating that a cooking vessel is subjected to (Rye 1976). Such fabrics tend to split and splinter on heating as the stresses cannot be redistributed. Cooking pot fabrics are generally fired at low temperature, are often hand made, and have temper of igneous rock fragments, organics or calcareous material such as shell (*ibid*).

These general points must be set beside the evidence on the vessels themselves. Signs of sooting on the bases do occur in the E ware assemblage, but it is necessary to be clear of the difference between sooting, fuming, and staining or burning. These effects are often confused and are particularly difficult to distinguish in the case of E ware, which has a basically white fabric but one which is highly susceptible to environmental discolouration, in firing, during use, and after deposition. Firing discolourations produce patches of reduced grey and black fabric which are sometimes extensive. This discolouration is very similar to that produced over an open fire, but tends to form irregular patches and does not have carbon deposits. It is only on fairly complete vessels, such as E108 from Iona (Pl 14), that the form of these patches can be seen to be due to kiln conditions. E ware also tends to take up colours from the surrounding soil and as it is often buried in black midden soil, it tends to be stained black. This is apparent in the many cases where different sherds from a single vessel join but are of totally different colours (Pl 14). In this case also no carbon deposits are found. Sherds are also occasionally burnt, but they tend to take on a reddish colour (E73 from Dunadd for example).

Taking these factors into account, it can be seen from Table 3 that less than one-third of the known E1 bases show signs of sooting indicative of use in a hearth. At first sight this might seem fairly strong evidence in favour of the cooking-pot function, but a closer examination shows a more complex picture. For example, several of the E2 and E3 forms also have heavily sooted bases though these vessels are quite unsuited in size or form for use as cooking vessels, and this was clearly not their original function. It is certain that these vessels were being *reused* for different purposes, possibly for medicinal or industrial use. It is therefore possible that the E1 jars with sooting were being reused in the same way, having originally functioned as containers. There is some other evidence to support this view. A vessel from Loch Glashan (E139) has had the upper part trimmed off to produce a shallow bowl which has then been heavily sooted on both the interior and exterior, with this sooting extending over the trimmed surfaces, proving the secondary usage. It is possible that this vessel was used as a lamp. Another vessel, from Port y Candas (E171) is also a cut-down base with heavy sooting covering extensive spalls, again suggesting secondary use. Finally, the purple stains of dyer's madder found in several vessels may be indicative of the original contents of the vessels, or of reuse as dye containers (Chapter 5.6), but in either case a cooking-pot function is not indicated and reuse is likely. Furthermore, the lack of sooting on many vessels is a clear indication that these were never used for cooking, as the white fabric would show sooting immediately. This group of jars therefore must have had some other function.

Direct evidence that the E ware jars were used as containers comes from the chemical analysis of the interiors which show traces of purple dyestuffs (Chapter 5.6; Appendix 4). Although only a few examples have been certainly identified, post-depositional changes tend to remove the obvious purple stains, suggesting that many more were used for this purpose. This is shown on some sites where of two joining sherds, one shows purple staining and the other does not. It is suggested below (Chapter 5.6) that other exotic materials which have been found closely associated with E ware were also transported in E ware jars.

There are also indications that E ware was often

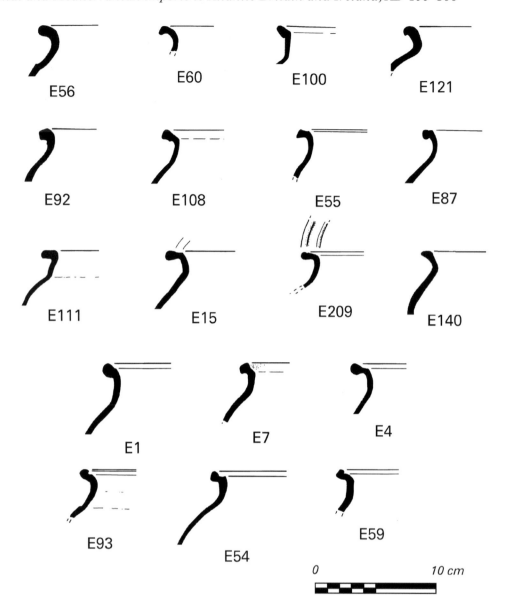

Fig 36 Rim forms of E1 jars. Simple: E56, E60 Dunadd; E100 Gransha; E121 Lagore. More elaborate: E55 Dunadd, E87 Garranes; E92 Garryduff; E108 Iona. Flat-topped: E15 Carew Castle; E111 Kildalloig Dun; E140 Loch Glashan; E209 Whithorn. Lid-seats: E1 Ardifuir; E4 Ballinderry no. 2; E7 Ballycatteen; E54, E59 Dunadd; E93 Garryduff

associated with industrial activity. This evidence ranges from a general association of E ware with metal working areas on sites (outlined in Chapter 7), to specific instances of glaze-like deposits on sherds from the Mote of Mark, and analysis of some sherds from Dunadd showing abnormally high sodium and potassium ratios indicative of alkalis (Table 21), both of which may be due to contact with wood ash or other alkali-rich material.

There are other objections to the view that the primary purpose of the importation of E1 jars was as cooking vessels. The extremely small number of vessels and their concentration on high-status sites make it clear that the use of these items would have been restricted to a few individuals of high status. However, all the literary evidence for this period suggests that cooking and eating, at least on high-status sites, was a communal shared activity. The *topos* of the cauldron in the hall pervades the literature of the period, both in Wales (Davies 1982, 29–30) and Ireland. Given this ethos and the small capacity of the E1 jars, sufficient only for a meal for one or two persons, it is difficult to imagine someone in a royal court preparing and eating an 'individual portion' from an E ware vessel. It also has to be remembered that cooking-pots have a very short life span, which anthropological studies suggest is a few months at most (DeBeor and Lathrop 1979, table 4.5) and E ware vessels do not have the ideal fabric for use as cooking ware. This would suggest that if the purpose of the importation was to supply and

Table 3 Sooting on E ware bases

Form	sooted	not sooted	indeterminate
E1/1B/1C	13	30	2
E2	4	17	2
E3	2	5	1
E4/4B	1	1	–

sustain a habit of using pottery, then it was an extremely ineffective system. Even at the major centres there is only enough E ware to sustain a couple of years' use for one or two persons. On the breakage of these vessels there would have to have been a return to the use of metal or leather cooking vessels. It has been suggested that the presence of E ware vessels suggests that there was a move towards more individual cooking practices at this time amongst the aristocracy (Wooding 1988), but this is a circular argument which ignores the evidence for multi-functional use of E ware. However, Wooding is right to dismiss Mytum's reading of a 9th-century text, *Bethu Brigte*, as referring to E ware, as it is more likely to refer to a glass vessel (Mytum 1986, 375–6).

It could be argued that the exotic nature of the imported pottery would confer prestige on the user, and that this factor would outweigh any practical or cultural considerations in the use of this pottery. Thus an item of low value and status in its place of origin, as an E ware vessel undoubtedly was, could acquire high status in a society which did not produce such items. This can be described as the 'beads for the natives' theory but it is doubtful if early medieval Atlantic societies were as unsophisticated as this. In the Roman period, and in later medieval times, the types of pottery recognised as being 'special' outside the normal marketing area were the glossy, highly decorative vessels, such as samian ware, Tating ware, or lustreware, all of which required special skills to manufacture. It was these wares which were exported to the 'peripheral' cultures and there seems no reason to suspect that in the intervening early medieval period the fashion was any different.

There is of course a danger of transferring modern values onto past societies, but I think it is possible to show that E ware vessels would not have had any great intrinsic value to the early medieval Atlantic societies. Although no pottery was produced in most of western Britain and Ireland at this time, it is not true to describe these areas as aceramic. It is obvious from the use of clay for a wide variety of purposes that craft workers had an exact and wide-ranging knowledge of ceramic technology. At Dunadd, for instance, different clays and tempers were deliberately selected for different tasks with fine clays being used for moulds, heavily quartz-tempered clays for crucibles, and special tempers for tuyères (Lane and Campbell 2000, 106–49).

Elsewhere in the Hebrides, organic- and rock-tempered ware was produced for cooking vessels throughout the first millennium (Lane 1990) and in Ulster ceramic cooking vessels were in use from the 8th to 12th centuries. This ceramic knowledge was widespread, and similar examples can be quoted from many other sites.

Ceramic objects were not then the products of an exotic technology as far as the early medieval Atlantic peoples were concerned. They were quite capable of producing adequate cooking vessels, as they later did in Ulster (Ryan 1973) and Cornwall (Hutchinson 1979). The reasons they did not at an earlier period were presumably cultural and practical: cultural, because of a tradition of communal cooking; and practical, because the damp climate is poorly suited to making pottery while metal, wooden and leather vessels were more practical and longer lasting.

In conclusion, it seems most likely that the E_1 jars were imported as containers and that the empty vessels were then sometimes reused for a variety of purposes, including industrial processes, lighting and possibly cooking. By this time the vessels would have lost their 'luxury' cachet as it was the original contents of the vessels which were important. There are, however, some E_1 jars which seem to have been used primarily as cooking ware. It is possible that some sites producing quantities of E ware were used by Continental traders rather than being centres of importation. It has already been noted that some sites do not share the high-status characteristics of most of the major E ware centres. These sites are mainly in the south-west, particularly in Scilly (Table 16), and it is tempting to see these as traders' settlements or temporary stop-over points (Chapter 9.3). This is particularly the case in Scilly, as the islands are probably too small to have produced enough surplus to exchange for luxury goods. It is interesting that Thomas has suggested a similar trading function for the putative Scilly harbour in the Roman period (Thomas 1985, 165–72). It has been suggested that Dalkey Island is another of these trading settlements (Hodges 1982, 61; Doyle 1998), and more recently Dunnyneill Island (Campbell forthcoming b). This is again possible as Dalkey Island does not seem to be a high-status site, though it continued to receive high-status jugs in the medieval period (Liversage 1968, 186–90). It is noticeable that the only certain E_5 lids came from Dalkey Island and Scilly. In addition, the lid E11 from Bar Point, Scilly, is pierced in the centre, suggesting use for cooking rather than as a container lid.

If the E ware on some sites was used by traders, this raises the possibility that the E ware found on other, high-status, sites was the personal property of traders. Such a situation seems highly unlikely as elsewhere in Europe at this period traders and merchants had their own settlements or trading places where trading took place (Hodges 1989,

69–114). These places were never within existing high-status settlements. It was in the interest of royalty to control trade, both because of the revenue from taxation, and because of the power available through control of access to prestige goods. It was also in the interest of merchants to keep to separate areas where they might have some protection, royal or ecclesiastic. Because merchants were not kin they were not protected by customary law in Celtic society (Doherty 1980, 79). The essence of such places, whether they are described as *emporia*, ports of trade or gateway communities, is that they were neutral in terms of political/legal associations and therefore non-kin could meet in relative safety. They were also situated in places where merchants could stay close to their vessels with their valuable cargoes. It is therefore difficult to see traders operating within high-status settlements in Atlantic society, cooking for themselves with their own kitchen utensils. Apart from the safety aspect, this would violate the rules of hospitality of Celtic society, which compelled the person in residence to cater for guests (Kelly 1988, 139–40; Simms 1978).

The E2 beakers present more of a problem in the interpretation of their function. This form is usually described as a drinking beaker as it fits the hand comfortably and has a simple rim, enabling easy drinking. However, some of the sharply carinated forms would be extremely difficult to drain completely. It is possible, of course, that like E1 jars, they could have had a variety of functions. It is not clear whether they could have functioned as containers as it might have been possible to seal these forms using a cloth and twine, as with the E1 vessels. They could then be used to carry small items such as nuts, beads or even honey. This use as containers could explain their wide distribution and the fact that they sometimes occur on sites not in association with other E ware vessels. If, however, they were drinking vessels, it is difficult to explain their redistribution from the major centres. It has been suggested (S Driscoll pers comm) that the E2 beakers had a partly symbolic function, showing that the recipient had shared drink with the overlord who gave the gift. This would be unlikely if the argument above concerning the perceived worth of E ware vessels is accepted. It could be suggested that the beakers were supplied as accompaniments to wine supplied in barrels, as part of a package associated with drinking, but the distribution of beakers does not coincide with that of jugs and pitchers, which tend to be restricted to high-status sites. The function of these vessels in an Atlantic social context remains unclear.

The less common forms cannot be regarded as containers. The E4 and E4B jugs and pitchers are obviously designed for serving liquids. The E3 bowls are apparently tableware but it is possible that they could also have been used for drinking. Drinking from bowls is mentioned in some of the early literature such as the *Gododdin* (Jackson 1969). The subsequent use to which many of these vessels were put (see above) shows that they were not highly regarded even when complete. Yet these vessels are quite clearly associated with each other and with high-status sites (Table 2). It may be that these vessels were part of a package of goods. If wine was being imported along with E ware, then perhaps it was normal to provide the jugs necessary for refilling drinking vessels from the barrel. As the jug form of vessel does not appear to have been used in Late La Tène metalwork and cannot be made in wood perhaps these jugs were supplying a lack in the local range of domestic equipment.

3.3 Miscellaneous wares

There are a variety of unclassified wheelthrown wares which are almost certainly imports as they are found in association with other imported wares on Atlantic sites (Chapter 5.3; Fig 49). It is difficult to identify specific types as each seems to be unique, and it is not practical to erect a new series of import wares without further evidence that they were widely imported. Some of these may be unusual residual Roman wares, but a few can assigned to the early medieval period with some certainty. Most are featureless sherds, but a few show some features of their form. Some of these may be the wares classified by Thomas (1959, 100, 110; cf 1981, 25) as Classes F and G, but these labels are best dropped as they cover heterogeneous material, not all of proven early medieval date, and some now known to be of medieval or Roman origin. One distinct group of similar wares can be identified, which I have termed late white gritty wares, and the rest are a miscellaneous group, mostly comprising single vessels, of which I have not made a systematic study (see Chapter 5.3).

Late white gritty wares

These vessels are apparently related to E ware, in that they have a whitish, quartz-gritted fabric. The forms are quite different, however, and the vessels are much thinner, have different rims, and some have tiny spots of yellow glaze (Fig 37). The group was first noted and published by Lloyd Laing (1974, 187–9, fig 3). It is found on at least two western Scottish sites, Lochlee (initially reported as Lochspouts) and Little Dunagoil, both sites which also have E ware. Laing reported other material from Stranraer as well. He suggested these wares might be dated to the 10th century, but they could be earlier as yellow glaze appears on vessels in western France as early as the 8th century (eg in Tours). There are early medieval (?7th-century) vessels from Poitiers (Campbell 1991, fig 55, CU4) which are the same form as

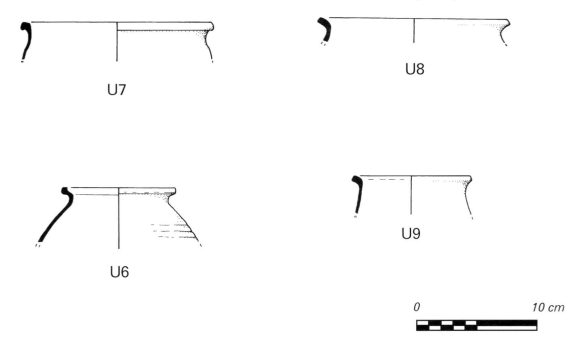

Fig 37 Late white gritty wares. U6 Little Dunagoil; U7–U9 Lochlee

those from western Scotland (Fig 37, U6–9). This enigmatic group appears to post-date E ware but possibly was produced in the same general area. Featureless individual sherds can be very difficult to distinguish from E ware. As none of the material is well stratified, it is possible that these are some form of medieval Scottish white gritty ware, which can also be very difficult to separate from E ware. The group of sites around the Firth of Clyde is difficult to explain, but perhaps ties in with the late form of E1 from Loch Glashan (Pl 20) discussed above.

4 Imported glass: Groups A–E

4.1 Introduction

Imported glass has received much less study than the pottery discussed in the last two chapters. Part of the reason for this is that for many years the glass sherds found on Altantic sites were considered to be the result of the import of broken vessels as sherds for cullet, intended for melting down to produce beads (Campbell 2000a, 33). Glass of the period has in the past sometimes been discarded because it looks 'modern'. It is also perhaps true that glass is more difficult to study than pottery and requires different techniques of analysis, particularly the fragmentary glass from settlement sites. It is therefore still common for discussion of imports in the Atlantic West to concentrate on the pottery and ignore the glass, Alcock (2003) and Wooding (1996b) being exceptions. However, glass has turned out to be a major import in the early historic period, occurring on 45 sites and accounting for more than 300 vessels, more than E ware.

There have also been major advances in ideas about the chronology and provenance of the glass in recent years (Campbell 2000a), which have increased the usefulness of the material. In that review paper I divided the imports into five traditions of glass making, labelling them Groups A–E to help differentiate and discuss the material. It is important to realise that unlike pottery 'wares', these 'groups' do not imply a common restricted production source area or particular kiln site. In fact some vessels could belong in several of these traditions. In that paper I also reviewed the history of glass studies in the Atlantic West, and readers are directed to that paper for background information. In summary, the groups are as follows.

Group A: Vessels in the Late Roman tradition, particularly with wheel-cut, abraded or engraved decoration of figurative scenes and/or inscriptions. High-quality metal (the technical term for the 'fabric' of the glass), often colourless (decolourised), bowls, cups and flasks.

Group B: Vessels in the Anglo-Saxon or Germanic tradition. Wide variety of characteristic forms such as claw beakers, squat jars, palm cups, along with beakers and bowls. Metal often bubbly, thick, green or brown.

Group C: Vessels in the 'Atlantic' tradition, decorated with marvered opaque white trails, in horizontal bands (Ca), chevrons (Cb) or festoons (Cc). Mainly cone beakers (Fig 38A) and some bowls, all with fire-rounded and thickened rims. Metal of very high quality, thin, very pale yellowish, occasionally other shades.

Group D: Vessels in the 'Atlantic' tradition, but without decoration.

Group E: Vessel copying Group C but with unthickened rims. Bag-shaped cone beakers, decorated with opaque white trails, feathered up and down, not always marvered (Fig 38B). Metal poorer, thicker, sometimes amber/pink dichroic, or pale green/yellow. So far found only at Whithorn and possibly made there.

In the catalogues, vessels have been assigned to these groups where possible, but it can be extremely difficult with small sherds to be sure of the group attribution. It was for this reason that I differentiated Groups C and D. Group C vessels can be ascribed with more certainty to the group (because of the distinctive decoration) than the plain vessels of Group D, which can be mistaken for Group A or B vessels. The advantage of differentiating these two groups, rather than labelling them one 'Atlantic' group (cf Wooding 1996b, 87, Class 3), is that it enables chronological differences to be discovered. This was clearly shown at Whithorn, where it was possible to show that different batches of vessels of different types were chronologically separate (Hill 1997, 322–6).

Fragments of glass vessels have been found on many settlement sites in western Britain and Ireland (Fig 39) in contrast to the situation in Anglo-Saxon England where most of the known glass is complete vessels from cemeteries. This difference is not due to a difference in status of sites which have been excavated. The royal palace sites such as early Saxon Yeavering produced only one sherd (Hope-

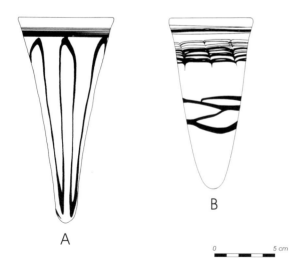

Fig 38 Reconstructions of: A, Group Cb cone beaker from Dinas Powys; B, Group E cone beaker from Whithorn

Taylor 1977, fig 86); late Saxon Cheddar had none (Rahtz 1979, 258–62); while mid-Saxon Northampton had only two (Williams *et al* 1985, 73–4). It will be suggested that this difference is due to cultural differences in attitudes to rubbish disposal.

The glass vessels found in the Atlantic West are, with a few exceptions, different in form, metal and decoration to those found in Anglo-Saxon England. Where the form can be ascertained the vessels are mainly beakers, most of which are probably cone beakers though those with vertical rims could be tumbler-shaped, with fewer bowls and occasional examples of other forms (Table 6). The colours found are principally a very pale yellow to colourless, with smaller amounts of very pale green, and only occasional examples of other, deeper colours (Table 4). This is quite different from the mainly greens and browns of Anglo-Saxon and north-western Continental material, showing it must be from a different source. The metal is generally of exceptionally high quality, very thin (0.2–1.0mm) and shows no signs of decay. The decoration on the Atlantic finds is principally of marvered opaque white trails, though a substantial number of vessels were probably plain (Table 5). As Harden originally pointed out, white-trailed decoration is rare on vessels from Anglo-Saxon and Frankish cemeteries, though he did not make the logical jump which would suggest the Atlantic vessels were from a different source or of different date, preferring to suggest that white-trailed glass sherds had been specially chosen to bring to the west as cullet (Harden 1963, 179). Marvered white trails seem to be an even rarer feature for which I can find few parallels. Marvering is the process where trails or other decorative elements, in a colour other than the main body of the vessel, are impressed into the vessel wall by reheating and rolling on a flat plate. The white-trailed decoration is principally of horizontal windings in a band just below the rim, with the threads varying from hair-thin to a few millimetres in thickness, but there is also an important group with vertical chevrons, and some with combed festoons (Table 5). Some of these individual types will be discussed below. As a whole the glass in the Atlantic group is remarkably uniform in vessel type, decoration and metal quality, suggesting a restricted

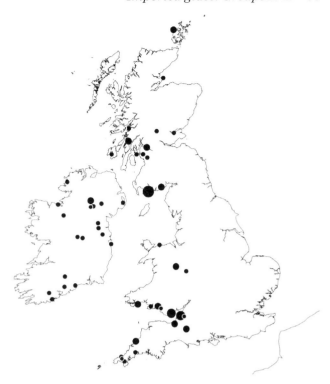

Fig 39 Distribution of glass imports

source and possibly that specifically selected types were being exported to these areas.

It was during my PhD study of the Dinas Powys glass assemblage that I began to question the conventional picture of glass in the Atlantic West, which had been propounded by Harden in the original site report (Harden 1963). Since that period little had been published on western glass although there had been several studies of Anglo-Saxon glass by Harden (1972; 1978), Evison (1972; 1982a; 1982b; 1983), Hunter (1980) and Cramp (1970). Henderson (1989) had reported technical evidence of glass making in Ireland. Evison (1982a; 2000) in particular revised parts of Harden's overall classification of Anglo-Saxon vessels. The study by Hunter (1980) and Hunter and Heyworth (1998) of the glass from the 8th- to 9th-century trading centre of *Hamwic* is the only substantial body of material from a Saxon

Table 4 Distribution of colours amongst glass groups
(expressed as % of Group total, with vessel numbers in brackets)

	Group A	Group B	Group C	Group D	Group E
Light yellow	44% (7)	11% (7)	44% (52)	67% (36)	67% (10)
Light green	6% (1)	17% (11)	32% (37)	17% (9)	
Light blue	6% (1)	27% (17)	7% (8)	4% (2)	
Honey/amber		2% (1)	7% (8)	7% (4)	33% (5)
Deep blue		14% (9)			
Deep green	6% (1)	14% (9)	3% (3)	2% (1)	
Brown/black		11% (7)		4% (2)	
Colourless	38% (6)	5% (3)	8% (9)		

Table 5 Types of decoration in glass groups

	Group A	Group B	Group C	Group D	Group E
Plain	1	2		13	2
Opaque white horiz. trails	3		76		10
Opaque white chevrons			17		
Opaque white festoons			11		
Self-coloured trails		13			
Moulded		9			
Bichrome		2	1		

settlement site and has provided a useful comparison with Dinas Powys.

The most important breakthrough for glass import studies came with the excavation of the monastic site at Whithorn Priory from 1984–91. Here a long sequence of deposits covering the 6th to 8th centuries produced the largest collection of glass in the Atlantic West, together with some evidence for glass vessel production (Group E), and examples of almost all the pottery import groups. The stratigraphic sequence included 22 sub-phases covering the two centuries of the imports, enabling a detailed picture of the relative chronology of the different wares to be constructed. There are difficulties in interpreting the stratigraphy, or rather the taphonomic deposition processes. There is clearly much residuality, caused by contemporaneous disturbances such as grave cutting, building foundations and pits. There is also intrusion of material into earlier contexts caused by factors such as unrecognised later disturbance, and over-digging. This is not surprising given the thinness of the deposits, and the difficulties of the excavation. However, the general picture is clear, and Hill has identified four phases of importation within the 6th to early 8th centuries (Hill 1997, 322–6). The details of the sequence are discussed later (Chapter 7.6), but the Whithorn evidence gives the best opportunity for calibrating the sequence of imports.

Harden considered that the Dinas Powys glass, and the glass from other Celtic sites such as the Mote of Mark, was datable to the 5th to 6th or early 7th centuries (Harden 1963, 179). This assessment has dominated the dating of glass in the Celtic areas ever since. The basis for his date-range was a combination of the range of forms found in the west, belonging to his Phases 1 and 2, and the abundance of white trailing in the material, which he assigned to a 5th- to 6th-century horizon, based on the assumption that the Dinas Powys vessels were the same type as the Anglo-Saxon vessels with white trails. As I shall demonstrate, this is not the case, and anyway the comparison with English data is only valid if the glass is assumed to have come from England. However, the characteristic Dinas Powys cone-beaker with white chevrons is unknown in Anglo-Saxon England.

4.2 Group A: Late Roman/Mediterranean tradition (Pl 21; Fig 40)

Vessels with wheel-cut, abraded or engraved decoration are a feature of Late Roman Britain and the Continent (Price 1995), but they are also found in post-Roman contexts in Britain, for example in 5th- and 6th-century Anglo-Saxon graves (Price 2000a). It is therefore difficult to be sure that examples from Atlantic areas belong to the post-Roman rather than the Roman period of importation. This is the same problem encountered with LR3 and Bv amphorae. Even where they are well stratified, it could be argued that they were curated Roman period material. With the fragmentary material found on Atlantic sites, it is usually impossible to ascertain the design and form of vessel, making it difficult to ascribe a certain date to it. Despite these problems, enough evidence has now accumulated to be fairly certain that Group A vessels were imported in the 6th century alongside other pottery and glass imports, even though they are not common finds.

The evidence from Whithorn has been the key to establishing the 6th-century date of Group A. Here fragments of eight vessels, all bowls, were found, five with wheel-cut decoration of scrolls and inscriptions (Campbell 1997, 300–1, illus 10.4). Three vessels without wheel-cut decoration, but with bands of opaque white trails, were ascribed to this group on the basis of their decolourised metal, a specifically Roman technique. This was confirmed by their stratigraphic association with the other vessels (Fig 76). Most of these vessels can be assigned to early 6th-century contexts, appearing in contexts with LR2 amphorae, but below ARS and LR1. It seems reasonable to suggest that these vessels were imported from the Mediterranean alongside the other imports. Two other significant import sites have produced similar material, Cadbury Congresbury (3 vessels), and Tintagel (6 vessels), as well as Trethurgy (1 vessel). Most of these were effectively unstratified, but large pieces of a flagon were found in 1998 in stratified contexts at Tintagel (Campbell forthcoming a, vessel 6) alongside a range of other imports, confirming the Whithorn dating.

The form of these vessels seems to be restricted to bowls and flagons, similar to those found in more

Imported glass: Groups A–E 57

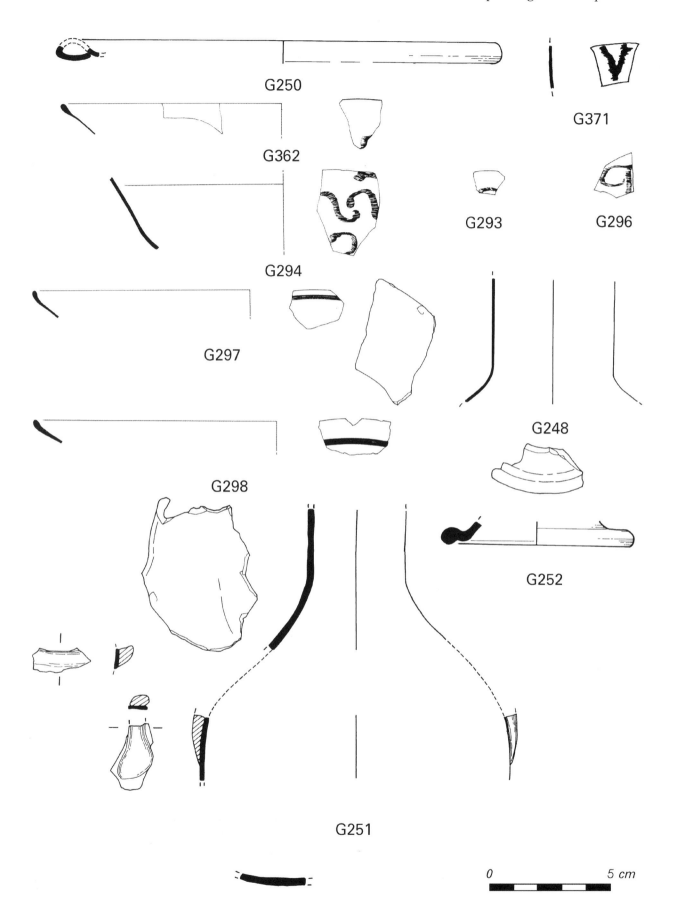

Fig 40 Imported glass from Insular sites. Group A, Mediterranean tradition: G248, G250–2 Tintagel; G293–4, G296–8, G362 Whithorn; G371 Dunnyneill Island

complete forms in Anglo-Saxon contexts. The **bowls** are similar to the well-known example from Holme Pierrepont, Nottinghamshire (Price 2000a, fig 9, pl 7), a truncated conical bowl with basal kick, which has a frieze of peacocks with an inscription above, and a band of circles below. Vessels G293–6, 362 from Whithorn, G267 from Trethurgy, G263 from Tintagel, and G16 from Cadbury Congresbury, are all probably of this type. G17 from Cadbury Congresbury may be from a segmented bowl, similarly decorated. Price discusses these in detail (2000a, 24–5), showing that the form is unknown in Late Roman contexts, but occurs in the 5th and 6th centuries on the Continent. They are particularly common in Iberia, with examples from Conimbriga, Portugal. Other significant concentrations are found in Bordeaux. Both these sites are on the sea routes to the Atlantic West. G297–9 from Whithorn have no abraded decoration, but were grouped with these vessels on the basis of the quality of the metal. Parallels for the form and white-trailed decoration can be seen amongst the Bordeaux 6th-century material (Foy and Hochuli-Gysel 1995, fig 14, 9–13).

Other vessels include flagons, goblets and plates. G251 from Tintagel could be partially reconstructed to show that it was a **flagon**, apparently undecorated, in thick yellow glass, with an unusual oval-sectioned rod handle. Handled vessels do not appear to have been produced in the post-Roman industries of north-western Europe. None are recorded from Anglo-Saxon England, and only a handful from Frankish cemeteries on the Continent (Feyeux 1995, 114). Production of the common Roman handled forms of bottles and flagons appears to have continued in areas further south, however, for example in the south of France well into the 5th century (Foy 1995a, pl 21) and in Aquitaine possibly till the early 6th century (Foy and Hochuli-Gysel 1995, 157), but the published descriptions of these vessels do not correspond to the thick glass, wide neck and simple handle of the Tintagel vessel. A closer comparison is with southern Spanish vessels which may imitate local ceramic forms (Gamo Parras 1995, 306). Two illustrated forms are from sites in Málaga and Cádiz in 6th- to 7th-century cemeteries (*ibid*, pl 4.1 and 3). Without examining these finds it is impossible to be certain of attributing a Spanish origin to this vessel, but given the trading links between the Mediterranean and Tintagel, it remains a strong possibility. G248 and G252, also from Tintagel, are also from bottles or flagons. G252 has a flattened and infolded rim. Examples can be quoted from 5th-century Carthage (Tatton-Brown 1984, fig 67.70) and the south of France (Foy 1995a, pl 6.33). Harden (in Radford 1956, 70, vessel b) apparently thought this was from a bowl, and related it to vessels from Karanis with which he was familiar, suggesting it was an Egyptian import. However, the diameter is far too small, and the flattening of the underside of the rim shows that it was oriented wrongly by Harden. It is possible that this is not a rim sherd, but the base-ring of a stemmed goblet. Stemmed vessels are not as rare as flagons, but are nevertheless uncommon, particularly in England (Harden 1956a, 139). Stemmed beakers are found in post-Roman cemeteries in the 5th and early 6th centuries, but these are formed in one piece, by folding in the base of the vessel. G252 differs in that the foot was separately blown, with its own infolded and rounded rim, to be attached to the main body of the glass. This technique is not found in any of the north-western European assemblages that I know of, but it does occur in the Mediterranean, developing from the single-piece footed vessel in the 6th century in southern France (Foy 1995a, 207, pl 15), and also appearing in Italy in the 6th century (Sternini 1995, fig 19). Infolded rims are very rare in these footrings, however, but one was found at Cadbury Congresbury, G51, which may belong in Group A rather than D. There is one more certain **goblet** in this group, G52 from Cadbury Congresbury (Price 1992, fig 98, 46), represented by part of the solid stem.

The last vessel to be discussed is a tubular-rimmed vessel, from Tintagel, G250, probably from a **tubular-rimmed bowl or plate**, depending on the orientation of the rim, which is difficult to determine from the fragment. Shallow tubular-rimmed bowls are found in Roman Britain at a number of periods (Price and Cottam 1999, 110–11), but none seems very close in form to G250. More obvious parallels are found in the Mediterranean region, and Harden thought this was a 4th-/5th-century 'eastern' import. They are fairly common at Carthage in the 5th and particularly 6th centuries (Tatton-Brown 1984, 195, fig 65.4), and are also found at Conimbriga in Portugal in 4th-/5th-century contexts (Alaraçao *et al* 1976, 193, nos 198–9, pl xci), southern France in a 5th-century context (Foy 1995b, pl 7, 58) and in southern Spain (J Price pers comm).

The origin of all these vessels is obscure at present, though the parallels can be found throughout the western Mediterranean, Iberia and western France. They quite possibly come from a variety of sources, but seem to be securely associated with the 6th-century phases of imports. The forms are all tablewares: decorative bowls, flasks, goblets, flagons and possibly plates. They were presumably space fillers in the amphorae cargoes, and occur in similar numbers to the ARS and PRS tableware which they accompanied.

Fig 41 (opposite) Imported glass from Insular sites. Group B, Germanic tradition: G300–303 Whithorn; G83, G95 Dinas Powys; G217–18 Moynagh Lough; G219 Mullaroe; G211 Mote of Mark; G169 Lagore; G77 Dalkey Island; G372 Dunnyneill Island

Imported glass: Groups A–E   59

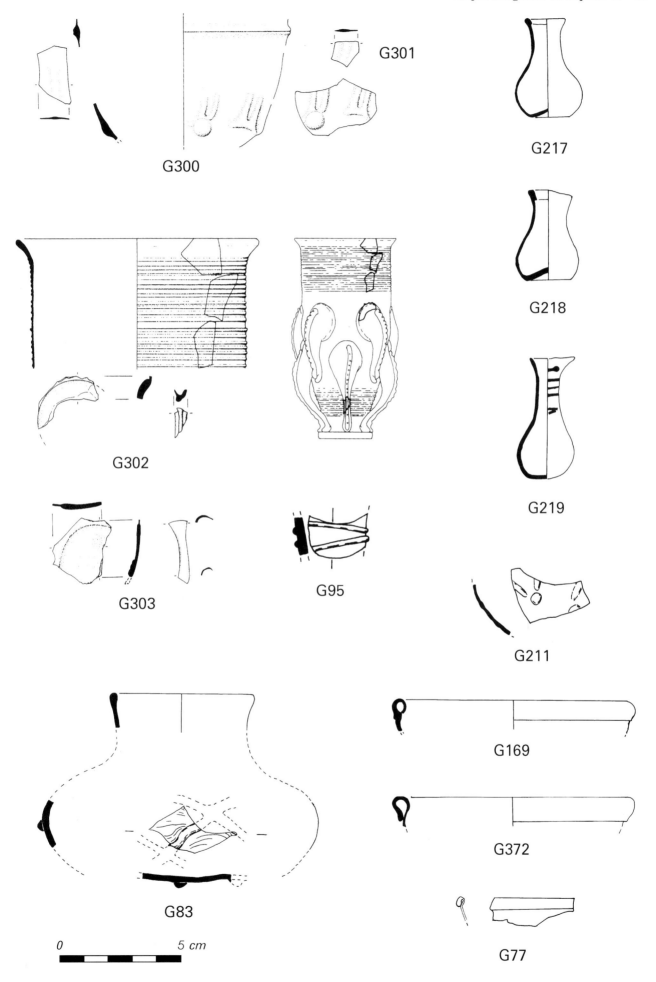

4.3 Group B: Germanic tradition (Pls 22–30; Fig 41)

Glass vessels belonging to the 'Germanic' tradition (labelled 'Teutonic' by Harden) have been familiar to archaeologists since the period of antiquarian collections of pagan Anglo-Saxon grave goods. They are characterised by a wide variety of vessel forms, few of which survive from the Late Roman period (Evison 2000). New introductions include claw beakers, palm cups, bell beakers, horns and globular beakers (squat jars). Evison (*ibid*, 47) notes that most of these forms are not tableware as such, being unstable forms, but were drinking vessels. Techniques of manufacture are also different, for example fire-rounded rather than knocked-off rims. Finally, the actual glass metal itself is in different colours from Roman glass, and often of poorer quality: thick, bubbly and full of inclusions. Glass vessels found in the Atlantic West can therefore be ascribed to this group on the grounds of either form, technology, colour or a combination of these qualities. For example, claw beakers are characteristic of Anglo-Saxon and Continental pagan grave assemblages, but are unknown in Late Roman or Atlantic traditions. Again, deep (cobalt) blue is characteristic of a proportion of Germanic vessels from the late 6th century, and deep reds, greens and blacks become common from the 8th century onwards. Decoration of self-coloured trailing is common from the 5th century, and although it is found in Group C vessels it is uncommon there and many examples in the west can be ascribed to Group B.

Small amounts of Group B material are found on many western sites, being much more widespread than Group A, though there are few in Ireland (Fig 48). As will be seen, the chronological range is also wide, though there is nothing that can be securely ascribed to the 5th century. Given that much of this material may have entered the Atlantic West overland from England, the exchange mechanisms by which it reached these areas may be quite different from the rest of the glass imports.

Claw beakers

Claw beakers are perhaps the easiest type of Germanic vessel to recognise in fragmentary form, as even a tiny sherd of a claw cannot be mistaken for any other vessel. There are two fragments of claw beakers at Dinas Powys. G93 (Pl 22) is a brown claw (Harden 1963, fig 40, 9) which has been classified by Evison (1982a, 64) as belonging to her Type 3c, the largest of the English groups (see also Evison 2000, 65, as Group 37), having characteristic nicked vertical trails. She dates vessels from this group to the middle of the 6th century (Evison 1982a, 58), and believes they could have been manufactured in England, probably in East Anglia, as few are found on the Continent. The distribution of this type suggests that the Dinas Powys example should have arrived at the site via the Upper Thames area. Evison suggested that this type of claw beaker was made for redistribution as the widespread distribution contrasts with other types of glass (*ibid*, 58). Most of the claw beakers in English cemeteries come from rich graves and, rather surprisingly, four are from female and three from male graves. This suggests that these glasses were more a symbol of wealth and power than purely functional accompaniments to drinking and feasting. Hawkes has also suggested that Kentish objects found in the Upper Thames area were diplomatic gifts (Hawkes 1985). The other fragment (G95) was not drawn by Harden. It is from towards the base of a pale yellow claw beaker. This colour is not found in the putatively English-produced claw beakers. There is one beaker of this colour from Coombe, but it is probably of Continental manufacture (Evison 1982a, 50). The sherd is from a narrow vessel of conical form. The body is thick, with thick spiral trails. There is no sign of attached claws within the one-third of the circumference that survives. It cannot be assigned to any of Evison's types or dated more generally than to the 5th/7th centuries.

Whithorn also produced two claw beakers. The best preserved was G302, which like G93 from Dinas Powys probably belonged to Evison's Type 3c (Campbell 1997, illus 10.5, 11). Although the short length of vertical trail surviving does not appear to be nicked, the lower parts of some trails in vessels of this group are hardly nicked, as in a vessel from Islip, Northants (Evison 1982a, fig 11c). The very pale green colour is unusual in Anglo-Saxon vessels, but does occur. The other claw fragment, G303, is a dark yellow-brown like G93, but its fragmentary nature precludes assignment to any of Evison's groups (Campbell 1997, illus 10.5, 12). A colourless neck sherd, G304, may also be from a claw beaker, but could also be from other forms. All these were found in early contexts at Whithorn, around the stage of the earliest LRA imports, before the ARS of the mid-6th century. A date in the first half of the 6th century is likely. The Dinas Powys vessels are not securely stratified.

An important new find comes from Dunnyneill Island, Strangford Lough (Pl 25), the first occurrence in Ireland (G370). This vessel is an unusual colour, greenish-blue, more characteristic of the 7th and 8th centuries than the more common 5th- and 6th-century forms. This type of colour is found in a series of vessels from Scandinavian burials of the 7th and 8th centuries, some of which may have been produced in England. The fragmentary nature of the vessel means that it cannot be placed easily in Evison's typology. Its form seems to be tall and narrow with fairly flat claws, and should be conical. However, two sherds show quite strong vertical curvature, which would be unusual in a claw beaker, though these may have been distorted by attachment of the claw. It is possible that two different vessels are represented, but the metal is identical in both. The claws have vertical nicked trails applied to them, which shows that the vessel does not belong to the latest phase of development of claw beakers in the 8th century. The closest parallel is with some of the vessels from the 7th-century Taplow princely burial, Evison's Group 50. One sherd has a wavy trail above a claw, a feature not seen in other claw beakers, though some of the Taplow beakers have a nicked trail in this position, and one from Vendel has a wavy trail within nicked borders (Evison 1982a, pl VId; XIIa). The Taplow beakers are of a different colour, but an unusual bag beaker from Dry Drayton, Cambs., shares the same colour of glass as the Dunnyneill beaker and has been dated to the late 7th/8th century by Evison (2000, 72). Overall a 7th-/8th-century date and Anglo-Saxon origin seem likely.

Kempston-type beakers

This type of cone beaker with vertical looped trails under a band of horizontal trails, all self-coloured (Evison 2000, 62, Group 26), is the most numerous type of cone found in England. The beakers can be dated to the 5th and early 6th centuries, and distribution suggests they were manufactured both in Kent and in the Rhineland (*ibid*, 62; cf Evison 1983, 87).

Cadbury Congresbury has produced the largest collection of Germanic glass in the Atlantic West. Price claimed at least eight Kempston-type beakers in the assemblage, but illustrations suggest that not all of these belong to this group, and only three, G20, G23 and G24 (Price 1992, 141, nos 14, 17, 18) are accepted by Evison (2000, 74). Even though not certainly Kempston-type cones, the other vessels described by Price still belong in the Germanic tradition. Another possible example of a Kempston-type beaker occurs at Whithorn, G270 (Campbell 1997, 302, illus 10.5, 14, wrongly orientated). As at Cadbury Congresbury, there are some other sherds with self-coloured trails which might belong to this or other types of Germanic beakers, G271 and G304 (Campbell 1997, 302, illus 10.5, 13, 15). Finally, at Cadbury Castle, there is another collection of very fragmentary glass vessels, two of which, G241 and G242, have been claimed to be Kempston-type beakers (Price and Cottam 1995, 101, illus 7.1, Gl21). Evison does not list these in her catalogue, as they are not certainly from this type of vessel. As at the other sites, there are other sherds which may belong to this type, G243 and G244, but these are even less diagnostic.

Blue globular beakers (squat jars)

Globular beakers are another common type in England. They have a wide variety of decoration, and have been classified into nine sub-types by Evison (2000, fig 3, 68–9). These are later in date than the vessels previously discussed, assigned to the period 550–700, and are mainly confined to Kent where a large concentration around Faversham suggests a production centre (*ibid*). The only certain examples in the Atlantic West come from the south-west. An almost complete deep blue vessel, G231, was found in a well associated with a disused Romano-British temple at Pagans Hill, Chew Stoke, Somerset. The find has been thoroughly discussed (Evison 1989; Evison 2000, 69, Group 67) and attributed to the 7th century. At Dinas Powys, another deep blue vessel, G83 (Pl 23), belongs to a different type (Evison 2000, Group 66), which can also be dated to the 7th century (Campbell 1989b). There is also another sherd at Dinas Powys which belongs to another vessel, G84, with pulled knobs and thin opaque white trails. The form of the vessel is unknown, but this is not a normal type of decoration on Anglo-Saxon vessels, though it does occur on some bell beakers and it is more common on the Continent. There is one example of a globular beaker with this form of decoration from northern France (Feyeux 1995, pl 15, T90.1cpd), so a provenance there is possible.

Other deep blue vessels

Deep blue globular vessels seem to have been of particularly high status, and I have pointed out how they are confined to high-status sites outside of Kent (Campbell 1989b, 241–2; Dickinson 1974), being found in four 'princely' graves. The recent discovery of another pair of examples of this sub-type in the 7th-century princely grave at Prittlewell, Essex, confirms this picture. It seems clear that these special vessels were distributed from Kent to the surrounding kingdoms, and made their way to the south-west by the route of the Thames valley (Campbell 1989b, 243, fig 2). I also suggested that these blue squat jars were made under royal control in Kent and distributed as diplomatic gifts to surrounding, and possibly client, kingdoms, perhaps reflecting Ethelbert's position of dominance in the early 7th century.

There are other deep blue fragments found on Atlantic sites, though none can be attributed to definite forms. These occur at Cadbury Congresbury, G19; Cannington, G59; Clogher G68 and G69; Dalkey Island, G80; Dinas Powys G84; Drumacritten, G123; Garranes G147; Hen Gastell, G164; and Little Dunagoil, G380. Of these, the Cadbury Congresbury and Hen Gastell chips are completely undiagnostic, and the Drumacritten sherds have not been located. The Cannington stemmed vessel is unique, and may belong to Group A. The Dalkey Island sherd could be from a bowl or jar, but is otherwise undiagnostic. One Clogher example, G68, may be from a beaker but the other, G69, is from a flat-bottomed bottle or phial of a mould-blown type not found in England or other Germanic areas (Bourke 1994, 170) and again may belong to Group A. The Little Dunagoil sherd could be from a cone beaker with trails, but is too small for this to be certain. Finally, the Garranes vessel has a simple rim, and could be from a globular beaker, but too little remains for any certainty. Some of these may also be 7th century, or later, but without diagnostic forms it would be unwise to read too much into their distribution. Dinas Powys, Garranes and Clogher are known or suspected royal sites, and a case could also be made for Hen Gastell, reinforcing the suggested association of the deep blue vessels with aristocratic sites.

Palm cups/funnel beakers

The palm cup is another type newly appearing in the period 550–700 in England and the Continent, though a developed form continues later, morphing into funnel beakers by the 9th century. The only certain example is from Whithorn, G300 (Pl 30), which has characteristic mould-blown decoration. This belongs to Harden's Group Xai, dated by him to the 6th century on the basis of Continental examples. These vessels were reclassified by Evison as Group 54, accepting them as Continental imports. The Whithorn context seems to belong to the first half of the 6th century. G301, also from Whithorn, has a mould-blown rib and may belong to a similar vessel but is too small to be diagnostic. A number of other sherds may belong to palm cups but can be less certainly assigned. G77 from Dalkey Island has a rim folded outwards forming a slight hollow rim. This is a characteristic feature of palm cups. Bourke calls this a late palm cup, suggesting it is close to the transition to funnel beakers (Bourke 1994, 173), and therefore, presumably, 8th century in date. However, funnel beaker rims are always folded *inwards* (Hunter and Heyworth 1998, 8), and there are good parallels for this form of rim in palm cups in 7th-century contexts (Evison 2000, 68). At *Hamwic*, however, there is a series of what are described as bowls with out-folded rims (Hunter and Heyworth 1998, 19, fig 14), which are likely to be of late date. G169 from Lagore also has a characteristic hollow rim, but in this case folded inwards, though Bourke (1994, 173, cf 204) implies that it is folded outwards. The blue/green colour and metal of this vessel is distinctive, not like anything else in the Atlantic West, and it is possible that it belongs to the later palm cup/early funnel beaker series of the 8th century or later. This piece is important as it was securely stratified in Period 1b, along with E ware (E121 and E124) and many other finds. Dating of this key site's phases has been the subject of debate (for summary see O'Sullivan 1998, 113), so the possibility that Period 1b lasted into the 8th century is significant. The last site to have possible palm cups is the Mote of Mark, with two possible examples, G210 and G211. G211 is the most certain, being part of a base with mould-blown bosses at the bottom of vertical ribs, probably from Evison's Group 54. Like G300 from Whithorn, it is a characteristic 6th-century form. G210 has mould-blown ribbing, and may belong to a similar vessel. Both are from old excavations and unstratified. G14 from Buiston crannog, discussed below, may also be a palm cup. G8 from Birsay has a hollow rim and may be from a palm cup or a funnel beaker, but is too fragmentary to distinguish.

Phials and flasklets

Small phials and flasklets are very rarely found in western contexts, but paradoxically include the only complete vessels found in this area. All the known examples are discussed in this section, though it is by no means certain that they all belong in the Germanic Group B tradition. The general form was fairly common in the Late Roman period, and some of the examples below are likely to belong to Group A. Phials are not found in the Anglo-Saxon assemblage, though there are a few larger bottles known (Evison 2000, 65–6), but are found in Frankish burials on the Continent, and in Late Antique contexts in the south of France and the Mediterranean.

Six vessels are of the same type, and all were found in Ireland. All have similar yellowish or yellow/green metal, rather bubbly with inclusions. Two complete undecorated examples, G217 and G218, came from crannog excavations at Moynagh Lough in what appears to be an early 7th-century context (Bourke 1994, 168). These are simple forms, though with infolded rims. Another complete example came from an undated context in a souterrain at Mullaroe, Sligo, G219 (Pl 24). This example has decoration of an unmarvered opaque white spiral trail around the neck. This feature relates it to Continental Group B examples. The incomplete examples include G233, part of a base which came from an Early Historic context on a crannog at Rathintaun (*ibid*, 168); G148 another incomplete base from Garranes, stratified above Mediterranean wares; and G122 another incomplete base from Dooey. Bourke (*ibid*, 169) suggests that a ground-down disc from Garranes, G149, may also be from a similar vessel. There is one possible example from outside Ireland, G340 from Whithorn, which was found in a late 6th-century context. These bases all share a characteristic kick which is not found in other forms in the Atlantic West. Rademacher (1942, 318–19, taf 71, 20) illustrates examples from the Rhineland, some with neck trails, which he dated to the 5th/6th centuries. Other small flasks of slightly different forms are known from northern France (Feyeux 1995, pl 2, type 22), dated to the 7th century, and Bordeaux (Foy and Hochuli-Gysel 1995, fig 15, 20) from a 7th-/8th-century context. A much closer parallel comes from Marseille (Foy 1995a, 213, pl 19, 241), again from a 7th-/8th-century context, which shares the infolded rim of G217 and G218. In total, this evidence suggests that small flasklets were being produced on the Continent from the 6th century onwards in small numbers, and although the provenance of this group of examples found in the Atlantic West must remain unclear at present, the quality of the metal suggests links with Group B rather than A or C/D. The form suggests use as unguentaria for perfume or oil, or possibly as containers for holy oil or water. The context of the finds suggest a 7th-century date in Irish contexts, though the Whithorn example is earlier, in the 6th century. It is surprising that almost all of this group come from Ireland, perhaps hinting at some different exchange mechanism taking them there. They are widely distributed, but three are from sites in the west of Ireland (Dooey, Rathintaun and Mullaroe), notably beyond the range of finds of Continental pottery. As these vessels are not found in Anglo-Saxon England, their origin may lie in western France, like the Group C/D vessels, despite the differences in metal and decoration.

The other possible flasklets are rather different in metal. G190 from Longbury Bank appears to be from the neck of a flasklet, in a fine greenish-blue metal, but it is not certainly ancient and was unstratified. G69 from Clogher is the circular flat base of a mould-blown phial or small bottle in deep blue glass. Although the colour is characteristic of some 7th-century Anglo-Saxon vessels discussed above, no parallels can be cited, and this may be a Late Roman vessel, even though it was found in an Early Historic context. The final vessel from Llanelen, G173, has a knocked-off rim rather than the fire-rounded rims of all other vessels found in the Atlantic West (Campbell 1996c). Knocked-off rims are found in Late Roman vessels, though none of this form are known from Roman Britain (J Price pers comm). The date of the context of the vessel is unclear, though the site also produced a Group C rim. The context pre-dated the 12th-/13th-century chapel, and may have been associated with a foundation grave of the 6th/7th century (Schlesinger and Walls 1996, 112–14). This is the only example of a flasklet from a religious site.

Late vessels in deep colours

Technological developments led to the introduction of a set of new deeper colours and some decorative techniques in the mid-Saxon period (Evison 1982b; 1983; 2000, 71–2, 84–6). The first of the new colours, the deep cobalt blue of the 7th century, has already been discussed, and this period also saw the beginnings of the bichrome vessels which were to become prominent in the 8th and 9th centuries. These colours include vivid green/blue and blue/green, emerald, red, black and other very dark colours. Reticella rods were used for decoration, as well as trails in different coloured glass. Only a small amount of this glass has been found in the Atlantic West, and it is all very fragmentary, but the distinctive colours enable secure identification of the period, if not the vessel type. The metal is much finer than in the Group B vessels of the 5th/6th centuries, in some cases being exceptionally fine.

Only two examples of vessels decorated with reticella rods have been found, G366 from Whithorn, and G7 (Pl 26) from the Brough of Birsay, though reticella rods are known from other import sites such as Iona and Dunnyneil Islands. G366 was a dark green/black vessel with opaque yellow and green reticella trails. By this period Whithorn was an Anglo-Saxon monastery and material of mid-Saxon origin is not unexpected. A close parallel, but with opaque white reticella, comes from an 8th-century level at Barking Abbey, Essex (Webster and Backhouse 1991, 92, 67r). A number of other deep colours were found at Whithorn. A vessel in opaque blue, G367, with a mould blown rib may be from a palm cup. Another vessel in opaque blue also came from Whithorn, G327, apparently from a 7th-century context. The Brough of Birsay sherd was found with a variety of other sherds in vibrant colours, all of 8th-/9th-century appearance (Pl 28). Similar colours are seen in sherds from York (Webster and Backhouse 1991, 147, illus 108d) and Barking Abbey (*ibid*, 92, illus 67t) in a mid-Saxon context. Almost black vessels are found at a number of other sites. Tintagel has produced a rim in black, G262, and Dumbarton a rim decorated with horizontal self-coloured trails, G127.

Another characteristic of this late glass is the use of dark red, either as body colour or as streaks and swirls within other colours (Evison 1990). G172 from Lagore is opaque black to dark red/maroon. This may be a piece of window glass, as one edge appears grozed, but there is slight curvature suggesting that it originally came from a vessel. The colour is not found before the 8th century, confirming that Period I continues to that date. There is another possible window glass sherd from Lagore, in deep blue (G368), but not certainly ancient. Dundurn has produced a bright red vessel, G142, unfortunately again of unknown form. This came from the final phase of the stone rampart on the terrace, Phase 3B, stratified well above an E ware sherd (E80) from Phase 1B, and perhaps of the same phase of importation as an unstratified unclassified Continental import (U14). It is probably of 8th- or 9th-century date. Harden (1956a, 150) reported that one of the Mote of Mark sherds was 'pale wine coloured'. This is in fact pink (G194) and possibly related to the Whithorn pink vessels. A sherd from the Brough of Birsay, G13, has dark red streaks characteristic of the 7th/8th centuries, in very high-quality reddish-brown/maroon glass (Pl 27). This red streaking had begun to be introduced by AD 600, as a rim from Buiston crannog, G14, was securely dated to AD 598–604 by dendrochronology. This may be the earliest attested use of this technique, which is also seen in the Pagans Hill blue globular beaker.

The Brough of Birsay produced a collection of sherds which are rather different in colour from others in the west. These include various shades of bright blue/green, G6, which has an opaque yellow trail (Pl 28), and vibrant turquoise, G10. This bright turquoise is also seen at Castle Hill, Dalry, G64; and at Dunadd G137 (Pl 29), both from old excavations. As with other colours, they can be paralleled at mid-Saxon sites such as York, Barking Abbey and Brandon, Suffolk, as well as in Scandinavian glass. G8 from Birsay may be from a funnel beaker with hollow rim and is in an aquamarine colour.

These fragmentary later vessels reveal a more widespread distribution of mid-Saxon vessels than has been appreciated hitherto. Glass vessels clearly continued to be imported from England to the Atlantic West into the 8th or even 9th centuries, well after the end of E ware importation. The route(s) by which they reached the west is less clear. The earlier Group B vessels may have come overland via the Thames valley. Those at Dundurn and the Brough of Birsay may have followed the eastern coastal sea route. Sites such as Dunadd and possibly Buiston are known to have had overland contacts with Anglo-Saxon England, but some others, particularly those in Ireland, may have been supplied from western English sites across the Irish Sea (Fig 48). A similar scatter of coins and metalwork of English origin are also found in these areas, and were probably brought by the same mechanisms (Campbell forthcoming b). The sites involved in this late phase of importation are mainly high status secular or important religious sites.

4.4 Group C: decorated Atlantic tradition
(Pls 31–6; Figs 42–4)

Group C, with around 120 vessels, is the largest glass import group. Along with the around 60 vessels of Group D, the vessels in the Atlantic tradition account for two-thirds of all classified glass vessel imports. The rationale for dividing the Atlantic tradition into two groups was that the decorated examples can certainly be ascribed to this tradition, but there can be more doubt with undecorated examples.

Group C vessels are distinguished by their fine metal with few bubbles or inclusions, their very pale yellow or yellow/green colour, shiny surfaces, thin walls (often paper-thin), and their marvered opaque white decoration (Pl 34). The opaque white trails often decay in acid soils, sometimes disappearing completely leaving grooves which have been mistaken by some for lines of abraded decoration. Close examination of the opaque glass often shows that the glass is full of bubbles, the frothiness causing opacity. These bubbles by themselves can produce opacity, but there are often white particles as well as, or instead of, the bubbles. Chemical analysis shows this opacifying agent to be tin oxide rather than calcium antimonite (Henderson 1993, 47). This is significant, as tin oxide was used in the Early Historic period in Ireland, while calcium antimonite was in use in Scandinavia (*ibid*). Unfortunately there are no comparable analyses of French material which might help to confirm the production area of Group C vessels. The chemical composition of the translucent body glass of Group C/D falls into the general pattern of soda-lime-silica type which persisted from the Roman period into the Early Historic. There are differences from the normal Roman type, however, in higher magnesium oxide and potassium oxide levels (*ibid*, 46, table 2). This shows that the glass was not merely recycled Roman cullet but was probably being produced from raw materials. Again, lack of comparable analyses prevents comparison with Continental material.

Cone beakers

There is little typological variation in the Group C material as the vast majority of forms are cone beakers (92 vessels plus ten uncertain). Bowls form a small minority of vessels (six plus two uncertain). The only other forms present are a possible palm cup from Longbury Bank, G176, and another possible cup, G203, from the Mote of Mark. The details of the form of the cone beakers are difficult to reconstruct from the fragmentary material available (Pl 31). Only in a few cases can profiles be suggested, such as G98 from Dinas Powys (Fig 38, A). A feature of these cones seems to be that the base is very narrow, meaning that the overall shape is a cone with concave walls, rather resembling a funnel beaker shape. This can also be seen in the material from Longbury Bank, for example G181. However, other cones such as G97 from Dinas Powys appear to be the more common triangular shape. It might be thought that this could suggest that the funnel beaker developed from the cone beaker, but it has been fairly conclusively shown that they developed from the late palm cup (Ypey 1963; Evison 2000, 79–80). The form and height of these cones is very close to that of vessels described as funnel beakers from *Hamwic* which are straight-sided and not funnel-shaped (Hunter and Heyworth 1998, fig 10, 36/333). It has to be admitted that it can be difficult to distinguish cone beakers, palm cups and funnel beakers on the basis of small rim sherds, if there are no other distinctive features. The rim diameters range between 6 and 10cm, though most are 7–9cm. Heights can only be estimated for one example, G98, at around 16cm.

Bowls

The Group C bowls are wider, with rim diameters around 14–16cm, but no profile can be reconstructed. The possible palm cup from Longbury Bank, G176, has a height of around 6.5cm and a rim diameter of 8cm. It is decorated with a band of marvered trails below the rim, and irregular spiral unmarvered trails around the base. The olive green colour is unusual in Group C vessels. A 7th-/8th-century date for this vessel was suggested in the original publication, and it is perhaps relevant that similar forms were found at Bordeaux in 7th-/8th-century levels (Foy and Hochuli-Gysel 1995, fig 15, 3 and 10). The dominance of the cone over all other forms is unusual, and certainly differentiates the Atlantic material from Anglo-Saxon, which has a wide variety of forms, at least until the 10th century (Evison 2000, figs 2–4). At Bordeaux, in contrast, cones and bowls were the dominant forms in the 6th-century vessels decorated with opaque white trails, though a few other forms were present (Foy and Hochuli-Gysel 1995, 160–1, fig 14). It seems possible that the cones were specially selected for export, perhaps because of their use as drinking vessels.

Decoration of cones and bowls

The decoration of the Group C vessels can be divided into three schemes:

a) a band of opaque white marvered trails just below the rim (Fig 42);
b) vertical running chevrons (merrythought), also with a band below the rim (Pl 31; Fig 43) (Thorpe 1935, 69);
c) combed or dragged festoons, also with a band below the rim (Pl 35; Fig 44) (cf von Pfeffer 1953).

Occasionally, as in G176, there is an additional spiral band of unmarvered trails on the base, and a few other less regular schemes exist, for example on Group E vessels at Whithorn. It is difficult to be sure of the relative proportions of these schemes. No certain example of chevrons or festoons has been found without a horizontal band below the rim. Vertical chevrons outnumber festoons by around 22 to 13. As already discussed in Chapter 4.2, the only parallel for the vertical chevron scheme comes from Bordeaux (Foy and Hochuli-Gysel 1995, 160–2, fig 14, 23, 24; fig 15, 23). Festoons are also found in the Bordeaux material (*ibid*, fig 14, 20), but neither of these schemes appears to be common. Again this may indicate special selection of vessels for export, or an alternative source of supply somewhere in the same region of France with a slightly different tradition of decorative schemes.

The technique and sequence of application of the trails can be determined by close examination. The vertical chevrons were the first to be applied, as the vessel was slowly rotated while still attached to the paraison. The horizontal band was applied next, sometimes by applying a new gob of opaque white glass (G102), but often by picking up the still viscous glass from the top of a chevron (G97). The vessel was then spun quickly so that very a fine thread of glass was produced and laid in a tight spiral. Such a process involved very considerable skill to keep the thread from cooling and breaking. The lower parts of the vessel would then have been marvered by rolling on the marver block. The glass vessel was then attached to a pontil rod on the base using a gob of glass, and broken off from the paraison. The pontil scar (circular or oval) can often be seen overlying the basal parts of chevrons (Fig 43, G1). The vessel was then ready for marvering the upper part, and reheating the rim to fire-round the broken-off edge. Finally the vessel was removed from the pontil rod. The whole process indicates that the glass blowers had full control of their material and equipment, were able to regulate temperatures of their furnaces, and were therefore operating in a sustained tradition of glass vessel production. A fuller discussion of the origin of the Group Cb cones is given in Appendix 3.

Bichrome vessels

This small group of vessels appears to belong to a late phase of Group C production, having features which relate them to the technological advances of the late Group B vessels discussed above. They all have a thick band of differently coloured glass applied to the outer part of the rim, completely marvered into the body of the vessel. In four of the examples, G120 from Dooey, G200 and G201 from the Mote of Mark, and G305 from Whithorn (Pl 34), the applied colour is opaque white, while in G326 from Whithorn it is translucent blue (Pl 33). The use of opaque white glass for most of these vessels links them to Group C vessels, and in fact at least three also have further bands of typical horizontal opaque white trails in the normal position below the rim. The reason for considering these vessels as late in the Group C sequence is that bichrome rims are a feature of 8th- and 9th-century glass vessels, though these were often made from reticella trails (Evison 2000, 85). Many examples of these reticella rims are known from mid-Saxon *Hamwic* (Hunter and Heyworth 1998, figs 7 and 8) and Scandinavian sites. The use of bichrome techniques in general also dates to this period (Evison 1982b). The use of white and blue for rims would appear to be a feature of Group C vessels which may have pre-dated the reticella type of rim decoration. Examples of blue rims are now known from the south of France in 7th-century contexts (D Foy pers comm) and a green vessel with a blue rim is known from a Carolingian deposit at St-Denis, Paris (Evison 1991, 144, no 60a). The blue-rimmed vessel G326 came from a late 7th-century grave at Whithorn (Period I/4.3). The excavator considered, on rather dubious distributional grounds, that this sherd had been disturbed from underlying late 6th-century deposits (Hill 1997, 308), but it is perhaps as likely that it is contemporary with the digging of the grave. G305 came from the same Period I/10 deposits as the bulk of the E ware vessels and the Group C glass vessels with chevron decoration, suggesting that the occasional use of white bichrome rims was well established by the early 7th century in the Group C tradition.

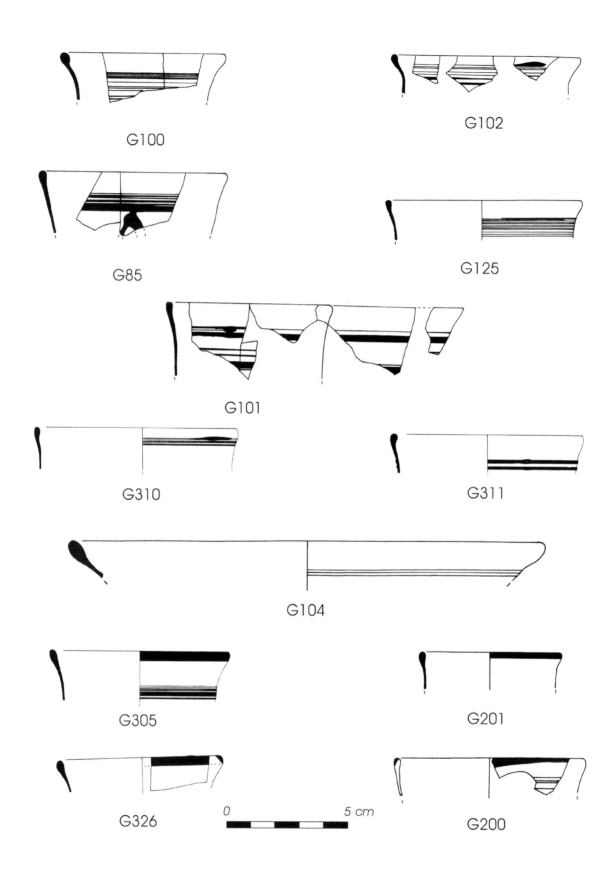

Fig 42 Imported glass from Insular sites. Group Ca, decorated Atlantic tradition, band of trails at rim. Cones: G85, G100–102, G125 Dinas Powys; G310–11 Whithorn. Bowl: G104 Dinas Powys. Solid coloured rim: G200–201 Mote of Mark; G305, G326 Whithorn

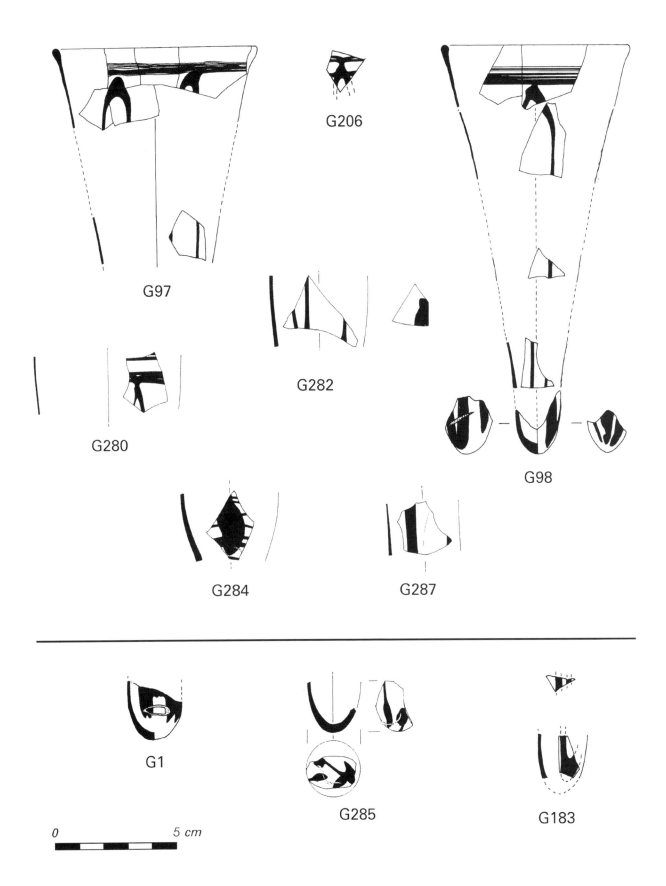

Fig 43 Imported glass from Insular sites. Group Cb, decorated Atlantic tradition, cones with vertical chevrons. G97–8 Dinas Powys; G206 Mote of Mark; G280, G282, G284, G287 Whithorn. Bases: G1 Armagh; G285 Whithorn; G183 Longbury Bank

68 *Continental and Mediterranean imports to Atlantic Britain and Ireland, AD 400–800*

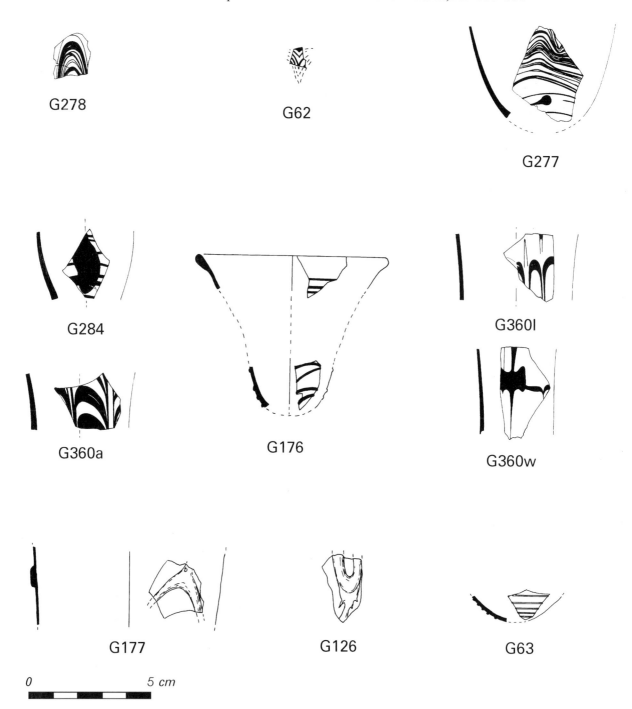

Fig 44 Imported glass from Insular sites. Group Cc, decorated Atlantic tradition, cones with festoons: G62 Castle Hill Dalry; G277–8, G360 Whithorn. Horizontal basal trails: G284 Whithorn. Vessels with unmarvered trails: G63 Castle Hill Dalry; G126 Dumbarton Rock; G176–7 Longbury Bank

Chronology

The chronology of the Group C vessels is difficult to establish. Only at Whithorn is there a good stratigraphic sequence. Here there is a clear differentiation between the vessels with vertical chevrons and those with only horizontal trails (Fig 76). The vessels with vertical chevrons appear in the same late 6th-/7th-century contexts as most of the E ware, while those with horizontal bands also occur in mid-6th-century deposits with the bulk of the Mediterranean amphorae and ARS ware. Festoons are rare at Whithorn except in Group E vessels. The Group C glass thus appears to span both import systems, with some being brought in alongside Mediterranean wares and others with the Continental pottery. The glass may not therefore be such a good chronological indicator as the pottery, though if the association of chevron-trailed glass with E ware is substantiated at other

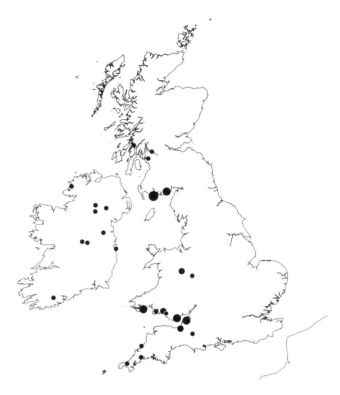

Fig 45 Distribution of Group C glass

sites, this particular sub-group may mark a better chronological horizon.

Taphonomy

The question of whether these glass sherds are cullet or vessels is discussed in relation to Dinas Powys (Chapter 6.3) where it is shown that, there at least, complete vessels were present on the site (Pl 31; Campbell 1995a). A similar pattern emerged at Whithorn, where the size of the assemblage enabled parts of vessels to be reconstructed (Campbell 1997, illus 10.10, 71). It follows that the sherds from the other sites probably also represent imported complete vessels, but there is no way of knowing if this is true in any particular case as there is not sufficient information about find spots on other sites. Most specialists now accept that the glass on western sites represents broken complete vessels (eg Bourke 1994, 180).

Distribution

In distributional terms the Group C glass is concentrated on western British sites (Fig 45), where all the main concentrations of vessels occur, with relatively few in Ireland. This is especially the case with chevron-decorated vessels with only one known from Ireland, G1 from Armagh. This may be due to chronological factors, if most of the E ware on Irish sites is 7th- rather than 6th-century in date, but this is discussed further in Chapter 9.3.

4.5 Group D: undecorated Atlantic tradition
(Fig 46)

All the characteristics of Group C are present in Group D vessels, apart from decoration. Indeed, because of the fragmentary nature of many vessels, it can be difficult to be sure if undecorated vessel sherds represent an undecorated vessel, or are merely the undecorated part of a decorated vessel. It is probable then that the proportion of decorated to undecorated vessels was originally higher than 2:1.

The same range of forms, colours and metals as in Group C are found in Group D vessels. The distribution is also similar in general geographic terms, and Group D vessels are often found on the same sites as Group C vessels. In terms of chronological distribution, only Whithorn provides any evidence. There the Group D vessels appear in two stratigraphic groups. The early examples, G329, G331, G334 and less certainly G337 and G328, are found in early 6th-century contexts with the Mediterranean pottery imports. The later group examples are contemporary with the main deposits of E ware in the late 6th/early 7th century, or in later 7th-century contexts. However, it is noticeable that most of the early group has particularly bubbly metal, and it may be that these really belong to Group B, which is also found in these deposits. These particular vessels were classified as Group D because they had none of the distinctive decorative features of Group B, but with such fragmentary material attribution to a group can only be tentative.

Typologically, there seems to be a higher proportion of bowls to cones amongst the Group D vessels. Of the identifiable vessels, 28 are cones, and 20 are bowls. One of the bowls, G325, has a flat base, the only example which survives. Similar flat-based bowls are seen in the Bordeaux assemblage (Foy and Hochuli-Gysel 1995, fig 14, nos 13, 15). Most other bowls of the period had either rounded or kicked bases. A few kicked basal fragments are known in the Atlantic assemblage, though none can be certainly ascribed to bowls or Group D.

4.6 Group E: Whithorn tradition (Pl 37; Fig 47)

This group can be related to the Atlantic tradition on the basis of the decorative techniques and the quality of metal, but is restricted to an unusual assemblage of vessels from Whithorn which may have been produced there, copying Group C vessels (Campbell 1997, 310–13). Although at first sight the Group E vessels look like Group C cone beakers, close inspection reveals a number of differences. Firstly, the rims are fire-rounded, but not thickened internally. The internal surfaces of the rims retain the marks of the pincers used to fashion them. These marks are lost in Group C/D vessels due to internal thickening. The vessels tend to be thicker than

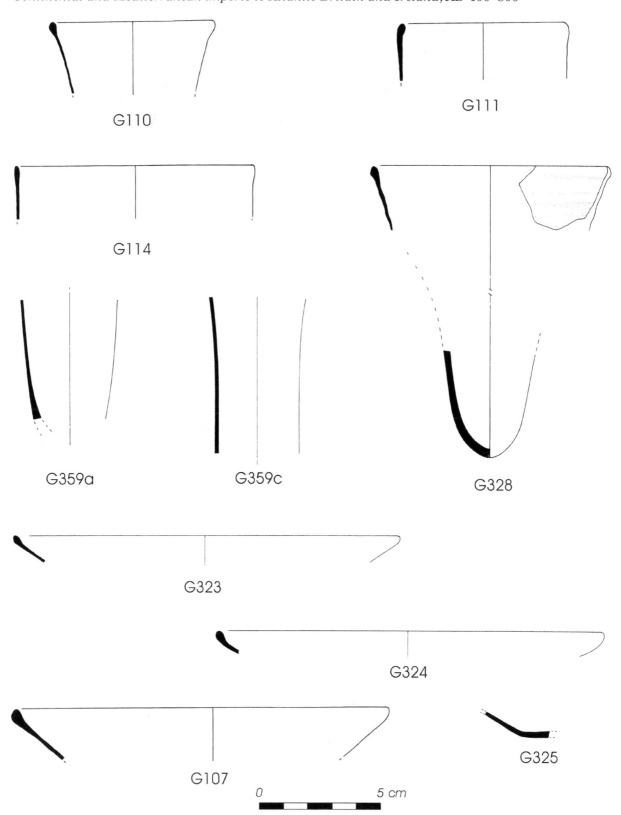

Fig 46 Imported glass from Insular sites. Group D, undecorated Atlantic tradition. Cones: G110, G111, G114 Dinas Powys; G328, G359 Whithorn. Bowls: G107 Dinas Powys; G323–5 Whithorn

Group C/D vessels, at around 1.5mm, as opposed to around 0.5–1.0mm. Some of the vessels have a distinctive amber or honey colour with pink streaks which may be due to traces of metallic copper.

The form and decoration of the vessels is also characteristic. Around fifteen vessels can be identified, G242–360, all of which are cone beakers. Like Group C, they are decorated with opaque white trails, but

Imported glass: Groups A–E 71

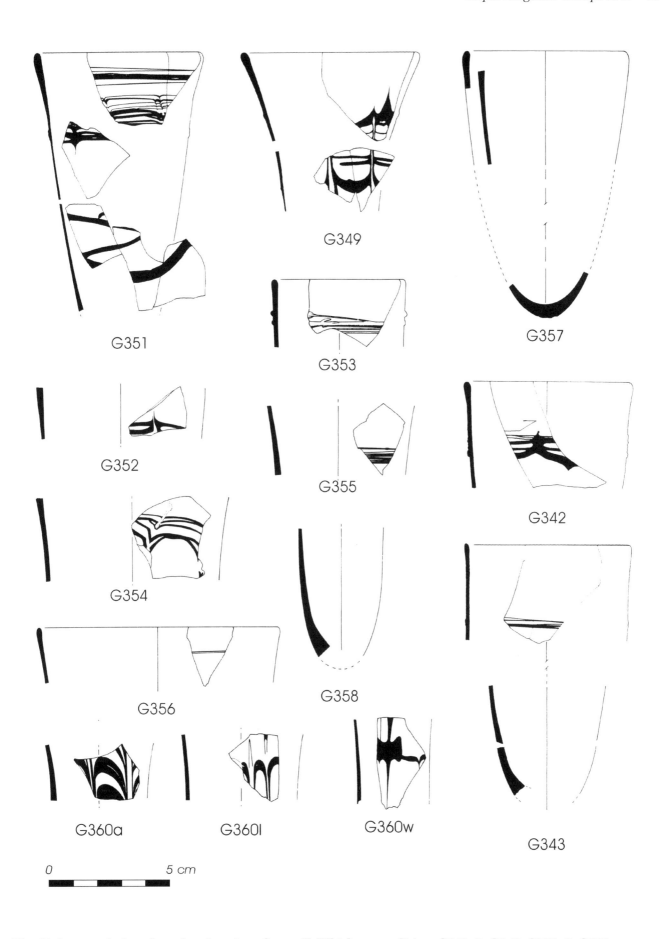

Fig 47 Imported glass from Insular sites. Group E, Whithorn tradition: G342–3, G349, G351–8, G360 Whithorn

Table 6 Forms of imported glass vessels

	Group A	Group B	Group C	Group D	Group E	All
cone	–	13	102	29	17	161
bowl	11	1	8	20	–	40
phial/flasklet	–	5	–	–	–	5
claw beaker	–	6	–	–	–	6
palm cup	–	7	–	–	–	7
goblet	2	–	–	–	–	2
flagon	2	–	–	–	–	2
beaker	1	4	–	–	–	5
squat jar	–	2	–	–	–	2
jar	–	2	–	–	–	2
cup	–	2	2	1	–	5
funnel beaker	–	1	–	–	–	1
others	2	2	1	1	–	6
Total	18	45	113	51	17	244

the spiral band around the rim is unmarvered. Below this band there are often thicker horizontal trails which have been dragged with a point upwards and/or downwards to form partial festoons (Pl 37). The trails seem to have been viscous when dragged, creating a rather different effect from that seen in Group B or Group C vessels. The form of the cones is also distinctive, with a constant rim diameter of 7cm, and a rather bag-shaped form, less conical than Group C cones. A similar form is seen in some of late 6th-/7th-century cones from Bordeaux (Foy and Hochuli-Gysel 1995, fig 14, 20, 21).

The vessels come from a restricted stratigraphical range, Period I/2.2, which can be dated to the later 6th century between the main Mediterranean and Continental pottery import phases at the site. A number of pieces of melted and folded glass vessels were found in the same area (Campbell 1997, 314), providing possible evidence of manufacture. It is, however, possible to interpret these as vessels which were accidentally burnt in a fire, rather than deliberately melted down for reuse. The main evidence for manufacture here lies in the distribution of the vessels being restricted to Whithorn, and their concentration in one stratigraphic unit at the site. Only recovery of crucibles with glass residues can confirm this hypothesis. Although the Group E vessels are rather cruder in manufacture than Group C/D, they are technically competent, and the metal is finer than that in Group B vessels. They appear to have been made by someone trained in the Atlantic tradition of glass-blowing. An alternative explanation is that they are the product of a particular glass kiln or glass-blower on the Continent, which only exported one batch of material. This is not impossible, though the weight of evidence points towards the possibility of a Continental glass-blower at work at Whithorn.

4.7 Form and function

There are significant differences between the groups in terms of the forms represented (Table 6). Group A, as we have seen, is dominated by bowls, alongside a variety of forms not found in the other groups, such as flagons and goblets. This is the most striking illustration of the different cultural background of this Mediterranean group of vessels. Many of the vessels are decorated, and were intended as tablewares displaying wealth and cultural affinities. Group B, in contrast, has a majority of cone beakers, along with other drinking forms such as claw beakers, squat jars and palm cups, with bowls noticeably absent. Again this reflects the traditions of the areas of production. Groups C and D should be considered together, for the reasons outlined above. There is a much more restricted range of forms, mostly cones, with a much smaller proportion of bowls. This may reflect a suite specially chosen for export, as the range of vessel types in northern France is much greater, but the excavations at Bordeaux seem to show a similarly restricted range of forms in the 6th/7th centuries. Group E vessels are restricted to copies of the commonest Group C form, the cone beaker.

The cone beaker form would not stand up by itself, of course, leading some commentators to consider that the entire contents had to be drained in one draught. It is equally possible however that these vessels were carried by a cup-bearer who would hand it to their lord on demand. Illustrations of cup-bearers holding conical drinking vessels are seen in some late Saxon manuscripts, for instance the Harley Psalter, f.51b (Backhouse et al 1984, pl 19). There may be a contemporary illustration of a cone beaker in the *Book of Kells*, folio 188r (Meehan 1994, illus 94). An alternative possibility is that the cones

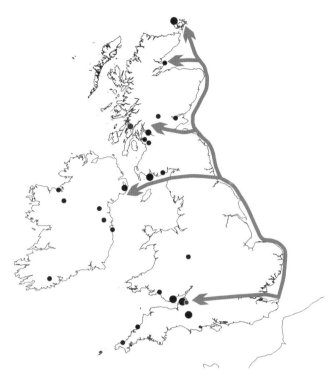

Fig 48 Distribution of Group B glass and possible supply routes from Anglo-Saxon England

were used as lamps. Most lamps used in the Mediterranean world were conical forms, sometimes with three or six handles (eg Tatton-Brown 1984, 202, fig 66, 57–60). It has been suggested that Anglo-Saxon cones could have functioned in the same way (Clark 2005, 6), though there is no evidence for this. As with the pottery, it is possible that there could have been several functions. In Italy, glass lamps at this period were confined to ecclesiastical sites (Newby 2005, 6), and so this might explain the presence of vessels apparently associated with luxury and the consumption of wine at sites such as Whithorn. It could be argued that researchers have been overly influenced by the imports' associations with the putative wine trade, and have ignored this possibility. It is noticeable, however, that lamps in the Mediterranean world are always undecorated, while many of the conical beakers, including the Group E ones from Whithorn, are decorated with white trails, which might militate against this interpretation.

4.8 Conclusions

The discussion above has shown that the glass imports have a much more complicated chronology, pattern of production and distribution than the pottery discussed in earlier chapters. The Group A vessels, of Late Roman or Mediterranean tradition, probably accompanied the Mediterranean pottery imports as space fillers, rather like the PRS and ARS pottery vessels, and like them, date to the first half of the 6th century. The Group B vessels of Germanic tradition have the most diverse dating and production source. Some appear in early contexts at Whithorn, contemporary with the Mediterranean pottery, but it seems unlikely that they were part of the same cargoes, as the Mediterranean imports are not found in any Anglo-Saxon areas. It is possible that these vessels reached the Atlantic West by a variety of overland routes from Anglo-Saxon England (Fig 48). This is fairly certain with some vessels, such as the blue globular jar from Dinas Powys, G83, which can be seen to have arrived via the upper Thames valley on distributional grounds. The other sites in the south-west, at Pagans Hill and Cadbury Castle, were presumably supplied by the same route. The Whithorn, Dumbarton, Dunadd, Mote of Mark and Buiston material may have arrived overland from Northumbria. Some of these sites have known links with Northumbria revealed by documentary sources and/or other finds (Campbell and Lane 1993b). The finds from Clatchard Craig and Dundurn may have been supplied directly by east coast trading contacts. The later finds from Ireland are more difficult to account for, but may indicate contacts with the west coast of Mercia across the Irish Sea. None of this Group B material appears to be accompanied by any other bulk traded material from Anglo-Saxon England, and may be the result of casual personal contacts by travellers, or diplomatic or marital gifts, rather than any sustained trading network. The chronological range of this material, from the early 6th century through to the 8th and possibly 9th centuries, supports this interpretation.

The Group C/D vessels appear to have a production source close to that of DSPA and E ware, and might be expected to have been imported alongside these vessels. However the Whithorn evidence shows that some of these vessels overlap with the earlier Mediterranean wares, and the relative lack of distribution in Ireland compared to E ware supports the idea that they represent some kind of transitional phase of importation between the two main pottery phases. This will be discussed in Chapter 9.3. Nevertheless, quite a high proportion of the Group C vessels, those with vertical chevrons, do appear to be associated with the E ware phase of importation at Whithorn. The Group E vessels seem to represent production in Scotland by a Continental glassworker, but this needs to be confirmed.

The evidence of the glass vessels therefore has to be used cautiously, with clear differentiation between the various groups, and even of sub-types within the groups, before drawing any conclusions on the mechanism of importation.

5 Miscellaneous material

Although the focus of this corpus is on pottery and glass, a few other items can be shown to have been imported from the Mediterranean or the Continent, or have been claimed as such imports (Fig 49). These are listed and discussed here, though the sites are not listed in the same detail as the pottery and glass in the appendices unless they also have these imports. Much of the material is from antiquarian collections or metal-detector stray finds, both of which sources can be compromised by known processes of false attribution, salting of sites, and competitive collection (Boon 1991, 39).

5.1 St Menas flask (Pl 38)

These little ceramic *ampullae* were used by pilgrims to contain holy oil taken from the lamps burning over the shrine of the Christian martyr Menas, though holy water from the same site is another possibility. Menas's shrine was situated at the famous pilgrimage site of Abu Mena, near Alexandria in Egypt. The *ampullae* are found widely throughout the Middle East and Europe from the 4th to 7th centuries. The only example from a fairly secure context in Atlantic Britain is from Meols, on the Wirral peninsula. It was found in 1955 in a peat layer in the same area as a huge 19th-century collection of Iron Age, Roman, post-Roman, Anglo-Saxon and later medieval finds from eroding coastal deposits (Griffiths 2003, 68). Meols was clearly an important trading place over a long period of time, but unfortunately most of the material is unstratified.

The flask has moulded decoration showing St Menas flanked by the two camels which reputedly brought his body to his burial place. The form of the Meols flask is 6th- or 7th-century. The presence of this object at Meols is very interesting, particularly as the site has produced no Mediterranean or Continental pottery or glass imports. It might be argued that the antiquarian collectors would not necessarily have kept such commonplace material, but as some Roman and medieval pottery was kept (mainly brightly coloured or glazed sherds), the absence may be genuine. Items such as the flask were possibly personal possessions, though there is increasing understanding of trade in holy relics in early medieval Europe (Geary 1994; Theuws 2004). What the flask does show is that Mediterranean connections reached areas outside the core area of import sites in the Atlantic West. Whether or not Meols was a trading place in the 6th and 7th centuries, as it undoubtedly was at earlier and later periods, must await the results of the large project underway to re-evaluate all the old material and undertake new research (Griffiths 2003, 65–8). The recent discovery of three 6th-/7th-century Byzantine coins nearby may suggest that there was direct contact with the Mediterranean, but some doubt attaches to the reliability of these coins as ancient losses (Philpott 1998, 201; see below). A recent suggestion that the flask may have reached Meols overland from Anglo-Saxon England has considerable merit, as the distribution of these flasks throughout Europe suggests they were not brought by the Atlantic sea-route from the Mediterranean (Harris 2003, 68–9). There is another stray find of a Menas flask further up the Mersey, from Preston on the Hill, Cheshire (D Griffiths pers comm).

5.2 Coins

One of the biggest contrasts between the Atlantic West and Anglo-Saxon England is the lack of coinage in the Early Historic period. No coins were minted in Ireland, Wales or Scotland during this period, and very few coins from outside this area have been found as stray finds. It is important to note that none have been found on any of the excavated sites which produce imported pottery and glass. There is no

Fig 49 Distribution of miscellaneous imported material. P, pottery; G, non-vessel glass; D, madder dye; O, other; C, coins; M, metalwork

doubt that coins played an important symbolic role, as well as a purely economic one (Aarts 2005), shown for example by the deposition of late Roman coins at Newgrange in what is clearly a votive deposit (Fig 81). However, the stray coins known from the area, whether antiquarian or modern metal-detector finds, are difficult to interpret as they are so sparse. As with the pottery, the coins fall into two broad groups, Merovingian and Byzantine, which will be discussed separately.

Byzantine coins have been found near to Meols, as mentioned above, and at around 80 other locations, often Roman towns such as Caerwent and Exeter. These bronze coins were studied by George Boon, who produced convincing arguments that most were recent losses, for example by soldiers returned from duty in the Middle East, or by tourists (Boon 1958; 1991). The giveaway is the type of patination on the coins, most of the known examples showing a Middle Eastern type indicating initial burial in that region, and subsequent collection by dealers. Boon accepted only one coin from Princetown, Devon, two from Ilchester, and the *Hamwic* and Moreton coins discussed below, as genuine losses. Gold coins are much rarer, and, although they are found in Anglo-Saxon graves, there they are usually converted into pendants (Harris 2003, 153, colour plate 25) and may never have been used as currency. They are not relevant to this discussion as none has so far been found in the Atlantic West except for one possible *solidus* of Maurice Tiberius (582–602) found in unknown circumstances in Gloucestershire, in any case post-dating the Mediterranean trading system (Harris 2003, 153).

Boon's conclusions on the low-value coinage have been questioned in more recent discussions (Dark 2000, 162–3). Low-value coinage is of course more likely to be indicative of direct contact than high-value coins of precious metals, as its only use is as a means of exchange in a monetary economy, while gold and silver coins can be exchanged for their intrinsic value. Dark (1994, 200–6) has argued for continued use of a 'hotch-potch' currency of late Roman issues in 5th- and 6th-century Britain, but most numismatists and Romanists would disagree (eg Reece 1993). The lack of such coins in good stratigraphic contexts with the pottery and glass imports studied here seems conclusive evidence that there was no monetary economy in the Atlantic West. While some late Roman coins are found in post-Roman graves, for example at Cannington cemetery (Rahtz *et al* 2000, 365), these are either accidental associations of residual material, or keepsakes picked up from Roman sites and used as fortuitous grave goods. The one Roman coin from a certain 7th-century grave at Cannington was pierced and used as a pendant in a child's grave (*ibid*).

Harris (2003, 152–4), on the basis of the Byzantine coins from the Wirral, suggests that these coins, and the Menas flask, could have reached the Wirral from Anglo-Saxon England (cf Griffiths 2003, 69), and this is possible. She also points to a relative lack of Byzantine coins in France, despite documentary evidence for large quantities of these coins being imported to France (Harris 2003, 153). However, Byzantine coins are found in the areas of southern France which we know from ceramic evidence had trading contacts with north Africa and the eastern Mediterranean (Morrisson 1999; Lafaurie and Morrisson 1987). The three coins from near Meols are interesting, but several aspects advise caution. Firstly, the find spots are actually at Moreton, about 3km inland from Meols. More damaging is the condition of the Maurice Tiberius *follis* (AD 600/1), which shows signs of having been crudely cleaned in the past. This was a metal-detector find along with another *follis* of Justin I (AD 518–27), both possibly dredged from river silts. The condition of the former coin shows it was cleaned at some point, suggesting it was part of a recent collection rather than an ancient loss, thus throwing the other coin found with it into doubt as well. The third coin is a *decanummium* of Justinian I (AD 540/1), from the Carthage mint, found in a garden. There are no questions over the source of this coin, but it would be as well to remember Boon's caution that the most suspect finds are those 'from allotments, gardens, towns and near ancestral seats' (Boon 1958, 318). The two separately found Ilchester coins might fit into that category, but Boon accepts them on the basis of the patination. Both are early 6th-century issues of Constantinople. Although unstratified, they have been accepted more readily because of the supposed presence of 6th-century LRA in the town (Boon 1991, 41). These supposed LRA sherds from Ilchester are often quoted in support of a Roman town continuing in occupation into the 6th century (Rahtz 1974, table 1; Alcock 1982, 381). However, the basis for this statement is an unsupported suggestion by a local antiquary that some sherds found in a pipe trench were similar to sherds from Tintagel (Cox 1956, 170). This uncorroborated suggestion cannot be regarded as having any validity, given the lack of expert identification, the unavailability of the sherds for study, and the presence of some types of LRA in late Roman urban contexts.

The danger of over-interpreting these stray finds is shown by the only Byzantine coin to have been found in a good stratigraphic context, at *Hamwic* (Metcalf 1988, 25). This mid-6th-century copper *decanummium* of Justinian (AD 540/1) was found in a mid-Saxon pit dated to around 750–900, buried at least two centuries after its minting. How it reached *Hamwic* is a matter of debate. Lack of wear on the coin suggests that it had not been long in circulation after minting. The mint was Carthage, a rare mint place amongst Mediterranean coin assemblages at this period. A group of both Vandal and Justinian coins of the Carthage mint have also been dredged from the harbour at Bordeaux (Boon 1991, 42; LaFaurie and Morrison 1987, 69). It is therefore possible that this coin was brought by the Atlantic sea-route, but whether it came in the mid-6th century or later is not clear. Its date, just after the

Justinian reconquest of north Africa, and Carthage origin, would tie in with the importation of ARS and B*v* amphorae in the mid-6th century, so it would be unwise to dismiss completely all Byzantine coinage as recent losses. A possible complication is that coins of the Carthage mint are unusually common in southern France, not just in the 6th century but also the 7th, because of close trading links between Carthage and southern France (Morrison 1999). As the garden-found coin from Moreton is identical to *Hamwic*'s, a contemporary origin is possible. It is also noticeable that the hoard of Carthage mint coins of Justinian from the Gironde are the earliest of the Byzantine series found in western France, and are in a location close to Bordeaux, which has LRA. These are the only coins which fall within the period of importation of the Mediterranean imports.

The later 6th-century Carthage coins (ie of emperors later than Justinian) in western France are also in intriguing locations. One at Abbartez has been mentioned as it was found in a tin mine, and potentially dates tin extraction in Brittany. This is a tantalising hint of support for the hypothesis of tin as a driver of the Mediterranean trade. Other single coins come from further up the major western rivers, at Orléans on the Loire and Casteljaloux on the Gironde (LaFaurie and Morrison 1987, 64–74), routes likely used by merchants. It is noticeable that all these Carthage mint coins, except those from Meols, *Hamwic* and the Gironde, post-date the period of importation of Mediterranean ceramics to Atlantic Britain. However, they may reflect continuing contact and trade with the Mediterranean, but contact that did not extend to Britain and Ireland.

The occasional deposition of such coins at local shrines or sacred places by Byzantine merchants would not be unusual. This may explain the *follis* of Anastasius I from the chambered tomb of Porthellick in the Scilly Isles (Dark 2000, 162). Others may have been passed to customers as trinkets, or retained by pilgrims on return from the holy places of the Near East. On the other hand, to extrapolate this evidence to suggest coin-use for payment in the west would be wrong (cf Dark 1994, 206) and misinterprets the nature of the documentary evidence of the *Life* of St John the Almsgiver (see Chapter 9.2).

Merovingian coinage is much rarer in the west, not surprisingly as this was of gold, and later silver, denominations. Two gold tremisses, Merovingian civic issues of early 7th-century date, are known, from Trim, Co Meath, and Portlaoise, Co Laois, in Ireland, but neither is in any archaeological context. The coin from Trim (Rigold 1975, no 66A) was minted at Beaufay, and that from Portlaoise (*ibid*, no 70) at Le Mans, both in the *département* of Sarthe. There is no means of knowing if these are genuine contemporary losses, though they are accepted as such by Rigold and also by Metcalf (pers comm). The coin from Le Mans is described only as coming from 'near Maryborough' (ie Portlaoise) (Anon 1863, 245), but it is interesting to note that the major royal fortress of Dunamase lies only 5km to the east of Portlaoise (S 531982). The site is documented as an Early Historic stronghold, and by the 10th century was in the control of the kings of the Loígis (Smyth 1982, 34, 101). The many Byzantine copper coins in Britain and Ireland have generally been dismissed as modern losses, as discussed above. Bateson (1973) has shown that many of the disputed Irish examples are found in garrison towns and it may be significant that Portlaoise was a garrison town in the post-medieval period. On the other hand gold coins are not as easily lost or discarded as copper coinage, and the western mint sites would not conflict with a source for E ware in western France, as the Sarthe is a tributary of the Loire, and the early date coincides with the *floruit* of E ware. However, as with Byzantine coins, no Continental imports are found on these sites; indeed Portlaoise lies in a notable blank spot in the distribution of Continental imports, though Trim is close to Lagore. Although most gold or silver coins would have been melted down, the lack of Merovingian coinage in hoards contrasts with their abundance in the Late Roman and Viking periods in Ireland, suggesting that the lack of these coins is real. The contrast with the quantity of Merovingian gold coinage found in Anglo-Saxon England in the 7th century is also striking.

One further coin needs to be discussed, the only Anglo-Saxon coin known from an import site in the west, except for sites such as Whithorn where later Saxon occupation levels with coins overlie levels with imports. This is a forgery of a mid-7th-century Anglo-Saxon gold *thrymsa* from Buiston Crannog (Grierson and Blackburn 1986, 162). In this 'peripheral' area, the coin may be a locally made copy, but it is perhaps more likely to have reached Buiston from Anglian Northumbria, along with other Anglo-Saxon finds from the site (Campbell 1991, 169; Crone 2000, 144). It thus falls into the same type of distribution as the Group B Germanic glass.

5.3 Unclassified pottery (Fig 50)

At Dunadd three fabrics were found in addition to DSPA and E ware, all in deposits containing E ware. The sherds in Dunadd Fabric A2, a soft pinkish micaceous fabric (Lane and Campbell 2000, 102–3, illus 4.1, 900 and 1739), appear to be the only examples of Class 'F ware' (Thomas 1959) which are genuine early medieval imports (Duncan 1982, 51). Comparison of the fabric with the imports from Southampton showed a very close similarity to *Hamwic* Fabric 195 (Timby 1988, 102–3), which is a rare import there, found in late 8th-century contexts. Its source is unknown. The Dunadd sherds appear to be from a single vessel of closed form such as a jug (Fig 50, U3). Dunadd Fabric A3 (Lane and Campbell 2000, 103) is a red quartz-gritted

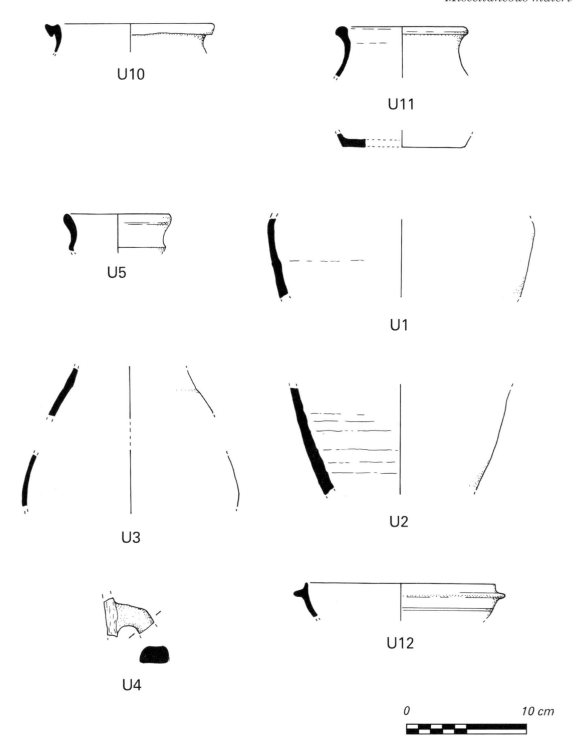

Fig 50 Miscellaneous imported pottery. U1–5 Dunadd; U10 Mote of Mark; U11 Bruach an Druimein; U12 Whithorn

ware, with a similar surface appearance to E ware but with well-sorted sub-rounded grains. In thin section apart from quartz the inclusions include rare calcite, quartzite and feldspar. The general similarity to E ware suggests it is a Continental import, but the fabric is not matched at *Hamwic*. Two different vessels appear to be represented (Fig 50, U1–2). Dunadd Fabric A4 is a soft pink ware. The handle sherd is unusual in that it is pulled rather than wheel-thrown like E ware and most other Continental wares (Fig 50, U4). An origin cannot be suggested.

The Mote of Mark has produced a soft micaceous vessel with an unusual rim (Fig 50, U10). This may be related to the Dunadd Fabrics A2 and A4, which are also soft and micaceous.

At Whithorn, there were two unidentified fabrics, one of which is of a flanged bowl, a form common in ARS (Campbell 1997, 332, illus 10.2). However, the fabric differs, though there may be traces of a red slip. It is possible this is a late Roman ware, like some of the late red slipwares originally identified by Thomas as Class G.

Other import sites have produced unidentified wares, but rarely is the stratigraphy clear enough to be sure they are imports and I have not examined these in detail. Examples include: buff wares from Clogher (R Warner pers comm); an unusual form of hard red ware at Armagh (Brown and Harper 1984, 143, fig 18, 100); numerous fabrics amongst the large collection of imports from Dalkey Island; and a sherd possibly of 8th-/9th-century Rhenish ware at Dundurn (Alcock *et al* 1989, fiche 2: G11). A number of sherds of a single vessel from Cadbury Congresbury were published as 'Gaulish' (Rahtz *et al* 1992, 181–3, fig 134). These have a superficial similarity in fabric to E ware, but the round-based form cannot be easily paralleled in Merovingian forms, and it may be a local Iron Age product as suggested by Peacock (in Rahtz *et al* 1992, 182).

These miscellaneous wares are so rare that they cannot help to elucidate any pattern of trade. They may have been brought as part of the import systems described above, but may represent individual travellers returning with the odd vessel or sherd picked up on their travels.

5.4 Other Byzantine finds

The site of Cefn Cwmwd, Anglesey, produced a rare Byzantine haematite intaglio. The jewel would have been originally set in a signet ring, and is decorated with an incised scorpion (Harris 2003, fig 43). It has been dated to the 6th or 7th century. Whether the jewel was originally imported as a signet ring, or just as an individual stone setting, is impossible to say, so it would be premature to build a hypothesis of official signatures on documents at this period in Wales (cf Denison 2000). The site also produced DSPA ware, so the stone may have reached Anglesey via western France, but it adds to the list of items in the Atlantic West derived from the Byzantine Empire.

Two other items come from Somerset. The most spectacular is a leaded brass censer from Glastonbury, close to the Early Historic abbey (Rahtz 1993, 100, fig 69). This is a 6th-/7th-century type and is an unusual item of liturgical metalwork. Unfortunately this is another stray find and is not certainly an ancient loss, though a similar one is known from Spain (Harris 2003, 144). The other is a 6th-century Byzantine coin-weight from near Taunton, found in unknown circumstances (Entwhistle 1994). This suffers from the same problems as the coins discussed above, and again may be a recent loss, though three other examples are known from Anglo-Saxon graves.

From Dunadd comes a single glass mosaic tessera with inlaid gold leaf (Pl 39). Such tesserae were Byzantine in origin and were imported into Scandinavia from the 8th century for use in inlay work on jewellery and in quantity from the 9th century for melting down to make beads (Bencard *et al* 1979). However, the Dunadd tessera came from a certain 7th-century context and must have been imported via the Atlantic coast along with other Mediterranean pottery and glass. Another example of glass mosaic tesserae is from Birsay in the Orkneys (Curle 1982, 122, no 645) though this is without gold leaf. It is possible this was part of a pre-Viking trade from Scandinavia to northern and western Scotland. There is a group of thirteen from Whithorn (Hill 1997, 296), though only one is from a pre-Anglian phase and again has no gold leaf. There is another possible example from the Mote of Mark (Campbell 2006). These could also be Byzantine, but are less distinctive than the gold leaf tesserae which were used to decorate wall mosaics in major Byzantine churches in Constantinople and Ravenna.

In contrast to Anglo-Saxon England, no Byzantine silver bowls or plates such as those from the Sutton Hoo ship-burial are known from the Atlantic West, but a silver offcut from Longbury Bank may be from such a vessel (Campbell and Lane 1993a, 30, fig 5). The acid soils of the west are generally inimical to the preservation of silver (Longbury Bank is unusual in being sited on limestone), and since such vessels would have been recycled rather than deposited in graves, it is possible that silver vessels were reaching high-status sites in the west.

One other item needs to be mentioned here for its reputed Byzantine connections, an inscribed Class 1 stone from Penmachno, Gwynedd. This inscription has been interpreted as reading IN TEMPORE IUSTINI CONSULIS and referring to the consular system of dating in the Roman and early Byzantine Empires. If accepted this would imply someone familiar with the system, and up to date with consular changes in Byzantium, with all that implies. However, there are many problems with the reading of the inscription, and it cannot be seen as evidence of direct Byzantine influence on north Wales in the 540s (Knight 1996, 116).

5.5 Other Continental finds

A similar scatter of supposed Continental metalwork has been claimed for sites in the Atlantic West, but the quantity is surprisingly small given the scale of commercial contacts shown by the pottery and glass.

A Salin's Style 2 enamelled disc from Dunadd, decorated with interlace ornament, has been claimed to be 'Frankish' (Craw 1930, fig 4), but is almost certainly Anglo-Saxon (Lane and Campbell 2000, 245–6, illus 7.10). Also claimed as 'Frankish' is a scramasax from Lagore (Hencken 1950, 94, fig 25, H). The type is not very distinctive, however, and may be influenced by Anglo-Saxon examples, as are several of the swords from the site. Thomas (1990, 19) admits these may be Anglo-Saxon but suggests that another sword from the Boyne ten miles north of Lagore can be paralleled in Trier, and also suggests four shield-bosses and a bridle-bit as Frankish rather than Anglo-Saxon. The shield-bosses resemble Dickinson's Group 8, some of which may have been imported from the Continent (Dickinson and Harke 1992, 21–3, fig 15c), but we do not know what Irish shield-bosses were like at this period. Thomas's basis for dismissing Anglo-Saxon influence in Ireland is that this is an unlikely direction of contact, but there is growing evidence for exchange between eastern Ireland and England at this period. This is shown in the Germanic glass found at Lagore and other sites (Chapter 4.3), and the strong influences on Irish metal working styles, seen for example on various buckles and the Moylough belt-shrine (Youngs 1989, 58–9). Similar contacts and influences are seen at western Scottish sites such as Dunadd (Campbell and Lane 1993b; Campbell forthcoming b), equally distant from Anglo-Saxon England, so there seem no *a priori* reason to dismiss England as a source for this type of material in Ireland.

A small cruciform ring-ornament from Tintagel has been claimed to be 'Merovingian' by Dark (1994, 80, fig 22). Again this is a stray with a number of possible origins. The general type is Roman, but Dark suggests a Continental origin on the basis that the specific sub-type is rare in Britain. However, as he quotes no Continental parallels, and the object has never been properly studied, this conclusion is dubious. Another small belt-fitting, from Tean in the Scilly Isles was claimed by Thomas (1985, 195–6, fig 88) to be possibly Merovingian. This also is a late Romano-British type and has no quoted Continental parallels, again throwing doubt on the attribution.

5.6 Miscellaneous material

If, as we have seen, pottery and glass were being imported as space-fillers amongst larger, more perishable cargoes, then perhaps other goods were also being imported. One would expect that these would also be luxury items, or at least items scarce or lacking in western Britain and Ireland. But before looking at the evidence for these goods it is necessary to say something about the possible perishable bulk goods for which no evidence survives.

Wine

It has often been suggested that E ware was an adjunct to wine importation (Thomas 1959, 100; 1976b; 1981; Hodges 1977). It has been argued that northern wine was transported in barrels which are perishable (Thomas 1976); that wine was exported from France; that there was a market for wine amongst the nobility and ecclesiastics; that there is evidence in the later Middle Ages for the import of wine and fine pottery from Saintonge to western areas; and that there is a wealth of literary evidence to support this view. There is no doubt that this is an attractive theory; indeed I think it is probably partly true. Unfortunately none of the evidence cited above stands up to further examination, as Wooding has shown in a detailed examination of the documentary sources (Wooding 1996b).

Taking these points in turn, it is true that barrels rather than amphorae were used to store and transport wine in north-western Europe, but no evidence of this can be pointed to at an Insular site. Thomas claimed wine barrels were found at Lagore and Lough Faughan with E ware, and that Adomnán mentioned wine oozing from a crack in a barrel (1976b, 252–3). At Lough Faughan the supposed barrel staves are in fact bucket staves as they have only one end with a groove for a base (Collins 1955, fig 12, 77). There is a barrel stave from Lagore, but as local barrels were in use in Ireland for other purposes at this period the association is meaningless. Wooding has pointed out that Adomnán only refers to a *vassis*, or 'vessel', and the whole image is possibly to wine oozing from cracks in a jar or amphora. In any case the image is probably an allusion to classical literature and may not therefore refer to contemporary conditions (cf Callender 1965, xx, n 1). The comparison with the later medieval trade in Saintonge ware is also misleading. Allan (1983), using the evidence of port books, has shown that wine and pottery from Saintonge were not imported in the same ships in the post-medieval period and he suggests that the nature of ship-borne trade is such that a similar situation obtained in the earlier medieval period.

The main attraction of the wine theory lies in the supposed historical evidence, originally propounded by Zimmer (1909). Zimmer's outdated theories were based on supposed literary evidence for contacts between Gaul and Ireland in the 5th century. Wooding has recently comprehensively discussed and dismissed Zimmer's view of these documents (Wooding 1983, 54–63; 1987; 1996b). However lacking the historical evidence for wine trade, there is no doubt that wine was in use at this period. Adomnán mentions wine as 'necessary for the most holy mysteries' (Anderson and Anderson 1961, 197), though it is not clear whether communion wine had to be made from grapes, nor how often it was necessary. Locally made wines could presumably have been produced throughout the Celtic West using native fruits. The need for communion wine does not imply that the churches organised a wine trade as Hodges has inferred (1977) since the wine trade could be articulated through secular settlements under royal control. By the 8th century in Ireland wine is mentioned in commentaries on the Sea Laws, the *Muirbretha*, as a cargo (O'Mahany and Richey 1873, 427; Kelly 1988, 276–7) and the *Book of Armagh* mentions wine used during festivities in AD 807 (Gwynn 1906).

Salt

Wine is just one of a likely variety of bulk cargoes. Salt, which was not produced in Ireland before Norman times (Scott 1981a, 115), is equally likely. Major sea-saltings were in use in Brittany and near the mouth of the Loire from the Iron Age onwards (Nenquin 1961). The saltings in Brittany seem to have gone out of use in the Late Roman period (Galliou 1986, 60; Sanquer and Galliou 1972, 119) but those closer to the Loire are attested in the early medieval period and are of considerable economic significance (Davies 1988, 53, 166; Wooding 1996b, 70–1). The few literary references to Irish trade and travel which can be shown to be contemporary with the E ware trade are all localised around the Loire (James 1982; Wooding 1996b), which is of course on the sea-route from south-western France to Atlantic Britain. It should be borne in mind that some salt may have come from England, as the salt springs at Droitwich were still in production. Despite the evidence of Continental sceattas from nearby, hinting at overseas trade, most production seems to have been directed to the south-east (Maddicott 2005, 44–5). Salt is of course a more prosaic item than wine, and must have been traded widely at all periods. The tract on the Sea Laws mentioned above also specifies salt as a cargo on 7th- or 8th-century ships. Salt was used extensively for preserving meat in early medieval Ireland as is shown by numerous references in the *Críth Gablach* of the 7th century (MacNeill 1923). It is likely that wine and/or salt were the major bulk items of trade, with the pottery, glass and other items merely being added-value space-fillers.

If small luxury items were being brought into western areas along with E ware, glass and some bulk cargo, these items should turn up on sites with E ware. It is perhaps surprising how few obviously Continental items have been found in the Celtic West. Those which can be identified include dyestuffs, beads and possibly some items of metalwork. The 8th-century Irish text of Sea Laws (*Muirbretha*) and its commentaries include lists of items which might be cargo on ships of this period, including hides, buffalo horns, feathers, iron, salt, foreign nuts, goblets, and an *escup* vessel of wine or honey (O'Mahany and Richey 1873, 427; Wooding 1996b, 68–72). While the first four of these could be local items being exported, the others are most likely to be imports and salt has already been discussed. The 'goblets' could possibly refer to the glass vessels which I have shown were imported, while the foreign nuts could have been carried in E ware jars. The reference to an *escup* vessel of wine or honey could also refer to E ware, and recalls the charter of St-Denis which links wine and honey as traded items (Appendix 5). However, as Wooding (1996b, 70) points out, only E4 jugs could possibly have been used for measuring wine, and this is perhaps unlikely. Honey could have been carried in E ware jars, but again this seems unlikely. In later medieval times honey was carried in boxes. Other small items which might have been carried in E ware vessels include spices such as cinnamon, pepper and cloves, and nuts such as almonds, pistachios and dates, which are all mentioned in a Frankish document of around 700, Marculf's *Formulatory* (James 1988, 189), as well as the dyes and other materials discussed below.

Dyes

The evidence for dyestuffs comes from the analytical study of some E ware vessels which show a purple colour on the interior (Walton Rogers 2005; Appendix 4 gives full details). The analysis of this dye shows it comes from dyer's madder (*Rubia tinctorum*), a plant native to south-eastern Europe. This dye was found on vessels from Dunadd, Buiston and Teeshan. There is documentary evidence that it was exported from France at least in the 9th century. A forged charter of this date, though purporting to be 7th-century, of St-Denis Abbey near Paris, mentions foreign merchants and people from Rouen and Quentovic coming to the St-Denis market to buy wine, honey and dyer's madder (Pertz 1874, 140–1; but note new translation by Percival in Appendix 5). This is a significant group of goods, though it is not possible to project their export back to the 7th century when the market was founded by Dagobert in AD 634/5 (Lebecq 1989). It is not entirely clear whether the dye would be transported already ground up and mixed with a mordant or as a pigment, or as whole roots. The reference in the charter to a measure of *quarrada* (cartload) for madder suggests it was traded whole, but this may be a mistake for the measure *quarta* (Appendix 5). Whichever was the case the association with E ware is indisputable and helps to confirm a Continental origin for E ware as the plant was not grown in Britain until late Saxon times at the earliest.

Another colourant which may have been imported along with E ware was the yellow mineral orpiment (arsenic sulphide). A piece of this mineral was found at Dunadd in association with E ware in the 1981 excavation (Campbell 1988a, 113; Lane and Campbell 2000, 212). This mineral must have come from the Mediterranean, the only sources in classical times being Vesuvius in Italy and Asia Minor (Dana 1883, 28). It is possible that a whole range of colourants were imported, both for manuscript illustration and as dyestuffs. An 8th-century letter from one Continental bishop to another mentions an enclosed package of pigments including orpiment, lapis lazuli, madder and malachite amongst others (Roosen-Runge and Werner 1960, 261–2). In normal circumstances of preservation dyestuffs are extremely difficult to detect, and it is only luck that has preserved some madder on E ware.

Organic produce

As mentioned above, Marculf's *Formulatory* (James 1988, 189) suggests a range of exotic organic foodstuffs which might have been exported from Gaul, and several have indeed been found on sites in association with E ware. At both Buiston (Crone 2000, 152–3) and Whithorn (Hill 1997, 124), fruits of coriander (*Coriandrum sativum*) and dill (*Anethum graveolens*) have been recovered in 6th-/7th-century contexts. Neither of these are native species, and must have been imported, presumably alongside E ware, if not actually carried in the pots themselves. It is likely that other exotic spices will be recovered as routine palaeobotanical analysis takes place on more excavations. Other produce which may turn up includes other spices, dried fruits such as figs, raisins and olives, and nuts, such as those mentioned in the *Muirbretha* (O'Mahany and Richey 1873, 426–7).

Non-vessel glass

Beads have been traded since the earliest times and are notoriously difficult to attribute to sources or dates. Beads of supposed Continental origin are found on western Insular sites. Dunadd has produced a Frankish bead of the 6th to 7th century, at least according to Guido (Lane and Campbell 2000, 176), but few others can be confidently said to be imports in the present state of knowledge. One type which seems to be certainly of Near Eastern origin is the segmented metal-in-glass bead (Boon 1977; Guido 1978, 93–4; Guido 1999, 78–80; Brugmann 2004, 75, type 8.2.3). A notable example of the gold-in-glass type is from Dinas Powys (Alcock 1963a, fig 41, 5), where it was found in a 7th-century context (Campbell 1991, 432). Others from a necklace in a burial overlying the forum in Wroxeter, may be of 6th-century date (Boon 1977, 199), though they could be later. Originally described by Harden as 'Coptic', Boon considered on distributional evidence that they were also manufactured in the late and post-Roman period in the Rhineland (*ibid*, 201), while Guido (1999, 79) suggested a wide spread of sources from around Gdansk to Dacia.

More recent work has shown that the type was certainly manufactured in the eastern Mediterranean, with a 5th- to 7th-century Byzantine workshop being excavated in Alexandria (Rodziewicz 1984, 242). It is likely that they continued to be produced into the Islamic period, as the glass analyses are similar to those of Islamic glasses. There appears to have been a change from the use of gold foil to silver at some time around the 8th century. In Scandinavia such beads are commonest in the early Viking period, and occur along with other segmented beads of a variety of colours, including blue and yellow. Recent work on the well-stratified deposits at Ribe, Denmark, has shown that the metal-in-glass beads there are all silver-in-glass beads, and that they are confined to the late 8th and early 9th centuries at that site (Sode and Feveile 2002, fig 3). It had previously been considered that these were manufactured in Scandinavia, due to the numbers of deformed beads found at sites such as Birka, Kaupang and Helgö, but the analyses and technological details of the beads from Ribe show that they were probably manufactured in Alexandria (*ibid*, 12). A broken silver-in-glass bead from Loch Glashan (Pl 40) is therefore likely to date to the late 8th or 9th century and to have come via Norse trading networks (Crone and Campbell 2005, 72).

Decorative glass. Other glass items which might belong to this phase are bichrome twisted glass rods which were used in Scandinavia to decorate 8th- to 10th-century glass vessels. Their occurrence in Britain is coastal (Näsman 1984, 79–80; Evison 1982b, fig 2). Three of these rods have been found in western contexts. The first comes from Iona, from a pit with other industrial material with a ^{14}C date of CAL AD 600–760 (Barber 1981, pl 14). The second comes from Movilla Abbey, again in a craft working deposit associated with decorative moulds and souterrain ware (Ivens 1984, fig 15, 3). The third is from Dunnyneill Island, found in association with E ware and imported glass. These rods may have been used to make beads, such as the cable beads which incorporate twisted rods, and may again be Viking or pre-Viking in origin. It is equally possible, however, that they were imported from the Continent or even produced in Ireland as recent discoveries at Dunmisk have shown (Henderson 1989).

A unique decorated glass plaque (Pl 41) comes from the Mote of Mark (Curle 1914, fig 17, 13). This thick flat oval plaque (originally circular) of green glass has inverted conical spots of white and yellow inserted in the upper surface. There are traces of an iron band round part of one edge (Pl 42) and the glass is layered, suggesting that it was made by pouring glass onto a flat surface bounded by the iron band. It seems to have functioned as a plaque to be inset in some piece of decorative mosaic, metalwork, or possibly to be suspended from a chain. Harden recognised its uniqueness and described it as part of an inlay, but was wrong in saying no original edge survived (Harden 1956a, 151, no 23). The pale green body colour is similar to Roman glass, but the use of opaque white and particularly opaque yellow might point to a mid-Saxon date, when these colours were used to decorate glass vessels with trails and spots (Evison 1982b, 13–14). It is possible this is from a Continental or Mediterranean context originally, as there are no parallels in Insular contexts. It may have been part of a decorative glass inlay in a floor panel, as the upper surface seems abraded.

Millefiori is another type of glass rod used for inlay work on jewellery. The origin of post-Roman millefiori is a matter of controversy. It is found on many Irish objects and clear evidence of the use of millefiori rods has been found at Garranes, Lagore and Dinas Powys. A stray find comes from Luce Bay Sands (Cramp 1970, 333, fig 1g). Millefiori was also used in some Saxon metalwork. The Sutton Hoo gold and garnet jewellery shows clear signs of using millefiori specially designed to fit the scheme of decoration, but this was suggested to be reused Roman slices (Bimson 1983). No actual evidence of manufacture of millefiori has been found in Ireland despite frequent mistaken claims that this is the case at Garranes (Henry 1956; Näsman 1984; cf Henderson 1989). At Garranes there is evidence that millefiori rods were chopped up to provide inlay pieces, but this is not evidence of manufacture. The recent evidence of glass making from Dunmisk mentioned above is unfortunately undated. At Dunadd there may be evidence of millefiori rod manufacture (Lane and Campbell 2000, 173–4, 215–16).

It is quite possible the millefiori rods were traded, like the reticella rods. Youngs (1989, 21) suggests that the reintroduction of millefiori occurs around 600. We have seen that the rod from Dinas Powys is stratified in a 7th-century context with E ware. The only zoomorphic penannulars with millefiori which came from excavated contexts, at Gransha, Ballinderry No. 2 and Lagore, are also all associated with E ware (Newman 1989, 14). It seems possible that millefiori rods were exported to western areas along with the Continental pottery. Evison has suggested the export of millefiori beads and of the technique for their manufacture from the Mediterranean region to Ireland in the late 6th century (Evison 1982b, 10–11). However, recent analytical work opens up the possibility of the manufacture of millefiori in western Celtic areas (Henderson 1989) and the situation is unresolved.

5.7 Conclusions

These miscellaneous finds are relatively few, geographically scattered, and often of dubious provenance or attribution. Where they occur on sites with pottery or glass imports they are more likely to be acceptable imports, but the majority of the finds in this category are of unclassified pottery. Of the other material, the coins have the greatest potential to illuminate commerce rather than mere communication, but they suffer particularly from problems of provenance and only a few are likely to have been lost in antiquity. Overall, this material does illustrate some of the kinds of goods which would be incidental accompaniments to the main cargoes carried by Byzantine or Continental traders, or the result of personal keepsakes or pilgrim trophies, but none seem to be important items of trade in their own right. Only salt and wine, for which no evidence survives, and dyestuffs, for which some scientific evidence exists, seem likely to have been important goods in their own right.

6 Patterns of consumption: taphonomic studies at Dinas Powys

The previous chapters examined the imported sherds, and what they can tell us about the production side of the exchange process; this one will consider their distribution within individual sites because the patterns of deposition and recovery are potentially informative about the social function of the pottery and glass. This type of taphonomic study is essential to the understanding of any assemblage of material, but has only become standard practice fairly recently. When I first carried out this work in 1983 there was little published on ceramic taphonomy. I used the distributions of material at Dinas Powys hillfort as a test case to help develop systems for looking at the small quantities of pottery and glass found on Atlantic sites. These small numbers pose different problems of analysis from the larger volumes of pottery found on many other sites (Orton et al 1993, 166–81), and require a different approach to make best use of a scarce set of data (see Chapter 1.4). A summary of the techniques and results is given below.

The Dinas Powys material was key to understanding the processes involved in the deposition of the imported material. I was able to use Leslie Alcock's original site archive to locate all the finds due to the excellent standard of recording for the time (the site was excavated 1954–58). Most finds could be located to within 6 feet (1.8m), and some were three-dimensionally recorded. This enabled detailed distributions to be drawn up for all classes of artefact (Campbell 1991, illus 87–125). One surprising result of this horizontal stratigraphy was that it forced me to reinterpret the vertical stratigraphy of the site, resulting in its rephasing as a multi-phase Early Historic site (Campbell 1991; 1993; cf Dark 1994, 68–9, illus 17). The distributions are shown in relation to the two buildings on the site, Building 1 being larger than Building 2, both enclosed within Bank 1, which can now be shown to be of late 6th-/early 7th-century date. Both buildings were identified only by eaves drip gullies (Pl 43), with no signs of timber or stone superstructures. They may originally have been turf-walled, or of timber sill-beam construction, like other buildings of the period in Wales (Campbell and Lane 1993a, 25–6). The Dinas Powys evidence is summarised below (from Campbell 1991) as it is the key to discussing other sites with less extensive amounts of imported pottery and glass. The evidence which led to the reconstruction of some vessels from the site, and the subsequent rejection of the 'glass cullet hypothesis', is also given in detail as this has only been previously published in summary form (Campbell 1995a). Full discussion of the finds from the site, including a large quantity of material not published in the original report, is given in Appendix 6. Details of the sizes and contexts of the pottery are given in Appendix 7.

6.1 Techniques of analysis

The techniques used in this study are all very simple. They consist of horizontal distribution plans, maximum sherd size curves and vessel-to-sherd ratios. These analytical aids have all been used before in pottery studies, but as I have developed the use of maximum sherd size curves this technique is discussed in more detail.

Horizontal distribution plans (Campbell 1991, illus 87–125)

The information from the excavation records enables finds from Dinas Powys to be localised generally within a number of recording 'squares', which are either the original excavation cuttings (Cuts 1–31) or are subdivisions of those cuttings based on the stratigraphic information in the site notebooks (Campbell 1991, illus 86). The exception is in parts of Cuts 1 and 4, where the position of most of the finds was recorded three-dimensionally. This accounts for the apparently patchy distribution of finds within these areas. Some other finds can be accurately positioned when they come from postholes or gullies. This information is particularly useful for the drip gullies of Buildings 1 and 2. On the plans, symbol sizes indicate pottery sherd size or glass weight. This enables an assessment of the significance of any occurrence to be made. Also for the pottery and glass, sherds belonging to individual vessels are identified by different symbols. As discussed in Chapter 1.4, the attribution of sherds to individual vessels could be carried out confidently, and turned out to be a key factor in determining taphonomic processes. The distribution of individual vessels is discussed below. The significance of distributions other than pottery and glass are detailed in Appendix 8.

Maximum sherd size curves

One of the most useful ways of looking at pottery on the Atlantic sites that I have developed is a graph showing the maximum size of the sherds. Other quantitative methods of looking at ceramic assemblages have concentrated on sherd weight, volume, minimum number of vessels and estimated vessel equivalents (Vince 1977; Orton 1975; Orton

84 *Continental and Mediterranean imports to Atlantic Britain and Ireland, AD 400–800*

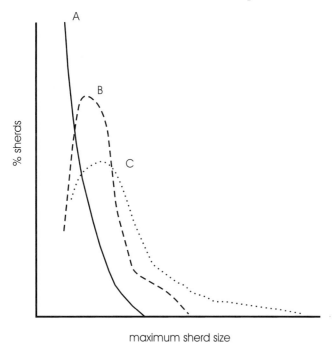

Fig 51 Theoretical sherd size curves for A, low-fired prehistoric ware; B, small well-fired vessels; C large well-fired vessels. Based on data from Dinas Powys

assemblages, particularly in view of the importance of this pottery in dating other material in Britain and Ireland. The size of the sherds is a fundamental characteristic and is very useful because the size is mainly determined by the amount of degradation the vessel has undergone since discard. When I developed this methodology I was not aware of experimental American work on the same lines (Kirkby and Kirkby 1976). Taylor (2000) has subsequently used a similar analysis in relation to ploughsoil processes.

It is worth looking at this principle in more detail. Pottery vessels are almost always curved in one or two planes. When a vessel is broken a number of sherds of widely differing sizes are formed. If these sherds are not immediately sealed (for example by being thrown in a pit or dropped down a well), they become subject to further processes such as trampling, redeposition or plough action, and the sherds are broken down further. Obviously there is a limit to how far this process can go. In other words there is a minimum size of sherd which is approached the further the process is taken. In practice this minimum size seems to range between 1 and 2 cm for earthenware, ignoring the effects of chemical weathering and tiny spalls from the edge of breaks (Fig 51). Experimental studies on modern pottery support this observational data (Kirkby and Kirkby 1976, table 3). Below this size hard-fired sherds are very difficult to break except by hammering. The reason for this is that when a person stands on a curved sherd the pressure is concentrated in the centre, leading to breakage. As the sherd becomes smaller by this process, the curvature is reduced and it becomes more difficult to break. This is the reason why the maximum size

and Tyers 1990; Orton *et al* 1993). These aspects of quantification are suitable for dealing with comparative quantification between sites, but sherd size curves tell us more about taphonomic processes within sites. It is obviously necessary to extract as much information as possible from these small

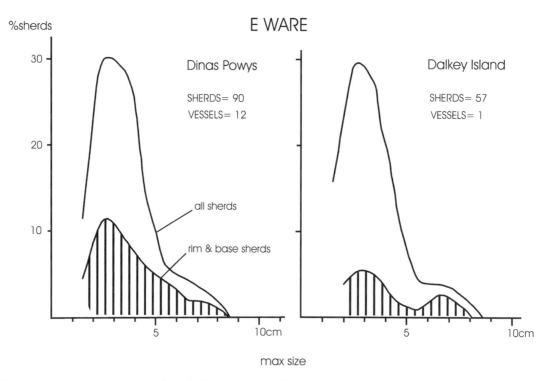

Fig 52 Maximum sherd size curves for all E ware from Dinas Powys and a single trampled vessel (E27) from Dalkey Island

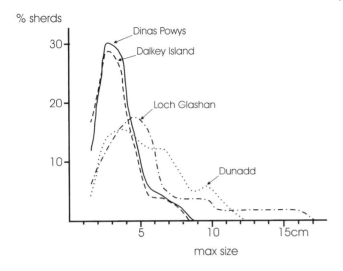

Fig 53 Maximum sherd size curves for E ware from sites with different depositional histories

(that is, the maximum chord) is of such importance and is used here as the standard measurement for sherds.

Two other factors influence the size of sherds. One is the sherd thickness, as the thicker the sherd the more difficult it is to break. This means that rim and base sherds, being thicker, tend to produce larger sherds than body fragments. Rim sherds in particular do not break easily because the rim tends to act as a strengthening rib, and also redistributes some of the stress. Handles are also strengthened in this way. Figure 52 shows how the larger sherds in a maximum sherd size curve are dominated by rims and bases. The other factor influencing the degree of breakage is the physical competence of the fabric itself. In practice however there seems to be little difference in the behaviour of all types of kiln-fired earthenware. For instance the curve for E ware from Dinas Powys, which is almost a stoneware, is little different from D ware, which is a much softer earthenware (Campbell 1991, illus 129–30). There is however a significant difference between low-temperature clamp-fired wares and kiln-fired wares. Figure 51 shows that the prehistoric pottery from Dinas Powys has a much smaller minimum size than the import wares, and a steeper fall-off curve. Part of this difference is due to the physical strength of the sherds, but also to post-depositional breakdown by physical and chemical weathering.

Measurements are taken across the maximum chord of the sherd for the reasons outlined above. The maximum measurement possible is the diameter or height of the vessel. Measurements are taken to the nearest centimetre both for speed of use and so as not to give spurious accuracy. The measurements for each size-band are then expressed as a percentage of the total number of sherds in order to make comparisons between groups. The curves have been plotted with smoothed averages between the bands which eliminates any false peaks caused by biased measuring, and provides a simple visual profile of the sherd size distribution.

One problem with using these curves is that of separating the effects of different breakage properties of differing wares and forms from the effect of differing degradational histories. To overcome this I have compared the same ware, in this case E ware, from different sites with different depositional histories (Fig 53). The curve from Dalkey Island represents a single vessel which is known to have been heavily trampled *in situ*; at Dunadd the pottery is from mixed industrial/domestic contexts excavated at a variety of dates; and at Loch Glashan much of the pottery was dumped over the edge of the crannog and subject to little degradation. These curves show that as the amount of degradation increases the median shifts towards the minimum sherd size, while at the same time the median value increases and the skewed tail-off also becomes shorter. These principles of degradation would appear to apply to other kiln-fired wares that I have studied (for example Romano-British wares) and are not confined to E ware.

The other problem in interpreting sherd size curves lies in having a 'standard' sample of a degree of degradation. Obviously it is not possible to smash complete ancient pots and trample them in order to see what happens, as can be done with modern pots (cf Kirkby and Kirkby 1976; Nielson 1991). Fortunately with E ware it is possible in one case to have a standard. The Dalkey Island excavation produced an area of trampled occupation surface upon which were scattered the remains of an almost complete E ware vessel (Fig 25, E27). The sherd size curve of this vessel (Fig 52) provides a standard for a heavily trampled E ware vessel. In fact this curve agrees almost precisely with the E ware curve from Dinas Powys, suggesting that a similar degree of trampling had taken place there, even though the Dinas Powys curve represents the remains of at least twelve vessels.

Using the criterion described above it is possible to arrive at an estimate of the degree of degradation of an assemblage (Fig 54). This is of the utmost importance in considerations of residuality and degree of association with other objects, problems which have beset early medieval archaeology for many years. Few pottery studies have used sherd size information in the past but DeBeor and Lathrop (1979) used this method to define a pathway in a modern settlement and they suggested that this example could be extrapolated to archaeological sites. This would necessitate a combination of distribution and sherd size analysis. Bradley and Fulford (1980) illustrate examples of the use of the size of sherds in terms of the percentage of rim and also of sherd weight. Fischer (1985) has made interesting comments on the distribution of Iron Age pottery from Winklebury Camp, Hampshire. He does not quantify or give details of his data for sherd sizes, so it is difficult to be sure of the basis for his claims. He seems to be claiming that large sherds and

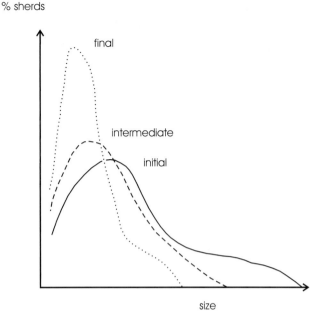

Fig 54 *Theoretical sherd size curves for a single assemblage through successive phases of degradation*

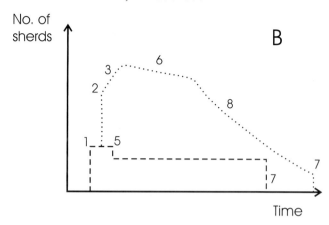

Fig 55 *Two possible sherd size curves for different parts of the same vessel, one buried in a rubbish pit after breakage, and the other trampled, scattered and ploughed before being recovered. 1 breakage, 2 discard, 3 trampling, 5 burial in pit, 6 burial by further deposits, 8 ploughing, 7 excavation*

high pot densities can be used to indicate material which is not residual and therefore can be associated with particular structures (*ibid*, 177–9). This is a dangerous assumption, given the anthropological and archaeological evidence that abandoned dwellings are often used as middens. The example of the LRA wares at Dinas Powys (see below) provides an interesting example of a concentration of large sherds which are probably secondary rather than primary rubbish (Fig 58). Use of this type of data is now more commonplace in field surveys (Frankovitch and Patterson 2000; Given and Knapp 2003).

Vessel-to-sherd ratios (Tables 7–8)

Vessel-to-sherd ratios are difficult to establish in large assemblages, especially where mass-produced wares are common, but at Dinas Powys and other Early Historic sites this is fairly easy as E ware and the other imports tend to be variable enough to distinguish individual vessels. This variability is partly caused by production and partly by usage. The theoretical basis for using vessel-to-sherd ratios can be explained as follows. When a pot is broken its sherds go through a series of processes culminating in recovery at the time of excavation. These processes are exactly analogous to the processes which affect animals when they die: death (equivalent to breakage); disarticulation (breakdown of sherds by trampling); transportation; and final burial. Palaeontologists were the first to investigate this system of taphonomy, and in recent years prehistorians, particularly palaeolithic specialists, have used taphonomic studies to look at bone assemblages and flintwork. Interest in the taphonomic processes affecting pottery is more recent and springs from a realisation that the context of a find is of fundamental importance in its interpretation (Moorhouse 1986, 85).

The various stages of the degradation of a vessel can be illustrated graphically with a horizontal axis of increasing time and a vertical axis of the number of sherds (Fig 55). The number of sherds rises fairly quickly as the pot is first broken (primary refuse), then swept up and redeposited on a midden (secondary refuse). With further exposure to human and natural processes such as ploughing, building, digging, animal burrowing and colluviation, the sherds become scattered and tend to be removed from the immediate system. The longer this process goes on the less of the pot will be recovered. Figure 55 illustrates the situation where a broken vessel undergoes a variety of these processes before being recovered by excavation. Part or all of a vessel could be removed from this system at any point by the normal activities taking place on a human settlement such as burial in pits, incorporation in earthworks or floors, or reuse for some other purpose.

Vessel-to-sherd ratios have not been much used by archaeologists. Indeed the only example that I know of is Burrow's work on Cadbury Congresbury (Burrow 1979; 1981). Burrow's data provided a useful comparison with Dinas Powys (Table 7), particularly as he also dealt with import wares. The ratios were particularly useful in discussing the problem of the residuality of the Romano-British wares at Dinas Powys (see Appendix 8). Vessel-to-sherd ratios give a measure similar to that which Orton *et al* (1993, 169) define as the *brokenness* of a vessel. What they define as the *completeness* of a vessel cannot be measured without using EVEs, though in some cases it can be estimated (see Chapter 7). The huge variation in vessel-to-sherd

Table 7 Vessel-to-sherd ratios for different categories of pottery at Dinas Powys, compared to Cadbury Congresbury (CadCong) and Cadbury Castle (CadCastle)

Type	Sherds	Vessels	Ratio	CadCong	CadCastle
Iron Age	56	13	1:4.3	–	–
R–B	69	37	1:1.9	1:2.7	–
samian	18	6	1:3	1:9.3	–
ARS	18	4	1:4.5	1:16	–
PRS	40	4	1:10	1:11.1	1:3.3
LRA	184	c.6	1:31	1:34	1:10.3
DSPA	46	9	1:5.1	–	1:1
E ware	73	12	1:6.1	–	–

Table 8 Vessel-to-sherd ratios for E ware from different sites

Site	Sherds	Vessels	Ratio
Ballycatteen	51	3	1:17
Clogher	40	5	1:8
Dalkey Island	88	8	1:11
Dinas Powys	73	12	1:6.1
Garryduff	81	9	1:9
Gwithian	50	5	1:10
Loch Glashan	25	5	1:5

ratios for imported vessels seen at different sites illustrates the inappropriateness of sherd counts as a quantitative method. For example, Dinas Emrys produced 44 sherds, representing 1 vessel (1:44), while Longbury Bank had 61 sherds representing 6 vessels (1:10) and Dumbarton 7 sherds representing 4 vessels (1:2). Dumbarton is more like Longbury Bank than Dinas Emrys in terms of its access to imports (Tables 17 and 19), with the difference in vessel-to-sherd ratio merely resulting from taphonomic and excavation processes.

6.2 Pottery distributions (Figs 56–62)

Using the techniques described above, the distributions of the different classes of pottery and glass at Dinas Powys were analysed to produce an understanding of how the vessels were used and discarded. As already mentioned, this analysis led to a reinterpretation of the chronological sequence of occupation on the site, the full details of which are available in Appendix 9. Details of the distributions of other materials is given in Appendix 8.

Samian

The small quantity of samian sherds means that it is difficult to be sure that their distribution is meaningful. Subjective examination of the distribution appears to show a lack of correlation with the other Romano-British finds (Campbell 1991, illus 94–5). This is supported by the low correlation co-efficient between the wares (*ibid*, table 17). In fact the samian seems to have two concentrations, a major one in the south-west and a smaller one in Cut 6. It is noticeable that the samian sherds from Cut 6 are very fresh and glossy compared with the rest, and that there are some fragments of spindle whorls cut from samian sherds in the same trench. It seems probable that these sherds were brought to the site to produce spindle whorls and that this work was carried out in the adjacent Building 1. It was in this building that spinning and weaving seems to have taken place, on the basis of the distribution of artefacts related to these processes (*ibid*, 74–5). The use of samian for spindle whorls has been identified as a very Late Roman/post-Roman practice, with possible religious connotations (Cool 2000, 53–4, fig 30), so the Dinas Powys evidence fits into this pattern.

The other main concentration of samian is in the south-western metal working area. The sherds here are noticeably abraded. It is possible that these sherds were specially brought to this area in order to be used in some industrial process. Samian sherds are found on a variety of non-Roman sites in the Roman, early medieval and medieval periods. Numerous suggestions have been put forward as to their purpose, ranging from medicinal or talismanic use to a primitive form of exchange token (Warner

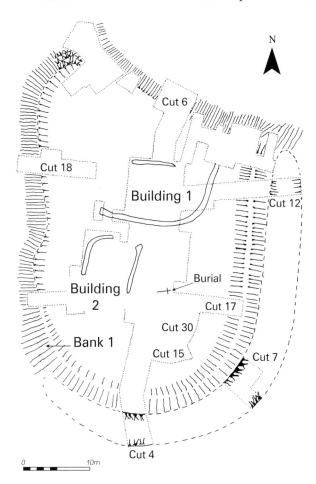 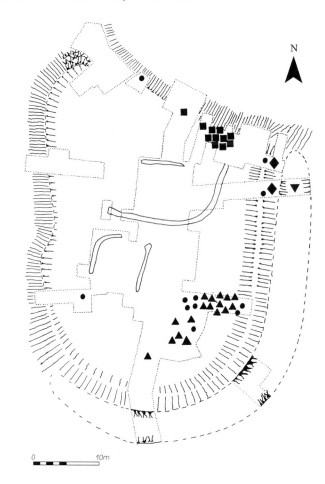

Fig 56 Main features of Dinas Powys, showing the inner rampart (Bank 1), the two buildings outlined by drip gullies, the child burial, and the main excavation trenches (cuts) referred to in the text

Fig 57 Distribution of individual PRS vessels at Dinas Powys: P13 ▲; P14 ◆; P15 ■; P16 ▼; unassigned sherds ●

1976; Bradley 1982; Hansen 1982). If the Dinas Powys sherds were being used in an industrial process, it is possible that they were being ground down to produce a red colourant.

Most of the other Romano-British pottery on the site had a very low vessel-to-sherd ratio (Table 7), suggesting the sherds were derived from ploughsoil, perhaps brought to the site in turfs from nearby Romano-British farmsteads such as Biglis (Robinson 1988).

Phocaean Red Slipware

The PRS has the highest vessel-to-sherd ratio (1:10) of all the non-amphora imports (Table 7). This is almost certainly due to the delicate nature of the ware, which has very thin walls (2–3mm) that on breakage produce many sherds. There is no doubt that the PRS was brought to the site as vessels rather than as sherds. One vessel (P13) has been reconstructed and is on display in the National Museum of Wales.

The sherd size curve shows that the sherds tend to be larger than those of E ware despite their fragility (Campbell 1991, illus 128). This must mean that the PRS dishes have not suffered much trampling. The explanation for this seems to lie in a different means of disposal of these vessels. The evidence of the distribution of vessel P13 (Fig 57) shows that the vessel was discarded in the open spaces of the settlement in the Period 2a phase, and not on a midden, presumably because there was more room within the enclosure then. The overall distribution indicates that both buildings were in use in this phase, with the pottery being discarded in two different areas.

Functionally the PRS was a tableware, perhaps standing on tables as serving dishes rather than being used for eating from. It seems as if these vessels were disposed of immediately on breakage, rather than being left to be trampled underfoot within the buildings as is postulated for the E ware (see below).

African Red Slipware

The small number of sherds makes it difficult to make definite statements about this ware. However, the vessel-to-sherd ratio, at 1:4.5, is about the same

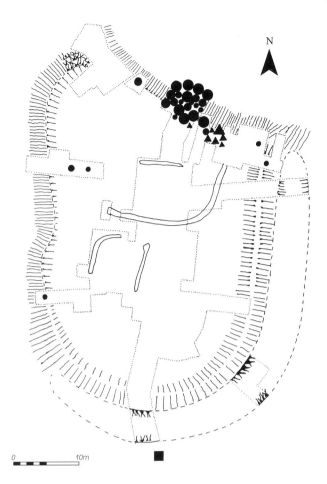

Fig 58 Distribution of sherds from three LRA vessels at Dinas Powys: LR2 (B34) ●; LR1 (B36) ▲; LR4 (B39) ■

as that of D and E ware and slightly less than the PRS (Table 7). Perhaps this is because these wares are generally thicker than the PRS. There are not enough sherds to give a meaningful sherd size curve. The distribution of the sherds (Campbell 1991, illus 98) is similar to that of PRS. As with the PRS, the distribution suggests that both buildings were in use during the currency of the ARS. The ARS is also a tableware like the PRS.

Late Roman amphorae

The large size of the imported amphorae means that they produce large numbers of sherds when they are broken, explaining the very high vessel-to-sherd ratio of 1:31. This factor also accounts for the large size of individual sherds and the long tail-off in the sherd size curve (Campbell 1991, illus 129). This makes comparison of sherd size data with the smaller tablewares meaningless. The distribution of the sherds and vessels, on the other hand, is highly significant. From Figure 58 it can be seen that the amphorae are concentrated overwhelmingly on Cut 6, with some spread eastwards along the northern edge of the site. Occasional sherds are found outside this area, particularly in the later metal working area in the south-east corner of the site. It is possible that the amphora sherds found in this area were brought there deliberately for use as trays to keep scrap or metal objects on while work was in progress. Only one LR1 vessel (B37) shows a preponderance of sherds in this area. A number of sherds of this vessel are found within the make-up of Bank 1 in Cut 17, so it is possible that one vessel was discarded in the south-eastern area at an early date. All the other amphorae are strongly associated with Cut 6. This concentration of vessels cannot be explained as merely reflecting the area of rubbish dumping for Building 1. As Figure 57 shows, the contemporary tablewares are spread out along the northern edge of the site, but appear to be excluded from Cut 6. It is clear that the amphorae were treated differently from the other wares. Functionally, they were containers for wine or oil, but, being sturdy, they were unlikely to be broken in use. They could have been reused as liquid containers after the original contents had been used up. A noticeable feature of the site is the lack of a water supply (Alcock 1963a, 3). As water must have been stored somewhere, it is possible that the amphorae could have been used for this purpose, and stored in the region of Cut 6.

An alternative explanation is that the amphorae were broken during periods of feasting and drinking (if indeed they held wine). The association of the amphorae in Cut 6 with a concentration of glass sherds from at least ten drinking vessels, and the handle of an E ware jug, and vast quantities of bone, might be taken as support for this idea. It would of course fit the *topos* of the feasting hall so vividly described in the *Gododdin* (Jackson 1969), but leaves the difficulty of explaining the absence of tablewares, which would also have been used in feasting, from Cut 6. This cannot be due to chronological factors, as these tablewares were contemporary with the amphorae.

DSPA

The DSPA has a similar vessel-to-sherd ratio, at 1:5.1, to that of E ware, at 1:6.1, and it is clear from the distribution of sherds from individual vessels (Fig 59) that they were in use on the site. This is of importance as no other Insular site has more than a few sherds of DSPA, and these could possibly be regarded as stray sherds if it were not for the Dinas Powys evidence. The sherd size curve (Campbell 1991, illus 129) shows that the median size of the sherds tends to be larger than in E ware, ARS and PRS because of the thickness of most of the sherds, which is often around 10mm. Otherwise the profile of the curve is similar to the other tablewares, but rather flatter, probably because this ware is less easy to break.

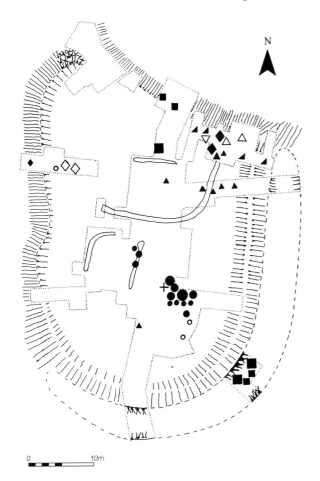

Fig 59 Distribution of DSPA vessels at Dinas Powys: D2 ●; D4 ◆; D5 ◇; D6 ▲; D7 △; D8 +; D10 ▲; unassigned ○

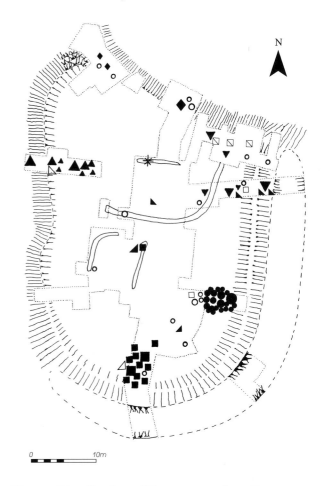

*Fig 60 Distribution of E ware vessels at Dinas Powys: E37 ●; E38 ■; E39 ▲; E40 □; E41 ◆; E42 ▼; E43 ▲; E44 △; E45 ▶; E46 ◺; E 47 ◨; E48 *; E49 ○*

The distribution of individual vessels shows clearly how the broken pots were discarded from the buildings. The sherds of D2 fan out from the side of Building 2 towards the periphery of the site, while D10 shows the same process in Building 1. In the eastern area, the horizontal distribution of DSPA does not overlap with that of E ware. In fact DSPA is nowhere found on the midden areas on the rear of Bank 1. It is also missing from beneath Bank 1, except for one sherd in a disturbed layer in Cut 23. This makes it very difficult to assess the chronological relationship of DSPA to E ware, though it does suggest that they were not contemporary.

Most of the vessels are associated with Building 1, though D2 was obviously used in Building 2. One surprise is the presence of several large sherds of D3 in Cut 7, in the ditch outside Bank 1. At least one of these sherds was found in the causeway rubble. It seems possible that these sherds were brought from the interior to Cut 7 in rubble during the building of the causeway. The other sherds of this vessel are found in the north of the site. Functionally the DSPA wares are all tablewares, the forms being plates, bowls and mortaria.

E ware

The vessel-to-sherd ratio at about 1:6 is similar to that of the PRS, ARS and DSPA. The concentration of sherds from individual vessels in coherent groups shows that the vessels were in use on the site (Fig 60). The sherd size curve has a high peak at about the 2cm size (Fig 52), with the few larger sherds in the 'tail-off' consisting of rims and bases. Confirmation of the heavily trampled nature of the assemblage comes from comparison with the curve from Dalkey Island referred to above. At Dalkey most of a large E ware vessel was found scattered on a trampled occupation layer (Liversage 1968, fig 39). The sherd size curve of this vessel is remarkably similar to that of E ware from Dinas Powys, despite the fact that this curve represents about twelve vessels rather than the one at Dalkey Island. It is obvious that the Dinas Powys E ware has undergone a considerable period of post-depositional breakdown. However, this poses something of a problem as sherds from some vessels retain coherent distributions. It is also the case that E ware is mainly found on the rear slope of Bank 1, outside the main areas of trampling revealed by other data (Campbell 1991, illus 122). The implica-

Patterns of consumption: taphonomic studies at Dinas Powys 91

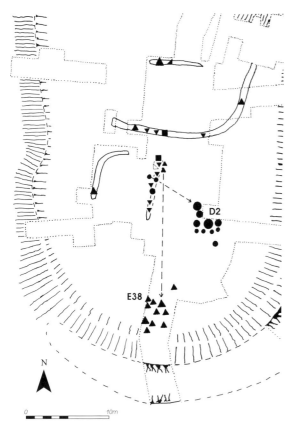

Fig 61 Distribution of sherds in building drip gullies, showing fanning out of material from artefact traps around Building 2 to the midden areas: E ware ▲; DSPA ●; LRA △ ; PRS ◢ ; samian ■; glass ▼

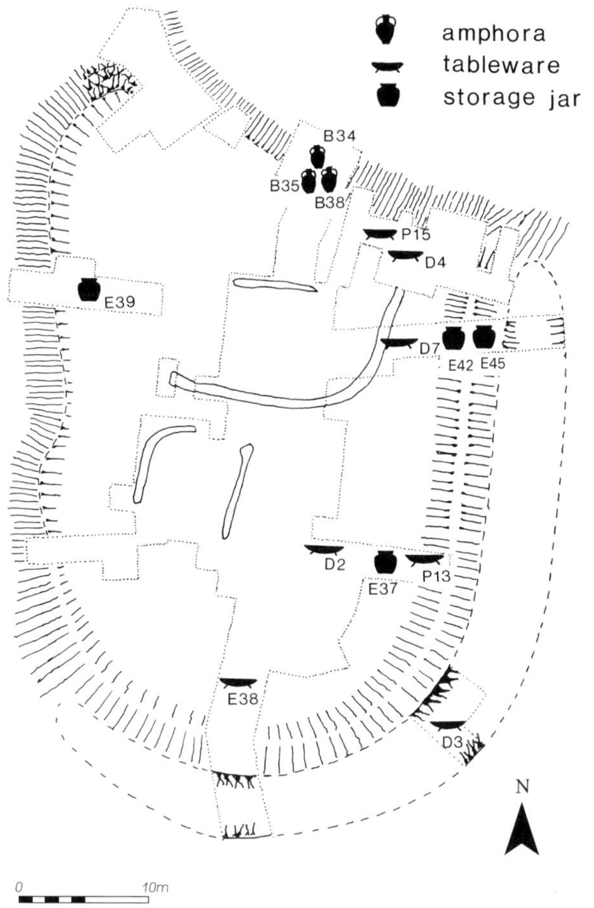

Fig 62 Dinas Powys distribution of pottery vessels by function

tion is that E ware suffered some trampling within the buildings before being swept up with organic floor refuse and dumped, still in fairly coherent groups, on the rear of Bank 1. The distribution of vessels such as E38 shows that this is a likely pattern of rubbish disposal, as small sherds have been trapped in the eaves drip gullies of Building 2. This is an interesting difference from the DSPA ware which appears to have been swept less far from the buildings. Presumably the presence of Bank 1 (making the interior of the settlement smaller) when E ware was in use justified the slightly greater effort needed to take the rubbish here.

Looking at the overall distribution there are two concentrations. The northern one is all around Building 1, including to the west in Cut 18. None of the other imports are found to the west of this building. There may have been an addition or alteration to the west of Building 1 during the currency of E ware. Unfortunately the west end of Building 1 was not excavated so this must remain pure speculation. The second concentration is in the south-east corner. Here the distribution can be seen to fan out from the centre of Building 2 (Fig 61). There are more vessels associated with Building 1 than Building 2, which may be an indication of different status.

The function of E ware vessels was discussed in Chapter 3.2, where it was argued that E_1 jars were used as containers for imported commodities, rather than as cooking-pots. None of the vessels from Dinas Powys has any sign of sooting on their bases, which tends to confirm their storage function. Presumably after the original contents had been used up, the vessels could have been used for the storage of other items. The only tablewares in the E ware assemblage at Dinas Powys are the E_4 jug (E41) and the E_3 bowl (E38). It is possibly significant that the E_4 jug handle was found in Cut 6 along with the remains of amphorae and glass drinking vessels. If E ware jugs were associated with the drinking of imported wine, this association would reinforce the speculation outlined above that Cut 6 was used as a special rubbish disposal area for material from feasting. However, as all the evidence suggests that E ware was not contemporary with the amphorae (Chapter 2.5) the association may well be fortuitous. The E_3 bowl is associated with Building 2. There are six large and two small E ware storage vessels associated with Building 1, but only one large and two small ones associated with Building 2 (Fig 62). The association of E ware with the major building on the site suggests that the material stored in these vessels was valuable, as Building 1 must have been the principal residence of someone of high status, however that is defined.

The inter-relationship of the imports

Most of the information on the relationships between the imports is given in the stratigraphic discussion. The horizontal relationships can be summarised as follows (Fig 62).

- Most of the import sherds are found to the north and north-east of Building 1 and to the south-east of Building 2 in midden areas.
- The amphorae are concentrated in a discrete area of the northern boundary (Cut 6), and other imports were somehow excluded from this area.
- Most of the vessels of tableware function (ARS, PRS, DSPA) and storage function (E ware) are associated with Building 1. The liquid containers (LRA, E4 jug) were exclusively associated with Building 1.
- The E ware was more widely distributed and more heavily trampled than the other imports. It seems to have been disposed of differently in that it was mainly dumped on middens while the tableware was apparently broadcast into the public areas of the settlement.
- Although Building 2 has few vessels associated with it, these include vessels of PRS, ARS, DSPA and E ware. This tends to confirm the assumption that Buildings 1 and 2 were in contemporary use.

The distributions are clearly patchy. As very little of the peripheral areas, as opposed to the central area, was excavated, the distribution of finds outlined may be misleading to some extent. A large amount of material has also probably been lost over the northern cliff-edge. However, it does seem clear that Building 1 was the most important of the two buildings, but that they both shared generally similar functions and periods of occupation.

6.3 Glass distributions

The Dinas Powys assemblage of some 250 sherds is important as Alcock's interpretation of this glass as cullet came to be used as a model for the whole region. Before discussing Alcock's theory it is worth pointing out the corresponding situation in contemporary Anglo-Saxon England. Here glass is relatively abundant in inhumation and cremation cemeteries, though graves with glass vessels appear to be of high status (Arnold 1980). About 430 vessels from around 100 sites are known overall (Harden 1956a; Huggett 1988; Evison 2000, 50). On Anglo-Saxon settlement sites the picture is very different with glass being very rare, even on palace sites, and usually consisting of only a few fragments. Only one site, the mid-Saxon trading centre of *Hamwic*, has produced any quantity of glass. Despite the greater spread of glass on settlement sites in the west, it was generally agreed when this study commenced that glass vessels were never used in the west (Laing 1975, 267; Mytum 1986, 376). The reasons for this apparent dichotomy lie partly in the prominence given to the Anglo-Saxon grave-good assemblages in Anglo-Saxon archaeology, but can possibly also be attributed to the widely held paradigm amongst Anglo-Saxon archaeologists that the Early Historic Celtic West was indeed poor, dark and barbaric, what Alcock (1992) termed 'the dark side of the moon'. Ironically, Alcock's own interpretation of the Dinas Powys glass appeared to provide evidence to reinforce this prejudice.

Alcock (1963a, 52–3) put forward the idea that the glass sherds were a collection of cullet, intended for melting down to make small items such as studs and beads. This idea seems to have first been put forward as a casual remark in the report on the excavation at Lagore (Hencken 1950, 129). It is quite certain that glass melting *did* take place on Celtic sites: at Garryduff glass globules were found (O'Kelly 1962, 77); at Lagore there were moulds with glass studs *in situ* (Hencken 1950, 129–30); at Armagh there were crucibles with glass residues (Brown and Harper 1984, 145); and at Dinas Powys itself there were quantities of fused and bent glass (Alcock 1963a, 187). The evidence is overwhelming that glass melting took place on sites which had glass vessel sherds available (Campbell 1991, table 13). Julian Henderson has recently summarised the evidence for Ireland, and points out the difference between glass melting and glass making, which is a technically much more advanced process, at present known only in the Atlantic West from Dunmisk, Co. Tyrone (Henderson 1989), and there only for bead making, not glass vessel blowing. It does not follow, however, that the glass sherds were brought to these sites as cullet, rather than as vessels. The evidence presented below shows that glass vessels were in use at Dinas Powys, and that they were melted down *after* breakage of the vessels on the site.

Before presenting this evidence, it is necessary to summarise Alcock's arguments in favour of the cullet theory. Firstly, he pointed to the pieces of fused glass from the site as evidence of glass melting. Secondly, he noted that a high proportion of the sherds had opaque white trails, a type of decoration rare on Anglo-Saxon glass vessels. Alcock therefore agreed with Harden's suggestion that these sherds were 'specially chosen for bringing to the west' (Harden 1963, 179). Thirdly, he pointed out that there was a disproportion of bases and rims in the assemblage, as there was only one true base compared with about 25 rims (Alcock 1963a, 53). Alcock argued that the thick bases would be more likely to survive than the delicate rims, and that therefore a preponderance of bases should be expected on a settlement site.

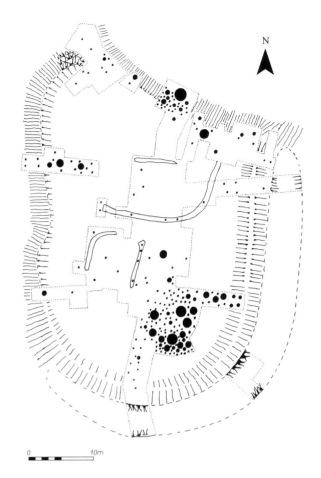

Fig 63 Distribution of glass vessel sherds at Dinas Powys, size of symbol proportionate to size of sherd

Alcock's theory was a pioneering attempt to come to terms with the problems of the taphonomy of a glass assemblage, but his explanation raises several difficulties. Firstly, why should there be a lack of bases in a collection of cullet? The bases contain a large part of the weight of glass in a vessel because they are so thick, and so one would suspect that they would be preferentially collected for reuse. Secondly, why should white-trailed sherds of pale yellow colour be chosen for importation to the Atlantic West? Melting of these sherds would produce an almost colourless glass. There is no evidence from surviving beads and metalwork that this colour of glass was particularly sought after, or indeed much used at all in the west. Thirdly, if so much trouble had been taken to bring this material to the site, why was so much then discarded and spread over the site? Fourthly, why is there such a date-range amongst the glass? The present reappraisal of the glass shows that there may be vessels from the late 5th or early 6th, mid-6th, early 7th, and possibly late 7th centuries. In addition, the publication of the glass from *Hamwic* (Hunter 1980; Hunter and Heyworth 1998) gave a yardstick against which to measure the Dinas Powys material. It turns out that the *Hamwic* assemblage is also lacking in bases compared with rims (Campbell 1991, table 24).

With these problems in mind while studying the distribution of the Dinas Powys glass, I began to suspect that vessels had been in use on the site. In order to find criteria which would distinguish between Alcock's explanation and my own I treated the glass assemblage in a similar manner to the ceramics.

Techniques

Unlike the ceramics, maximum sherd size did not appear to be a useful measurement as so many of the glass sherds were so small and delicate. Accordingly the sherds were weighed to the nearest 0.1g, and this measurement was used in the distribution maps. Joining sherds were extremely difficult to identify due to the smooth breaks and tiny size of the sherds. The mid-parts of the vessels are often paper-thin, and individual sherds are difficult to orientate. Some indication of position on the vessel can be gained from the orientation of the included bubble trails which follow a standard pattern in most vessel shapes. Colour has been shown to be a useful discriminant (Hunter 1980, 71–2). Some vessels could be distinguished by a distinctive colour, or quality of metal, or distinctive decoration, but there remained a large quantity of pale yellow sherds which could not be assigned to any particular vessel or even form. The analysis of the material was thus hampered by the intractable nature of fragmentary glass, but some important results were obtained. Horizontal distributions of all the glass, and some of the individual vessels, could be constructed. Enough of some rims could be reconstructed to provide important evidence on vessel form and use. In addition, analyses of the different sherd to vessel ratios of different colours of glass proved to be significant.

Sherd size

Most body sherds weighed less than 0.5g, with very few large sherds. Unlike the E ware, there is no outside standard to compare with the sherd size curve, but subjectively it appears to be a degraded assemblage. Most of the sherds seem to be far too small to have been worth collecting for melting down. Only the rims, bases and claws from claw beakers would have provided sufficient glass to make even a few beads. Almost all the larger sherds over 1.0g are concentrated in the south-east area (Fig 63), contrasting with the LRA.

Vessel-to-sherd ratios

As already mentioned it was impossible to assign most of the pale yellow sherds to particular rims. However, taking the group of pale yellow sherds together and comparing them to the brightly coloured glass produced interesting results (Campbell 1991, table 24C). The interpretation of the difference between these two groups will be discussed below, but it is clear that the fairly high vessel-to-sherd ratio of about 1:10 amongst the pale yellow glass is an indication that these vessels at least could have been in use on the site. The actual number of sherds per vessel for the brightly coloured glass is very low, most of the vessels being represented by only a few sherds. Interestingly, this accords with the situation at the contemporary settlement at Eketorp, Öland (Näsman 1984, 61, fig 5). Scandinavian archaeologists have never suggested that the glass fragments found on their settlement sites were cullet, but have accepted that complete vessels were used, despite the fact that only odd sherds have been found there. As in Anglo-Saxon England the occurrence of complete vessels as pagan grave-goods made this view easy to accept, despite the fact that Scandinavia is further from the centres of production of the imported vessels in the Rhineland than the Atlantic West is from south-western France. The exception to this is the site at Ribe where glass mosaic tesserae have been shown to have been imported for melting down (Bencard *et al* 1979).

Horizontal distributions

Around half of the sherds are concentrated in the south-eastern corner of the site with two smaller concentrations, one in Cut 6/6w, and a less defined one in Cut 18 (Figs 63–4). It is also noticeable that there is a scatter of small sherds in the area of the two buildings and their gullies. As other artefacts are noticeably missing from these areas (Campbell 1991, illus 87), it seems that these tiny sherds escaped the cleaning process by virtue of their size. It is clear that the major concentration of glass is associated with either Building 2 or the metal working area in Cuts 15/30. This contrasts with the pottery distribution which centres in the area around Building 1.

The difference between the south-eastern concentration and other areas can be illustrated in a number of ways. I have already mentioned that the large sherds (>1.0g) are concentrated in the south-east. There is a much higher proportion of these sherds in the south-east than would be expected on the basis that only half the sherds are found there. Conversely, there are proportionately fewer of the brightly coloured sherds in the south-eastern area (*ibid*, table 24E).

Looking at the distribution of sherds from individual vessels it is apparent that they are more scattered than is the case with the pottery vessels (*ibid*, illus 105–6). There are several possible reasons for this dispersion. One is the small size and weight of the sherds, which could easily be picked up in the mud on shoes, and thus be carried around the settlement. Another reason could be that the intrinsic brightness of the sherds led children and others to pick them up, as playthings or curios. Hayden and

Fig 64 Distribution of individual Group C glass vessels with chevron trails: G97 ▲*; G98* ●*; G117* ■*; unassigned* ○

Cannon (1983, 132) give some interesting examples of children's propensity for dispersing and collecting odd objects. Thirdly, as will be seen below, some of the sherds were reused and taken to specific areas for remelting.

The distribution of vessels with joins (Fig 64) shows that the south-east has a concentration of coherent groups of sherds from single vessels, similar to that found with the DSPA and E ware in the same area. Three vessels in particular (G97, G98, G101) have large proportions of their rims surviving, and the forms of the vessels can be reconstructed (Fig 38). As pointed out above, the sherds in the south-east also tend to be larger and to have a higher vessel-to-sherd ratio. Taken together these factors seem to show that vessels were broken in this area. It is not merely the number of sherds belonging to individual vessels which shows that they must have been broken on the site. The three vessels with reconstructable rims have respectively 90, 120 and 190 degrees of their rims surviving. This fact more than any other seems to show that complete vessels were in use on the site, as it is extremely difficult to believe that large curved pieces of glass could have survived intact as cullet since they would have to have survived the successive processes of breakage,

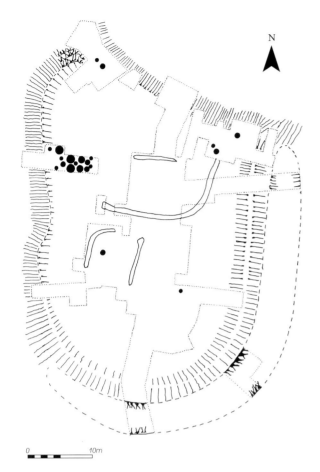

Fig 65 Distribution of fused glass at Dinas Powys, size of symbol proportionate to size of sherd

discard, collection, packaging, transport, unpacking and further dispersal before reaching their find spots. It does not seem conceivable that the sherds from individual vessels were kept together in groups during these processes, and then redeposited in groups at Dinas Powys. Whithorn and Cadbury Congresbury have similar patterns of deposition.

Fused glass

The distribution of fused glass, in contrast to that of the glass sherds, is confined to the eastern end of Cut 18 (Fig 65; see Fig 56). The fused material can be seen to be melted vessel glass, but most is not globules or droplets produced when pouring molten glass. It is not only the distribution that is striking. The colours found in the melted glass are almost entirely the deep hues of brown, deep blue and dark green, with almost none of the pale yellow which makes up the bulk of the glass sherds from the site. In fact a high proportion (60–80%) of the glass of these deep colours is found in a fused state, in contrast to the pale glass (5%) (Table 9). The obvious conclusion is that only the bright colours were wanted for melting down while the pale yellow and opaque white vessels were discarded. This conclusion explains a great deal about the peculiarities of the glass sherd assemblage mentioned in the previous section. Firstly, the low vessel-to-sherd ratio amongst the deep-coloured glass could be a result of attempts to collect as many sherds as possible from vessels of these colours after their breakage. The sherds that remain are those that have escaped detection, usually only one or two per vessel. Similarly the high vessel-to-sherd ratio amongst the pale yellow glass can be explained because little of this colour was collected for reuse. This process also explains why there are larger sherds in the south-eastern area where most of the pale yellow glass is found, and why it is only here that vessels can be reconstructed. It could also be the case that the apparent dominance of the glass from Building 2 is illusory, as despite the differing number of sherds there are roughly the same number of *vessels* represented in Cuts 6/6w and Cut 15.

In conclusion, it seems clear that there was a glass working area in Cut 18. Presumably small items such as beads were being made. The small brown bead (Alcock 1963a, fig 41,6) could have been made from the dark brown glass of the claw beaker (Harden 1963, no. 9). The pale yellow bead could have been made from the common pale yellow glass from the site, a small quantity of which was fused. The two dark blue glass rods from Cut 15 and possibly the dark blue bead from Cut 10 could have been made on the site from the dark blue fused glass. It seems likely that the dark blue fused glass was derived from the 7th-century blue squat jar (G83), the only dark blue vessel on the site. A small sherd of this vessel was found in Cut 18, so it is probable that glass melting was taking place at least in the early 7th century or later. The other deep colours are rare in 6th-century glass, the normal colour being a pale brown or green (Evison 1982a, table 1). The association in Cut 18 of glass melting and E ware may also point to a 7th-century date for this activity.

In contrast, the presence in the south-east area of three glass rods, two dark blue and one millefiori (Campbell 1991, illus 107), suggests the possibility

Table 9 Weight (g) of fused and unfused glass at Dinas Powys

	Fused	**Unfused**	**% fused**
Blue	21.8	4.9	81.6%
Green	6.9	6.0	53.5%
Brown	10.3	7.5	57.9%
Pale yellow	4.5	95.0	4.5%

that inlay work took place near the bronze casting area, rather than in the glass melting area of Cut 18.

Conclusion

Where does this leave Alcock's arguments in favour of the cullet theory? The presence of the fused glass has been explained. The predominance of white-trailed glass compared with Anglo-Saxon assemblages can be explained on two counts. Firstly, the pale yellow and white glass was not wanted for melting down and so is over-represented in the assemblage. Secondly, as is pointed out in Chapter 4, the white-trailed vessels do not come from Anglo-Saxon England, but from a production area where white-trailed glass was much commoner. It is still possible white-trailed glass was specially selected for export to the Atlantic West, but as vessels not cullet. Finally, the apparent lack of bases has to be accounted for. As was mentioned in the introduction, bases also seem to be lacking at the Saxon settlement of *Hamwic* (Campbell 1991, table 24A), where some of the glass vessels may have been manufactured (Hunter and Heyworth 1998, 61). Hunter and Heyworth (*ibid*, 59) believed that the glass sherds from *Hamwic* were derived from broken vessels and were not cullet, though the recovered sherds may be the result of 'de-selection' from a larger assemblage, as happened at Dinas Powys. Other support for a general lack of bases on settlement sites comes from the Mote of Mark (one base in eighteen vessels) and Eketorp, Öland (Näsman 1984). The explanation for this phenomenon is a matter of speculation, but Hayden and Cannon (1983, 151) have shown from modern studies in a Peruvian village that glass has a high 'nuisance value' and that it tends to be carefully collected and removed from the occupation area. As the bases of the cone beakers are the only really substantial pieces of glass in the Dinas Powys assemblage, these may have been preferentially removed from the site. The body and rim sherds are very thin compared with modern glass, and might not have been a significant problem. A base such as G98 (Fig 43), however, would not crush if stood upon, and might pierce a leather shoe. One positive piece of evidence for the removal of bases from an assemblage comes from the hoard at Tatershall Thorpe, Lincolnshire, which included along with smith's tools and metal scrap the base of a deep blue 7th-century bag beaker, clearly picked out for its thickness and colour (Evison in Hinton 2000, 76–83).

All the evidence presented seems to prove that glass vessels were in use in the Atlantic West. There is corroborative evidence for this in the contemporary literature. Adomnán, in his *Life of Columba*, written at the end of the 7th century, tells the story of Columba visiting King Brude of the Picts in his fortress. The king's magician is represented as drinking from a glass cup (Anderson and Anderson 1961, 400–1). This detail is incidental to the story, and there is no reason to doubt Adomnán on this point. The 7th-century heroic poem, the *Gododdin*, also mentions glass vessels in use in royal courts (Jackson 1969, 34–5). These poetic images have been dismissed as poetic exaggeration or anachronism (Foster 1965, 234), based on the mention of gold 'torques', which he mistakenly equated with those of Iron Age Celtic culture, but this single example does not invalidate the other details of the poetry, most of which can be shown to be archaeologically correct (Alcock 1983a). Perhaps the most persuasive evidence, however, is archaeological. At Mullaroe in Co. Sligo a complete glass vessel (G219) of 7th- to 9th-century date was found in a souterrain (Harden 1956a, pl 19h). Fragments of another identical vessel were found a few miles away at Crannog 61, Loch Gara (G233), and more recently another two complete vessels were found at Moynagh Lough (G217, G218). This positive evidence that vessels were in use in the Atlantic West was explained away by Mytum (1986, 376) as 'an exception'! It is clear that the prejudices mentioned above are difficult to remove.

The implications of the proof of the use of glass vessels in the Celtic West are considerable. Firstly, it supplies us with an entirely new class of imports with which to identify and date Early Historic sites. Although many of the sites so far identified have other, ceramic, imports, many do not (Table 13). The provenance of the glass vessels may also give some indication of the provenance of the Continental E ware. Finally, these rare and delicate vessels reinforce our view of the high status of the sites on which they are found.

6.4 Reinterpretation of the phasing of Dinas Powys

The plotting of the horizontal distributions of sherds from individual vessels showed that many formed coherent groups. When these groups were then related to the vertical stratigraphy, it became obvious that there was a clear stratigraphic distinction between the Mediterranean and Continental imports. This was best seen in Cut 17, where it was possible to localise the positions of the sherds fairly closely from information in the site notebooks (Fig 66). The fact that the groups of sherds from individual vessels showed a horizontal and vertical integrity proved that their deposition must be contemporary with activities before and after the construction of Bank 1. Bank 1 therefore had to date to the later 6th century, and not the 11th/12th century as Alcock had proposed. Alcock's explanation for the presence of 6th- and 7th-century material in his putative Norman earthwork was that this material had been scraped up from the occupation deposits associated with the Early Historic buildings and dumped to produce the medieval rampart. The coherence of the groups of sherds from individual

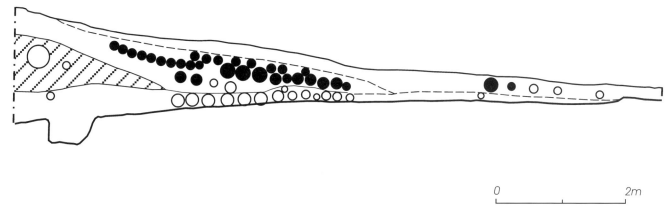

Fig 66 Cut 17 at Dinas Powys. Schematic section with individual imported vessels, showing stratigraphic differentiation between Mediterranean (open circles) and Continental (solid circles) imports

vessels, and the stratigraphic separation within the rampart, showed that this explanation was impossible to sustain. Full details of the argument are given in Appendix 9. Although the relative sequence of events deduced by Alcock remained valid, a new phasing scheme had to be introduced (Figs 67–8). In summary this was:

- Period 1 Late Bronze Age unenclosed settlement (Alcock Phases 1 and 2)
- Period 2a Initial early medieval settlement enclosed by Bank 2 – 5th century (Alcock Phase 4)
- Period 2b Retraction in area and building of Bank 1 – later 6th century (Alcock Phase 5)
- Period 2c Multiplication of defences, Banks 3–5 – late 7th/early 8th century (Alcock Phase 6)

6.5 Social interpretation of distributions

General points

It is difficult to say much about the pre-Bank 1 phase of activity at Dinas Powys as very few areas of certain early activity were excavated, or indeed preserved. However it is possible to come to some tentative conclusions. Concentrations of animal bone and shellfish show that a midden area was located under Bank 1 in the north-east of the site (cf Gilchrist 1988). At this period this was a metal working area, where the lead die for a zoomorphic penannular brooch was found (Appendix 6; Graham-Campbell 1991). As the later metal working area in the south-east of site was also sited in a midden area, this suggests continuity of cultural practices between Phase 2a and 2b. The Mediterranean tablewares, which belong to this phase, were scattered over the eastern part of the site, rather than being piled on the rear of the enclosure rampart (Bank 2), as in the succeeding phase.

The material from the gullies is interesting both for the stratigraphic dating of the buildings, and because it illustrates the range of material which was in use within the buildings (Fig 61). One noticeable concentration is the collection of objects in the north end of Gully 6 (Pl 43). Almost every class of object found on the site is represented here. This raises the possibility that this might be a votive deposit of some kind as it is reminiscent of the pit at Cadbury Congresbury filled with almost all the artefact classes present on that site, including prehistoric and Roman flint, slag, glass and pottery, and a sherd of cross-stamped ARS (Rahtz et al 1992, figs 44–5, 244). It was suggested that this collection of objects was symbolic in some way, like the items found round holy wells in Ireland. This is not the only parallel on post-Roman sites in the west. Inside the round at Trethurgy in Cornwall there was a small stone-lined feature, filled with clean sand and containing fragments of imported pottery of types LR1, LR2 and PRS, as well as samian and Oxford ware, a feature interpreted by the excavator as a shrine of some kind (Quinnell 2004, 208–9, 236–8). Other indications that imported pottery sherds may have had some talismanic significance comes from the excavations at Dalkey Island and Cadbury Congresbury. At Dalkey Island, a sherd of a LR1 amphora had been placed beneath a hearth slab in what was believed to be a deliberate manner (Liversage 1968, 121). At Cadbury Congresbury two pits were found near the entrance to the circular building interpreted as a shrine. One pit contained 'votive' bone plaques and the other had two different handles of LR1 amphorae (Rahtz et al 1992, 242–4, fig 172).

While these examples give some indication that imported material could have some talismanic or amuletic function, at Dinas Powys the evidence is against such an interpretation. Firstly, the 'collection' of objects is in fact spread out along the gully and through its fill, rather than being in a 'hoard'. Some pieces are in the bottom silt and others in the rubble filling. More significantly, one sherd of DSPA from the bottom silt joins another from the ground surface immediately adjacent to the gully. It seems most likely that the pottery and other items found in this gully were lying on the surface when the

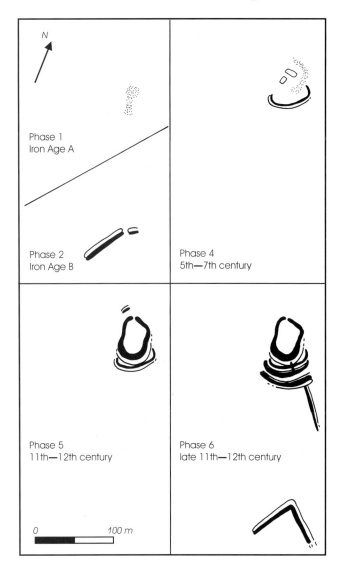 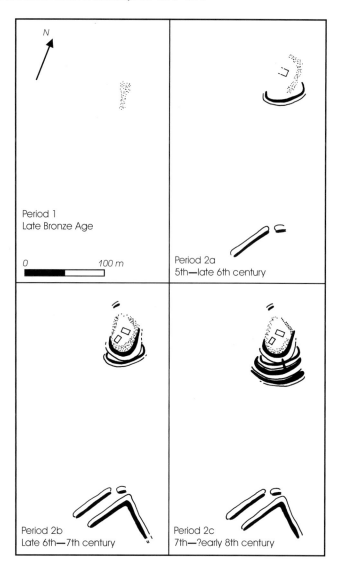

Fig 67 Alcock's original phasing of Dinas Powys

Fig 68 Rephasing of Dinas Powys

gully was dug and so became incorporated in its fill, some falling in when the gullies were open, some deliberately incorporated in the stone packing. A large sherd of E ware (Fig 60, E48) was noted in the site book as having been 'packed in with the stones laid longitudinally along the gully'. Secondly, the items tend to be small and insignificant looking. The glass in particular consists of minute slivers, and the samian ware is a very small abraded sherd. These pieces do not look like specially selected items. Finally it should be pointed out that the gullies round the houses are purely functional features, unlike the pits at Trethurgy and Cadbury Congresbury which have no obvious utilitarian function. The conclusion from these arguments must be that the material in the gullies is a sample of the material which was in use in the area of the buildings when the gullies were in use. The material in the gullies was protected when the other rubbish was swept out to the perimeter, acting as 'artefact traps' (Sommer 1990, 53). This conclusion has implications for the stratigraphic dating of Building 2, showing it was in use during the currency of E ware and Group Cc glass in the 7th century.

The overall density of finds on the site in terms of objects per m² for all classes of material except animal bone, slag and other metal working debris illustrates the strikingly peripheral nature of the find spots (Campbell 1991, illus 87). The central area is remarkably free of artefacts. One concentration of artefacts was along the northern palisaded edge of the site. Anthropological studies provide parallels for this type of accumulation along the margins of regularly cleaned enclosures (De Beor and Lathrap 1979, fig 4.6). The other main area of artefact accumulation was on the rear slopes of Bank 1 on the eastern side of the site.

The most obvious difference between the early (Phase 2a) and later (Phase 2b/c) phases is the reduction in the size of the enclosed area. In fact, in the later phase the available space within the enclosure was almost halved from 1650m² to 850m², and the enclosing bank was brought much closer to the buildings. In Phase 2a the enclosing bank

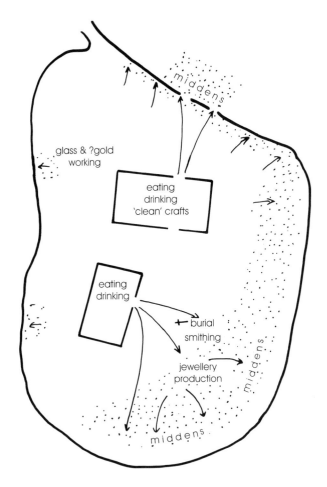

Fig 69 Suggested activity areas at Dinas Powys

sleeping, which could have taken place in both buildings, there is evidence of spinning and weaving and other 'clean' crafts in or around Building 1. The south-east corner of the site had most of the bronze melting and iron smithing activities. Here also large quantities of domestic rubbish were dumped, and a child was buried. In the north-west there was another industrial area where less noxious activities took place. This seems to have involved the melting of glass and possibly gold working. The areas around the buildings were kept clean, as were the floors of the buildings. The metal working areas, particularly the iron working area, would have been rather anti-social areas, both in terms of noise and fumes. Not surprisingly, these areas are to be found to the leeward side of the buildings, given a prevailing south-westerly wind. These metal working areas seem to have been seen as areas where domestic rubbish could be dumped, presumably because they were already seen as 'dirty' areas.

Processes of rubbish disposal

Having looked at the distribution of material in some detail, it is necessary to consider the problem of the actual processes of rubbish disposal. As we have seen, some of the industrial debris is probably primary refuse (crucibles, bronze clippings), or *de facto* refuse (hearth bottoms), or recycled refuse (fused glass). Most of the other material such as bones, pottery, glass, personal and domestic items is probably secondary refuse. Much of this material must have been discarded and broken originally within or around the buildings. There are several clues as to how this material was transferred to the site perimeter. Firstly, most of the finds came from layers described as black and sticky, so must have had a high organic content which cannot be explained in terms of the animal bone content. A likely source of organic material would be rotting flooring and bedding material. Contemporary literary references make it clear that rush-strewn floors were found in high-status buildings. The 7th-century '*Lament for Cynddlan*' describes a luxurious hall as having 'fresh rushes beneath my feet till bed-time' (Clancy 1970, 89). Bedding was probably also organic, bracken being mentioned in other, later sources. This organic material would have to be cleaned out periodically. Any material which had been dropped amongst this debris would be removed at the same time. The bulk of this material would necessitate its removal from areas where people walked. It would therefore be carried to the back of the enclosure bank or dumped over the edge of the crags.

This process of sweeping up and dumping material in discrete areas would explain one puzzling feature of the taphonomy of the pottery. As has been pointed out, the E ware appears to have been heavily trampled, and seems to be secondary refuse, yet sherds from some vessels form coherent spatial groups. Two of these vessels (E37, E38) are found on

(Bank 2) lay at some distance from the buildings. Pottery seems to have been broadcast away from the buildings, but not to any specific area. Thus some of the DSPA is quite close to the buildings, while some of the PRS is further away. As has been pointed out above, the rear of Bank 2 was not used as a midden area but there was a midden area in the north-east of the site, and fine metal working seems to have taken place there.

When Bank 1 was constructed in Phase 2b the area around the buildings became very cramped. To avoid cluttering the activity areas pottery and other refuse was deposited on the rear of Bank 1 where it would not be walked upon, or else it was dumped over the cliff at the northern edge of the site. This reduction in the area of the enclosure may even have been an incentive to keep the area around the buildings swept clean in the later phases.

Areas of activity

A synthesis of the information given in the previous sections is presented in Figure 69. Here it can be seen that the two buildings appear to be differentiated, with a wider variety of functions being associated with Building 1. Apart from eating, drinking and the rear slope of Bank 1 where they were unlikely to have been trampled *in situ*. The explanation seems to be that the pottery was broken and trampled for a time within the buildings. It was then swept out in a coherent mass and dumped on the periphery. Larger pieces, especially thick rims and bases which would be uncomfortable to walk on, could have been thrown out immediately. This might explain the large DSPA ware sherds close to Building 2. The amphorae present a special problem. This type of vessel tends to be long lived as it is usually kept static in one particular location. Hayden and Cannon (1983, 131–9) give ethnographic data which show that large vessels tend to be left for some time when they are broken, because a special effort is needed to remove them. It may be that the explanation for the mutually exclusive distributions between the amphorae and the tableware is due to this process. The concentration of amphorae in Cut 6 may then represent a period of 'spring-cleaning', removing an awkward pile of broken, or no longer used, amphorae at a period some time after they had been in use as water vessels. This might explain why none of the contemporary tableware appears to have been discarded with the amphorae.

The child burial

An intriguing feature of the south-eastern metal working area is the shallow grave with the skeleton of a female child lying between Hearths J and K. Alcock pointed out that this burial is either contemporary with, or later than, the metal working, as there was a crucible fragment in the grave-fill (Alcock 1963a, 30). It is possible to suggest two reasons why it is likely that the burial took place during the occupation of the site. Firstly, the burial had been disturbed as the feet had been cut away and were missing. This suggests that the burial was in existence during the period of activity in this area as there would have been no reason to disturb the burial after the abandonment of the site. Secondly, the area of the burial has a high concentration of finds (Campbell 1991, illus 87). If the grave was inserted after the abandonment of activity, it is likely that more finds would have been incorporated in the fill of the grave. The grave also seems to have been placed deliberately between the two hearths. If it is accepted that the body was buried while the site was still occupied, this gives important information on the inhabitants' attitude to death and burial.

The association of the burial with the 'dirty' area of rubbish disposal is surely significant, and would suggest that the person buried was also 'dirty' in some way, as it is the only burial on the site. It could be suggested that the person buried was regarded as being outside the normal community, and therefore not fit to be buried in the normal places. Examples of such 'outsiders' would be outlaws, foreigners, pagans or perhaps those with illness or deformities. As this was the burial of a young, apparently normal female child, most of these possibilities seem unlikely. I suggest it is possible that this was the child of a female slave, perhaps a foreigner or a pagan. A Saxon female slave is mentioned in one of the Llandaff charters of the 8th century as part of the price for an estate in the Welsh kingdom of *Ergyng* (Davies 1979, no 185). Slavery was apparently common in Wales in the early medieval period (Davies 1982, 64). Burial within a settlement is recorded elsewhere in the Celtic West. At Dalkey Island there was a child burial in the ditch during the early medieval occupation (Liversage 1968, 100). Hamerow (2006, 27) has shown that infant burials are common amongst 'special deposits' in north-western Europe at this period, and were often placed in liminal areas.

Structuring of disposal patterns

Having assembled and analysed the data on the distribution of material on the site, we are now in a position to look for any underlying structure in the patterning. However, there are immediate difficulties. There is no absolute archaeological indication of the position of the entrances to the buildings, or even the position of the walls. Although the site entrance in the later phase is clearly in the north-west, its position in the previous phase is less clear. No internal divisions can be seen in the buildings and there are virtually no finds in or near the buildings. This means that most comparisons with ethnographic sites are virtually useless. However a few points can be made.

Firstly, the interior of the site can be divided into public 'front' and 'back' areas in terms of Goffman's analysis (Portnoy 1981). The area around the buildings is kept clean and free from debris and must be seen as a front area. The back area is peripheral to this, stretching along the rear of Bank 1. It is here that the 'dirty' activities took place and rubbish was dumped. There is no sign of corresponding private front and back areas. The living accommodation appears to have been communal within the site. The entrance in the north-west led directly into the front area by the supposed entrance to the main building. There was no elaboration of this entrance or attempt to prevent access to the main body of the hall, which opens directly onto the public front area. In terms of access analysis (Hillier and Hanson 1984) there is no hierarchical arrangement of access, unlike that which Foster has shown in her analysis of the access patterns in the Scottish later Iron Age buildings (Foster 1989). Recent research looking at the site from a post-colonial perspective has suggested that its layout may mirror that of Late Roman villas in the Cardiff area, such as Ely, reflecting a memory of past Romano-British ancestry (Bowles 2006).

If the site is a high-status one, this is not reflected in the internal spatial arrangement. However, the strong encircling defences could be seen as visual symbols of isolation and high status. It is possible to see this situation in terms of what we know of Celtic society. Feasting and drinking in the hall are a common theme of the early medieval Welsh literature (Davies 1982, 29–30), and it seems that cooking was communally arranged. Society was kin-based and hierarchical only in a broad sense. The king belonged to the noble class and was not theoretically different in status from its other members. Society was not hierarchical in the feudal sense, with the king at the summit of a pyramid of economic relationships. Openness and hospitality were required of all, but particularly the upper classes (Davies 1982, 130; Kelly 1988, 139–40). Thus the societal relationships of Early Historic Wales may be reflected in the openness of the spatial arrangements at Dinas Powys, at least for those allowed access in the first place.

6.6 Conclusions

The methodologies developed here have shown their potential and limitations when applied to the Dinas Powys case study. A number of significant research problems were answered satisfactorily using the techniques of taphonomic analyses presented here. Some of these were of specific relevance to the site, while others had more general implications. These included:

- Confirmation of the practice of working samian sherds for spindle whorls in the Early Historic period, using distribution maps. This supports the idea that the practice was a Late Roman/post-Roman feature (Cool 2000, 53–4).
- Confirmation that Buildings 1 and 2 were occupied at the same time, from the association of Mediterranean and Continental imports with both, but Building 1 was exclusively associated with LRA, and Building 2 more associated with Continental pottery and glass.
- Indications that the different Mediterranean imports had different disposal patterns, from their different distributions. In particular, the Late Roman amphorae were concentrated in one location, suggesting they had been stored together. This has implications for the stratigraphic interpretation of other sites which have not been fully excavated.
- Confirmation from horizontal and vertical distribution studies that glass vessels were in use on the site, and not brought as broken cullet as had been thought previously.
- Realisation that deeply coloured glass sherds were specifically chosen for remelting from collections of broken glass vessels of various shades. This has implications for the interpretations of relict assemblages on other sites as sherd counts could produce seriously misleading pictures of the initial quantities of vessels on these sites.
- Characterisation of trampled secondary refuse assemblages from a study of the sherd size curves and vessel-to-sherd ratios of E ware. This potential is explored in reference to other sites in Chapter 7.
- Redating of the entire Dinas Powys sequence of defences and occupation, using a combination of horizontal and vertical stratigraphic analyses.

Some of these results could perhaps have been expected, others were more surprising. The discovery of the use of complete glass vessels on the site required overturning a paradigm on the nature of 'Celtic' society and trade relationships. However, this seems to have been accepted by most people working in the field with little difficulty. The redating of the Dinas Powys sequence is perhaps more controversial, especially as the excavator of the site has argued strongly that an excavator's opinion of stratigraphic matters cannot easily be reinterpreted by others who were not present at the time of excavation (Alcock 1978). The original phasing has been upheld by the Royal Commission review of the site (RCAHMW 1991), despite some caveats. As the original site report has been a classic text for student discussion, perhaps it will continue to provide ammunition for both sides of the debate. It is important to note that it was often the combination of two methods of analysis which produced better interpretation of distributions, as has been pointed out by Orton *et al* (1993, 22).

The limitations of this type of study are also clear. The lack of good data on building layouts (doors, rooms etc) made it difficult to relate patterns of deposition to patterns of activities, though some attempt was made. More disappointingly, there was no sign of any deep structuring principle to the distribution of midden material, as might have been suspected from anthropological studies such as those of Moore (1982). Most distributions could be seen as functionally determined, but comparative information from other well-preserved sites may reveal more consistent patterning related to metaphorical structures.

7 Patterns of consumption: taphonomic studies at other sites

The Dinas Powys analyses presented above provide some general techniques of analyses and a comprehensive comparative case study for the analysis of other Early Historic Atlantic sites. They illustrate the necessity of careful study of the vertical and horizontal distribution patterns of imported material before it is possible to understand the chronological or social context of the material. Such studies have much to contribute to issues such as the nature of the 5th-century 'transition' in western Britain (Collins and Gerrard 2004; Wilmott and Wilson 2000). The question of residuality is the key to understanding the material culture of this period as, unless we can recognise residual material in these putative 5th-century contexts, there is no means of establishing continuing occupation from the latest datable Roman contexts. There have been some recent attempts to address this problem in general terms, with important papers by Hilary Cool identifying a distinct very Late Roman finds assemblage (Cool 2000), and Gerrard arguing for continuing pottery production in the south-west (Gerrard 2004), but key sites such as Wroxeter are noticeably lacking in such studies. The case studies below isolate one particular aspect of each site which has been illuminated by these studies.

7.1 Tintagel

The maximum size curve for the fine tablewares (ARS and PRS) from the 1930s' Tintagel excavations shows that the sherds are almost entirely rim and base fragments, and biased towards larger sherds (Fig 70). This curve contrasts markedly with sites such as Dinas Powys where all sherds were collected (Fig 52). This must mean that there was a selection of sherds during (or after) Radford's excavations, with almost all small undecorated body sherds being discarded. This is perhaps not surprising, given the period of excavation, and use of labourers to dig the site, but does show clearly the problems of using quantification of material from older excavations. Rather surprisingly, this discard process is not so apparent in the LRA material, at least in the case of a small amphora such as LR3 (Campbell 1991, illus 134). The overall site distribution of the recovered PRS/ARS sherds may therefore be somewhat biased. Nevertheless, from Site A came fifteen sherds, all but two of which were rims, bases or decorated sherds. Many of the sherds are unabraded, suggesting little movement after breakage. The distribution of the fineware sherds shows marked concentrations on Site A, the terraces on the north side, and below the Inner and Lower Wards of the medieval castle.

The Site A finds must represent an area of usage of the vessels, as there would be no point in carrying midden material up the steep slopes to the summit area. Dark (1985, 10–11) suggested that the imports on Site A were probably associated with Radford's Period 1 structures, consisting of two rectangular buildings set at right-angles to each other and measuring about 9m by 4m internally (*ibid*, fig 2). These buildings were irregular in nature, the walls composed of clay with slate. The distribution and nature of the finewares suggests that this is a likely explanation.

The vessel-to-sherd ratios of the LRA are in the range 1:20. At Dinas Powys it was shown that a single amphora would produce at least 100 sherds on breakage, so we can estimate that around four-fifths of the Tintagel sherds must be unrecovered. As there is no indication that large numbers of amphorae sherds were discarded during Radford's excavations, this is a salutary reminder of the pottery losses even on a prolific site. Given the steepness of the slopes where most of the LRA sherds were found, it seems reasonable to conclude that the rest of the sherds were dumped over the cliff edges along with other midden material, or were washed over by colluvial processes, and indeed large quantities of imports have been found in cliff-edge falls and recent examinations using ropes. The distributions of the various amphorae show that the flat summit has a scatter of finds, especially around Site A, but that most came from the area of the Inner Ward and terraces around Sites B, C and the Iron Gate. The north African amphorae are hardly found on the summit. It is possible that the large size and

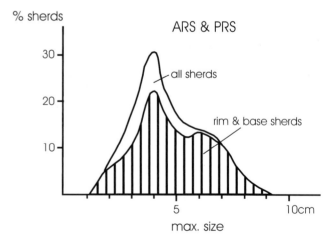

Fig 70 Maximum sherd size curves for ARS and PRS from Radford's excavations at Tintagel, showing preferential retention of a selection of rims, bases and decorated sherds

Patterns of consumption: taphonomic studies at other sites 103

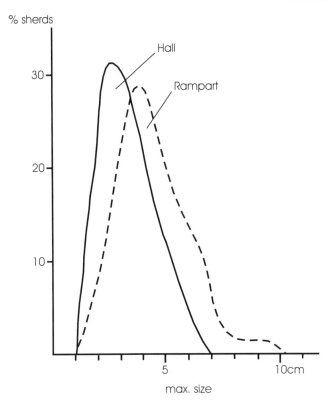

Fig 71 Maximum sherd size curves of LRA from Cadbury Castle

weight of these amphorae mitigated against their being carried up the steep slope to the summit. The distribution evidence, and the size and freshness of many of the sherds, does not support the idea that most of the sherds on the terraces have been washed down from the summit. It seems that the major site of Early Historic occupation may have been in the sheltered area of the Island Ward, where relatively small excavations have produced large amounts of imports (Thomas 1989), and on the eastern and southern terraces.

7.2 Cadbury Castle

Professor Alcock himself has pointed out how the PRS and LRA sherds cluster around Structure L1, the putative Early Historic hall (Alcock 1982, 374, table 2), confirming his interpretation of the date of this building and its function as a hall where feasting took place. In order to test Alcock's hypothesis, and to confirm the pattern of maximum sherd size distribution found at Dinas Powys, I analysed the sherd sizes from the area of the hall itself (Areas L, S, P) and the areas on the back of the rampart (Areas K, D). This analysis was taken up in the final site report (Alcock 1995, 118–24). As well as a concentration around Structure 1, there is another around a possible structure in Site C, indicated by a concentration of LR2. The results (Fig 71) show that the sherds from the hall area have a typical heavily trampled shape of curve, peaking at a low size for such thick sherds (2.5cm) and falling off rapidly with no large sherds. On the other hand the sherds from the rampart have a much larger peak (at 4cm), with almost no sherds of 2cm size, and with a long tail-off containing some large sherds. The difference in mean size between the hall deposits and those of the rampart is statistically significant. The interpretation of these curves seems clear. In the area within the hall, broken vessels were heavily trampled, resulting in many very small sherds which were caught in artefact traps (*ibid*, 120, illus 2.24), while the larger sherds were removed with other rubbish to the middens on the rear of the rampart. The material scattered around the hall may represent subsequent scattering during later occupation. The distribution of sherds at Cadbury Castle seems to show that the site of Early Historic buildings can be identified by distributions of imported pottery even if no structural features are present, and contradicts the scepticism of some authors about the existence of the Early Historic hall (Arnold 1988, 305). The concentration of small sherds within the confines of the postholes outlining the hall is striking. It is possible that another building exists on site C, perhaps the six-post structure C6 which is in a parallel alignment with the hall and is surrounded by LR2 sherds. This has important implications for identifying buildings on sites such as Longbury Bank where most of the structural features seem to have been destroyed.

There is a notable difference in the distribution of the LR1 and LR2 sherds, with LR2 widely distributed, while LR1 is mostly confined to the area of the hall. If these two types of amphorae are contemporary the difference in distribution must reflect some difference in use and/or disposal of the vessels. It could be suggested that LR2 vessels were associated with drinking and LR1 with cooking, and that different areas were associated with each activity. Alcock (1995, 39) reported that an ancillary structure S1, to the north of the hall, may have been a kitchen. However, it is not clear why both types of vessel should be found within the hall. If LR1 amphorae are associated with cooking, one would not expect them to be broken within the hall, or if they were, one would expect the resultant rubbish to be disposed of in the same place. An alternative explanation would be that the LR1 and LR2 vessels were in use at different times. It will be interesting to see if any other sites share the differentiation. There is no sign of this at Tintagel, and there are insufficient sherds at Dinas Powys to be sure that the difference seen there is real. Recent finds at Bantham indicate that there may be spatial or chronological differentiation between LR1 and LR2 at other sites.

7.3 Longbury Bank

Longbury Bank, near Tenby in Dyfed, was excavated in 1988 and 1989, and proved to rival Dinas Powys in the variety of imported pottery and glass (Campbell and Lane 1993a). Severe plough erosion in the medieval period resulted in the loss of most features, and only one possible building was found, a small hut occupying a rock-cut platform on the sloping side of the promontory (*ibid*, fig 3). In general, the imported artefacts on the flat summit were only found in hollows in the bedrock, where they had been protected from plough erosion. Despite this, the overall distribution of the material must be of significance, as hollows were found over the entire site but finds were restricted to certain areas. Studies of the movement of artefacts in plough soil have shown that ploughing causes little horizontal displacement of objects on flat sites (Crowther 1983, 34).

The major concentration of finds is in Trench E and does not extend as far west as Trench H. The other major concentrations are in Trench B and in Stephen Green's excavations north of Trench E (Campbell and Lane 1993a, fig 12). Both of these lie down the slope from the summit area. Taking all these areas into consideration it is possible to suggest that the main occupation of the site lay to the east of Trench H, on the narrow point of the promontory. The area between Trenches H and E is the most level part of the field and the most obvious site for a major building. Trench E also had the most convincing posthole found on the site. If there was a major building here then it seems that midden material was thrown over the edges of the ridge, and perhaps into the shaft leading to Little Hoyle cave.

The size of the sherds is generally small but two concentrations of larger sherds were found. One of these was a collection of joining LR1 amphora sherds from the floor of the small structure in Trench B, indicating that an amphora was broken *in situ* on the floor of this building. The position of this building, on a slope below the main ridge, suggests it may have been a store of some kind. A series of rock-cut steps led down from the summit to the building. It is possible that amphorae and other stored food and drink were kept in this building, with the rock-cut floor and sheltered position keeping the stores cool. It is certainly difficult to see the structure as a dwelling as there is no hearth.

The other concentration of larger sherds is in the cave shaft excavated in 1878 where a large part of a PRS bowl was found. This had been thrown into the shaft along with much midden material, described as black soil mixed with shells and bones. A number of prehistoric human skeletons of at least eleven individuals including children were also found in this deposit. The shaft was obviously a convenient location to dispose of rubbish. The concentration of finds in Green's 1986 trench, which is not directly under the cliff edge of the promontory, may represent the spoil heap of the 1878 excavations where the midden material dug out of the shaft had been dumped. The few odd sherds closer to the cliff in the 1958 and 1984 trenches probably represent material thrown or ploughed directly over the edge.

The amount of imported material from Longbury Bank is not large enough to engage in the kind of detailed study undertaken for Dinas Powys, but it does enable a number of important observations to be made. Comparisons with Dinas Powys show that both the sites are of roughly the same area and shape. The finds of glass from the central area of Dinas Powys are of similar density to those at Longbury Bank (*ibid*, fig 11). These tiny glass sherds or micro-refuse may be all that is left after the normal sweeping-up processes used to keep sites clean when they were occupied. If this is so, almost all the distinctive finds will have been removed from the main areas of occupation on these sites, with the original positions of activity areas being indicated by 'ghost distributions' of material fortunately caught in hollows or too small to be swept away. From this ghost distribution it is possible to postulate that a building or buildings similar to Building 1 at Dinas Powys once stood between Trenches E and H (*ibid*, 62). Without the comparative work at Dinas Powys, it would have been difficult to be confident of such a conclusion given the absence of excavated features indicating the presence of a building.

When concentrations of larger sherds are found within features on the site, as with the structure on Site B, it enables us to be virtually certain that these are contemporary features, datable by the age of the vessels. The structure on Site B is therefore an important addition to the small corpus of Early Historic buildings in western Britain. Interestingly it bears many similarities to Saxon sunken-featured buildings, with gable-end posts and a sunken floor. Similar types of construction were found at Cadbury Congresbury (Burrow 1981, fig 11) and Glastonbury Tor (Rahtz 1970, figs 8–10). Radiocarbon dates from a carbonised post in structure B gave a 5th-/6th-century date (Campbell and Lane 1993a, 53), confirming the association with LR1.

7.4 Trethurgy

Trethurgy is a key site for many aspects of Atlantic Romano-British and Early Historic studies, particularly as it is the only site fully excavated to modern standards (Quinnell 2004, viii). The full excavation of the interior and entrance enable us to be sure that all the import sherds within the enclosure were recovered. None of the exterior areas, where middens might be expected, were excavated, partly due to financial constraints (*ibid*, 3).

Although a variety of imports were found, there were very few sherds from each vessel. Using the figures from other sites it is possible to estimate roughly the original number of sherds which would have been present when the vessels were first discarded (Table 10).

The difference between the number of sherds recovered and those originally present must show the large numbers of sherds which were removed from the interior of the site, presumably to middens or fields. The table clearly shows that there are great variations in recovery levels between indi-

Table 10 Numbers of imported vessels at Trethurgy with numbers of sherds recovered tabled against possible original number of sherds

Import type	MNV	No. sherds	Estimated original no. sherds	Percentage recovery
PRS	2	6	60	10%
LR1	2	47	200	24%
LR2	2	15	200	8%
LR3	1	2	70	3%
E ware	1	1	50	2%
Glass	3	5	150	3%

vidual vessels, but that these variations are due to post-usage processes, and not to the supply of vessels to the site. The use of MNV can therefore be shown to be much more useful than sherd count, which would be seriously misleading. However, it is also possible to use the distribution patterns to estimate what the figures for MNV would have been if only part of the site had been excavated. Dividing the site into quadrants shows that if only one quadrant of the site had been excavated, the site would still have produced examples of most of the imported vessels (based on Quinnell 2004, fig 88), and would still have ranked as an intermediate site in terms of quantity of imports. The Trethurgy evidence allows us to extrapolate to other sites which have had only partial excavation, in order to assess the original scale of importation with more confidence.

7.5 Loch Glashan

The crannog of Loch Glashan, Argyll, was excavated in 1960, but has only recently been written up and published (Crone and Campbell 2005). The site produced five E ware vessels, but no glass or other imports, except for a glass bead of Mediterranean origin. As most of the site was excavated, the distribution of finds gives a good comparison to other well-recorded sites such as Dinas Powys or Trethurgy, but in a very different burial environment. The site posed considerable difficulties of interpretation, and the published report suggests that the excavated deposits are a conflation deposit formed from the degradation of substantial thicknesses of organic build up. This interpretation is based on modern studies of crannogs as well as the relationship between the finds and the structure of the crannog, and a series of radiocarbon dates. Accordingly the site can now be seen to be a multi-phase site with long-term occupation throughout the first millennium AD. The original excavator's recognition of a substantial rectangular building is rejected, necessitating revision of the interpretation previously put forward (Scott 1960; RCAHMS 1988, 205–8; Campbell 1991, 165; Campbell 1999, 26–7). One further aspect of the site was the direct dating of some of the E ware vessels from radiocarbon dating of carbonised residues (Chapter 3.2).

The horizontal distribution of the E ware differs from that of the other artefacts, which are almost all organic. The organic artefacts, mainly wood and leather, cluster in a small area in the lee of the crannog, lying between the crannog and the shore (Crone and Campbell 2005, fig 7). Some of the E ware is also in this area, but other sherds lie along the interior edge of the crannog in the same quadrant. These latter sherds are almost the only artefacts from within the crannog palisade. The concentration of organic artefacts, originally interpreted as a midden, is now believed to be a deposit washed off the degrading crannog over many years, and contains material dated from the 2nd to 8th centuries AD. The sherd size curve of the E ware is markedly different from that at other sites (Fig 53), containing a very high proportion of large sherds. It is therefore clear that the E ware has suffered almost no post-depositional breakage or trampling. In that sense it could be considered 'primary' refuse in Schiffer's terms (1972), though it has been moved slightly from its place of breakage. It seems likely that the pottery has been preserved from degradation by being thrown or swept to the side of the crannog, where it accumulated against the palisade. Ethnographic study shows that settlement edges and fences form similar artefact traps caused by sweeping patterns (Hayden and Cannon 1983, fig 4.6). Joins between sherds in this area and those in the leeward deposit might show that rubbish which accumulated around the palisade margin was periodically thrown over it into the loch for disposal. Alternatively, these patterns may indicate that there was an opening in the palisade in this area, and the join patterns recall those at Dinas Powys where vessel sherds fan out from a postulated doorway in Building 2 (Fig 61). The most complete vessel (E140), is unique amongst the E ware assemblage in being almost intact, and must represent the final stage of abandonment of the site, Schiffer's *de facto* refuse.

The sherd size curve and horizontal distribution patterns therefore give valuable insights into disposal patterns, and show that sherd size curve on its own can be interpreted safely as an indicator of the taphonomic status of assemblages.

106 *Continental and Mediterranean imports to Atlantic Britain and Ireland, AD 400–800*

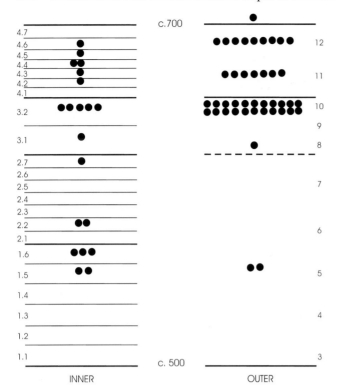

Fig 72 Whithorn stratigraphy, showing actual position of E ware vessel sherds

7.6 Whithorn

Given the quantity of imports from Whithorn, and the standard of excavation recording, this site should have the potential to produce insights into taphonomic processes. Unfortunately, the complex stratigraphy of the site, which was so useful in elucidating the chronology of the imports, causes difficulties when trying to interpret depositional processes. The site has a succession of building phases in a very concentrated area, and it is not possible to be sure which midden deposits relate to activity in which buildings. Even in cases where the distribution of material seems to respect the outline of buildings (eg Hill 1997, illus 10.24), it is possible to suggest that the building could post-date the material as easily as pre-dating it, if the floors were aggressively cleaned to disturb the very shallow stratigraphy. Aggregation of data over all of the site's phases would not be acceptable, except for the most general of conclusions. Despite these difficulties, some use can be made of the taphonomic data.

Horizontal distributions of individual vessels were used by the excavator to show coherent groups of sherds, indicating areas of rubbish deposition in patterns similar to those from Dinas Powys (*ibid*, illus 10.3–10.24). These coherent patterns were used to 'reunite' sherds which had been stratigraphically, but not horizontally, displaced from their original place of deposition by

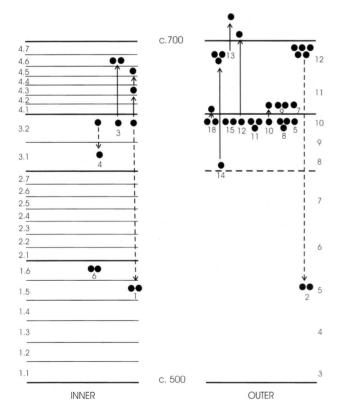

Fig 73 Whithorn stratigraphy, with individual E ware vessels and processes of dispersal upwards and downwards. Residual sherds shown by full lines, intrusive by dotted

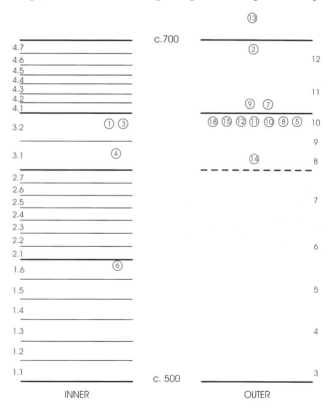

Fig 74 Whithorn stratigraphy, with first occurrence of E ware vessels

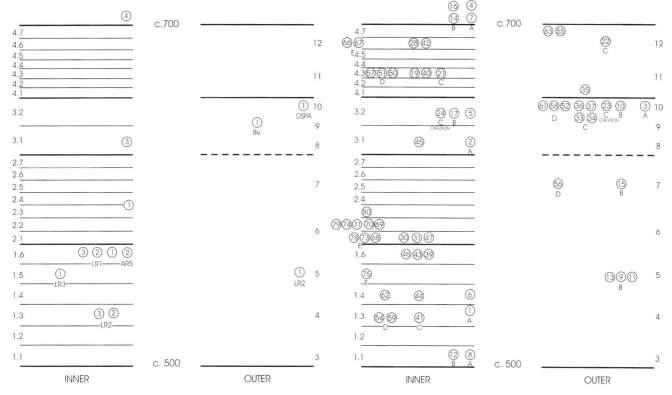

Fig 75 Whithorn stratigraphy, showing first occurrence of Mediterranean vessels, as in Fig 74

Fig 76 Whithorn stratigraphy, showing first occurrence of glass vessels, as in Fig 74

later disturbances such as grave digging or animal burrows. Using these data it has been possible to show this vertical displacement graphically (Figs 72–6). This system of illustration can be compared to that proposed by Brown (1985) for the specific case of joining fragments of vessels. The data can be presented in a number of ways. Figure 72 shows the actual vertical distribution of E ware sherds over the stratigraphic phases. At first glance this appears to show material spread through most of phases 1.5 to 4.6, and is difficult to interpret. By separating the material into individual vessels, Figure 73 shows how material from one vessel can be spread upwards (full lines) by processes such as grave digging which intrudes into lower deposits, or downwards (dotted lines) by intrusion caused by burrows and stratigraphic confusion. By re-presenting the data to show the stratigraphic unit where the vessel first appears in the record, the picture is considerably simplified (Fig 74). After undertaking the same process for each import group, the first appearances of each group can be combined to produce a relative chronology of the groups. This graphic technique immediately highlights anomalies, such as the case of E209 (vessel 2), two sherds of which appear very early in the sequence. In this case, the excavator accepted that the sherds probably belonged to the later of two intercutting contexts (Hill 1997, 321). The overall sequence presented here does differ in some cases from the excavator's opinion, but only where there are possible cases of contamination or stratigraphic confusion. The results presented are a salutary reminder of the complexities of stratigraphic processes and the problems of residuality and intrusion on sites with continuous long-term occupation. It is clear that only detailed investigation of a site's taphonomic processes can be used to create a secure chronology for it. Hopefully the techniques described here can contribute to the understanding of these processes at other sites.

The Whithorn material provides some other means of using the distribution data. The two stratigraphic sequences in Period 1 at the site, in the outer (divided into twelve sub-phases) and inner (22 sub-phases) precincts, have no direct stratigraphic link between them. However, a glance at Figure 74 shows that in both there is a restricted period of deposition of most of the E ware, and Group C glass with chevrons, in both sequences. This enables a fairly secure link to be established between the two stratigraphic blocks in the later part of the sequence, with Phase 3.2 equivalent to Phase 10 (*ibid*, 119, table 3.37). The earlier part of the outer sequence is impossible to correlate using the imports, as only a few sherds of Mediterranean imports are found here, not enough to be sure they are contemporary with the deposits they are found in. The use of pottery from individual vessels to link separate stratigraphic sequences has been reported before from medieval sites (Moorhouse 1986, 88–97). In the Whithorn case, there are no actual vessel links between the two areas, just similar sudden appearances of vessel types in both areas. This clearly represents episodes of deposition, and there is no guarantee that this would have taken place at the same time in different parts of the site. However, the appearance of two different types of vessel, E ware and Group C chevron-decorated glass, in quantity in both sequences strongly suggests there is some link between the two episodes of deposition.

The excavator took this analysis further, and suggested that the episodic nature of the *deposition* related to an episodic *supply* of imports to the site (Hill 1997, 323). Stages which had few imports deposited were seen as times when no imports were reaching the site, and a complex sequence of supply was outlined with four main stages and ten sub-stages each perhaps representing 'successive cargoes of trade goods' (*ibid*). The evidence presented for other sites such as Dinas Powys, and from ethnographic parallels, suggests that episodes of deposition cannot be directly related to supply, but are the result of a variety of social processes, which could occur at unknown intervals after the supply of the material to the site. Hill's stages of supply are probably generally correct, but the sub-stages are too dependent on the vagaries of human action to be fully acceptable.

7.7 Conclusions

The evidence presented above from a selection of import sites shows the usefulness of taphonomic analysis in the small assemblages found on Early Historic sites. It is also apparent that each site brings its own problems of interpretation, but also the possibility of understanding the processes at work in the use and disposal of the imported material. The Dinas Powys evidence is particularly clear in showing that buildings were normally kept clear of debris, and that concentrations of pottery and glass seem to indicate 'inactivity areas' (ie middens), rather than activity areas. Metal working debris, on the other hand, often represents activity areas. It is also clear that midden material is often removed entirely from the interior of sites, presumably for use as manure, though there are other possibilities. This can be seen clearly at sites such as Trethurgy discussed above, or Kildalloig Dun (Campbell 1991, illus 172). The implication is that the midden deposits found at sites like Dinas Powys may represent a stage in the transference of material from the interior of buildings to off-site locations, and the full process has been interrupted. Sometimes buildings were used as convenient temporary dumping grounds for midden material, as at Late Roman Trethurgy Structure U (Quinnell 2004, 175). In these cases it is important not to link the activities indicated by the midden material to the structure where they were found. However, this functional interpretation of midden deposits is not the only one possible. Work in the Western Isles of Scotland has shown that in some cultural settings midden material can be seen as a sign of status, and therefore something to be displayed, for example by the entrance to a site (Parker Pearson 2004, 80). This can perhaps be seen at Kildalloig Dun. Only detailed excavation of a larger sample of sites will enable socially significant patterns such as this to be recognised.

Plate 1 Phocaean Red Slipware with stamped hares, Dinas Powys P13

Plate 2 African Red Slipware, Whithorn A29–32

Plate 3 LR1 complete vessel, Turkey

Plate 4 LR1 amphora with red-painted graffito, Whithorn B245

Plate 5 LR2 amphora with graffito, Whithorn B242

Plate 6 LR3 amphora, Whithorn B246

Plate 7 DSPA, Dinas Powys

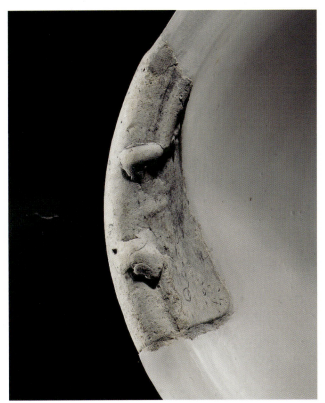

Plate 8 DSPA mortarium showing crudely formed pouring spout, Dunadd D11 (© Trustees of the National Museums of Scotland)

Plate 9 E ware fabric in thin section, Dunadd E79

Plate 10 (right) E ware showing string cut-off on base, Buiston E12 (© Trustees of the National Museums of Scotland)

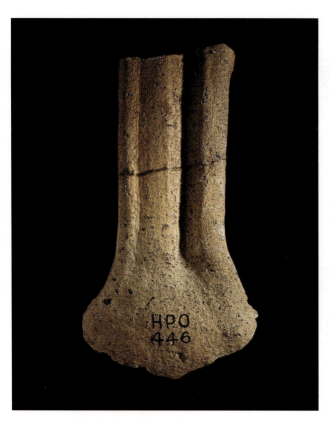

Plate 12 E ware spout showing finger-smearing and attachment method, Buiston E13 (© Trustees of the National Museums of Scotland)

Plate 11 E ware handle showing wheel-thrown profile, Dunadd E74 (© Trustees of the National Museums of Scotland)

Plate 13 E ware handle, showing finger-smearing attachment, Dunadd E76 (© Trustees of the National Museums of Scotland)

Plate 14 E ware showing orange oxidised firing marks on exterior, and grey reduction patch on interior, Iona E108 (© Trustees of the National Museums of Scotland)

Plate 15 E1 jar, Dunadd E56 (© Trustees of the National Museums of Scotland)

Plate 16 E2 beaker, with sooting showing secondary reuse, Buiston E12 (© Trustees of the National Museums of Scotland)

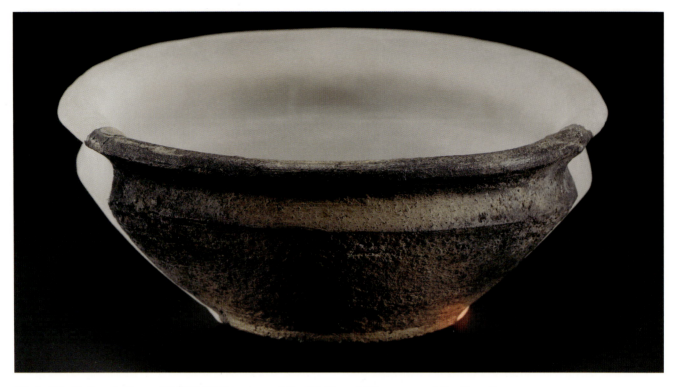

Plate 17 E3 bowl, Dunadd E69 (© Trustees of the National Museums of Scotland)

Plate 19 E4B spouted pitcher, Buiston E13 (© Trustees of the National Museums of Scotland)

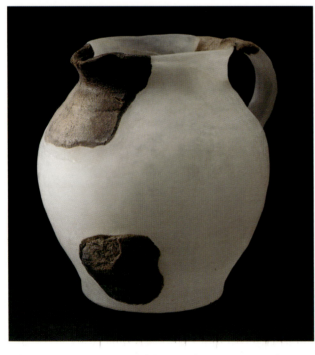

Plate 18 E4 jug, Dunadd E76 (© Trustees of the National Museums of Scotland)

Plate 20 Late form of E1 jar, Loch Glashan E140

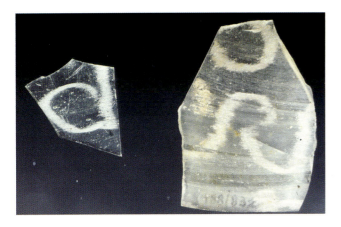

Plate 21 Glass Group A, with wheel-engraved letters, Whithorn G294, 296

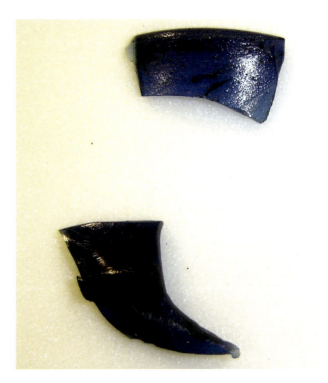

Plate 23 Glass Group B, squat jar, Dinas Powys G83

Plate 22 Glass Group B, claw beaker, Dinas Powys G93

Plate 24 Glass Group B, complete phial, Mullaroe G219 (National Museum of Ireland)

Plate 25 Glass Group B, claw beaker, Dunnyneill Island G370

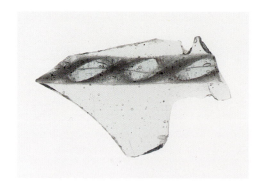

Plate 26 Glass Group B, reticella vessel, Birsay G7 (© Trustees of the National Museums of Scotland)

Plate 28 Glass Group B, bichrome green/yellow vessel, Birsay G6 (© Trustees of the National Museums of Scotland)

Plate 27 Glass Group B, opaque red/brown streaky glass, Birsay G13 (© Trustees of the National Museums of Scotland)

Plate 30 Glass Group B, moulded ribs of palm cup, Whithorn G300

Plate 29 Glass Group B, turquoise vessel, Dunadd G137 (© Trustees of the National Museums of Scotland)

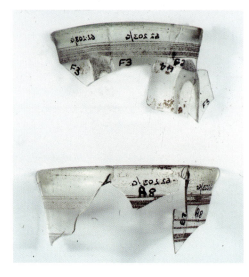

Plate 31 Glass Group Cb, reconstructed cone beaker rims, Dinas Powys G98, 101

Plate 32 Glass Group Ca, rim of cone beaker with opaque white trails, Mote of Mark G274 (© Trustees of the National Museums of Scotland)

Plate 34 Glass Group C, vessel with white rim, G305 Whithorn

Plate 36 Glass Group C, Whithorn, pink/amber diachroic G276

Plate 33 Glass Group C, bichrome vessel with blue rim, Whithorn G326

Plate 35 Glass Group Cc, Mote of Mark, decoration of festoons (© Trustees of the National Museums of Scotland)

Plate 37 Glass Group E, Whithorn, G342, showing unmarvered white trails dragged alternately up and down

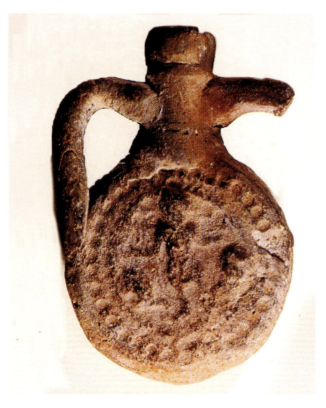

Plate 38 St Menas flask, Meols M1 (D Griffiths)

Plate 39 Gold-leaf glass tessera, Dunadd G140 (© Trustees of the National Museums of Scotland)

Plate 40 Silver-in-glass bead, Loch Glashan M13

Plate 41 Polychrome plaque, Mote of Mark M4 (© Trustees of the National Museums of Scotland)

Plate 42 Polychrome plaque, Mote of Mark M4, showing original edge with iron staining (© Trustees of the National Museums of Scotland)

Plate 43 Dinas Powys, drip gully of Building 2 which acted as an artefact trap (L Alcock)

Plate 44 Dunadd, looking west (Crown copyright: RCAHMS)

Plate 45 Ardifuir, looking south down the Sound of Jura from the interior of the dun (Crown copyright: RCAHMS)

Plate 46 Loch Glashan from the west (Crown copyright: RCAHMS, Horace Fairhurst collection)

Plate 48 Dumbarton Rock from the Clyde, looking north (Crown copyright: RCAHMS)

Plate 47 Dunollie, looking north (Crown copyright: RCAHMS)

Plate 49 Iona Abbey, looking east from Torr an Aba

Plate 50 Little Dunagoil, Bute, looking west

Plate 51 Mote of Mark, looking north (reproduced by courtesy of David Longley)

Plate 52 Whithorn Priory, site of main excavations

Plate 53 Deganwy, looking west along the north Wales coast

Plate 54 Hen Gastell during excavation

Plate 55 Tintagel, general view looking north

Plate 56 Tintagel, the harbour

8 Patterns of distribution: import site characteristics

Crucial to any understanding of the exchange processes which brought the Mediterranean and Continental imports to the Atlantic West is an appreciation of the type of site where they occur, and the relationship between these sites. This chapter, therefore, moves on from intra-site to inter-site distribution patterns. After first looking at the type of sites where the imports are found, and possible relationships between sites, it is possible to begin to understand how the distribution process operated. This leads to a discussion of the trading networks which lay behind the distribution of the imports (Chapter 9). A full discussion of each import site is presented elsewhere (Campbell 1991, 110–73; see also Dark 1994). Here the conclusions are presented in the form of a series of tables listing the characteristics of each site (Tables 16–19), and a summary of each major region. It is important to stress that the characteristics arise from the review below, and are chosen features common to the actual *import* sites, not a set of characteristics theoretically believed to be distinctive of high-status sites. The abundant Irish sites provide a model which can be used to interpret the other regions, and are therefore discussed in more detail.

Before looking in detail at the different regions, there are a few general topographical observations to be made. It has already been mentioned that the distribution of material is markedly coastal, with 82% of all imported vessels, and most of the sites with numerous vessels, being found less than 10km from the sea. There is a steep fall-off away from the coast, though thereafter there are small subsidiary peaks from 30 to 70km depending on the type of import. Three sites with above average quantities of imports buck this coastal trend and lie far inland: Cadbury Castle; Clogher; and New Pieces. The significance of the imports at these sites is considerably enhanced by the added difficulty in transporting material to these sites from the coast. In terms of height above sea level, the vast majority of sites lie below 100m OD, and New Pieces is quite exceptional in being located at 300m OD. This is a general indication, confirmed at particular sites such as Dunadd (Lane and Campbell 2000, 255–8), that import sites are associated closely with good agricultural land, rather than being in primarily defensible locations.

8.1 Ireland

The Irish Early Historic sites with import wares differ in a number of respects from those in Britain. They are the most numerous of all the Atlantic regions, with almost 50 known sites. A glance at the distribution maps (Figs 16 and 34) will show that the imports are dominated by the Continental wares. In fact only three sites, Garranes, Dalkey Island, and Clogher, have substantial quantities of Mediterranean imports. Another immediate impression gained from the maps is that the distribution is not predominately coastal, in contrast to Scotland, Wales and south-west England. It is likely that this difference is due to geographical factors, as the best arable land is coastal in the other western areas, but more widespread in Ireland. Consequently it is possible to analyse distributions of Irish sites in a more meaningful way than is possible for areas such as Scotland, where the constraints of topography outweigh any possible patterning in inter-relationships between sites. It is for this reason that the E ware fall-off curves discussed in Chapter 9 are confined to Ireland.

The only major Irish site for which I have detailed data on artefact distributions is Dalkey Island, which has already been discussed in Chapter 6 in relation to sherd size analysis (Fig 52). Distributional data have been obtained for a few other sites but all of these have only a few vessels of E ware. An interesting feature of the Irish evidence is the number of small enclosed sites of the period (raths) which have been more or less fully excavated. These include sites such as Gransha and Lisleagh as well as crannogs such as Moynagh Lough and Lough Faughan. As with Trethurgy in Cornwall it is evident that these small sites never had more than a few E ware vessels. This in itself is clear evidence for a hierarchy of sites with imports, ranging in ascending order from those with none, to those with a few vessels and finally to those with a quantity of vessels.

This ranking of import sites in Ireland can be analysed according to the type of site and other attributes, combined with an assessment of the amount and type of excavation and number of vessels from the site. These data are given in Table 18 for almost 50 sites with imported pottery or glass. Only six of these sites have more than five vessels: Clogher, Dalkey Island, Garryduff, Garranes, Lagore and Dunnyneil Island. As already discussed, Dalkey Island appears to be a special case, resembling the Scilly sites in the island siting, lack of defences (the bank is hardly defensive), and the use of E ware vessels as cooking-pots. It is suggested here that Dalkey Island was a trading site on a neutral, safe island, rather than a major habitation site. Dunnyneill Island is in a similar geographic situation, and could prove to be a similar type of site if further imported pottery turns up there. The four other major sites all share the characteristics of import centres in Britain such as Dunadd: they are probably royal sites, have strong defences and/or enclose large areas, and show evidence of the use of precious metals, weapons and jewellery production. These four centres are not the only possible major centres. On distributional grounds there appears to be a missing centre in the area of County Down where there is a concentration of lower grade sites. It is possible that one of the larger sites in the area which have received only small-scale excavation could be this missing centre. There are two obvious candidates, Scrabo and Downpatrick. Both are large hillforts fairly close to the sea, and it is possible that both were major centres. The presence of a spouted pitcher at Scrabo lends credence to its interpretation as a major centre but Downpatrick is more centrally placed with regard to the other County Down sites. It is unfortunate that there is no context for the single sherd from Downpatrick itself (E50). Scrabo has no known royal association but Downpatrick was a royal centre (Byrne 1973, 108), further strengthening the case for this site as a major import centre.

Clogher is clearly a site of major importance, not just because it has more imports than any other Irish site. As with Cadbury Castle it is situated far from the coast (70km) and although it does not enclose a large area (0.5ha) it is situated within an Iron Age hillfort with complex earthworks and an occupation lasting from the late Bronze Age to the 8th century AD (Warner 1988). Historical references make it clear that this was an important royal centre, probably reconstructed in the later 6th century (Warner 1979, 38). The distance from the coast means that the number of vessels should be increased by a multiplication factor related to the difficulty of transporting pottery overland. Studies of Roman sources suggest that overland transport is economically more expensive than sea transport by a factor of 20:1. Transporting E ware vessels to Clogher from Lough Foyle would therefore be equivalent in economic terms to transporting them by sea from France. Of course it is possible that purely economic factors were not operating in this part of the transport system but it is still probable that Clogher was a more major centre of importation and redistribution than the relatively small number of vessels, compared to sites like Whithorn or Dinas Powys, would at first sight suggest. This multiplication factor should not be applied to all inland sites, but only to sites which appear to have the characteristics of other primary importation centres. Secondary redistribution to more minor centres would not have taken place by trade but by gift exchange which was not constrained by cost factors, especially in small portable items.

The other major Irish sites are all near the coast. Lagore is a large crannog with occupation lasting from the 7th to 10th centuries. The amount of timber which went into the construction of a structure measuring 40m by 50m must have been immense. It implies that the builders of the crannog had control of a large workforce and extensive timber resources, the effort involved being equal to that of constructing a strongly defended fort. Lagore has historical references to it being a royal site of the Brega, a distinction shared at a later period with Knowth. Garryduff is a small strongly defended fort with abundant evidence of jewellery making and a fine filigree gold bird ornament. Although this site has a fair number of vessels it does not have the known royal associations or large size found in sites such as Clogher or Dunadd. The number of vessels may be a product of the almost complete excavation of the site. In size and function Garryduff seems closer to Dinas Powys than Clogher, and although it may have been a centre, it was perhaps a minor one. Two other sites in the Cork area deserve mention as major sites. Garranes is a large triple-banked fort which has substantial quantities of Mediterranean amphorae and tableware. It was clearly a major centre for imports in the first half of the 6th century, but occupation seems to have halted not long after the introduction of E ware. There is some evidence that Garranes was succeeded by the similarly triple-banked fort of Ballycatteen sited much nearer the coast. Both sites have possible royal associations but Ballycatteen lacks any of the earlier Mediterranean imports, suggesting that it was not founded until the 7th century. The reason for the small number of E ware vessels at Ballycatteen may lie in the scale of excavation there, which covered about one-quarter of the interior. However, as the excavations did cover most of the area of black midden deposits identified in a series of trenches around the perimeter it seems unlikely that a large quantity of E ware was missed. Thus while Ballycatteen could have been the successor to Garranes as an import centre, it was probably not a major centre. Either Garryduff or an unknown site may have been the centre for distribution to the other sites in the Cork area.

Import site characteristics

This attempt to identify the major centres of redistribution illustrates some of the problems in defining high-status sites in terms of a set of characteristics. Any archaeological aspects of a site are subject to the usual losses of evidence due to erosion of the site, the extent and character of the excavation, the degree of preservation of artefacts, and lack of publication. Similarly the number of sites known from historical sources to be of royal status must be a small fraction of the original total, even in Ireland where these sources are the most comprehensive for this period. Table 18 lists all the Irish sites with the characteristics which might indicate their status and function. The features chosen include the size of enclosure, which should give some indication of the labour involved in construction. The overall area of the site is used rather than the area enclosed as the former seems more relevant to assessing the amount of labour involved. An Irish Law tract of the 7th–8th centuries, the *Críth Gablach*, lays down a set of requirements for the size of dwellings of different grades of society, which include a rampart and ditch for a king's fort (MacNeill 1923, 305). While these rules are probably idealised versions of reality, they do indicate that stronger defences were a characteristic of royal status. Direct literary reference to a site's royal status is rare and it is often difficult to identify positively sites mentioned in the Annals and other sources. Clogher seems to have been the royal seat of the Airgialla from the ?4th to 8th centuries (Warner 1988). Lagore is attested as the capital of the southern Brega from the 8th century, apparently jointly with Knowth from the 9th century (Byrne 1968; 1973, 87). Downpatrick is noted as the capital of the Dál Fiatach branch of the Ulaid (Byrne 1973, 108) before it moved to Duneight in the 9th century. Garranes has been tentatively equated with the *Raithliu* of the Uí Eachach branch of the Eóganacht kings of Munster (Ryan 1942).

Another possible characteristic of high-status sites is the presence of weapons. In most heroic societies weapons are the prerogative of the warrior classes, and Ireland seems to have been no exception. Swords in particular were only used by the highest grades of society, partly no doubt because of the difficulty of manufacture of good-quality blades. In fact weapons are rare on any settlement site of the period, but are found on three of the higher status sites in the list. Two of these, Lagore and Ballinderry no. 2, have swords, a feature shared with Dunadd amongst the British high-status sites of the period.

There is abundant evidence in the early Irish Law Tracts that gold and silver were to be associated with the highest grades of society. For example only a king, a senior church dignitary or an eminent person of the court could pledge an object of gold (Kelly 1988, 164; Etchingham and Swift 2004, 46), while the *Críth Gablach* notes that one of the attributes of a lord is a brooch of precious metal (Richey 1879, 323; MacNeill 1923, 297). It is also noticeable that craftsmen who worked gold and silver had a high status in society (Kelly 1988, 63). Table 18 shows that only the highest status sites have produced evidence of gold objects, with gold working at Clogher and Knowth. It may be that gold working has been overlooked in the past on some sites, as my own examination of crucibles has found unrecorded gold at Dinas Powys and Dumbarton Rock, but the correlation of gold and royal sites seems very clear. Silver in Ireland in the pre-Viking period is rather scarce (Ryan 1981), as it does not tend to survive well in acid soils, but may have been more widespread socially than has been believed in the past (Etchingham and Swift 2004, 47; cf Nieke 1993, 128).

Finally there is evidence for the production of decorative jewellery in the form of moulds and crucibles. Although there is no clear literary evidence for such activities being restricted to royal sites, there is evidence that goldsmiths in particular had a much higher position in society than other craftworkers (Kelly 1988, 63) and were associated with kings. The Welsh Laws of Hywel Dda and other sources also point to the special status of craftworkers (Gillies 1981, 76). Table 18 shows that the circumstantial evidence for such an association is high, but that monastic sites also took part in this production. The only possibly lower-status site with brooch moulds is Dooey, a site of unknown function and status.

Taking all these characteristics together it is possible to distinguish a group of sites with 'royal' characteristics. It can be seen from Table 18 that this group is restricted to forts and crannogs. Although not all of these sites have all the characteristics, the general principle of looking at a 'bundle' of attributes to define high-status sites seems to hold true. It can also be seen that these sites correspond to those with the higher quantities of imports, especially when the factors of distance from the sea and amount of excavation are taken into account. This correlation does not imply that all high-status sites will necessarily be import centres. Sites such as Moynagh Lough have all the characteristics of royal sites (and possible royal references) but only a few import vessels. Other sites of the period, such as Deer Park Farms, Antrim, have produced no imports at all. Quite clearly a number of factors other than availability would govern which sites became import centres. Two of these factors are the siting of harbours and the political control of resources by individual kingdoms. Before leaving the question of how to define high-status sites and import centres it should be noted that the characteristics discussed for the Irish sites seem to hold true for the sites in northern Britain and Wales (Tables 17 and 19).

Trading routes

Working from Admiralty pilots and charts Warner (1976, fig 3) illustrated the safe harbours of the pre-industrial era for Ireland. Combining this evidence with the tidal flow pattern and areas of treacherous water (from Davies 1946) it can be seen that any sea route from the continent to Ireland would be restricted by physical factors (Fig 77). The west coast of Ireland would probably be avoided altogether because of the lack of safe harbours and exposure to Atlantic gales. At this period navigation was mainly by landmarks and vessels preferred to keep within sight of land where possible. As will be discussed, Scilly would probably have been the setting-off point for all vessels intending to trade up the west coast of Britain and Ireland.

Figure 77 shows the suggested routes and possible stopping places. West of Cork and Kinsale any vessel would be heading into the prevailing winds. The preferred route would be up the east coast, taking advantage of the tidal flow but not stopping between Wexford and Dublin because of the lack of harbours. This may in part explain the lack of sites in Leinster. Occasional voyages may have taken the western

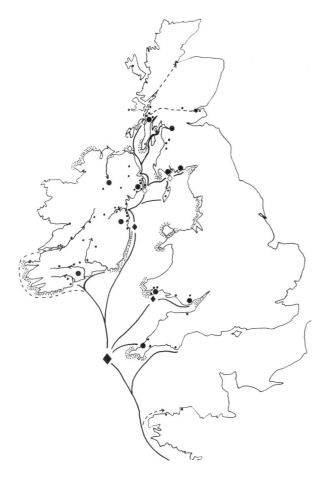

Fig 77 *Suggested trading routes for E ware, showing areas of dangerous water or lack of natural harbours stippled. Island trading settlements, solid diamonds; putative, open diamonds; primary import centres, large dots; secondary import sites, small dots*

route, and the excellent harbour at Valencia would have been a key stopover, close to the site of Caherlihillan. Rathgureen and Dooey are lonely outposts on the western coast. Between Dublin and Belfast there are a number of good harbours but from the distribution of finds it looks as if only Dublin Bay, the Boyne estuary and Strangford Lough were utilised. It is unlikely that foreign vessels would venture west of Rathlin Island which has severe tidal flows around it. This may explain the lack of sites associated with the good harbour of Lough Foyle and the lack of imports from sites such as Deer Park Farms which might be expected to have had imports because of its proximity to the coast. South of Rathlin is the obvious point to set out for Scotland as the Mull of Kintyre is visible here from Ireland, and the prevailing winds would enable vessels to make for western Argyll (and Dunadd) or for the Firth of Clyde (and Dumbarton).

What these maps imply is that only rulers whose area of influence extended to the coast between Cork and Wexford in the south, and Dublin and Belfast in the north, would have had easy access to Continental imports. These rulers could therefore control the flow of goods to inland kingdoms. The overall distribution of import sites and the siting of major centres would not conflict with this interpretation of the sea routes. Only Clogher stands out as anomalous in its inland situation, and the few sites in the west may represent stray vessels blown off course reaching the Shannon estuary. Alternatively these sites would have been supplied by exchange from kingdoms in the east.

If the overall distribution of sites in Ireland is due to the constraints of the realities of coastal trade in small sailing vessels, then this might explain a curious feature of the British distribution of E ware (Fig 34), namely that no sites are known between south Wales and southern Scotland. This may be because of the dangerous waters around Pembrokeshire, the Lleyn peninsula and Anglesey, coupled with the longer route around Cardigan Bay, the north Wales coast and north-western England. The shifting sands of the Cheshire and Lancashire coasts would also be forbidding, though the evidence that Meols was a longstanding trading centre suggests that there were political factors at work as well as geographic.

Irish political geography

Returning to the Irish situation, it is instructive to look at the distribution of sites in relation to the known political divisions of the period. We are fortunate that in Ireland the literary sources enable a fairly complete picture of the mosaic of small kingdoms and sub-kingdoms to be delimited. Recent scholarly work, particularly by Byrne (1973), enables the changing fortunes of the Irish dynasties to be charted. Although the boundaries of these kingdoms cannot be established precisely (and they may never have been very precise) the general area of each has been mapped by Byrne. If these maps are used as a base on which to plot the import distributions, some surprising results emerge. Firstly, imports are almost entirely lacking in two of the five ancient divisions of Ireland, Leinster (*Laigin*) and Connaught (*Connachta*). I have already suggested that the reasons for this are purely geographical but for Leinster the situation is compounded by a lack of excavation on sites of all periods. From the sea-route evidence, sites might be expected near Waterford and Wexford and the surrounding areas of south-western Leinster, and these may appear if excavations take place in this area.

Looking in detail at eastern and northern Ireland, it appears that the import sites are confined to particular dynastic groups within the ancient divisions of Ulster and Meath (*Mide*). In Ulster one concentration of sites lies within the territory of the Dál Fiatach, with its capital at Downpatrick, and its minor branch in the Ards peninsula (Fig 78). These sites are: Lough Faughan, Scrabo, Rathmullan, Langford Lodge, Ballyfounder, Spittal Ballee and

Patterns of distribution: import site characteristics 113

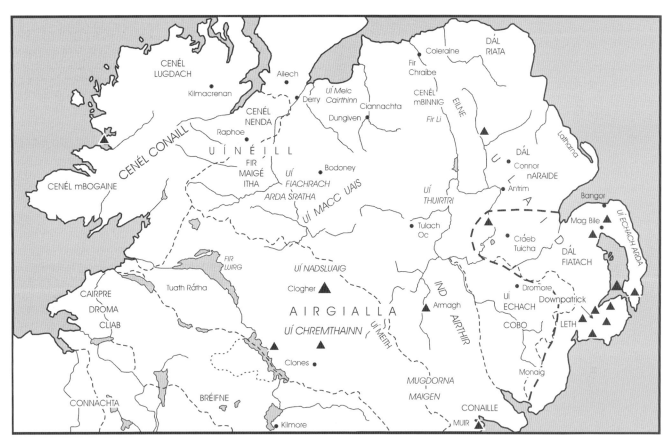

Fig 78 Political map of Ulster in the Early Historic period, with E ware sites

Downpatrick itself, along with Dunnyneill Islands. There is a notable lack of sites in the neighbouring Ulaid territory of the Dál nAraide despite the geographical similarity of the regions, the only possible site being Teeshan crannog which lies on the borders of Dál Riata, Eilne and Dál nAraide. Both regions have similar concentrations of raths, the commonest field monument of the period, and similar concentrations of sites with souterrain ware datable to the 8th to 12th centuries (Fig 79; Ryan 1973; Baillie 1986). It is therefore unlikely that the differences are due to differences of recovery of information. It might be argued that the work of the County Down Survey has led to over-representation of sites in the Dál Fiatach area, but only one of the import sites was excavated in the course of this survey, and much recent work in Antrim has failed to produce new E ware sites. Sites are also missing from the territory of the Dál Riata in northern Antrim and the Uí Echach Cobo in eastern County Down, both areas bordering on the coast and where import sites might be expected (Fig 78). The lack of sites in Dál Riata is especially notable given the quantities of imports in Scottish Dál Riata. Possibly also associated with the Dál Fiatach is the site at Upper Marshes, Co. Louth. There was a small subsidiary kingdom of the Dál Fiatach (*Muirthemne*) in just this area in the 7th century (Byrne 1973, 118). Politically, the Dál Fiatach were the dominant power in Ulster at the beginning of the 7th century (Ó Chróinín 1995, 48),

with their power centre at Downpatrick. They were also a noted seapower, attested by entries in the annals relating to seagoing activities, and this may have contributed to their control of the sea trade.

The other sites in Ulster fall within the territory of the Airgialla with its centre at Clogher: Armagh,

Fig 79 Ulster sites with souterrain ware (○) and E ware (●), showing political boundaries

Drumacritten and Lisdoo. It is interesting that Armagh fell under the control of the Airgialla (*ibid*, 82). The sites within the large Airgialla territory are confined to the southern portion. This may suggest that Clogher received its imports from the coast at Dundalk or Carlingford Lough rather than from the north at Lough Foyle where the sea is slightly closer. The northern part of the Airgialla territory fell under the control of the expanding Uí Néill dynasty by the 9th century. Imports are lacking from the Uí Néill territory despite its ultimately dominant position in the north.

Moving south to the area north of Dublin there is a concentration of sites within the kingdom of the Brega. The Brega came to be dominated by the Síl nAedo Sláine from the 7th century. This group had major centres at Lagore, *Raith Airthir* (Oristown) and Knowth. Nine sites lie within this territory: Lagore, Knowth, Moynagh Lough, Colp West, Gracedieu, Lusk, Smithstown, Loughshinny and Randalstown. These sites can be supposed to have been supplied from Dalkey Island which lies just outside the Brega on the boundary of *Laigin* and *Mide*. The concentration of sites in the Boyne valley suggests this was the route of supply to Knowth. Inland of the Brega there are three sites, Ballinderry no. 2, Clonmacnoise and Killucan. These sites lie within the territory of Clann Cholmáin whose notional capital was Uisneach. It is possible that the imports on these sites were the result of gifts from the Síl nAedo Sláine.

Irish historical context

These correlations between import distributions and tribal politics are extremely valuable evidence for political control of trade, but the Irish documentary evidence also gives some chronological perspective on the changing fortunes of individual kingdoms. It seems that those kingdoms which were expanding in the 7th century are precisely those which were involved in the importation of foreign luxury goods. Both the Dál Fiatach and Síl nAedo Sláine were expanding at this period according to Byrne (1973, 94, 119). Indeed the Síl nAedo Sláine came to exercise the position of 'mesne lords in the political hierarchy' (*ibid*, 94) and, as we have seen, the Dál Fiatach were the most important group in Ulster in the early 7th century with their kings being styled *rí Ulad* (kings of Ulster). These two examples enable us to construct a model for the function of imported goods in early medieval Ireland.

This model would see the imports as being used by rulers to bolster their status by controlling the supply and redistribution of luxuries to client chiefs and perhaps to neighbouring kingdoms. The kingdoms with coastal access (allowing for the constraints of geography discussed above) would be best placed to control this trade. Its mechanics could have been that Continental traders called at neutral, offshore sites such as Dalkey and Dunnyneill Islands, and resided there for some time while using their normal domestic pottery. Goods were exchanged with emissaries from the neighbouring kingdoms who took the imports back to the royal centres, such as Lagore and Downpatrick. At these centres some of the imports were used, with the pottery containers being reused for a variety of purposes. From these royal centres small quantities of the imports were redistributed to royal kin or clients who occupied settlements of lesser status, usually at some distance from the centre, in return for renders of surplus produce, which the ruler could use to exchange for the imports. This exchange probably took place at times of feasting. Gifts further afield to surrounding rulers may be a sign of political hegemony over these regions, as gifts imply reciprocal obligations. A model very similar to this has been proposed based on the evidence for Scottish Dál Riata (Nieke and Duncan 1988) and for the Mediterranean imports in the south-west (Thomas 1988b), but the Irish evidence presented above gives some historically attested substance to these archaeological models.

Social factors

The history of the Síl nAedo Sláine gives further insight into the possible function of imported goods in articulating power relationships. Byrne's work shows that throughout the early medieval period Ireland was a mosaic of small kingdoms and sub-kingdoms ruled by tribal chiefs. The fortunes of these dynasties fluctuated as kingdoms expanded, contracted, assimilated other kingdoms or disappeared, though a general tendency towards larger areas of hegemony becomes evident towards the period of the Norman conquest. Part of the reason for the fluctuations in fortune of particular dynasties was the Irish method of succession to the kingdom. This was based not on a father-to-son succession but to any member of the extended kin group of four generations (the *derbfine*) who had sufficient status. Consequently control of a kingdom could pass from one tribal group to another (sometimes switching between two groups alternately) meaning that any one group found it difficult to build a permanent power base.

The case of the Síl nAedo Sláine is instructive. In the 6th century the dynasty of Diarmait mac Cerbaill (544–565) was in danger of being excluded from the *derbfine* group associated with kingship. Yet the following century and a half saw this dynasty rise to become dominant in eastern Ireland. This happened at a period of some change in dynastic fortunes (Byrne 1973, 88). It seems possible that this dynasty latched on to the use of imported goods in order to bolster a social position which was under threat. It is possible that we are seeing here an illustration of Bourdieu's thesis of the existence of 'official kin' and 'practical kin' (Bourdieu 1977, 33–8). According to the idealised law codes the dynasty was about to be no longer 'official kin' of royalty, but it can be

Table 11 Pottery on early medieval sites in Ulster

Territory	Souterrain ware sites	E ware sites
Dál Fiatach	29	8
Dál nAraide	17	–
Dál Riata	14	–
Uí Echach Cobo	8	–
Eilne	2	?1
TOTAL	70	9

suggested that the control of imported goods was used to create 'practical kin' bound by practical obligation to the gift-giving dynasty.

There is no doubt that the establishment of stable dynasties was also encouraged by the Church. As has been pointed out for Saxon England (eg Hodges 1989, 46), the Church was involved in trying to alter social relations in order to alter patterns of inheritance to its own advantage. Similarly in Ireland there is evidence that clerics encouraged a model of dynastic kingship and power based on Old Testament exemplars which was at variance with the Celtic type of kingship. By offering spiritual legitimisation of this type of kingship the Church gained power and wealth in return. The gradual breakdown of the old kin-based social system meant that surplus production was diverted to the Church. It is at this period that kings began to change their role from dispensers of justice to that of law makers (Doherty 1980, 79). The *Muirbretha* or Sea Laws is an example of this new type of law, significantly in this case concerned with trade relations (*ibid*, 78–9). Subsequently, from the 8th century onwards, monasteries became independent centres of power and trade. However, in the 6th and 7th centuries there is no evidence that monasteries were trade centres. As already discussed, although a number of monastic sites do produce imports, these are only small quantities explicable as gifts from local rulers.

Discussion

The explanation of the import distributions offered above could be criticised in that it only discusses sites with imports and not other sites of the period. The apparent restriction of imports to certain areas would be stronger evidence if it could be shown that sites of equivalent status in the other areas did not have imports. Unfortunately it is normally the case that the import wares are the only means of securely attributing a site to the 6th or 7th century, so that a lack of these wares may be because the site was occupied outside this period rather than the imports not being available there. Nevertheless a few sites of the period, such as Deer Park Farms in Dál Riata, can be dated to this period by dendrochronology and do not have imports.

It has already been mentioned that sites with souterrain ware are found throughout Antrim and Down. There is no direct evidence that sites with this pottery (dating from the 8th to 12th centuries) were in existence in the 7th century but it is likely that many were. Of the eight sites in the Dál Fiatach region with 7th-century imports, at least five have souterrain ware in later occupation deposits, indicating a general continuity of use of sites. Using Ryan's (1973) data on sites with souterrain ware it is possible to compare the distribution of sites within Antrim and Down having imports and souterrain ware (Fig 79; Table 11). It is clear from this table that the apparent exclusion of imports from all territories except the Dál Fiatach is a genuine absence.

Two further points are of interest as far as Ireland is concerned. Irish archaeology is fortunate in that a distinctive type of monument, the rath, is characteristic of the early medieval period (Stout 1997). It has been estimated that there are some 45,000 raths in Ireland, with 1,300 recorded in Co. Down alone (Jope 1966, 108), and, although all may not have been in contemporary use, this gives some idea of the scale of population. The 50 or so sites in Ireland with imports contrasts markedly with this huge number of small farmsteads. Although it is much easier to recognise a rath than an import ware site there can be no doubt that there is a large discrepancy in numbers between the two categories. Each import ware site must have been supported by a large underclass of simple farmsteads, in a ratio numbering conservatively at tens or even hundreds to one. It is the surplus produce from these sites which would have enabled goods to be exchanged with Continental traders and which supported the upper classes of Celtic society and later the powerful monasteries. This underclass of small farmstead is almost archaeologically invisible in western Britain, leading to the unfair view that most sites of the period were of high status, and an inability to engage in a study of the development of settlement patterns in places such as Wales where place name evidence cannot be used (Edwards and Lane 1988, 2–3).

The Irish literary sources give us another type of site occupied in the 6th to 7th centuries, namely monasteries. Ó Chróinín has published a map of all monastic sites known from documentary sources to have been founded before 700 (Ó Chróinín 1995, 305; MacNiocaill 1972, 102). This shows a total of 60 sites, of which only two early sites, Clonmacnoise and Inishcealtra, and one later, Armagh, have produced any import ware. Admittedly, few of these sites have been extensively excavated, but it cannot be said that the evidence supports the view that the monasteries were the centres of importation (*contra* Hodges 1977). Part of the monastic interpretation of import centres rests on the *later* status of some monasteries as 'cities' with associated trading fairs or *oenach* (Doherty 1980, 81), an argument criticised by Valante (1998) and Swift (1998). Part also rests on Thomas's inclusion of Nendrum as a site producing E ware (eg Thomas 1981, 23). I am grateful to Richard Warner for confirming that no E ware exists in the Nendrum assemblage and that the 'red wares' mentioned in the original report are medieval (Jope 1966, 133, n 1). The belief in the existence of import wares from Nendrum was perhaps encouraged by a published drawing of Lawlor which shows a medieval vessel which bears a superficial resemblance to E ware (Lawlor 1925, fig 7). However, it is also true that some monastic sites have produced imports: Clonmacnoise, Armagh, Derrynaflan, Inishcealtra, Caherlihillan and Reask, but the quantity of sites, and imports on each, is small except for the unpublished Caherlihillan.

8.2 Scotland (Pls 44–52)

Imports are known from at least 21 sites in Scotland and a further two on the Isle of Man. Four sites, Craigs Quarry, Luce Sands Abercorn and Elie Links, reported by Thomas (1981, 21–2) are cases of confusion with Scottish medieval pottery. The Scottish sites are unusually interesting in that they are distributed between three peoples, the Scots, the Picts and the British (Table 19).

Scottish Dál Riata has nine sites: three forts (Dunadd, Dunollie, Little Dunagoil), two duns (Kildalloig, Ardifuir), two crannogs (Loch Glashan, Loch Ederline), one monastic site (Iona) and a sand dune site (Cruach Mhor). The finds from these sites are almost entirely of Continental origin, the only exception being one piece of ARS from Iona. Three of these sites have, unusually for Scotland, historical documentation for occupation in the 6th to 9th centuries. They include Dunadd, a 'nuclear' fort and probable royal centre of Dál Riata which has been recently re-excavated (Lane and Campbell 2000). This site has produced the largest collection of E ware of any site in Britain and Ireland with at least 25 vessels represented.

The seven sites in the British kingdoms comprise four forts (Dumbarton Rock, Mote of Mark, Castle Hill, Dundonald), two crannogs (Buiston, Lochlee), and one possibly enclosed trading/monastic site (Whithorn).

The five sites in Pictish areas are all from enclosed sites, but only a few sherds have been recovered from each. In the eastern Pictish region the three sites are large forts (Craig Phadrig, Clatchard Craig, Dundurn). One western site, Dun Ardtreck, is a dun probably in a Pictish area at this period, and the other (Birsay) an island settlement, possibly monastic.

The two Isle of Man sites are both small enclosures (Port y Candas, Kiondroghad). The Isle of Man seems to have switched between Irish and British control during the 6th to 7th centuries and the cultural affinities of the inhabitants are unclear (Byrne 1973, 109–12).

Even this brief survey of the Scottish evidence shows that there is a marked difference in the type of site with imports between Ireland and Scotland, with far fewer small enclosed sites in Scotland and more large forts. A possible inference would be that there was less distribution down the social scale in Scotland. Detailed on-site distributional evidence is available from a few Scottish sites, but most of these sites have only a few sherds. Only Loch Glashan provides important evidence of a total distribution on a crannog site. Dunadd and Whithorn will be discussed in some detail because of the importance of the assemblages and the sites.

Dunadd (Pl 44)

If Tintagel is the key site to understanding the Mediterranean phase of imports, then Dunadd fulfils a similar function for the later Continental phase. The outstanding volume and variety of artefacts from the older excavations have been supplemented by the picture gained from the modern excavations of the metal working area, and the environmental and scientific analyses of artefacts (Lane and Campbell 2000). Dunadd has produced the largest quantity of E ware from any Atlantic site despite being one of the furthest from the suggested source. The site is also of great importance politically, as a major power centre of the Gaelic kingdom of Dál Riata, the precursor of the medieval Kingdom of the Scots. It was also important as the site of inauguration of the kings of Dál Riata, with Dunadd as the centre of a richly symbolic landscape (Campbell 2003).

The metal working area of Site 3 (enclosure D) produced material showing the wide exchange contacts the site enjoyed. Material was present from the central valley and southern uplands of Scotland, Anglo-Saxon England, Ireland, south-west England, western France, and various Mediterranean sites. Materials used included gold, silver, copper, tin, and a variety of minerals, most of which are not available in the area. The workshop produced quantities of fine brooches, including large penannular brooches similar to the Hunterston Brooch. These were used as status symbols, and were one mechanism of social differentiation and elite control of resources (Nieke 1993). Much of the surplus wealth of the Dál Riata kings can be seen to have been invested in the production of these items, which were then gifted to noble clients to reinforce social ties of allegiance. Other imported material may have been kept for exclusive use by the kings, for example, the madder dyestuff, traces of which were found in several E ware vessels at Dunadd and Loch Glashan (Chapter 3.2). Red clothing was a prerogative of the sons of nobles and purple of the sons of kings according to the 8th-century Irish Laws (Kelly 2000, 263).

The site also illustrates the burgeoning symbiotic relationship between the Church and secular power centres. Orpiment, used for the yellow colour in illuminated manuscripts such as the *Book of Durrow* and the *Book of Kells*, was found at Dunadd, presumably en route for the major monastic centre of Iona where these two manuscripts were quite probably produced (Lane and Campbell 2000, 247). A stone disc inscribed 'INOMINE' came from the old excavations, showing someone literate could have been present on the site (*ibid*, 253), while the form of the cross-marked quern illustrates more contacts with Iona (Campbell 1988a). It is likely that the E ware from Iona also passed through Dunadd, like the orpiment a royal gift to the powerful monastery. The recent discovery of the leather book satchel from Loch Glashan may indicate further links with a literate community.

Within the good agricultural land in the immediate vicinity of Dunadd which provided the surplus to sustain the site, there is a cluster of sites which must be client settlements (Lane and Campbell 2000, illus 1.35). The crannog at Loch Glashan has produced evidence of being a craft working settlement, particularly dealing with leather working, but with links to Dunadd in the form of the E ware and access to precious materials such as a Mediterranean silver-in-glass bead (Crone and Campbell 2005, 71–2). It can be seen as one of number of specialist sites supplying goods to Dunadd, in this case leather goods, and perhaps dyed textiles, which would have been exchanged for imported material by the royal inhabitants of Dunadd.

Taking these aspects together, Dunadd can be used to create a model of how an import centre would have functioned as an articulation point between the Continental trading system and the developing local economy. Local surplus produce, given as tribute or renders from clients, was used by the rulers to exchange for exotic goods from the Continental merchants. Some of these luxury goods were used solely to bolster the king's position as controller of access to these items by restricting their use to defined groups (red dye for the nobles, pigments for the Church, glass vessels for his own retinue). Others were used to manufacture fine jewellery which in its turn was distributed as gifts to clients of various grades. We see here the start of a process of fusion of economic, political and ritual power in the hands of petty kings, a process which was to lead to the formation of the medieval state.

Whithorn (Pl 52)

Whithorn has the largest assemblage of glass from any Atlantic site, and is very important in understanding the nature of exchange with the Continent. Unlike Dunadd, and all the other supposed centres of importation, it appears to have been a religious site. We have already discussed Whithorn in terms of the importance of the stratigraphy (Chapter 7.6), but the nature of the site is also important. The excavator has little doubt that Whithorn was a monastic 'town' site, and has proposed that it had a concentric layout, with inner and outer zones, similar to some Irish sites (Hill 1997, illus 2.2–2.4). Whether the outer zone was under direct monastic control is difficult to say and the function of this part of the site remains unclear. Clearly some part of the site always had strong Christian associations, presumably including a church. The *Latinus* stone indicates this had been in existence probably as early as the 5th century. Craft activities were widespread, including gold, silver and copper working, mainly producing pins (*ibid*, 37). It is not clear whether these were intended for local use, or to be sold or exchanged elsewhere, as no specifically religious items were found. The quantities of fine imported glass vessels might seem excessive for such an ascetic environment and are not matched on other contemporary monastic sites such as Clonmacnoise or Portmahomack, both of which had extensive metal working areas. Another possibility is that it may have been a community of craftworkers and merchants around an important cult site with a regular fair (such as at St-Denis, Paris). It may therefore be best regarded as a trading site though, unusually, it is set inland, some 4km from the sea.

These two very different sites show that the Continental trading system articulated with the local population in a significantly different way from that of the earlier Mediterranean system as exemplified by Tintagel. The Continental import centres seem to be centres of production, have important ritual associations (with inauguration of kings at Dunadd), and increasing links to the Church (as at Whithorn). These features can be seen as part of the process of increasing centralisation and royal control which preceded state formation.

8.3 Wales and the Marches (Pls 53–4)

Wales is the area with the greatest overlap between the distributions of the Mediterranean (seven sites) and Continental (thirteen sites) imports, with both groups appearing together on five sites. The sixteen sites known to be occupied in this period in Wales are dominated by the high-status sites with imports (Table 17). These high-status sites are all newly defended or refurbished hillforts (Dinas Powys, Dinas Emrys, Deganwy, Hen Gastell, Coygan Camp, Carew Castle), except for the unenclosed Longbury Bank. Those forts which were refurbished (Dinas Emrys, Deganwy, Coygan Camp) all seem to have been occupied in the Late Roman period, and show signs of exceptional richness of finds which point to them being of high status at that period. There is a second rank of sites with fewer imports, probably receiving imports by redistribution from the major sites. These minor sites include the monastic sites of Llandough, Wenlock Priory, possibly Margam Abbey, and the church at Llanellen, as well as secular sites at Cefn Cwmwd, Lesser Garth and New Pieces. In the case of Lesser Garth, the E ware vessel (E128) has an unusual rim form which is paralleled exactly at Dinas Powys (E43), suggesting that it was supplied from Dinas Powys, the closest major import site. Caldey Island may be an offshore trading place protected by the monastery there, as the imports are not from the site of the monastery itself, and Linney Burrows may also be a coastal sand dune trading site. The difficulty of identifying Early Historic sites in Wales which do not have imports restricts the number of sites to those with radiocarbon dates or metalwork finds. There is also a scatter of stray finds of metalwork of the period not from occupation sites (Campbell 1991, illus 201). The distribution of these sites is generally restricted to the coastal areas of south and north Wales, with a scatter along the Marches. There is not a sufficient number of sites to enable a picture of settlement distributions within particular landscapes to be drawn. The more minor sites without imports tend to be small settlements of Romano-British origin (Pant-y-Saer, Cold Knap, Drim, Ty Mawr) or coastal sand sites (Kenfig, ?Goodwick) or caves with Romano-British occupation (Bacon Hole, Minchin Hole). Fuller details of these sites are given in Edwards and Lane (1988).

8.4 Somerset

Imported pottery is known from eight sites in this area, which is geographically linked to the south Wales area by the 'Severn Sea'. Indeed several of the sites are intervisible across the Bristol Channel. Three of the sites are reused Iron Age hillforts with possible Late Roman period occupation (Cadbury Castle, Cadbury Congresbury, Ham Hill); one is a newly occupied hilltop site, defensible but undefended (Glastonbury Tor); two are low-lying sites in the Somerset Levels (Glastonbury Mound, Athelney); one a sub-Roman cemetery with material derived perhaps from a nearby settlement or hillfort (Cannington cemetery); and one a suggested monastic site (Carhampton) (Table 17).

At Cadbury Congresbury and Cannington a direct link to sea-borne trade can be postulated due to the proximity to the Severn coast. The River Parrett afforded access to the interior of the Levels, at least as far as Langport near Athelney. Cannington hillfort commanded the entrance to this routeway, while Cadbury Congresbury commanded the River Yeo. Cadbury Congresbury is the major site in the area in terms of imports already recovered and those likely to remain on the site in unexcavated areas. Cannington hillfort is virtually unexcavated, though it may well have been occupied at this period (Rahtz et al 2000, 12, 424). However, the function of most of the Somerset sites is not clear. Cadbury Castle is a fortified site of abnormally large size and is obviously a site of the first rank in social terms. The presence of large amounts of imported pottery on this site, situated far from the sea, suggests that it had hegemony over the other Somerset sites, including Cadbury Congresbury and the Mendip metal mines, and that the inhabitants were able to afford the luxury of bringing heavy amphorae some 40km from the coast. The extent of this possible area of control is unclear but there are signs that it did not extend far beyond the bounds of Somerset. No imported pottery is known from areas north of Somerset, or indeed north of the west Wansdyke. Although it is difficult to argue from negative evidence, imports are not found on sites in this area which might have been occupied in the 6th century. These include the Roman cities of Bath and Cirencester, the hillfort of Crickley Hill and the temple site at Uley. These sites lie within the Bath-Cirencester-Gloucester area which may have been an independent political unit of the sub-Roman British political landscape. This is one possible interpretation of the *Anglo-Saxon Chronicle* reference in 577 to the battle of Dyrham where these three cities were claimed to have been gained as the result of a single battle. A similar patchy distribution of imports, governed by political control of territories, is more clearly demonstrated in Ireland (see Chapter 8.1).

If Cadbury Castle was the central place for much of modern Somerset, this suggests it was the major residence of one of the many rulers of small post-Roman kingdoms of western Britain. Cadbury Congresbury can then be seen as a combined trading/craft centre positioned close to the coast and handling the exchange of lead, silver and ?pewter to visiting Byzantine merchants. The other sites are of more problematical function. The lack of defences at Glastonbury Tor, the Mound and Carhampton could suggest monastic sites, but there is no positive evidence to support this. A class of weakly defended or undefended sites in defensible positions seems to be emerging from analysis of the import ware sites. Athelney may also belong to this class, but has later royal associations which may reflect earlier status (Hollinrake and Hollinrake forthcoming). The cemetery at Cannington seems likely to have served the population of Cannington hillfort, which may have been of similar status to Cadbury Congresbury.

Until recently it has been the case that there was no E ware from any of these import sites in Somerset, but the site of Carhampton has now produced E ware. The battles at Bradford-on-Avon in 627 and Penselwood in 658 mentioned in the *Anglo Saxon Chronicle* have been interpreted as signifying the extension of Saxon control to those areas of Somerset not already annexed after the battle of Dyrham in 577 (Rahtz 1988, 79). The period of the Saxon advance into or control over (not necessarily at the same period) the Somerset sites under discussion can be dated to the late 6th or 7th century. This does not conflict with the proposed date of E ware, and it is noticeable that Carhampton lies in the extreme west of the county which would have been the latest area to fall under Saxon control. Thus it could be suggested that it was Anglo-Saxon control over the area which caused the cessation of importation and consequent lack of E ware.

However, the date of the Saxon advance into Somerset is the subject of controversy (*ibid*). Burials with Anglo-Saxon grave goods from Camerton can be dated to the 7th century (Meaney 1964, 218; J

Hines pers comm), and an early 7th-century glass vessel from Pagans Hill, Chew Stoke (Rahtz and Watts 1989, 363), indicates that at least the northern part of Somerset and the Mendips was possibly in Saxon hands by this period. Further Saxon burials around Ilchester and Cadbury Castle (Rahtz 1982, fig 10.1), not to mention the 6th-century Germanic ring-buckle from Cadbury itself (Alcock 1995, 66–70, illus 5.1, 1), might be interpreted as showing that Saxon occupation of the area east of the Parrett was fairly widespread by the 7th century at least. However, the presence of Anglo-Saxon objects need not imply Anglo-Saxon political control, as this scatter of objects could be the result of trade or exchange (Campbell 1989b, 243–4; Rahtz and Watts 1989, 364), alliance or cultural hybridity (Bowles 2006). It could be argued that the battle of Dyrham represented a major victory for the Saxons which led to the collapse of the native British power centres throughout the south-west, without necessarily leading to immediate Saxon colonisation of the defeated areas. Although this is a possible scenario, the historical evidence is extremely meagre and we should be wary of putting too much emphasis on it, particularly as doubt has recently been cast on the interpretation of the relevant entry in the *Anglo-Saxon Chronicle* (Sims-Williams 1990, 23).

Finally, mention should be made here of the thesis proposed by Fowler (1971), that Roman material in hillforts in the south-west could be seen as an indication of post-Roman occupation. Burrow (1981, 150–1) cautiously supported this hypothesis, but his evidence from Cadbury Congresbury does not entirely support this view. The evidence presented in Chapter 6 on the pottery from Dinas Powys suggests that much of the Romano-British material could have been brought to these sites in the early medieval period, but only careful evaluation of the excavated material in its context could separate this process from contemporary Roman period deposition or the other models put forward by Burrow.

8.5 Cornwall and Devon

Cornwall and Devon have around 28 sites with imported pottery, mainly Mediterranean wares. As with Somerset, E ware sites are sparse, being confined to the southern coast of Devon, the coast of west Cornwall and particularly the Isles of Scilly (Table 16). Tintagel is the major site for imported Mediterranean pottery in Britain and Trethurgy is an almost unique example of a modern total excavation of an Early Historic site. These two sites will be discussed in detail, the rest in a more summary form.

Isles of Scilly

Taking all the Scilly finds together, they can be seen to be spread out over all the major islands, which were formerly part of one land mass. None are in defensive positions or are unequivocally religious sites, and nothing seems to distinguish them from the normal local Romano-British homestead. The concentration of sites, seven in an area of 8 by 5km, is far higher than any other area of Britain. Although a few Mediterranean imports are present, most of the wares are of Continental origin. This pottery occurs in substantial numbers of vessels. Both Samson, with twelve vessels, and Tean, with nine vessels, are only partial excavations on sites eroded by the encroaching sea and must have originally had more. May's Hill was fully excavated but four vessels from such a tiny structure is unusual. The other sites represent stray finds and it is impossible to estimate the original quantity of vessels. Taken as a group, the assemblage of 30 E ware vessels from Scilly is as large as the most productive site in the British Isles, Dunadd, and shares with such major sites a proportion of the rare forms other than E_1 and E_2. A further pointer to the nature of the Scilly assemblage is that most of the vessels show signs of being used as cooking vessels, a feature which is uncommon on E ware vessels in general (Table 3).

Clearly the circumstances of import and use of E ware in Scilly are different from those in most other western areas. Thomas, in his most recent discussion of Scilly, looks at the E ware distribution in terms of the introduction of Christianity to the islands, drawing parallels with the dedication of Cornish and Breton saints (Thomas 1985, figs 85, 87), and implying that both Tean and Samson are chapel sites. However, the detailed stratigraphy shows that the E ware from both sites occurs in pre-chapel phases, associated with domestic buildings (hearths, middens) (Campbell 1991, 145), as at the other sites.

An alternative explanation would see Scilly as an area where merchants from France resided for considerable periods of time, waiting for fair weather, local pilots or perhaps the arrival of British traders. The E ware sites could be seen as the temporary residences of these merchants, who utilised their own native pottery as cooking wares rather than as containers. This would account for the wide variety of wares found on the islands. However, as at least three of the E ware sites appear to have been occupied in the Roman period, it is perhaps more likely that these were native Scillonian sites and that the imported pottery was acquired (as pottery) from traders in return for provisions and possibly shelter. Sites such as Samson on the other hand may have been temporary camps of merchants. The plank-built hut suggests the use of imported timber, possibly ship's timbers. If this is the case it raises the possibility that other sites may have obtained E ware in a similar way. The immediately comparable site is Dalkey Island, but Caldey Island and Dunnyneil Island are possibly others. Such sites can hardly be called *emporia*, ports of trade or gateway communities (cf Hodges 1982, 67), although it is possible that such a site could have existed somewhere on

Scilly. They are on a much smaller scale than any *emporium*, their primary function being as service stations on the western sea routes, places where foreign goods might be exchanged but not necessarily having a primary function as trading places.

Tintagel (Pls 55–6)

Tintagel is the foremost site in Britain for the imported Mediterranean pottery, with quantities far in excess of any other site, and is therefore of key importance in understanding the nature of this trade. The site has been studied intensively in recent years and is currently undergoing excavation and a process of re-evaluation (Thomas 1988a; Nowakowski and Thomas 1990; Batey *et al* 1993; Harry and Morris 1997; Barrowman *et al* forthcoming). The site is situated on an isolated promontory joined by a narrow neck to the mainland. On the mainland side a large bank and ditch cut off this neck. Originally interpreted as a Celtic monastery by Ralegh Radford in the interim (*sic*) report on the site (Radford 1935), it has more recently been generally accepted as the fortified residence of a local ruler (Burrow 1973; Dark 1985; Thomas 1988a). More recently, Turner (2006, 58) has sought to restore a religious element to the site. Much of the imported pottery is effectively unstratified but is localised. However, recent excavations on the lower terraces have produced a clear sequence of deposits and small stone-walled structures dating from the Romano-British 4th century through to the 6th or even 7th centuries, with associated Mediterranean pottery (Harry and Morris 1997; Barrowman *et al* forthcoming). Other stratified deposits with imports have been found on the mainland in the churchyard of St Materiana, associated with cists and burial mounds (Nowakowski and Thomas 1990; 1992).

The pottery assemblage is huge, but is only a small fraction of what may be on the site. The fire in 1983 showed that pottery is scattered throughout the top and terraces of the island, and any small exposure on the site produces more imports. Mediterranean imports dominate, with the only Continental material consisting of a few DSPA vessels and a number of glass vessels. E ware is conspicuously absent, despite the presence of a few glass vessels which could be contemporary, and some radiocarbon dates which suggest some occupation into the 7th century (Harry and Morris 1997, 114, 120). Taken together this evidence suggests that the function of Tintagel changed with the cessation of the Mediterranean imports, and that it did not participate in the succeeding Continental trading system to any extent. The few DSPA and glass vessels from western France could have reached the site in the mid-6th century along with Mediterranean imports.

The distribution of the pottery from Radford's campaign is also of interest in giving some indication of foci of activity (Thomas and Thorpe 1988; Campbell 1991, illus 158–63). By far the largest concentration of vessels is in the Inner Ward of the medieval castle, where only small excavations have taken place. This sheltered area was clearly the site of a major focus of activity in the 6th century. Although quantities of LRA, PRS and ARS have been found in all areas of the island, north African amphorae (B*v*) are more or less confined to the Inner Ward area. There were other areas which were in use at this time. Site A, on the summit of the island, has a quantity of fineware sherds, many of which are fresh and unabraded. As discussed above (Chapter 7.1) this is only a selection of sherds, but does indicate use of the vessels on the summit. There would be no point in carrying midden material from the lower terraces up to this site. The lower terraces on Site C produced a fair amount of pottery, but not in the same quantities as at the Inner Ward or Steps area (Harry and Morris 1997, 122), and are noticeably lacking in finewares. Much of this could have fallen or been thrown down from the summit area above. The finds from around the burials in the churchyard are of a rather different character, and have been suggested to be the remains of funeral feasts (Nowakowski and Thomas 1990).

Apart from the quantities of imports, it is difficult to see any material remains connected with trading activities. Unlike other high-status sites, there is little sign of metal working or other craft activities on the site. Radford's material includes one crucible fragment, unlocalised and undiagnostic in shape. There is also a group of melted bronze fragments from Site Z, and a copper alloy sprue from the Steps area, but all of these could be of later medieval date. Stratified deposits have only produced minor iron working evidence (Harry and Morris 1997, 72–3), typical of that found on most sites of the period. It is possible that craft working took place in some so far unexcavated areas of the site, but the absence may well be genuine, raising questions about the nature of occupation. Environmental evidence also adds little to the picture. The lack of animal bone survival in the acid conditions leaves us with no idea how the site was provisioned. Charred cereal grains show that oats were an important part of the cereal assemblage, a feature noted at other contemporary sites such as Dunadd, but no exotic material was identified (Straker in Harry and Morris 1997, 99–101).

Despite the rocky nature of the coastline, there is no doubt that ships carrying amphorae landed at Tintagel, but the nature of the harbour (the Haven) appears to have been much altered by 19th-century slate quarrying activity (Thomas 1993, 37–43). The Iron Gate has been supposed to have been the Early Historic quay, having deep water beside it, but all rock-cut features here are believed to be modern. Recent diving exploration has not revealed any ancient works or wreckage. Access to the Haven would probably have required a local pilot, but there is little doubt that Byzantine vessels could have berthed in the Haven. Byzantine trading vessels were commonly less than 75 tonnes capacity, equivalent to about 1500 amphorae, though larger ships were built (Kingsley 2004, 85). Documentary evidence shows that ships up to 100 tons have berthed at the Haven in the recent past (Thomas 1993, fig 27).

Trethurgy

In contrast to Tintagel, Trethurgy is a small enclosure or 'round', a typical rural settlement of the Iron Age and Romano-British landscape of Cornwall, some of which survived into the Early Historic period before being replaced by unenclosed settlements (Preston-Jones and Rose 1986, 139–46). The full excavation and publication of the site (Quinell 2004) allow a unique opportunity to assess the evidence for continuing use of local ceramics from the Roman to post-Roman periods, and to assess the economic basis of a minor Mediterranean import site.

The round at Trethurgy enclosed a number of small structures which were repeatedly rebuilt and replaced over the six centuries of its occupation. By the period of the Mediterranean imports (Period 5, Stage 9) only one or two buildings were in use, one an oval stone-walled hut (House Z2), and the other an oval post-built structure (House A3). The import sherds were widely scattered throughout the interior, but there were concentrations in disused buildings which were used as temporary midden dumps (Structure U). As already discussed (Chapter 7.4), most of the sherds must have been removed from the site to surrounding fields. Although the excavator makes a strong case for continued use of local gabbroic wares in this period (*ibid*, 109–11), the data are not presented in a form which enable an assessment of the residuality of the gabbroic ware (*ibid*, table 5.2). Clearly, with the very large quantities of gabbroic ware on the site (over 6000 sherds), and continual rebuilding, a great deal of residual pottery would be expected in the late phases, a factor not fully considered by the excavator. Thus the claim that this pottery remained in production in the 5th/6th centuries remains unproven.

The economy of the site in the final phase of occupation is of great interest. A large tin ingot was found in midden material in the abandoned Structure U, dating to the late 4th century or later, and both silver and copper were also being worked (*ibid*, 74–6). Tin ore (cassiterite) was also found on the site in late phases, and a stone mould and mould cover (*ibid*, 142). From an earlier 4th-century context came a stone weight, a type paralleled at Gwithian (Quinell 1993), and presumably connected with trading activities. This evidence points to the production of tin as an important feature of the site. As Quinell points out, this must have been one of a substantial number of sites involved in tin streaming. The presence of Mediterranean imports on the site could then be explained in two ways. Firstly, the site could have had direct trading links with Mediterranean merchants, who supplied imports in return for small quantities of tin. Such an exchange could have taken place at a beach market such as that postulated at Bantham. More likely, the tin from Trethurgy and surrounding sites was taken to a central place such as Tintagel, presumably as a form of tax or render, where local potentates would have carried out any transactions with foreign merchants. Imports could then have returned to Trethurgy as gifts rather than as direct exchange for tin.

Other sites in Cornwall and Devon

Only a brief summary of the other sites with import wares in Cornwall and Devon can be given here. Most of these relate to the Mediterranean trade as very little E ware occurs in the south-west apart from Scilly. In fact only four sites, out of a total of eighteen with imports, have produced E ware. One of these is the residual sherd already mentioned from Trethurgy and the others are coastal sand dune sites. At Bantham a few E ware sherds have been found in midden material with large quantities of LR1 sherds, but no structures. The large quantity of amphorae has been interpreted as showing that it was the site of a beach market, and that other coastal sites such as Mothecombe may have functioned in the same way (Turner 2006, 74–5). At The Kelsies one E ware sherd came from another eroding midden, reportedly with LR1 sherds. The final site is Gwithian, the only one with a substantial number of sherds, from five vessels, associated with small stone-built huts. The stratigraphy of this site is discussed in detail elsewhere (Appendix 3). Other objects found include one piece of imported glass and various bronze objects (all unpublished), but there is no record of moulds or crucibles. The structures at Gwithian are reminiscent of those at May's Hill, Scilly.

All of the coastal sites except the Kelsies are in similar situations, in sand dunes overlooking tidal estuaries. All have been overwhelmed by sand in more recent times, but environmental work shows that in the past these areas were fertile grasslands (A Milles pers comm). It is difficult to see these sites as having any high status. It is possible that, as at sites on Scilly, small quantities of pottery were exchanged at harbour sites for provisions or minor trade. In this sense perhaps these could be trading places (cf Fox 1955). It is noticeable that all these sites have also produced Mediterranean pottery and that no new sites were established in the south-west in the period of E ware currency, unlike in Scotland or Ireland. It is possible that after the collapse of the major centres of the 6th century such as Tintagel, and associated sites such as Trethurgy, only a few coastal sites maintained any contact with traders, though on a reduced scale.

The other sites with Mediterranean imports alone can be discussed very briefly. Two of these are hillforts which could lay claim to be high-status sites. At High Peak, Devon, minor excavations showed that a small hillfort had been constructed in the post-Roman period. About 80 sherds of LR1 and LRA were recovered from small excavations, indicating that at least five vessels were present. Almost all of the site has been lost by erosion but this clearly could once have been a major site. Killibury is an Iron Age hillfort overlooking the head of the Camel estuary. Small-scale excavations produced a few sherds of LR2 from the interior at the base of ploughsoil. Again this is potentially a major site, emphasised by its position, which although 8km from the coast, is only 2km from the head of the tidal Camel estuary. The Camel was an important transpeninsular routeway in the early medieval period, as shown by the *Vita* of St Samson of Dol (Olson 1989, 13–17).

Chun Castle is an Iron Age stone-built hillfort reused in the post-Roman period. Although it overlooks the coast, there is no good harbour nearby. Signs of tin smelting were found associated with a few sherds of LR2. Although this is a large and impressive hillfort the secondary occupation does not seem to have been on a large scale and the site seems to be more similar to Trethurgy than Tintagel in scale.

Another site with similarities to Trethurgy is Grambla. This is a rectangular enclosure with large sub-rectangular or boat-shaped buildings. Occupation started in the 2nd century and continued into the 6th. Fragments of LR3 and PRS came from the area of Building 1. The site is some distance inland but only 2km from the head of the Helford estuary.

The remainder of the sites with stray finds are all from coastal locations. Some are associated with middens: St Michael's Mount, Perran Sands and possibly Padstow. The others are stray finds: St Michael Caerhays, Looe Island, Phillack church, Lydford and Mawgan Porth. The last two are residual finds on later sites and do not indicate contemporary occupation. Of these stray finds, Olson associates the Looe Island find with an early monastery (1989, 98–103). The finds from Perran are near another probable early monastery but not necessarily associated with it (*ibid*, 43). Those from Phillack church and St Michael's Mount are from the sites of medieval chapels which may be associated with early Celtic religious foundations, but the evidence is ambiguous (Turner 2006, 43).

8.6 Summary of Welsh and English sites

This brief survey of the south-western British sites illustrates a number of points about the context of imported pottery. Firstly, there is no direct relationship between early religious settlements and imported pottery as has been claimed in the past, though this does not rule out the possibility that cenobitic monasticism was introduced to Britain from the Mediterranean on the ships which carried the pottery (Thomas 1971, 22–7; 1976b, 251–2). Certainly both seem to appear around the beginning of the 6th century (Olson 1989, 105). On the other hand major monastic centres appear often to be sited close to possible major secular settlements, examples being Glastonbury Tor and Abbey; Dinas Powys and Llandough; Cadbury Congresbury and Congresbury; and Killibury and *Docco* (*ibid*, 14–16). Others are possible, such as Padstow Cove and Padstow (*ibid*, 48), reinforcing a picture already seen in Wales. However, Turner (2006, 58–9) has recently claimed that early monastic centres in Cornwall and Devon functioned as proto-urban centres, despite the lack of imports on known sites.

Secondly, as in Ireland and Scotland, the sites seem to be clearly ranked in terms of number of imports, size, defences and material culture. Large fortified sites, often reused Iron Age or Late Roman hillforts, have large quantities of imports, good defences requiring much labour to build and defend, and often have signs of aristocratic presence in terms of large halls, precious metals or jewellery making. It is noticeable that these latter features seem less evident in the sites with only Mediterranean imports. These sites are not necessarily coastal or near good harbours. They include Cadbury Castle and Tintagel. I interpret these as royal centres of local rulers. Related to these sites are those with similar or lesser quantities of imports, but smaller in size or with weak defences. Cadbury Congresbury and Glastonbury Tor fit this category and seem equivalent to the status of Dinas Powys. The artefacts on these sites also suggests aristocratic status, either of kings of small regions, or subsidiary royal centres, or subordinate princely or aristocratic sites within a larger kingdom. In the case of Dinas Powys there is some evidence that it was the seat of the kings of an unnamed small kingdom of the Cardiff region in the 7th century (Campbell 1991, 225; Davies 1978, 169–70; 1982, 93).

Below this category of sites are three groups of sites with fewer imports, no defences, and no signs of craft production or precious metals. In Cornwall one group, Trethurgy, Grambla and Chun Castle, are not coastal but may be associated with the collection of tin. This type of site may be peculiar to the circumstances of Cornwall. Another group consisting of unenclosed sites, usually with few imports, are found in mainly coastal locations, often near estuaries which would have provided safe anchorage, and in the Scilly Isles. These can be seen as trading sites of some kind, but without full excavation it is difficult to be sure of the scale of this activity. A third group consists of religious sites, not necessarily all monastic but including cemeteries, chapels and churches, such as Cannington cemetery, Looe Island and Phillack. It is possible that the wine from the amphorae found on these sites may have been used in communion services but this is clearly not a major element of the imported amphorae.

8.7 Summary of import site characteristics

This review of all the import sites has produced a number of significant results, with clear patterns emerging in the types of sites, their relative importance, their chronology and their regional distribution. With regard to the type of site producing imports, a limited number of classes can be recognised which I have styled forts, enclosures and unenclosed settlements, with stray finds probably belonging to the unenclosed settlement class. This classification is of course simplified, and ignores differences of scale between class members, but it does seem to coincide broadly with the other attributes listed in the tables of site characteristics (Tables 16–19).

In these tables *forts* are defined as enclosures where the bank(s) are of sufficient size to suggest a defensive function (though of course the purpose of these banks may have been for show rather than being purely functional). *Enclosures* are walled, ditched, banked or palisaded sites where the perimeter seems to delimit the extent of the settlement rather than being defensive. *Unenclosed* settlements are self-evident. A number of additional categories have been added to these basic divisions. *Monastic* sites are those with either documentary evidence of contemporary monasticism or clear archaeological evidence for such. A related subdivision is *cemeteries*, such as Cannington where monastic activity is possible but there is no evidence extant. *Crannogs* are a specific type of enclosure, protected by water, requiring considerable amounts of labour to construct. Some of these may be equivalent to forts but it is impossible to assess the amount of labour involved in their construction. *Duns* are stone-walled enclosures in Scotland which could be thought of as small forts. Indeed the Royal Commission makes an arbitrary division between forts and duns based on size, duns being classed as those enclosing less than 375m², though duns are usually sub-circular in shape. However, both the duns which do have imports appear to be Iron Age structures reoccupied in the Early Historic period, so that the original functions of these structures is perhaps irrelevant and they can be regarded as enclosures. There is also one *cave* site which again probably can be classed as an enclosure.

Although the classification outlined is simplified, it is striking to see the correspondence between forts and the sites with major import assemblages. In fact, apart from the sites in Scilly, almost all the sites with more than five vessels are forts, though the reverse is not true as several forts have only small quantities of imports. The tables also give the size of the enclosure, which I have defined as the maximum area of the site rather than the interior area. This measurement seems more likely to reflect the amount of effort put into the building of the defences than the usual measurement of the area enclosed. Thus Dinas Powys has a maximum area of *c* 5000m², as opposed to an internal enclosure of *c* 1800m², making it a more substantial fort than is commonly assumed. It seems clear from the tables that size in itself is not the determining factor as there is no direct correlation between number of imports and enclosure size. Forts range from the huge Ham Hill at 85ha, with two imports, to the tiny Mote of Mark at 0.04ha, with at least 32 imported vessels. The size factor is of course complicated by the fact that many of these forts have reused Iron Age or Late Roman defences which may not reflect contemporary resources. Another problem is that the larger the fort, normally the smaller the percentage of the area that has been excavated. These factors make a simple typological classification of settlement more appropriate than size to this type of analysis. One curious feature of these forts is that many are sited on small craggy hills with double summits (Campbell 2003, 55; cf Alcock 2003, 207). This can be seen at Dunadd (Pl 44), Dumbarton (Pl 48), Little Dunagoil (Pl 50), the Mote of Mark (Pl 51), Deganwy (Pl 53), Dinas Emrys, and Hen Gastell (Pl 54).

Following on from this typological analysis of the settlements is an attempt to construct a functional analysis of the sites in terms of their position in the import trade system. As with the size of settlements, the numbers of imported vessels cannot be taken directly as an indicator of status because of problems of partial excavation and recovery. I have therefore attempted in Tables 18 and 19 to assess how the amount and type of excavation would affect the original number of import vessels, and to classify the function of the sites accordingly. Again a simple classification is used: import *centres* are the primary locations for the arrival of imports; *secondary* sites are those which have received their imports from a primary centre; and *trading* sites are those where merchants may actually have resided for some time, or where exchange took place. The amount of excavation is arbitrarily divided into *Major* (more than 25% excavated); *Minor* (10–25% excavated); and *Trial* (less than 10% excavated). Other finds are *stray* and not from excavation, or *residual*, found in much later contexts than their production date.

Centres are defined as enclosed, usually fortified, sites which either have a large number of imported vessels, typically seven or more, or where further excavation might be expected to produce such amounts. Topographical situation and the known status of the site is also taken into account in these assessments. Some centres, such as Dunadd, seem to be quite clearly defined, but particularly in Ireland there seem to be some sites, such as Lagore, which have a fair number of imports but not large numbers. These differences may be regional, or due to the imperfect recovery of pottery, but it may be that with dual royal sites for one kingdom, such as occurs at Lagore and Knowth for the Brega, duplication of function led to a spreading of the valuable imports between sites. However, in general the correlation between import centre, fort and high-status site is remarkably good. *Secondary* sites are more clearly defined, almost always having only a few imports, with little possibility of more being present on the site. Possible *trading sites* are discussed below in connection with Dalkey Island and Scilly. Whithorn is another possible example of a trading site though its nature is still obscure. As already discussed, monastic sites in general seem to fall into the secondary category of importation but it is possible that Whithorn could be an exception.

Although some differentiation exists between sites which were involved in the earlier Mediterranean trade and those with the later Continental trade, this may be due to regional factors rather than chronological ones. In Cornwall and Devon only three out of eighteen sites are forts, and many of the secondary sites are unenclosed. Thus while Tintagel, the major early site of the region, has all the characteristics of the major centres associated with the later Continental trade, the gulf in apparent status between it and the lower tier of sites seems much greater than in other areas. This may reflect a local pattern of settlement which is less hierarchical than in other areas, as has been suggested for the 7th century onwards (Preston-Jones and Rose 1986). In those areas outside south-west England where the two distribution systems of imports overlap, sites with earlier imports usually also have later imports, and centres for the earlier system seem to continue for the later system This is the case at Dinas Powys, Longbury Bank and Garranes.

The sites producing imports in Cornwall and Devon are therefore somewhat different to those in other areas, but each major area has its own characteristic type of import site. In Wales and Somerset many of the sites have Late Roman period occupation, even if no continuity can be demonstrated between the Roman and Early Historic periods of use. This characteristic is shared by some of the sites in Cornwall and Devon, but is virtually absent from the Scottish and Irish sites. The Welsh sites are also distinctive in that several have a medieval masonry castle on the same site. In Ireland only one of the 50 sites has such a castle, in Scotland only three out of 20 sites, and in Cornwall and Devon two out of 28 sites. In Wales the figure is four out of sixteen sites, or five if Tenby is allowed for Longbury Bank. It is difficult to assess the meaning of these differences but the evidence suggests at least a continuing tradition of occupation on the Welsh sites. The siting of the seat of the Norman Lordship of Dinas Powys close to the Early Historic site, and presence of native Welsh castles at Dinas Emrys and Deganwy, both of which sites have medieval traditions of occupation by Early Historic figures, suggest deliberate use of the mythology of these sites in an attempt to legitimise later sovereignty.

In Ireland import sites are distinguished by their numbers, which are increasing at a rate of one per year. This may be due to the scale of excavation in Ireland and the ease of recognition of sites of the period. The small number of forts may be complemented by some of the larger crannogs, such as Lagore, which have known royal associations. It has been suggested above that the relatively high number of sites in Ireland is due to the visibility of early medieval settlements, which can be distinguished typologically from those of other periods. In Scotland the import sites are mainly forts but it has been argued that this is due to political factors, involving gift exchange between kingdoms, rather than the more normal type of redistribution within a kingdom (Campbell 1986a).

Despite the differences outlined above, the general pattern of types of site involved in the Continental import trade is sufficiently similar in all the areas studied to construct a model of trade and redistribution in the Atlantic West. This will be discussed in more detail below, but in essence it can be described as follows. Merchants from western France undertook trading voyages directed towards royal sites which were centres of power in the Atlantic areas. Trade took place at or near these centres, with Continental luxuries such as wine, honey, dyestuffs, spices and nuts being traded in exchange for surplus produce, perhaps leather goods, and probably slaves. The kings or princes of these sites used these luxuries directly in their royal strongholds, perhaps in feasting rituals, but also redistributed some of the goods by gift to lesser aristocrats. This process was used to articulate social relationships, enhance the standing of the ruler by his provision of luxuries, and to bind the receivers of these gifts in ties of mutual obligation to the ruler. Occasionally, as in Scotland, these luxuries may have been sent as diplomatic gifts to rulers in areas far from the western seaways such as Pictland. Actual trading settlements do not seem to have existed, but some island sites, such as Scilly, Dalkey Island and perhaps Dunnyneill, may have been used as safe havens for the traders, and could have been places of exchange (Fig 77).

The discussion of these centres of importation and the tables listing their characteristics show that they possess a set of attributes as a group which distinguishes them from other sites. All of these attributes may not be present at every site, but given the patchy nature of the archaeological record this is hardly surprising, and it can be assumed that the whole set of attributes were probably originally present at all of the sites. As a number of these sites in Scotland and Ireland are known to have royal associations it is reasonable to assume that the equivalent centres in Wales and south-west England were also royal even though the literary evidence does not survive to confirm this. It therefore seems reasonable to postulate that fortified settlements such as Dinas Powys and Tintagel were residences of royal personages in the 6th and 7th centuries.

9 Mechanisms of distribution

The previous three chapters have discussed in detail the taphonomy and function of the imported pottery, glass and other finds, and the nature of the early medieval sites on which they are found. In order to appreciate fully the significance of these finds, however, it is necessary to look at the overall pattern of trade and exchange systems of which they formed a part. It will then be possible to assess the relative significance of the imports and to gain some understanding of their function and status. This chapter will therefore be concerned with the changing patterns of importation and an attempt to provide some explanations.

The approach used in the following sections groups the various imports as part of a number of trading systems as identified in Chapters 2–5. Many previous discussions of the western pottery imports have been very general, grouping all imports together (Arnold 1984, 115–16; Bowman 1996), or have been divided up by the form of the vessel, such as red slipwares or amphorae (Thomas 1959; 1976b). This approach stems from a long-lived tradition of classifying archaeological artefacts by material. Thomas (1981, 3) has noted the difficulties of this system in relation to the imports, but did not implement the alternative system based on the areas of origin of the imports. It is this provenance approach which is used below to subdivide the imports. The justification is simply that wares from different areas are likely to have had different patterns of production and distribution, so it is necessary to look at each group separately.

9.1 The Late Roman background

In the later 4th century fine tablewares were imported to Britain from Continental sources: Mayen ware from the Rhine; Argonne ware from northern France; and *céramique à l'éponge* from western France (Fulford 1977; 1978). The distribution of these wares is concentrated in south-eastern England (Fig 80), though *céramique à l'éponge* is found in Exeter and around the Severn estuary. These distributions reflect the proximity of these areas to the Continental sources, and the relative prosperity of southern England in the latest Roman period. In addition there are a number of African Red Slipware vessels from Roman contexts (Bird 1977), and Late Roman amphorae from the Mediterranean (Tyers 1996). The date of the imports cannot be precisely defined, but it is possible to detect a stratum of late 4th- to early 5th-century wares. This stratum is made up of Argonne ware forms datable to the 5th century (Hübener 1968), African Red Slipware of similar date (from Bird 1977) and Mediterranean Late Roman amphorae (Peacock and Williams 1986; Tyers 1996).

In particular, amphorae are increasingly being found in the latest occupation layers of Roman urban sites. In London at the Billingsgate site there is a Palestinian amphora dated to post-400 but before a mid-5th-century brooch (Marsden 1980, 180–1) and at Bush Lane north African amphorae were found in a late 4th- to early 5th-century midden with sub-Roman pottery (*ibid*, 184). In Gloucester at the New Market Hall site north African and Palestinian amphorae were found in an early 5th-century context and also in 5th-century dark earths (Hassall and Rhodes 1974, 11). At York there was a quantity of amphorae in the latest contexts (Peacock and Williams 1986, 28). At Exeter again the combination of north African and Palestinian amphorae were found in late 4th-century dark earths, along with quantities of *céramique à l'éponge* (Bidwell 1979, 188). These contexts are all notably urban in

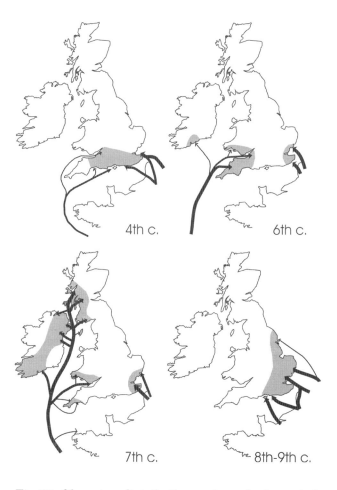

Fig 80 Changing distribution systems for imported pottery

contrast to the distribution of imported tablewares. There seems to have been an increase in the amount of Mediterranean imports towards the end of Roman urban life. Distributions show that these amphorae reached Britain by the Rhine/Rhone route (Tyers 1996, 2.15), as with the earlier amphorae (Fulford 1977). There are signs of a shift westwards in the distribution of imports at the end of the Roman period with Exeter, Gloucester, Cirencester and Chester all receiving late imports. A general increase in prosperity in the west can be seen in the deposition of many late coin hoards in areas such as Cornwall which had earlier used little coinage (Thomas 1976a). This prosperity may have been connected with an increase in the exploitation of tin and the manufacture of pewter in the late 3rd and 4th centuries. The contents of these amphorae are likely to have been oil and wine. It seems unlikely that any tablewares accompanied these amphorae as none has been found in associated contexts. It should be noted that the LR1 claimed by Dark at Gloucester and York (2000, 106, 199) appear to be phantom, possibly caused by confusion with other types of amphorae (cf Tyers 1996; Heighway 1984, 229; R Hall pers comm). Heighway refers to some sherds 'which have been identified as of Bii' from Gloucester, referencing Hurst (1976, 80), and others from St Oswald's Priory, but Hurst mentions only one possible sherd from St Oswald's and none from elsewhere. The primary source appears to be Peacock's report on the amphorae from the Roman tilery excavations at St Oswald's, but this does not specify the type as other than eastern Mediterranean (in Heighway and Parker 1972, 49, fig 10, 48). LR3, Palestinian and north African amphorae *are* found in these urban Late Roman contexts, but these are forms which can be dated to the late 4th/early 5th century, unlike the LR1, LR2 and LR3 found on Atlantic sites which belong to the late 5th/early 6th centuries. The actual end date of these Roman period imports cannot be assessed on typological or stratigraphic grounds, but the imports seem unlikely to have survived the collapse in Roman tax, monetary and ideological systems in the early 5th century (Esmonde Cleary 2000; Faulkner 2004). This is particularly so because there are no examples of Atlantic sites which have produced both Late Roman and Early Historic Mediterranean imports.

Another aspect of Late Roman trade relevant to the Atlantic areas is the evidence for trade between Britain and Ireland (Fig 81). This map shows all Late Roman objects from Ireland using information from Bateson (1973, 1976), Bourke (1994) and unpublished information from Richard Warner, myself and other sources. There is a clear concentration in eastern central Ireland and possibly a northern focus in Ulster. This pattern, and the British origin of some of the goods, shows that importation probably took place from England rather than the Continent. The lack of Late Roman pottery imports in the south of Ireland is particularly marked when compared with the distribution of the later imports. Some Irish archaeologists see these Late Roman

Fig 81 Late Roman material from Ireland (after Bateson 1973 and 1976 with additions). Coins ●; other objects ▲. Gold and silver: solid symbols

imports as the result of Irish raiding as described by St Patrick (Dolley 1976), but the use of neutral offshore sites such as Dalkey Island, and the deposition of objects at the ritual site of Newgrange, suggest a more bilateral exchange process.

All these Roman imports can be seen as part of the Late Roman imperial economy, closely associated with the administration of the Empire, rather than a true market economy, which could not survive the collapse of the Empire.

9.2 The Mediterranean trading system

Any discussion of the Mediterranean imports has to take place against the background of trade in the western Mediterranean at this time, so that we can see similarities and differences with the Atlantic trade. Fortunately, the results of many excavations have been admirably synthesised by Reynolds (1995) who has been able to present a detailed summary of trading patterns based on pottery studies. As discussed in Chapter 2, the Mediterranean imports fall into two sub-groups, an earlier one with a provenance in the north-eastern Mediterranean, and a later one with a provenance in north Africa, around modern Tunisia. However, there are good grounds for considering these to be part of one trading system and they will be discussed together here. A very small component of glassware (Group A) accompanied these pottery vessels. As we have seen (Chapter 2.5), the distribution of the north-eastern Mediterranean wares on Atlantic sites shows that they arrived as part of a 'package' of wares which were imported in a restricted period from c AD 475–550. Four types of post-Roman pottery found in Atlantic Britain are now known to have been manufactured in the Aegean or the north-eastern Mediterranean region: PRS tableware, and LR1, LR2 and LR3 amphorae (Fig 16). These four identified wares make up 71% of all the Atlantic Mediterranean imports, showing the importance of this trading system. In the western Mediterranean these wares are also often found in association with each other, but also with wares from the south-eastern Mediterranean, namely LR4–LR7, which are almost entirely missing from Atlantic sites (Reynolds 1995, 80). This 'package' of exported eastern Mediterranean wares was also recognised by Riley *et al* (1989, 151) as a feature of western Mediterranean sites. The north-eastern package of wares was supplemented by, or more probably replaced by, a package of wares from Tunisia for a short period around 525–550. This new package contained ARS tableware and B*v* north African cylindrical amphorae.

The lack of Gaza and Palestinian amphorae is not the only difference between the western Mediterranean and the Atlantic sites. LR2 is normally rare in western Mediterranean sites, accounting for a maximum of 7% of amphorae, but it forms 37% of the identified amphorae on Atlantic sites. The low proportion of ARS to PRS is also striking, and very different from the normal situation in the western Mediterranean where ARS dominates (Fulford 1989; Reynolds 1995, 135). The lack of Cypriot Red Slipware (LRD) is another important difference, as this is often found alongside PRS on western Mediterranean sites (Reynolds 1995, 36). The actual quantities of PRS found in Britain, measured by minimum number of vessels, are comparable with those on sites in Spain, despite their being much further from the source area. Finally, the date range of the Atlantic imports is more restricted than in the Mediterranean, where LR1 ranges from c 425–600, and LR2/PRS from c 450–600. These five factors immediately show that there is something peculiar about the Atlantic trading system, and that explanations for its existence must differ from those used to account for the western Mediterranean distribution, which can be explained by normal commercial activities involving the transport of commodities such as foodstuffs.

The questions which we might legitimately ask could include:

- by what route did the Mediterranean wares reach Britain, and was this direct or indirect?
- what ships were involved?
- what cargoes did the imports represent?
- what was traded in return?
- what was the scale of the trade?
- who carried out the trade?
- and what was the purpose of the trade?

Few of these questions can be answered directly, and they have been the subject of much debate.

Recent work on Mediterranean trading patterns revealed by ceramic studies (Keay 1984; Fulford and Peacock 1984; Reynolds 1995), shipping (Parker 1992; Kingsley 2004), other trading activities (Kingsley and Decker 2001b) and historical documentation for trade and traders (McCormick 2001), place these discussions on a much surer footing than previously.

Trading routes

The question of the route followed by the Mediterranean traders is perhaps the easiest of these to answer. Almost all recent commentators accept that the sea route through the Straits of Gibraltar was utilised (Campbell 1996a; Reynolds 1995, 135; Fulford 1989; Wooding 1996b, 51; Thomas 1988b, 13), and the distribution of PRS shows this clearly (Fig 6). Lone voices against this interpretation have been Story (1999, 425), following Bowman (1996, 101), who argue that the lack of western Iberian ceramics in the Atlantic assemblages must mean that the Narbonne/Carcasson Gap was used as an overland transport route from the south coast of France. Apart from the consensus by those specialists familiar with Mediterranean pottery distributions, this argument is refuted by the work of James (1977, 223–37) who showed that this overland routeway was closed at this period. If that route had been used, and if Bowman's argument was accepted, one would have expected the local southern French 5th-/6th-century pottery (DSPP and DSPL) to have been present in the Atlantic assemblages, which it is not. In any case the economics of overland transport of amphorae, which was up to 20 times as expensive as sea travel (Kingsley 2004, 36), effectively ruled out overland transport except for military purposes, or for high-value goods.

Within the Mediterranean, the sailing routes between east and west have been elucidated by Reynolds (1995, 135, fig 174) based on pottery distributions. This work shows that the main route from the north-eastern Mediterranean passed north of Crete and south of Sicily, then branched either to Carthage or southern Spain (Alicante), north-eastern Spain and southern France. Reynolds suggests that the detailed composition of the Atlantic assemblages, and in particular the lack of various eastern wares such as Bailey's lamp Q3339 and Fulford's Aegean casserole 35, shows direct contact with Britain, not stopping at Carthage or southern Spain (*ibid*). This conclusion applies to the north-eastern Mediterranean phase only, and has to be slightly modified in the light of the late north African phase identified above (Chapter 2.5). It appears that a stopover was made at Carthage in this late phase, or, perhaps more likely in view of the lack of late forms of PRS in the Tintagel assemblage, some late voyages originated there. The significance of this in terms of the motivation for the Atlantic trade is discussed below.

It is clear that the imports came by sea to Britain,

but was this by direct sailings, or a series of cabotage or tramping voyages, or a mixture of the two? There are strong arguments against a tramping model of distribution, and in favour of a direct sailing for at least the majority of the journey. The internal coherence of the 'Aegean' package, and the lack of LR4–LR7 amphorae and LRD tableware, shows a single restricted provenance for the cargoes reaching Britain, as does the lack of other amphora types which are commonly found on western Mediterranean sites. This suggests that the Byzantine trade was directed towards an Atlantic destination, and that though the vessels may have stopped and resupplied at intermediate ports, they did not trade during these stops. Recently, Cunliffe (2001, 479) has suggested that the Byzantine vessels may have offloaded their cargoes in Portugal, and that local vessels more suited to the rigours of Atlantic travel continued the voyages to south-west Britain. One argument in favour of this 'two-stage' voyage is the lack of evidence for Byzantine shipwrecks in British waters despite intensive diving exploration in these waters (S Kingsley pers comm). Byzantine anchors are of a distinctive cruciform shape (Kingsley 2004, 81–3) and would be recognised if they were found. This argument is suspect, however, as it is equally true that only one possible Roman anchor has been found in Atlantic waters, and that probably of 2nd-/1st-century BC date (Cunliffe 2001, 421, illus 9.39), despite the huge volume of Roman ship movements which must have taken place in these waters in the four centuries of Roman occupation. It is also difficult to see why such offloaded cargoes would be taken on to Britain, rather than distributed in Portugal. The proposal would only make sense if the Byzantine merchants continued on to Britain in the newly chartered vessels. As far as I know, there are no recorded examples of merchants and their cargoes changing ships in this manner. It is, however, possible that cargoes could have been offloaded at the Scilly Isles, or, alternatively, local pilots taken on board there. It is certainly true that the restricted harbour at Tintagel Haven (Thomas 1993, 37–43) would be difficult for a foreigner to find and negotiate safely without local support.

How long would a voyage from the eastern Mediterranean have taken? The return distance is in the order of 10,000km. We have contemporary accounts of the duration of shorter voyages (McCormick 2001; Kingsley 2004, 37) which show that the voyage could have been carried out in a couple of months in favourable conditions, making it possible to complete the return voyage in one sailing season, which normally lasted from April to October (Bowman 1996, 101). The suggested routes lie close to land, enabling frequent stops for supplies, so the voyages, although direct, would not have been non-stop.

Ships

This discussion has raised the question of the size and type of vessels likely to have made these voyages from the eastern Mediterranean. There is no way of assessing this from the archaeological evidence in Britain, but the study of Mediterranean wrecks shows the range of vessels which were in use at this time (Parker 1992). Most were fairly small, measuring up to 20m in length and carrying less than 75 tonnes (equivalent to about 1500 amphorae) (Kingsley 2004, 81–5). Larger vessels are known from literary sources, but whether they would have been suitable for Atlantic travel is unknown. The *Life of John the Almsgiver* mentions two types of ship trading from Alexandria in the 6th century, the *dromos* (runner), one of which traded with Gaul, and the *dorkona* (gazelle), one of which was reputed to have sailed to Britain and could carry 20,000 *modii* of grain, about 140 tonnes (Mango 2001, 96–9). The best known ship of the period is the 7th-century Yassi Ada B wreck (Bass and van Doorninck 1982), which carried a cargo of amphorae, mainly LR2, with lesser amounts of LR1, and a few LR3 and PRS dishes probably used by the crew. This cargo is of interest because it consists of the same package of types as found in Britain. Recent re-evaluation of the amphorae has suggested the cargo was owned by the Church and probably intended for supplying Byzantine troops on the Danubian frontier (Karagiorgou 2001). However, although most wrecked ships of the 5th–7th century were transporting cargoes consisting mainly of amphorae, the St Gervais B wreck was transporting mainly grain, with a small number of amphorae containing pitch, and other wrecks carried marble, millstones and metalware (Parker 1992). Documentary sources suggest that both low-value commodities and much higher-value cargoes were transported. Higher-value goods included silver, metalware, dried goods, textiles and medicines (Mango 2001, 98). The value of these cargoes was reputed to be very great, in one case over 200 pounds of gold. This type of cargo is not well represented in wrecks. Thus while a ship sailing to Britain could have carried mainly amphorae, it could also have had a mixture of other goods as well.

Cargoes

The nature of the possible cargoes carried can be approached in two ways – by looking at the contents of the amphorae found on Atlantic sites, and by studying the documentary evidence. Until recently it was thought that each type of amphora was designed to carry a specific product, so that, for example, LR2 held olive oil. As we have seen in Chapter 2.3, the picture is now believed to be more complicated. If form alone is not a guide to contents, only chemical analysis can confirm what cargoes were being brought to Britain. Unfortunately little work has been done on Atlantic amphorae. A preliminary study of some Tintagel amphorae has shown the presence of olive oil in some LR2 and B*v* north African amphorae, but also another unidentified commodity in LR2 (Jones in Barrowman *et al* forthcoming). There were no signs of tartaric acid which might indicate wine. What this does make clear is that wine was not the only commodity which the British received, contrary perhaps to the *topos* of the heroic feasting hall, or its supposed use for communion wine. Documentary sources show that amphorae held low-value contents (Mango 2001, 99), and it has been suggested that this would have made these voyages to Britain unprofitable. However, as Harris (2003, 54) points out, large profits would result from the exchange of goods which were of low-value in the eastern Mediterranean, but unobtainable in the Atlantic west, for goods which were readily available in the west.

A related question is whether amphorae and their contents were the main cargo carried. As we have seen, documentary evidence shows that both low-value foodstuffs and a variety of high-value goods were carried in the Mediterranean. However, there would be little point in sending high-value goods to the west unless they could be profitably traded, and low-value goods such as exotic oils and wine would give a much higher profit margin. The evidence of wrecks suggests that amphorae and grain were the main cargoes within the Mediterranean, but the special nature of the Atlantic trade means we cannot assume the same applied in the vessels which traded with the west. We could, however, envisage a mixed cargo consisting mainly of amphorae, but with some higher-value items intended either as gifts to those controlling the trade, or for exchange. Such items could include silks, books, 'dried goods' such as pepper or medicines, and other exotica (Mango 2001, 98). Whether or not silver and copper-alloy metalware were involved is unclear. Certainly none of these high-value goods has been recovered in the Atlantic West, and Harris (2003, 64–72) shows that the known silks and metalware from archaeological contexts in eastern Britain and north-eastern Europe were brought by another route entirely, via the Rhone and Rhine. The lack of grave goods in the Christianised west makes it unlikely that these types of goods would survive in the archaeological record, even if they had been imported.

The next question which has to be addressed is the nature of any exported goods exchanged for the imports. There is no archaeological evidence for any British goods being transported to the Mediterranean, with the exception of some reported British lead in Carthage (Farquhar and Vitali 1989), although this could have been recycled from earlier Roman imports. Slaves have often been mentioned as one possible export, and there is evidence that the slave trade was extremely profitable (McCormick 2001, 752–9). If later, 8th-/9th-century values, are anything to go by, slaves could have been worth about a pound of silver each, compared to the 70 *solidi* estimated for the value of the entire amphora cargo of the Yassi Ada B ship. These prices would have made transport of more than roughly ten slaves per ship very profitable. Cargoes of 63 and 221 slaves are mentioned in 9th-century sources (*ibid*, 759), and a *dorkona* could easily have carried at least 30 in its hold. Provisions, even on a long voyage, would have been cheap (Bass and van Doorninck 1982, 315) and not materially affected the profitability of the voyage. There is no doubt that a Byzantine ship could carry enough slaves to make the voyage to Britain very profitable. We do know that slaves from Britain were reaching Mediterranean markets from the 6th century, though Frankish, and later Slav, sources were more important (McCormick 2001, 738–9). It seems unlikely that a need for slaves drove Byzantine merchants to make the long voyage to Britain, when they were available from nearer sources, but slaves could have been a welcome additional part of a return cargo. Other organic materials have been suggested as Atlantic exports, including leatherware and sealskin, furs (of otters, martens, mountain hares), and eiderdown (Alcock 2003, 91).

The other commodity which has been put forward as a British export is tin (Campbell 1996a). The reasons for suggesting this lie in the close correspondence between the import sites and tin and other metal extraction areas in Britain (Fig 82). There is undoubted evidence that tin was being produced in Cornwall at this period (Penhallurick 1986, 212, 234), and ingots have been found on sites with imports, such as Chun (Thomas 1956a, 275) and Trethurgy (Quinnel 2004, 73). A cargo of tin ingots from a wrecked vessel has been recovered from near Mothecombe and Bantham, major import sites (Fox 1995), and others from Praa sands have been dated to this period (Biek 1994).

It is not just the association with tin which is important, but the scarcity of other supplies of tin at this period. Tin is a scarce metal in world terms, and there are few sources which are known to have been in production in the 6th century. Indeed tin is referred to in Egyptian 7th-century sources as the 'British metal' (Penhallurick 1986, 237). An examination of the sources of tin which were available in the 5th and 6th centuries shows that Cornwall and Brittany were the closest to the eastern Empire (*ibid* 1986), as the mines in Spain appear to have gone out of production in the 3rd century. Although small amounts of tin have been claimed to occur in Italy, Egypt and Asia Minor, it is important to stress that none of these have any substantiated evidence of tin *production* at this period. Only in Brittany is there the possibility of production shown by Merovingian coins in mine workings (Champaud 1957; Fleuriot and Giot 1977, 114). There is a contemporary caravan tariff list inscription from Anazarbus in Asia Minor which mentions tin amongst other commodities (Mango 2001, 104, n 67), and may suggest production there, though it could refer to transport of foreign tin. Archaeological evidence for tin production in this area has been claimed, but the evidence is far from clear or convincing. In any case, it is clear that tin was scarce in the Byzantine Empire. Low-value Byzantine coinage is reported as

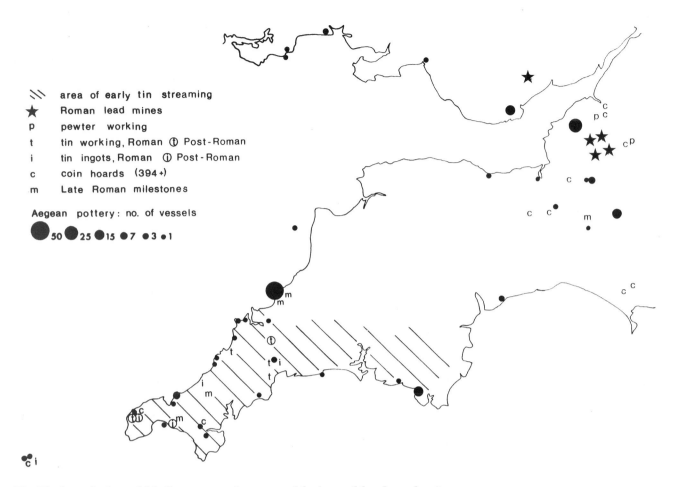

Fig 82 Association of Mediterranean imports with tin and lead production

ceasing to have any tin content after the reforms of Anastius in 498, with some brass used in the 6th century (Grierson 1982, 15). These reforms resulted in the introduction of a new low-value coinage, and millions of coins must have been struck and distributed. Interestingly, the weight of the new 'copper' coins increased to a maximum under Justinian in the period 539–42, thereafter decreasing. There would therefore have been an increasing demand for copper by the *procuratores monetarum,* who were the officials in charge of mints, throughout the first half of the 6th century.

Hammered copper sheet-metal vessels also become important at this period, with more expensive cast copper-tin alloy vessels being exported (Mango 2001, 93). There also seems to have been an upsurge in the volume of production of metalware for export in the 6th and 7th centuries (*ibid*, 89–95). Other sources note the stripping of Rome's metal statues and roofs by the Byzantine Empire, the break up of the Colossus of Rhodes, and scientific evidence for a decline in metal production (Kingsley 2004, 28). These are all signs of scarcity of supply, as are the low tin values in the analyses of cast metalwork of the period (Oddy and Craddock 1983). If there were tin mines in Asia Minor, they did not have sufficient output to meet demands, and Britain was the nearest alternative source. Who in the Byzantine Empire might have wished for tin, and for what purposes, is discussed below. Tin, however, would have been suitable ballast for a vessel, leaving plenty of room for additional goods, such as slaves, or other organic products like honey, furs or leather goods. It is also possible that other metals were exported at the same time. The association of Mediterranean imports not just with tin-producing areas, but also with areas of important Roman lead/silver mining in the Mendips and south Wales (Tyler 1982), and prehistoric copper mining in Ireland, is noticeable (Fig 82). These metals could have been useful adjuncts to tin in return cargoes, given the upsurge in demand for metals which seems to have occurred in the 6th-century eastern Empire.

Scale of trade

The scale of this trading activity is difficult to assess, and has been the subject of much discussion concerning questions of quantification of pottery assemblages, and how this might relate to the number of voyages undertaken (Thomas 1988b; Alcock and Alcock 1990, 119–39; Wooding 1996b, 48–50). Some of this discussion, based on the original Yassi Ada report, has been superseded by the new analysis of the amphorae from the wreck (Karagiorgou 2001). In this present study the quantification method used is MNV, whereas many Mediterranean assemblages are quantified by sherd count or weight. As amphorae pose their own problems of quantification, I have used the numbers of PRS finewares as a measure which enables comparison between the Atlantic and Mediterranean sites. The distribution map shows similar quantities in Britain and in southern Spain (Fig 6). While arguments could be made that different excavation or recovery strategies have distorted the figures, the detailed studies presented in Chapter 6 suggest that the MNV measure does give a good enough means of comparing the assemblages of different sites. This suggest to me that the scale of importation in the two areas was comparable, and we have no indication that the eastern Mediterranean trade with Spain was other than on a normal yearly commercial scale.

There are other reasons for suggesting that the trade was regular, rather than the occasional speculative voyage. The timespan of the trade over perhaps 50–75 years shows that several periods of voyaging was involved, *contra* the minimalist interpretations of Thomas (1988b; 1990). The collection of sufficient quantities of alluvial tin, its smelting to produce a cargo of say 50 tons of refined metal, and its collection at central sites, would all take a considerable period to organise. Any visiting Byzantine merchant would want to trade quickly and depart to enable the return journey to be completed before the winter storms, and would not like to wait while the whole process of assembling the tin was begun when they arrived. Sailing times show that the window of opportunity for trade would be quite small. Similarly, any British potentate would not wish to engage in the trouble of collecting tin (and possibly slaves) at a central site, and then have no market for the materials. Both parties would wish to be sure that the transaction would take place, which implies a regular cycle of contact.

Traders

The question of who carried out the trade is closely linked to that of the purpose of the trade. Harris (2003, 62–4) has argued that documentary references to Syrian traders in France and Spain can be taken at face value, and therefore that many of the Byzantine merchants were Syrian. However, this does not necessarily imply that Syria was the origin of the trading vessels, only that Syrian merchants controlled much of the eastern Mediterranean trade. As far as the Atlantic trade is concerned, the mention of '*Negotiatores graecos*' at Merida in the 6th century is of most direct relevance, and shows the presence in the west of actual merchants, or merchant-owners, rather than just ship captains (Wooding 1996b, 47). None of this is perhaps surprising in a Mediterranean context, but does not really take us much further with the question of the motivation behind the trade.

One literary source which has been utilised in discussions is the story in the *Life of John the Almsgiver*, referred to above and concerning a supposed voyage to Britain (Dawes and Baynes 1948, 216–18). Although the place referred to has been claimed as Brittany (Reynolds 1995, 135) or Galicia (Lewis 1978, 146), it is certainly Britain. Some commentators have accepted all the details of this story at face value. For example Mango (2001, 96–7) takes the mention of sale of half the cargo for 10,000 *solidi* as evidence for the existence of a cash economy in south-western Britain at this time. At the opposite extreme Knight (in Wilkinson 1995, 45) says the story is 'generally recognised as non-historic' and has the morphology of a standard folk-tale. In addition, he states that 'Britain' is often used in Late Antiquity as a *topos* for 'the ends of the earth' rather like the modern usage of Timbuctoo. Harris (2003, 151) and Wooding (1996b, 46) take a more central position, suggesting that the details of the story are confused or based on literary antecedents. What is certain is that the story was written in Alexandria, almost a century after the cessation of the Atlantic trade, and in a port which had never had contact with that trade. It is therefore likely that any details in the story merely reflect handed-down sailors' yarns of ships that used to trade with Britain, and that tin was somehow involved. Other details may reflect conditions in 7th-century Alexandria, or were taken from older literary sources such as Herodotus. This is not to say that some of the other stories in the *Life*, which give detailed accounts of other shipping ventures in the eastern Mediterranean, were not based on contemporary records.

This discussion of literary references brings us to another model for the Mediterranean trade, which is based on some references in Procopius, the Byzantine historian (Wooding 1996b, 46–7). These have been interpreted by Dark (2000, 130; 2003) and Harris (2003, 152) as evidence that the trade was diplomatic in nature, with 'merchants acting as diplomats and agents for the Byzantine authorities', in an attempt to bring Britain into the orbit of the Byzantine Empire (see also Middleton 2006). I find this particular interpretation of the sources unlikely for a number of reasons, though I do not discount a possible state involvement in the trade. Firstly, as we have seen, the trade continued over some 75 years during which five or six different Emperors ruled. This long date-range does not sit well with policy particularly associated with a single Emperor, Justinian. It would also suggest the supply over generations of very large quantities of 'gifts of money', but there is almost no sign of such coinage in the west (Chapter 5.2). The fragmented political situation in Britain and Ireland would also mitigate against any attempt to build alliances. At this period in Britain a mosaic of small polities were only beginning to emerge from the former

Roman Empire and no real state structures can be discerned for a further few centuries. In Ireland at this period there were at least 150 small 'kingdoms' (Byrne 1973) and even in south Wales at least seven (Davies 1982, fig 38). Forming an alliance with one or another temporary local warband-leader would be of little benefit to Byzantium, and again does not explain the longstanding nature of the contact with sites like Tintagel. There therefore seems little likelihood of diplomatic activity being the prime motivation for the Atlantic trade (cf Faulkner 2004, 7).

The presence of Christian symbols on some PRS dishes has led to speculation that there was a religious inspiration for the contacts with Britain, with wine for communion being imported in the amphorae and the PRS dishes being used as altar vessels (Radford 1956), or an association with the spread of monasticism (Haseloff 1987, 45). This interpretation was based on the stamps on the pottery, but Hayes' work on PRS shows that there was a changing fashion in the stamps. In the early period animals were the favoured symbols, such as the Dinas Powys hares, while after about AD 500 crosses and human figures predominate (Hayes 1972, 346–9). This is a general change and does not imply that the vessels had any religious function. In the case of communion wine, sources closer to Britain, such as France, could have supplied the Church, and indeed, must have done so after the cessation of the Mediterranean imports. These are minor points compared with the major objection to a religious motive of importation, which is that all the concentrations of the imports are on seemingly secular sites. Admittedly, in the past Tintagel was believed to be a monastic site, but this is now rejected by most authors (Burrow 1973; Dark 1985; Thomas and Fowler 1985; cf Turner 2006, 54). As we saw in Chapter 8, of all the sites with imports in the south-west only three have any evidence of a religious function. More significantly all the sites with concentrations of finds have indications of high secular status in terms of metal working, size of enclosure, defences or the presence of precious metals and glassware. This is not to deny that church leaders exchanged luxury goods, as there is good evidence for these practices, or that much early trade was involved in transporting the products of far-flung church estates to the major monastic centres. There is no evidence for these particular activities in 6th-century Britain.

A new trading model

Drawing all these strands of evidence together, it is possible to put forward a modified model which combines some elements of previous models. The starting point has to be the unusual combination of amphorae types found in the Atlantic West, with a larger percentage of LR2 than is normal. Karagiorgou (2001) has shown that this type is associated with Imperial supply to the military on the Danube, implying some kind of state backing to the venture. The directed nature of the trade, focusing on tin-producing areas, suggests that procurement of tin was its primary motivation. The evidence cited above for a scarcity of tin and other metals in the eastern Empire would explain the Empire's wish to keep supplies for official purposes, including the supply of copper-alloy items for military use. The late surge in north African imports, which can be dated to the second third of the 6th century, *could* be associated with Justinian's reconquest of Carthage in 533, when this important port came under Imperial control once more. After this date it might have been more practical to start the long voyage to Britain from Carthage, ensuring that the voyage could be completed in one sailing season. It might be that, on occasion, the existing trading links were utilised to make some sort of diplomatic initiative, however misplaced that might have been in practical terms, but this does not seem to have been the prime motivation for the trade.

Finally, we have to explain the sudden end of the trade, in the mid-6th century, when trade continued in the western Mediterranean ports until the 7th century. The one historical event which may have impacted on trade was the outbreak of the plague in the 540s. This had devastating effects on shipping and sailors, as it was recognised to have been transmitted by sea (McCormick 2001, 109). At precisely this time the plague reached Ireland, presumably brought by the Mediterranean traders in their vessels. The *Annals of Ulster* record diseases in 545, 549 and 554 (Mac Airt and Mac Niocaill 1983, 75–9) which killed numerous kings and abbots. The greatest effects would have been felt at the ports of entry of the Byzantine imports. Thus it may have been that the Byzantine merchants killed off their clients, especially the nobility at sites such as Tintagel. There are signs that the import sites in the south-west never recovered their position after this period. Wooding (1996b, 53–4) has criticised such economic explanations for social change as placing too much emphasis on the imports. However, if the imported commodities were being actively used to develop social stratification and engineer new power relationships, the loss of these exotica could have had serious short-term consequences. Certainly, few fortified sites seem to have continued occupation into the 7th century, as they did not participate in the succeeding Continental trading system. The combination of disruption to the official shipping in the Mediterranean, and social upheaval in south-west Britain and Ireland, may have been enough to break the cycle of the tin trade permanently.

9.3 The Continental trading system

As we have seen in previous chapters, the pottery imports from the Continent are mainly of E ware (*c* 230 vessels), with a very small component of

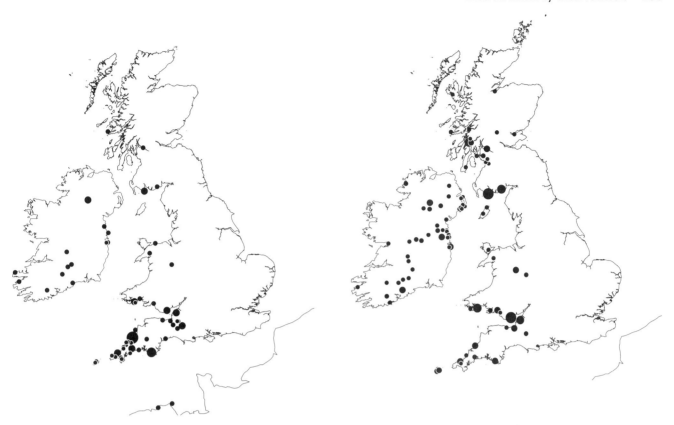

Fig 83 Comparison of distribution of all Mediterranean (left) and Continental (right) imports

DSPA (c 27 vessels), which may be transitional in date between the Mediterranean and Continental systems. Considerable quantities of glass (c 340 vessels) were also imported in this system, but it is more difficult to be sure that this material is all from the same source. Groups C and D are probably mainly of a similar provenance to the E ware and DSPA, but not every vessel can be securely placed in these groups. Accordingly, the discussion below concentrates on E ware, with additional comments on the other material where appropriate.

Unlike the situation with the Mediterranean trading system, where there is a large body of recent systematic work on the ceramics, there is no similar coherent body of research on western French material of the 6th/7th centuries, and the political situation in Aquitaine is also rather obscure. In this case, the distribution of the imports, and the analysis of the type of sites on which they are found, is the only basis on which to answer some of the questions raised by this exchange system.

Distribution of E ware

The distribution map of sites which have produced E ware shows immediately that there is little relation between the importation of this ware and the earlier Mediterranean wares (Fig 83). The sites occupy a broad swathe of Ireland and western Scotland, with sites in the south-west peninsula being mainly restricted to Scilly and the west of Cornwall. It is clear that whatever the nature of the mechanism of distribution of the two sets of wares, different processes were at work. E ware is found on around 80 sites, half of them in Ireland. It is in Ireland that the rate of discovery of new sites is greatest, with one site a year usually being discovered. To some extent this may reflect the much greater number of visible monuments (ringforts, enclosed cemeteries, crannogs) of the period in Ireland and the amount of archaeological activity associated with redevelopment, but it does seem that E ware was more widely distributed in Ireland than elsewhere. The apparent wide geographical spread in Ireland cannot disguise the fact that the overall distribution of E ware is basically coastal. Looking at the number of vessels, rather than the number of sites, it can be seen that 85% of these are found within 5km of the coast (Fig 34). It is clear that foreign traders did not venture into the interior, but stayed close to the relative safety of their ships.

There are around 230 vessels of E ware scattered over the 80 or so sites. This is a small number of vessels, though of the same order as the Aegean imports, or indeed 13th-century Saintonge jugs. An analysis of the number of vessels on each site shows that there were two, or possibly three, ranks of sites (Table 13). 75% of sites have only one or two vessels, but there are a few sites with a considerably greater number, and Dunadd is clearly the major site. It could be argued that this is merely a reflection of the amount or quality of excavation on individual sites, but the close analysis of the sites undertaken

Fig 84 Contoured distribution map of E ware

in Chapter 7 indicates that this is not so. Several small sites, such as Ballyfounder, Spittal Ballee and Kildalloig Dun, have been completely excavated and have produced only a few vessels, while many of the sites that have produced many vessels have been only partially excavated (eg Clogher, Dunadd, Dinas Powys). It does seem that there is a real difference in type of site as expressed by the number of E ware vessels found there (Tables 16–19). Sites with large, or potentially large, numbers of vessels are all either large forts or undefended sites. The undefended sites are mainly in the south-west, and, as will be discussed later, represent a different aspect of the trade. If we look at Ireland, Scotland and Wales, it seems that only large fortified sites were able to receive any quantity of vessels. Whithorn is the exception to this pattern.

A contoured distribution map of the number of vessels per site shows a number of centres with the distribution of vessels falling off with increased distance from these centres (Fig 84). These centres coincide with those identified in Chapter 8 as primary import centres, based on a suite of characteristics. It is also clear from this map that there is a 'missing' centre somewhere in the County Down area of Ulster which may be Downpatrick. Only very small-scale excavations have taken place there, so it is likely that larger quantities of imports would be recovered by further excavation. However, another possibility is Scrabo Hill, a fortified hilltop which has produced E4 and E4B jugs from very small excavations. This pattern in itself suggests that trade was controlled by these sites, and that merchants did not travel to the hinterland.

There is other evidence which supports the view that these primary centres were nexuses where imports were redistributed to surrounding client sites. Analysis of the fall-off curves for the common forms, E1 and E2, shows a marked double peak about 30km from the major centres, suggesting that the aristocrats of the primary centres distributed gifts to outlying client sites, or those in adjoining polities, as a means of social binding (Campbell 1991, illus 185). Polities in Early Historic Ireland were of the scale of tens of kilometres across. Clients residing closer to the centres could be entertained directly, so there was not the same need to give gifts. In addition, there are hints that particular batches of pottery can be identified which show this process in operation. At Lesser Garth cave, the E_{1C} vessel E128 has an unusual rim form, matched only by one from Dinas Powys (E43), the major centre lying near the coast. Lesser Garth lies on the edge of *Blaenau Morgannwg*, the upland area north of the fertile *Bro Morgannwg*, which probably formed the boundary of the unnamed early kingdom of south Glamorgan (Davies 1982, fig 32). At Loch Glashan, madder stains were found in E ware, just as at the nearby centre of Dunadd, seemingly more than a coincidence, and suggesting supply of the crannog from Dunadd (Crone and Campbell 2005, 122). The case of Loch Glashan shows that the redistribution pattern was not always at a considerable distance from the primary centre. In fact there is a group of three import sites encircling Dunadd, none more than 10km from the site. What is noticeable about this distribution is that these subsidiary sites all lie at access points to the low-lying area around Dunadd, the Kilmartin Glen, and probably controlled access to Dunadd (*ibid*). The geographical situation here in Highland Scotland was presumably the determining factor in the siting of important client sites.

As mentioned in Chapter 3.2, there are differences in the patterns of distribution of the various forms of E ware (Table 2). The primary centres defined above have a different profile of forms, having most of the unusual forms, E3 and E4, which are therefore concentrated in coastal areas. The minor sites in contrast have a relative preponderance of E2 forms, which have a wide distribution. Indeed the jug forms are almost a defining feature of primary centres, being otherwise found only on the suggested trading sites in Scilly, and in the monastic site at Whithorn. The profile of vessel forms at the suggested trading sites is also significantly different, reinforcing the view put forward based on sooting patterns (Chapter 3.2) that at these sites the pottery was being used by Gaulish merchants.

The patterns revealed by the distributions therefore are complex, reflecting a complex series of consumption and exchange mechanisms. The major centres were supplied directly by merchants, in some form of barter exchange. Here the consumption was related to feasting as a symbol of power and prestige, and the utilisation of the contents of the pots to produce symbols of wealth display such as red clothing. The secondary centres were supplied by gift exchange from the primary power centres. Some of these may have been diplomatic gifts, as was suggested for Clatchard Craig and Craig Phadrig in eastern Scotland, while others may have been reflections of political suzerainity (real or imagined). At the suggested trading sites, the occurrences indicate use by merchants of their own local pottery, reflecting Frankish social culinary usages, including use of cooking-pots with lids, bowls and jugs. Thus each category of site ended with a different profile of forms.

DSPA

The patterns revealed by the distribution of DSPA do not contradict the general pattern of E ware distribution, but the fourteen sites are concentrated on western British shores (Fig 17), and more towards south Wales than further north. This may reflect a chronological difference, as it has been suggested that the DSPA was transitional from the Mediterranean to the Continental system. However, as the DSPA forms are mainly tableware, including many mortaria, it is possible to suggest that culinary practices dictated the consumption pattern. As with E ware, the main concentrations are on primary centres, principally Dinas Powys. The only other concentration is at Hen Gastell, also on the south Wales coast. This site had little E ware, so may have gone out of use by the main period of its importation, but may have been an import centre for a brief period in the 6th century.

Glass

One of the major outcomes of this research on imports has been the recognition that imported glass is much more widespread than had previously been thought (Campbell 2000a, fig 1), being found on almost 50 sites, with up to 80 vessels identified on some sites (Fig 39). This contrasts markedly with Anglo-Saxon settlement sites of the same period where glass is very rare, with most vessels being recorded from pagan graves. The overall distribution of sites is similar to that of E ware, with concentrations on the same import centres. The only major anomaly is the large quantity of glass at Cadbury Congresbury, but this is almost certainly from Anglo-Saxon England rather than the Continental trading system. In tabular form this association between the two classes of Continental imports is clear (Table 13), with most glass sites producing E ware or DSPA. Of the sites with imported glass, only four have Mediterranean imports but no Continental imported pottery. On the other hand, of these 49 sites, 29 have produced DSPA or E ware. As several glass sites have produced no imported pottery at all this means that 90% of the glass sites which have imported pottery have DSPA or E ware as well. A further correlation is that those sites with the most glass vessels are also those with large concentrations of E ware, with the exception of Cadbury Congresbury, where most of the glass is Group B. It is clear that the glass, at least of Groups C and D, belong to the same Continental import system as E ware, though there are some differences which have to be explained.

The glass distributions, at least of the Groups C and D of certain Continental origin, fall in with the DSPA more than the E ware distributions, as they are concentrated in western Britain with rather less spread in Ireland (Fig 39). In fact, there are no major concentrations of glass at any sites in Ireland. This again may be due to chronological factors, but there is no indication from the stratified sequence at Whithorn that the glass ceased to be imported before E ware. It is noticeable that glass is also lacking in Gaelic Argyll, where a large quantity would have been expected at Dunadd. There may therefore be some social factors at work which discriminate against the use of glass vessels in Gaelic areas. As with the DSPA mortaria, these glass tablewares may have particularly appealed to Britons who wished to connect with an imagined Roman continuity of culinary usage.

The glass of Group B shares a generally similar pattern with that of Groups C and D. This might suggest that the supply route was similar, implying that glass was re-exported from western France after export from England or northern France. While this is not impossible in the light of later cabotage practices (Allan 1983), one might expect more variety in the pottery if these practices were widespread. It seems likely that some, or all, of the Group B glass might have been supplied directly from eastern Britain. Sites such as Whithorn, and those in west-central Scotland such as Buiston and Castle Hill have substantial signs of other contacts with Anglo-Saxon areas in the form of metalwork (Duncan 1982; J Graham-Campbell pers comm; Cessford 2000). Sites in northern and eastern Scotland such as Dundurn, Tarbat and Birsay are likely to have been supplied by the eastern coastal route. It has been suggested that the unusual high-status Group B vessel from Dinas Powys was a diplomatic gift from Kent via the upper Thames routeway (Campbell 1989b) and it could be argued that other vessels came by a variety of similar overland routes to western Britain. It is also noticeable that several of the Group B glass vessels in the interior of Ireland are not drinking vessels but containers (flasklets), which are otherwise very rare in the Atlantic assemblages. It may be that these were being imported for their contents, and this explains their occurrence in western areas which otherwise have little imported material. Some of the Group B material is of mid-Saxon date, and this material is most likely to have arrived directly from Anglo-Saxon England at a period when Anglo-Saxon influence was expanding into western Britain. The Group B material at sites such as Tintagel may be the result of this process. It should be acknowledged, however, that some proportion of the Group B glass may have been manufactured on the Continent, and found its way into the Atlantic trading system alongside glass of Groups C and D.

The Group A glass imports, of Mediterranean origin, are concentrated in the same area of southwestern Britain as the Mediterranean pottery imports, strongly suggesting they are part of that trading system. The only exceptions are Whithorn, which itself has a wide range of Mediterranean pottery, and the enigmatic site of Dunnyneil Island in Strangford Lough. Dunnyneil may have been a contact point for travellers moving between the Solway area and Ireland, and it may be that the Group A glass was redistributed here from Whithorn.

Mechanisms of distribution

Turning to the mechanism of distribution of E ware and the other Continental material, criticism of a concept of an 'E ware trade' can be levelled in terms of the small number of vessels found. Clearly, E ware was not the main focus of exchange in this system. I have suggested in previous chapters that the detailed taphonomic, residue and usage evidence suggests that E ware and glassware were imported partly as containers for their high-value contents, partly for traders' own use, and partly as low-cost 'added-value' goods accompanying a bulk trade in commodities such as salt and wine. The imports were then internally redistributed by a variety of processes, including gift and diplomatic exchange. The presence of imports on Atlantic sites, therefore, is merely an indicator of where exchange was taking place, rather than being the driving force behind that exchange. These arguments were based mainly on archaeological evidence, as were the estimations of the chronology and provenance of the wares.

The wider questions which this raises, such as who was carrying out the trade?, what was being exchanged in return?, what was the status of the consumers?, was this commercial exchange?, are more general issues which require the historical context to be taken into account. Several of these issues are inter-related. The relevant contemporary documentation is extremely sparse, and is conveniently assembled by Wooding (1996b). Previous theories of a documented link with the wine trade, first put forward by Zimmer (1909) and espoused by Thomas, have been effectively demolished by Wooding (1996a; 1996b), who has shown that the references are not contemporary sources. There are a few clues in the archaeological evidence, but it must be stressed that the following discussion has a much less secure basis than the issues outlined in the previous paragraph, and is more dependent on my own reading of the historical and social context.

The issue of who was carrying out the trade has been touched on in the discussion of the lack of variety in the imports. The pottery is dominated by E ware, most of which is an absolutely uniform technique and fabric (96% Fabric E1), suggestive of mass production in a single centre (see Chapter 3.2 and Appendix 2). If the trade was driven by traders coming from all the separate polities of Atlantic Britain and Ireland, it is difficult to see why they would go to one, and only one, particular site in Gaul for their goods. If this had been the case, we would expect a wide variety of pottery to have been picked up from different centres and brought back to Insular sites. There is some variety (the unclassified wares of Chapter 5.3), but it amounts to only around 5% of the total, and could be accounted for by personal possessions or goods picked up *en route* to western sites. The lack of variety is not so marked in the glassware, but 75% of identified forms are cones or bowls, and 60% are of Groups C and D. This is an especially homogeneous collection, given the huge variety of forms seen in assemblages from Frankish cemeteries (eg Feyeux 1995). Glass, as a much higher-value good than pottery, is also more likely to have been passed from one trader to another. This implies that the driving force for the trade came from western Gaul, and that the traders were Frankish merchants, or merchants based in that area. There is of course abundant evidence for a merchant class in this area, for example, the many references in Gregory of Tours, and charter evidence for taxes and tolls. Some of these merchants may have been of Mediterranean origin, whether 'Syrian' or not (Harris 2003, 59–64). In contrast, there is no mention of a trading class or persons in any of the extensive contemporary Irish legal documentation (Kelly 1988). This does not preclude the occasional voyage by British or Gaelic ships to the Continent, when trading may have taken place. This may be the context for the well-known account in the 8th-/9th-century *Vita* of St Filibert which mentions Gaelic (*Scothorum*) ships arriving at Noirmoutier, bringing leather shoes. The historical context may mask the reliability of the ethnic identification of the sailors (Wooding 1996b, 67), but it is a believable account of an actual exported cargo, given the quality of leather shoes found in Ireland and Scotland. It has been suggested that there was a transitional phase between the Mediterranean and E ware trading systems which may have been focused on the Bordeaux area. It is possible to speculate that merchants, some of whom may have Mediterranean connections, were familiar with the Mediterranean ships trading to Britain, perhaps having acted as intermediaries, translators or pilots, and who then used their knowledge of Insular sites, potential markets and sailing routes to undertake their own trade when the Mediterranean system collapsed.

There is an interesting comparison here with the slightly later situation at the mid-Saxon port of *Hamwic*. Here there is a huge variety of Continental pottery import types, amounting to almost 200 identified fabrics, believed to originate over a wide area of north-western Europe, though very little from western France (Timby 1988). Whatever the explanation of the presence of these 8th-/10th-century imports at *Hamwic* (Hodges 1981; Timby 1988; Brisbane 1988; Brown 1997), it is clearly a different place from any of the Atlantic sites with imports. The almost monotonous presence of E ware on these sites indicates a much more directed impulse from a particular sector of the Frankish economy than the more random, competitive situation revealed at *Hamwic* and other English ports. In this sense there is a comparison with the preceding Mediterranean trade, which I have suggested had an imperial drive behind it. It may be that there was some specific drive behind the Continental trading system, rather than just an expression of growing commercialism in Aquitaine.

It has been suggested that the ecclesiastics were behind the E ware trade (Hodges 1977). This is a possibility, as there is documentary evidence that important churchmen were moving large quantities of goods around Gaul, between their estates (James 1977, 223). They were also sending higher-quality goods, such as the package of colourants sent by one 8th-century Continental bishop to another (Rossen-Runge and Werner 1960, 261–2). There are good reasons for believing that this was not the main driving force behind the Continental trading system, however. Firstly, as we have seen in Chapter 8, very few imports have been found on ecclesiastical sites. While it could be argued that there has not been much large-scale excavation on monastic sites, the major site of Iona, which has suffered numerous campaigns of excavations (O'Sullivan 1999), has produced only one E ware vessel and no glass. Secondly, the evidence of the colourant orpiment from Dunadd shows that material which was intended for use in monastic *scriptoria* was being imported through this royal site. This ties in neatly with the only contemporary reference to Atlantic trade, the well-known story in Adomnán's *Life* of St Columba where Gallic sailors arrive at the *caput regionis* (Sharpe 1991, 132). What and where this place might be has been much discussed (Sharpe 1991, 291; Anderson and Anderson 1961; Alcock and Alcock 1987; Campbell 1988a), but the important and indisputable point is that it was *not* Iona that was seen by contemporaries as the articulation point for foreign traders.

If the Church was not the driving force, could the aristocracy, or royalty, have been involved? There is no evidence to suggest this, other than the very slight fact that the madder dye transported in E ware containers was being grown on royal estates in Carolingian France (Chapter 3.2). There is no indication, however, that trade in madder was a royal prerogative in Gaul, even if its use may have been restricted to the aristocracy in Gaelic society. There also seems little likelihood that the trade had a diplomatic function. It is too widespread, in time and region, to be the result of some unknown political initiative between Aquitaine and the Atlantic polities. The political history of Aquitaine at this period is obscure, but it seems to have been something of a backwater compared with the more dynamic Neustria and Austrasia to the north (James 1977, 13–14). It is possible that at this early period in the development of mercantile trade, large landholders had more control over trade than in later periods, and that there was some form of direction of trade based on a specific need of these landholders.

Almost no artefacts of British or Irish origin have turned up in France, which might give some clue as to the type of commodity being exchanged for the imports. As with the preceding Mediterranean trade, we are forced to speculate on the organic options. Leslie Alcock has compiled a list of products of these regions which might have been attractive to Frankish traders (Alcock and Alcock 1990, 128; Alcock 2003). These include the white furs of mountain hares, sealskins, eiderdown, freshwater pearls, quartz and garnets. These can be added to the leather goods already mentioned, and the perennial slaves. Whether any one of these was of sufficient value to have stimulated this trade is impossible to know.

The question of the type and scale of the exchange system involved has also been a matter of debate. If we look at the scale of distribution first of all, it is clear from the quantities and types of site that this is something more than a casual, random distribution of material picked up by travellers. Evison has put forward a model of the 'duty-free bottle' to explain the presence of small quantities of Frankish wheel-thrown bottles in Anglo-Saxon graves (Evison 1979). There is just too much E ware and glass to accept this model for Atlantic sites. However, it could be that occasional items could represent curios or talismans brought by pilgrims or travellers. Examples might be the ARS sherd from Iona, well outside its normal range, or the unique gold-leaf glass tessera from Dunadd, but this can only apply to a very few items.

As with the Mediterranean trading system, the time span of the Continental system militates against any minimalist interpretation of the exchange involved. As we have seen, the imports were arriving over at least a century, possibly more, showing some sort of structured trade. Wooding (1987; 1996b, 96) has suggested a tramping model, where merchants go wherever cargoes are available. I have termed this the '*Para Handy*' model, after the well-known Clyde puffer in the Neil Gunn stories (Campbell 1996a, 79). The decisive argument against this is the consistency of the import assemblages, particularly compared with assemblages from trading sites such as *Hamwic* discussed above. Any non-directed pattern of trade would produce a much greater variety of imports on Atlantic sites. The same arguments put forward in relation to the Mediterranean trade apply to the Continental – merchants and their clients would need a stable and accepted yearly time of trade to avoid unnecessary delays in the transaction process. I believe that the exchange process was a sustained pattern of trade, at least to the major import centres. The relatively small quantity of imports has been used as an argument against this view. It is interesting therefore to compare the quantities of imports in this system with those of another system in the same geographical area, the Saintonge green-glazed pottery trade (Campbell and Papazian 1992, 16–19). This system was also directed from western France, and was associated with bulk commodities of salt, vinegar and prunes, but not directly with wine (Allan 1983, 42). Quantification studies have shown that the quantities recovered from archaeological sites are a minute fraction of those recorded as being imported in documentary sources (*ibid*, 43–4). We could infer that the same might apply to the earlier system. In any case, the E ware and glass have been argued above to comprise only a small, visible, part of cargoes of other material.

The reluctance of some students to accept the possibility of any kind of sustained trade at this period in Atlantic areas may have its roots in a view of these areas as being less economically developed than areas further east. It is not really until the 8th century that the Anglo-Saxon trading centres develop, though there are indications of a beginning in the 7th. Many would be reluctant to see Atlantic areas as capable of this type of exchange at so early a period. However, the quantities of imports cannot be denied, and I believe the arguments detailed in the previous chapters show that some kind of sustained trade was taking place along the Atlantic coasts from the late 6th century.

9.4 Conclusions: changing distribution systems

From the preceding discussion it can be seen that the pattern of imported pottery distribution in the Atlantic West has been affected by a series of sudden and drastic switches in direction (Fig 80). In the Late Roman period pottery from the Continent and from the Mediterranean was arriving at major urban centres in southern England. Two routes seem to be indicated, one from western France (*céramique a l'éponge*) and the other by the Rhone/Seine/Rhine (Argonne ware, Mediterranean wares). It is noticeable that there is a shift into the south-west, as Exeter figures in this trade, whilst at earlier periods imports there were rare. At the same time there is an export (or re-export) of Late Roman material to Ireland (Fig 81) though not in sufficient quantities to suggest substantial trade. With the breakdown of the market economy in Britain in the early 5th century all this comes to a complete halt (cf Fulford 1977).

There is then an apparent gap until the late 5th century when an entirely new distribution centred on the south-west peninsula appears. In the intervening period contact must have been maintained between Britain, Ireland and the Continent, as it has been continuously since the Mesolithic period, but no trace of traded goods survives. Apart from isolated documentary references to religious contacts, one of the few pointers to continuous contact through the 5th century is the series of inscriptions on Welsh Class I inscribed stones (Nash-Williams 1950). These inscriptions have been matched to similar ones in France, in the Rhône valley and more particularly in the Loire valley (Knight 1984, 335). At Vienne these can be dated by consular attributions to the mid-5th century. Recently, however, Handley (2001) has shown that the Insular examples are of a general Late Roman type common throughout the western Empire, and cannot be localised to western France, or to this restricted time period. Despite this evidence of contact there seems to have been no impetus towards trade.

The new Mediterranean system lasted from the late 5th century until the mid-6th (Fig 85) and was centred on large enclosed sites of high status and possibly with royal associations, such as Tintagel, Cadbury Castle, Dinas Powys and Cadbury Congresbury, with redistribution to smaller sites. The imported goods are represented by an earlier phase of eastern Mediterranean or Aegean amphorae (LR1–3) and fine tableware, Phocaean Red Slipware, and a later phase of north African amphorae and African Red Slipware. The dynamic for this trade appears to have been generated by a need for the metals found in the south-west: tin in Cornwall; lead/silver in the Mendips and south Wales; and possibly copper in southern Ireland (Fig 82). The impetus for this trade must have come from the Mediterranean, possibly under imperial direction. Outliers to this south-western distribution, such as at Whithorn in Scotland or Clogher in Ireland, are likely to reflect a variety of types of contact redistributing goods within the Atlantic province.

In the last quarter of the 6th century a new system developed to bring goods to Ireland, western Scotland and the west coast of Britain (Fig 83). There may have been a short period of overlap in the interim period when pottery (DSPA ware) and glass, possibly from the Bordeaux region, is found on sites in both areas. This new distribution avoided the previous centres in the south-west but also concentrated on major high-status sites, often with contempoary documented royal associations (Dunadd, Clogher, Lagore, Garranes, Dumbarton Rock). These sites show signs of concentration of wealth in the form of precious metals, centralised production and craft specialisation. Concentration of power is shown in the labour-intensive defences, the presence of high-status weaponry and the control of redistribution. The imported goods are represented by E ware and glass vessels, but it seems likely that other bulkier goods such as salt and wine were the mainstay of this trade, and that the pottery vessels were containers for rare commodities such as dyestuffs and exotic foods. This trade was sustained and widespread in extent, and may have been articulated through neutral points of contact (Dalkey Island, Scilly, Dunnyneill) where the pattern of use of E ware indicates the possible presence of foreign merchants. It has been argued that the pervasiveness of this distribution system shows that the

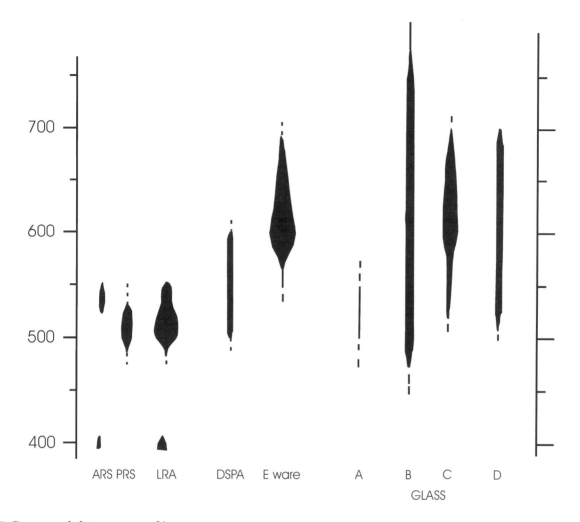

Fig 85 Suggested date ranges of imports

dynamics came from the Continent. It is unfortunate that the date of cessation of this system cannot be precisely established, but it does not seem to continue far into the 8th century (Fig 85). This is the period of expansion of the Saxon trading towns (*Hamwic*, Ipswich, London) and these may have siphoned off or undermined much of the trade. It may be that Continental trade lasted in an unorganised and minor form into the late 8th century, when the Viking raids heralded a new direction of distribution, this time from the north, and with development of new types of settlement, the Hiberno-Norse trading towns such as Dublin.

In summary it seems that the Celtic areas were constantly responding to external influence in the development of trade, but did not themselves initiate trade. This can be seen as a consequence of the peripheral nature of western Britain and Ireland compared with the economic core of the Frankish empire. This does not imply that the Atlantic polities were merely passive recipients of the products of the advanced economy of the Merovingian states. The fact that many of the recipient sites appear to continue to grow in the period after the cessation of the imports (eg Dunadd) shows that they were not dependent on foreign input for their existence, and that internal social development was taking place in these areas. For a variety of reasons this did not result in the development of an urban society, with coinage and a merchant class, as happened in other areas of north-western Europe, but this is not necessarily a sign of backwardness (Gondek 2003). Culturally, the area was at the forefront of artistic and literary merit, and it may be that surplus wealth was directed into these areas of endeavour rather than economic growth (Campbell 1996a, 91). However, it appears that the Continental trade did contribute to the enhancement and centralisation of power in the Celtic West and the gradual development of larger and more coherent kingdoms out of a mass of petty tribal divisions and post-Roman successor states.

10 Conclusions

This monograph set out to resolve some of the problems associated with the imports, and to give some explanation of their presence in the Atlantic West. Some questions have been resolved fairly satisfactorily. In Chapters 2–5, dealing with the production side of the cycle, the typologies and chronology of most of the wares were refined, and now provide a reliable framework for dating sites on which the imports occur. The production areas and routeways taken by the imports are now fairly well understood, though the continuing lack of kiln sites for E ware and glass hampers further progress in France. The analysis of depositional processes undertaken in Chapters 6 and 7, however, shows that more attention has to be paid in future to questions of taphonomic processes in interpreting the stratigraphy and consumption patterns of these sites. This is best exemplified by the case of Loch Glashan crannog, where inorganic artefact dating had suggested a 7th- to 9th-century date of occupation, but scientific dates showed that E ware was found in the same deposits as organic artefacts of 2nd- to 3rd-century date (Crone and Campbell 2005). In Chapter 8, analysis of the type of site, and associated material, where imports occur, showed a definite association of import centres with high-status, often royal, sites, which showed clear signs of craft specialisation and centralisation of certain activities such as fine jewellery making. In Chapter 9 a complex pattern of exchange mechanisms was reconstructed from the interplay of the intra- and inter-site distribution patterns, involving market forces alongside more traditional forms of gift exchange.

It was argued here and elsewhere (Campbell 1996a; 1999) that the imports formed part of the process by which the post-Roman successor states began to use their surplus wealth, at a precociously early stage, to develop more medieval types of hierarchical power structures. Ultimately, however, these did not develop along the lines that occurred elsewhere in Anglo-Saxon England, and a true market economy with coinage, a merchant class and towns failed to emerge. This is one of the unsolved aspects of the Atlantic economy.

Perhaps related to this question is another of the puzzling aspects of the Atlantic trade, what might be termed the 'Atlantic Curtain'. By this I mean the apparent barrier to distribution of the western imports to areas under Anglo-Saxon control. This is not just a geographical barrier. Even at sites on the west coast such as Whithorn, which had many imports in the 7th century, with the Anglo-Saxon takeover in the early 8th century, all Atlantic imports seem to cease coming to the site. The barrier however, was not impermeable to artefacts. As shown in Chapter 9, Group B glass was probably exchanged across Britain at a number of points from east to west (eg Campbell 1989b), and Anglo-Saxon metalwork followed similar routes to sites such as Dunadd (eg Campbell and Lane 1993b) and the Mote of Mark (Graham Campbell et al 1976; Laing and Longley 2006) and Dinas Powys (Graham Campbell 1991). Some metalwork did travel in the other direction, as finds of 'Irish' objects at Anglo-Saxon sites such as St Albans testify, and the zoomorphic penannular brooches found in pagan graves (Kilbride-Jones 1980), even if the evidence for hanging bowl production in Scotland is not accepted (Bruce-Mitford 1987; Youngs forthcoming). The 'curtain', then, seems to have been semi-permeable, open to people and certain types of artefact, but excluding the imports.

As the Anglo-Saxons were also receiving imports from the Mediterranean and different parts of the Continent at this period, there can have been no ideological barrier to the exchange of western imports with Anglo-Saxons. The only explanation is that either the western Gaulish traders had nothing the Anglo-Saxons wanted, or that the Anglo-Saxons did not have the goods which the traders wanted. The second seems the more plausible explanation, as the Anglo-Saxons did import some glass vessels, and wine, from north-western Europe. Hodges (1982, 87–94) interpreted the patchy distribution of Continental imports in southern England in terms of political control over trade areas by the competing polities of Austrasia and Neustria. In such a model, Aquitaine could be seen as having sole trading rights with the Atlantic areas. There is, however, no real evidence for such a system of trading areas, and it is difficult to see it applying rigorously to a site like Whithorn, which could only be supplied with bulk goods from the western coastal route. It is easier to imagine that geographic factors initially encouraged the links along the Atlantic façade (Cunliffe 2001). I have suggested (Campbell 1996b) that the growth of the Anglo-Saxon ports in the 8th century was a contributing factor in the demise of the Atlantic trading system, as these ports effectively siphoned off trade which would have flowed up the Atlantic seaways. This is not the whole story, however, and it seems possible that the unusual particularity of the E ware exchange system, identified in Chapter 9.3, left it vulnerable to political or economic changes in the production region. Such changes seem a better explanation for the collapse of the trading system sometime in the 8th century than the Viking incursions, which did not affect these areas until the early 9th century.

Part of the problem in understanding what was

going on in economic terms at this period is that it is a transitional phase, between, on the one hand, the mixed command/market economy of the Roman imperial system or the late prehistoric redistributive economies of Ireland and western Britain, and, on the other, the more familiar market economies of medieval Europe. In such a transitional state, it is not surprising that it is difficult to pigeonhole the type of activity we see recorded in the archaeological record into the static categories devised by economic historians. As at most periods, no single type of exchange dominated, and even what we think of as socially neutral market exchanges almost certainly involved a great deal of personal trust and social ties. The Atlantic peoples did not develop coinage of their own until outsiders began minting (the Norse in Ireland, the Normans in Scotland and Wales), but they did have systems of valuation for exchange. For example, the Irish Laws had a system based on the value of a milch cow or a female slave (*cumal*), though these later had equivalents in terms of ounces of silver (*sét*) (Kelly 2000, 58); the Welsh had a system also based loosely on the worth of cattle, though later a measure of silver became common (Davies 1982, 53–5). They were, therefore, familiar with the concept of payment for worth, and presumably the concept of coinage was known. Social factors probably prevented the development of coinage systems. It would be wrong, however, to infer that these societies were backward or 'failed states'. It has been suggested that surplus was directed into artistic and ecclesiastical directions rather than mass-production (Campbell 1996a; Gondek 2006).

The occurrence of the earliest-known household census in north-western Europe (Bannerman 1974; Campbell 1999, 39) in 7th-century Dál Riata shows very early signs of the development of the mechanisms of state bureaucracy.

The imports discussed here clearly throw some light on these issues at a time when documentary evidence is of little help. However, it has been claimed that archaeologists such as myself have made too much of the significance of the imports, and that they were never an important part of the economy. It is true that the imports were only a tiny part of the total economy of the period, and that the imports have been emphasised because often they are almost the only artefacts found on sites, and because of their chronological significance. Wooding (1996b, 5) has suggested that this has led to a 'maximalist' interpretation of the imports. Not surprisingly, perhaps, I believe that the imports are more important than their small quantity might suggest. What the imports do is shed a light, intermittent and difficult to interpret as it is, on the processes which were involved in the development of medieval state structures in western Britain and Ireland. Is it just coincidence, for example, that the Dál Riata, having hosted the major import site of the 7th century (Campbell 1996a, 87), became the leading polity in 9th-century Scotland? For this reason, perhaps more than the chronological precision they bring to the period, the study of the imports is of fundamental significance to any discussion of the period, and has general relevance in discussions of the factors involved in early state formation.

Bibliography

Aarts, J, 2005 Coins, money and exchange in the Roman world. A cultural-economic perspective, *Archaeological Dialogues*, **12**, 1–28

Adams, W Y & Adams, E W, 1991 *Archaeological typology and practical reality*. Cambridge: Cambridge University Press

Alaraçao, J, Delgado, M, Mayet, F, Moutinho Alaraçao A & Da Ponte, S, 1976 *Céramiques diverses et verres. Fouilles de Coimbriga*, VI. Paris

Alcock, L, 1963a *Dinas Powys, an Iron Age, Dark Age and early medieval settlement in Glamorgan*. Cardiff: University of Wales Press

Alcock, L, 1963b Pottery and settlement in Wales and the March AD 400–700, in Foster & Alcock (eds) 1963, 281–302

Alcock, L, 1978 Excavation and publication: some comments, *Proc Soc Antiq Scot*, **109**, 1–6

Alcock, L, 1981 Early historic fortifications in Scotland, in Guilbert (ed) 1981, 150–80

Alcock, L, 1982 Cadbury-Camelot: a fifteen-year perspective, *Proc Brit Acad*, **68**, 355–88

Alcock, L, 1983a Gwyr y Gogledd: an archaeological perspective, *Archaeologia Cambrensis*, **132**, 1–18

Alcock, L, 1983b The archaeology of Celtic Britain, Fifth to Twelfth centuries AD, in D A Hinton (ed) *25 years of Medieval Archaeology*. Sheffield: University of Sheffield, 48–66

Alcock, L, 1987 *Economy, society and warfare among the Britons and Saxons*. Cardiff: University of Wales Press

Alcock, L, 1992 A message from the dark side of the moon: western and northern Britain in the Age of Sutton Hoo, in Carver (ed) 1992, 205–16

Alcock, L, 1995 *Cadbury Castle, Somerset: the early medieval archaeology*. Cardiff: University of Wales Press

Alcock, L, 2003 *Kings and warriors, craftsmen and priests,* Soc Antiq Scot Monogr Ser, **25**. Edinburgh: Society of Antiquaries of Scotland

Alcock, L & Alcock, E A, 1987 Reconnaissance excavations on Early Historic fortifications and other royal sites in Scotland, 1974–84: 2, Excavations at Dunollie Castle, Oban, Argyll, 1978, *Proc Soc Antiq Scot*, **117**, 119–47

Alcock, L & Alcock, E A 1990 Reconnaissance Excavations on Early Historic fortifications and other royal sites in Scotland, 1974–84: 4, Excavations at Alt Clut, Clyde Rock, Strathclyde, 1974–75, *Proc Soc Antiq Scot*, **120**, 95–149

Alcock, L, Alcock, E A & Driscoll, S T, 1989 Reconnaissance excavations on Early Historic fortifications and other royal sites in Scotland, 1974–84: 3, Excavations at Dundurn, Strathearn, Perthshire, 1976–77, *Proc Soc Antiq Scot*, **119**, 189–226

Allan, J, 1983 Some post-medieval documentary evidence for the trade in ceramics, in Davey & R Hodges (eds) 1983, 37–45

Anderson, A O & Anderson, M O, 1961 *Adomnan's Life of Columba*. London: Thomas Nelson & Sons

Andrews, P (ed), 1988 *Southampton finds, volume 1: the coins and pottery from Hamwic, Southampton,* Southampton Archaeol Monogr **4**. Southampton: Southampton City Museums

Anon, 1863 Proceedings for the year 1863, *J Kilkenny South-east Ireland Archaeol Soc*, new series, **4**, 245–6

Appadurai, A (ed), 1986 *The social life of things*. Cambridge: Cambridge University Press

Arnold, C J, 1980 Wealth and social structure: a matter of life and death, in Rahtz *et al* (eds) 1980, 81–142

Arnold, C J, 1983 Review of Hodges 1982, *Scot Archaeol Review*, **2**, 80–3

Arnold, C J, 1984 *Roman Britain to Saxon England*. London: Croom Helm

Arnold, C J, 1988 Review of Alcock 1987, *Welsh History Review*, **14**, 301–5

Arnold, D, 1985 *Ceramic theory and cultural process*. Cambridge: Cambridge University Press

Arthur, P, 1986 Amphorae and the Byzantine world, *Bulletin de Correspondence Hellenique, Supplement*, **13**, 655–60

Astill, G, 1985 Archaeology, economics and early medieval Europe, *Oxford J Archaeol*, **4**, 215–31

Aston, M & Burrow, I (eds), 1982 *The archaeology of Somerset*. Taunton: Somerset County Council

Aston, M & Iles, R (eds), [1988] *The archaeology of Avon*. Bristol: Avon County Council

Backhouse, J, Turner, D H & Webster, L, 1984 *The golden age of Anglo-Saxon art 966–1066*. London: British Museum Press

Baillie, M G L, 1986 A sherd of souterrain ware from a dated context, *Ulster J Archaeol*, **49**, 104–5

Bannerman, J, 1974 *Studies in the history of Dalriada*. Edinburgh: Scottish Academic Press

Barber, J W, 1981 Excavations on Iona, 1979, *Proc Soc Antiq Scot*, **111**, 282–380

Barrowman, R, Batey, C & Morris, C, forthcoming *Excavations at Tintagel Castle, Cornwall 1990–1999*, Soc Antiq Lond Monogr. London: Society of Antiquaries

Bass, G F & van Doorninck, F H, 1982 *Yassi Ada, a seventh-century Byzantine shipwreck*. Texas: Texas A & M University Press

Bateson, J D, 1973 Roman material from Ireland, *Proc Royal Irish Acad*, **73C**, 21–97

Bateson, J D, 1976 Further finds of Roman material

from Ireland, *Proc Royal Irish Acad,* **76C**, 171–80
Batey, C E, Sharpe, A & Thorpe, C, 1993 Tintagel Castle: archaeological investigation of the Steps area, 1989 and 1990, *Cornish Archaeol,* **32**, 47–66
Bencard, M, Ambrosiani, K, Jorgensen, L B, Madsen, H B, Neilsen, I & Näsman, U, 1979 Wikingerzeitliches Handwerk in Ribe, eine Ubersicht, *Acta Archaeologica,* **49**, 113–38
Biddle, M, 1976 Towns, in D M Wilson (ed), *The archaeology of Anglo-Saxon England.* London: Methuen & Co, 99–150
Bidwell, P T, 1979 *The legionary bath-house and basilica and forum at Exeter,* Exeter Archaeol Rep, **1**. Exeter: Exeter City Council
Biek, L, 1994 Tin ingots found at Praa sands, Breage, in 1974, *Cornish Archaeol,* **33**, 57–70
Bimson, M, 1983 Coloured glass and millefiori in the Sutton Hoo grave deposit, in Bruce-Mitford 1983, 924–44
Bird, J, 1977 African Red Slipware in Roman Britain, in Dore & Green (eds) 1977, 269–78
Böhner, K, 1958 *Die Fränkischen Altertümer des Trierer Landes.* Berlin
Boon, G C, 1958 A note on the Byzantine Æ coins said to have been found at Caerwent, *Bull Board Celtic Stud,* **17**, 316–19
Boon, G C, 1977 Gold-in-glass beads from the ancient world, *Britannia,* **8**, 193–207
Boon, G C, 1991 Byzantine and other ancient bronze coins from Exeter, in N Holbrook & P Bidwell (eds), *Roman finds from Exeter.* Exeter, 38–45
Bourdieu, P, 1977 *Outline of a theory of practice.* Cambridge: Cambridge University Press
Bourke, E, 1987 *Glass vessels in Ireland c 100–1400 AD.* Unpublished MA thesis, University College, Dublin
Bourke, E, 1994 Glass vessels of the first nine centuries AD in Ireland, *J Royal Soc Antiq Ireland,* **124**, 163–209
Bowen, E G, 1969 *Saints, seaways and settlements in the Celtic lands.* Cardiff: University Wales Press
Bowen, E G, 1972 *Britain and the western seaways.* London: Thames & Hudson
Bowles, C, 2006 *Rebuilding the Britons: The postcolonial archaeology of culture and identity in the Late Antique Bristol Channel.* Unpublished PhD thesis, University of Glasgow
Bowman, A, 1996 Post-Roman imports in Britain and Ireland: a maritime perspective, in Dark (ed) 1996, 97–108
Bradley, J, 1982 'Medieval' samian ware – a medicinal suggestion, *Ulster J Archaeol,* **44–5**, 196–7
Bradley, R J & Fulford, M G, 1980 Sherd size in the analysis of occupation debris, *Bull Institute Archaeol Univ London,* **17**, 85–94
Brisbane, M, 1988 Hamwic (Saxon Southampton): an 8th-century port and production centre, in Hodges & Hobley (eds) 1988, 101–8
Brogiolo, G P & Ward-Perkins, B, 1999 *The Idea and Ideal of the Town between Late Antiquity and the Early Middle Ages.* Leiden: Brill
Brown, C G & Harper, A E T, 1984 Excavations on Cathedral Hill, Armagh, 1968, *Ulster J Archaeol,* **47**, 109–61
Brown, D, 1985 Looking at cross-fits, *Medieval Ceramics,* **9**, 35–42
Brown, D, 1997 The social significance of imported medieval pottery, in C Cumberpatch & P Blinkhorn (eds), *Not so much a pot, more a way of life.* Oxford: Oxbow Books, 95–112
Bruce-Mitford, R L S, 1975 *The Sutton Hoo Ship-burial,* vol 1. London: British Museum Press
Bruce-Mitford, R L S, 1983 *The Sutton Hoo Ship-burial,* vol 3, A Care Evans (ed). London: British Museum Press
Bruce-Mitford, R L S, 1987 Ireland and the hanging-bowls, in Ryan (ed) 1987, 30–9
Brugmann, B, 2004 *Glass beads from early Anglo-Saxon graves.* Oxford: Oxbow Books
Burrow, I, 1973 Tintagel – some problems, *Scot Archaeol Forum,* **5**, 99–103
Burrow, I, 1979 Roman material from hill-forts, in Casey (ed) 1979, 212–29
Burrow, I, 1981 *Hillforts and hilltop settlement in Somerset in the first to eighth centuries AD,* BAR, **91**. Oxford: British Archaeological Reports
Byrne, F J, 1968 Historical note on Cnogba (Knowth), *Proc Royal Irish Acad,* **66C**, 383–400
Byrne, F J, 1973 *Irish kings and high-kings.* London: Batsford
Callender, M H, 1965 *Roman amphorae.* London: Oxford University Press
Campbell, E, 1984 E ware and Aquitaine: a reappraisal of the petrological evidence, *Scot Archaeol Review,* **3**, 35–41
Campbell, E, 1985 Normandy Gritty Ware from Gateholm, Pembrokeshire, *Medieval and Later Pottery in Wales,* **8**, 79–80
Campbell, E, 1986a The Dark Age pottery – E ware, in Close-Brooks 1986, 155–6
Campbell, E, 1986b The post-Roman imported pottery, in Green 1986, 117–18
Campbell, E, 1988a A cross-inscribed quern from Dunadd and other evidence for relations between Dunadd and Iona, *Proc Soc Antiq Scot,* **117**, 105–17
Campbell, E, 1988b The post-Roman pottery, in Edwards & Lane (eds) 1988, 124–36
Campbell, E, 1989a New finds of post-Roman imported pottery and glass from South Wales, *Archaeologia Cambrensis,* **138**, 59–66
Campbell, E, 1989b A blue glass squat jar from Dinas Powys, South Wales, *Bull Board of Celtic Stud,* **36**, 239–45
Campbell, E, 1991 Imported goods in the early medieval Celtic West: with special reference to Dinas Powys. Unpublished PhD thesis, University of Wales, College of Cardiff
Campbell, E, 1993 Dinas Powys, in N Pounds (ed), The Cardiff Area, *Archaeol J (supplement),* **150**, 23–4

Campbell, E, 1995a New evidence for glass vessels in western Britain and Ireland in the 6th/7th centuries AD, in Foy (ed) 1995b, 35–40

Campbell, E, 1995b Early medieval pottery and glass, in P F Wilkinson 1995, 18–23

Campbell, E, 1996a Trade in the Dark Age West: a peripheral activity?, in B Crawford (ed), *Scotland in Dark Age Britain*. St Andrews: University of St Andrews, 79–91

Campbell, E, 1996b The archaeological evidence for contacts: imports, trade and economy in Celtic Britain AD 400–800, in Dark (ed) 1996, 83–96

Campbell, E 1996c Glass; and Copper alloy ornamental fitting, in A Schlesinger & C Walls, An early church and medieval farmstead site: excavations at Llanelen, Gower, *Archaeol J*, **153**, 125–7; 136–8

Campbell, E, 1997 The early medieval imports, in Hill 1997, 297–322

Campbell E, 1999 *Saints and Sea-kings: the first kingdom of the Scots*. Edinburgh: Historic Scotland/Canongate

Campbell, E, 2000a A review of glass vessels in western Britain and Ireland AD 400–800, in Price (ed) 2000b, 33–46

Campbell, E, 2000b The glass vessels, in Crone 2000, 264–5

Campbell, E, 2000c E ware from Dun Ardtreck, Skye, in E MacKie, Excavations at Dun Ardtreck, Skye, *Proc Soc Antiq Scot*, **130**, 395–6

Campbell, E, 2001 Were the Scots Irish?, *Antiquity*, **75**, 285–92

Campbell, E, 2003 Royal Inauguration in Dál Riata and the Stone of Destiny, in R Wellander, R, D Breeze & T Clancy (eds), *The Stone of Destiny: artefact and icon*, Soc Antiq Scot Monogr Ser, **24**. Edinburgh: Society of Antiquaries of Scotland, 43–59

Campbell, E, 2004 Early Historic imported pottery, in G Ewart & D Pringle 2006, 'There is a castle in the west...', Dundonald Castle excavations 1986–93', *Scot Archaeol J*, **26**, 90–2

Campbell, E, 2005 Pottery, in Cavers & Henderson 2005, 292–3

Campbell, E 2006 Early medieval imports: glass and pottery, in Laing & Longley 2006, 104–13; 120–32

Campbell, E, forthcoming a Glass, in Barrowman, Batey & Morris forthcoming

Campbell, E, forthcoming b Anglo-Saxon Gaelic interaction in Scotland, in J Graham-Campbell & M Ryan (eds), *Anglo-Saxon Irish relations before the Vikings*

Campbell, E & Bowles, C, forthcoming Byzantine trade to the edge of the world: Mediterranean pottery imports to Atlantic Britain in the sixth century, in M Mango (ed), *Byzantine trade (4th–12th century): recent archaeological work*

Campbell, E & Lane, A, 1989 Llangorse: a 10th-century royal crannog in Wales, *Antiquity*, **63**, 675–81

Campbell, E & Lane, A, 1993a Excavations at Longbury Bank, Dyfed, and early medieval settlement in South Wales, *Medieval Archaeol*, **37**, 15–77

Campbell, E & Lane, A, 1993b Celtic and Germanic interaction in Scottish Dalriada: the seventh-century metalworking site at Dunadd, in Higgitt & Spearman (eds) 1993, 52–63

Campbell, E & Papazian, C, 1992 The survey of medieval pottery and rooftile in Wales AD 1100–1600, *Medieval and later Pottery in Wales*, **13**, 1–107

Carver, M (ed), 1992 *The Age of Sutton Hoo: the seventh century in North-Western Europe*. Woodbridge: Boydell & Brewer

Carver, M, 1993 *Arguments in Stone: Archaeological research and the European town in the first millennium*, Dalrymple Lectures for 1990, University of Glasgow. Oxford: Oxbow Books

Carver, M, 2000 Town and anti-town in first millennium Europe, in A Buko & P Urbanczyk (eds) 2000, *Archeologia w teorii i w praktyce*. Warsaw, 373–96

Casey, J (ed), 1979 *The end of Roman Britain*, BAR Brit Ser, **71**. Oxford: British Archaeological Reports

Cavers, M G & Henderson, J C, 2005 Underwater excavation of a crannog at Ederline, Loch Awe, Argyll, Scotland, *Internat J Nautical Archaeol*, **34**(2), 282–98

Cessford, C, 2000 A possible Anglo-Saxon burial at Castle Hill, Ayrshire, *Anglo-Saxon Stud Archaeol Hist*, **11**, 187–9

Champaud, C, 1957 L'exploitation ancienne de cassitérite d'Abbaretz-Nozay (Loire-Inférieure) Contribution aux problèmes de l'étain antique, *Annales Bretagne*, **64**, 46–96

Chapelot, J, 1983 The Saintonge pottery industry in the later middle ages, in Davey & Hodges (eds) 1983, 49–53

Clancy, J P, 1970 *The earliest Welsh poetry*. London: Macmillan

Clark, R, 2005 Lighting and Anglo-Saxon glass, *Glass News*, **18**, 6

Close-Brooks, J, 1986 Excavations at Clatchard Craig, Fife, *Proc Soc Antiq Scot*, **116**, 117–84

Collins, A E P, 1955 Excavations at Lough Faughan crannog, Co Down, *Ulster J Archaeol*, **18**, 45–81

Collins, R & Gerrard, J (eds), 2004 *Debating Late Antiquity in Britain AD 300–700*, BAR Brit Ser, **365**. Oxford: British Archaeological Reports

Cool, H, 2000 The parts left over: material culture into the fifth century, in Wilmott & Wilson (eds) 2000, 47–66

Cox, J S, 1956 The government of the town, *Ilchester Hist Monogr*, **8**. Taunton

Cramp, R, 1970 Decorated window-glass from and millefiori from Monkwearmouth, *Antiq J*, **50**, 327–35

Craw, J H, 1930 Excavations at Dunadd and at other sites on the Poltalloch Estates, Argyll, *Proc Soc Antiq Scot*, **64**, 111–27

Crawford, O G S, 1936 Western seaways, in D Buxton

(ed) 1936, *Custom is king: Studies in honour of R R Marett*. London, 181–200

Crone, A, 2000 *The history of a Scottish Lowland crannog: Excavations at Buiston, Ayrshire 1989–90*. Edinburgh: Scottish Trust for Archaeological Research

Crone, A & Campbell, E, 2005 *Excavations at Loch Glashan crannog by Jack Scott in 1960,* Soc Antiq Scot Monogr Ser, **32**. Edinburgh: Society of Antiquaries of Scotland

Crowther, D, 1983 Old land surfaces and modern ploughsoils: implications of recent work at Maxey, *Scot Archaeol Review*, **2**, 31–44

Cunliffe, B, 2001 *Facing the ocean: the Atlantic and its peoples*. Oxford: Oxford University Press

Curle, A O, 1914 Report on the excavation in September 1913 of a vitrified fort at Rockcliffe, Dalbeattie, known as the Mote of Mark, *Proc Soc Antiq Scot*, **48**, 125–68

Curle, C L, 1982 *Pictish and Norse finds from the Brough of Birsay 1934–74,* Soc Antiq Scot Monogr Ser, **1**. Edinburgh: Society of Antiquaries of Scotland

Dana, J, 1883 *A system of mineralogy*, 5th ed. London

Dark, K R, 1985 The plan and interpretation of Tintagel, *Cambridge Medieval Celtic Stud,* **9**, 1–18

Dark, K R, 1994 *Civitas to kingdom: British political continuity 300–800*. Leicester: Leicester University Press

Dark, K R (ed), 1996 *External contacts and the economy of Late Roman and Post-Roman Britain*. Woodbridge: Boydell & Brewer

Dark, K R, 2000 *Britain and the end of the Roman Empire*. Stroud: Tempus

Dark, K R, 2003 Early Byzantine mercantile communities in the West, in C Entwhistle (ed), *Through a glass brightly: studies in Byzantine and medieval art and archaeology presented to David Buckton*. Oxford, 76–81

Davey, P & Hodges, R (eds), 1983 *Ceramics and Trade*. Sheffield: University of Sheffield

Davies, M, 1946 Diffusion and distribution of megaliths around the Irish Sea, *Antiq J*, **26**, 38–60

Davies, W, 1978 *An early Welsh microcosm*. London: Royal Historical Society

Davies, W, 1979 *The Llandaff charters*. Aberystwyth: National Library of Wales

Davies, W, 1982 *Wales in the early Middle Ages*. Leicester: Leicester University Press

Davies, W, 1988 *Small worlds*. London: Duckworth

Dawes, E & Baynes, N H, 1948 *Three Byzantine saints*. Oxford: Blackwell

DeBeor, W R & Lathrop, D W, 1979 The making and breaking of Shipibo-Conibo ceramics, in C Kramer (ed), *Ethnoarchaeology*. Columbia, 102–38

Delgado, M, Mayet, F & Moutinho de Alarcão, A, 1975 *Fouilles de Conimbriga*, IV *Les sigillées*. Paris

Denison, S, 2000 Gemstone evidence for late Roman survival: jewel points to trade between North Wales and the Byzantine Empire, *British Archaeology,* **52**, 4

Dickinson, T M, 1974 *Cuddesdon and Dorchester-on-Thames, Oxon: two early Saxon princely sites in Wessex,* BAR, **1**. Oxford: British Archaeological Reports

Dickinson, T M & Harke, H, 1992 Early Anglo-Saxon shields, *Archaeologia,* **110**, 1–94

Doherty, C, 1980 Exchange and trade in early medieval Ireland, *J Royal Soc Antiq Ireland,* **110**, 67–90

Dolley, M, 1976 Roman coins from Ireland and the date of St Patrick, *Proc Royal Irish Acad,* **76C**, 181–90

Dore, J & Greene, K (eds), 1977 *Roman pottery studies in Britain and beyond: papers presented to John Gillam,* BAR Internat Ser, **S30**. Oxford: British Archaeological Reports

Doyle, I, 1996 *Imported Mediterranean pottery in Ireland (A and B wares)*. Unpublished MA dissertation, Univeristy College, Cork

Doyle, I, 1998 The early medieval activity at Dalkey Island, Co Dublin: a re-assessment, *J Irish Archaeol,* **9**, 89–104

Doyle, I, 1999 A ceramic 'platter' of Mediterranean origin from the ringfort of Garranes, Co Cork, *J Cork Hist Archaeol Soc,* **104**, 69–76

Driscoll, S T & Nieke, M R (eds), 1988 *Power and politics in early medieval Britain and Ireland*. Edinburgh: Edinburgh University Press

Dufournier, D, 1981 L'analyse des matiers premiéres argileuses dans la recherche de l'origine de fabrication des céramiques, *Revue d'Archeometrie 1981*, supplement, 83–94

Duncan, H, 1982 *Aspects of the Early Historic Period in South-West Scotland*. Unpublished MPhil thesis, University of Glasgow

Earwood, C, 1992 Turned wooden vessels of the Early Historic period from Ireland and western Scotland, *Ulster J Archaeol,* **54–5**, 154–9

Edwards, N & Lane, A (eds), 1988 *Early medieval settlements in Wales AD 400–1100*. Cardiff & Bangor

Empereur, J-Y & Picon, M, 1989 Les régions de production d'amphores impérials en Méditerranée orientale, in A Hesnard *et al* (eds) 1989, *Amphores romaines et histoire économique; Dix ans de recherché*. Rome, 223–48

Entwhistle, C, 1994 Coin-weight from Somerset, in D Buckton (ed) 1994, *Byzantium: treasures of Byzantine art and culture*. London: British Museum Press, 86

Esmonde Cleary, S, 2000 Summing up, in Wilmott & Wilson (eds) 2000, 89–94

Etchingham, C & Swift, C, 2004 English and Pictish terms for brooch in an 8th-century Irish Law-text, *Medieval Archaeol,* **48**, 31–50

Evison, V I, 1972 Glass cone beakers of the 'Kempston' type, *J Glass Stud,* **14**, 48–66

Evison, V I, 1979 *A corpus of wheel-thrown pottery in Anglo-Saxon graves,* Royal Archaeol Inst Monogr Ser. London

Evison, V I, 1982a Anglo-Saxon glass claw-beakers, *Archaeologia*, **107**, 43–76

Evison, V I, 1982b Bichrome glass vessels of the seventh and eighth centuries, *Studien zur Sachsensforschung*, **3**, 7–21

Evison, V I, 1983 Some distinctive glass vessels of the post-Roman period, *J Glass Stud*, **25**, 87–93

Evison, V I, 1989 The glass vessel, in Rahtz & Watts 1989, 341–5

Evison, V I, 1990 Red marbled glass, Roman to Carolingian, *Annales du IIe Congrès de l'Association pour l'Histoire du Verre, Bâle, 1988*, 217–28

Evison, V I, 1991 Le verre carolingien, in Foy & Sennequier (eds) 1991, 137–48

Evison, V I, 2000 Glass vessels in England AD 400–1100, in Price (ed) 2000b, 47–104

Evison, V I , Hodges, H & Hurst, J G, 1974 *Medieval pottery from excavations: studies presented to Gerald Clough Dunning*. London: John Baker

Farquhar, R M & Vitali, V, 1989 Lead isotope measurements and their application to Roman lead and bronze artefacts from Carthage, *MASCA Res Papers Sci Archaeol*, **6**, 39–45

Faulkner, N, 2004 The case for the Dark Ages, in Collins & Gerrard (eds) 2004, 5–12

Ferguson, W, 1998 *The identity of the Scottish nation: an historic quest*. Edinburgh: Edinburgh University Press

Feyeux, J-Y, 1995 La typologie de la verrierre mérovingienne du nord de la France, in Foy (ed) 1995b, 109–38

Fischer, A R, 1985 Winklebury Hillfort: a study of artefact distribution from subsoil features, *Proc Prehist Soc*, **51**, 167–80

Fleuriot, L & Giot, P-R, 1977 Early Brittany, *Antiquity*, **51**, 106–16

Foster, I, 1965 The emergence of Wales, in I Foster & G Daniel (eds) 1965, *Prehistoric and early Wales*. London: Routledge & Paul, 213–35

Foster, I & Alcock, L (eds), 1963 *Culture and environment*. London: Routledge & Paul

Foster, S M, 1989 Transformation in social space: the Iron Age of Orkney and Caithness, *Scot Archaeol Review*, **6**, 34–54

Fowler, P J, 1971 Hillforts AD 400–700, in Jesson & Hill (eds) 1971, 203–13

Fowler, P J, Gardener, K S & Rahtz, P A, 1970 *Cadbury Congresbury, Somerset, 1968, an introductory report*. Bristol

Fox, A, 1955 Some evidence for a Dark Age trading site at Bantham, near Thurleston, S Devon, *Antiq J*, **35**, 55–68

Fox, A, 1995 Tin ingots from Bigbury Bay, *Proc Devon Archaeol Soc*, **53**, 11–23

Foy, D, 1995a La verre de la fin du IVe au VIIIe siècle en France méditerranéenne, premier essai de typo-chronologie, in Foy (ed) 1995b, 187–242

Foy, D (ed), 1995b *Le Verre de l'Antiquité tardive et du Haut Moyen Age*, Association Française pour l'Archéologie du Verre. Guiry-en-Vexin: Musée Archéologique du Val d'Oise

Foy, D & Hochuli-Gysel, A, 1995 La verre en Aquitaine du IVe au IXe sièlce, un état de la question, in Foy (ed) 1995b, 151–76

Foy, D & Sennequier, G (eds), 1991 *A travers le Verre du moyen âge à la Renaissance*. Rouen

Frankovitch, R & Patterson, H (eds), 2000 *Extracting meaning from ploughsoil assemblages*, Archaeology of Mediterranean Landscapes vol **1**. Oxford: Oxbow Books

Fulford, M G, 1977 Pottery and Britain's foreign trade in the later Roman period, in Peacock (ed) 1977c, 35–83

Fulford, M G, 1978 The interpretation of Britain's Late Roman trade: the scope of medieval historical and archaeological analogy, in J Taylor & H Cleere (eds) 1978, *Roman shipping and trade: Britain and the Rhine provinces*, CBA Res Rep, **24**. London: Council for British Archaeology, 59–69

Fulford, M G, 1989 Byzantium and Britain: a Mediterranean perspective on post-Roman Mediterranean imports in western Britain and Ireland, *Medieval Archaeol*, **33**, 1–6

Fulford, M G & Peacock, D P S, 1984 *Excavations at Carthage: the British mission* Vol 1(2) *The Avenue du President Habib Bourguiba, Salammbo: the pottery and other ceramic objects from the site*. Sheffield: University of Sheffield

Gabet, C, 1969 La céramique gallo-romaine receuillie à Pépiron (Charente-Maritime), *Gallia*, **27**, 45–70

Galliou, P, 1986 Céramiques: les problèmes de l'autochtonie, *Rencontres archéologiques de Nantes*. Nantes, 57–66

Galliou, P & Ménez, Y, 1986 La villa gallo-romaine de Kervéguen en Quimper, *Bulletin Société archéologique Finistère*, **115**, 43–78

Gamo Parras, B, 1995 Vidrios de época visigoda en España, una aproximación, in D Foy (ed) 1995b, 301–18

Geary, P, 1994 The ninth-century relic trade – a response to popular piety?, in P Geary (ed) 1994, *Living with the dead in the Middle Ages*. Ithaca, 177–93

Gerrard, J, 2004 How late is late? Pottery and the fifth century in southwest Britain, in Collins & Gerrard (eds) 2004, 65–76

Gerritson, F, 1999 To build and to abandon: cultural biography of late prehistoric houses and farmsteads in the southern Netherlands, *Archaeological Dialogues*, **6**, 78–97

Gilchrist, R, 1988 A reappraisal of Dinas Powys: local exchange and specialized livestock in 5th- to 7th-century Wales, *Medieval Archaeol*, **32**, 50–62

Gillies, W, 1981 The craftsman in early Celtic literature, *Scot Archaeol Forum*, **11**, 70–85

Given, M & Knapp, B, 2003 *The Sydney Cyrus survey project: social approaches to regional archaeological survey*. Los Angeles: UCLA

Gondek, M. 2003 *Mapping sculpture and power: symbolic wealth in early medieval Scotland 6th–11th centuries AD*. Unpublished PhD thesis, University of Glasgow

Gondek, M, 2006 Investing in Sculpture: Power in Early-historic Scotland, *Medieval Archaeol*, **50**, 105–42

Graham-Campbell, J, 1991 Dinas Powys metalwork and the dating of enamelled zoomorphic penannular brooches, *Bull Board Celtic Stud*, **38**, 220–32

Graham-Campbell, J, Close-Brooks, J & Laing, L, 1976 The Mote of Mark and Celtic interlace, *Antiquity*, **50**, 48–53

Green, S, 1986 Excavations at Little Hoyle (Longbury Bank), Wales, in 1984, in D A Roe (ed) 1986, *Studies in the Upper Palaeolithic of Britain and North-West Europe*, BAR Internat Ser, **S296**. Oxford: British Archaeological Reports, 99–119

Grierson, P, 1982 *Byzantine coins*. London: Methuen

Grierson, P & Blackburn, M, 1986 *Medieval European coinage: with a catalogue of coins in the Fitzwilliam Museum, Cambridge 1: the early Middle Ages (5th- to 10th-century)*. Cambridge: Cambridge University Press

Griffiths, D, 2003 Markets and 'productive sites': a view from western Britain, in Pestell & Ulmschneider (eds) 2003, 62–72

Guido, M, 1978 *The glass beads of the prehistoric and Roman periods in Britain and Ireland*, Res Rep Soc Antiq Lond, **35**. London: Society of Antiquaries of London

Guido, M, 1999 *The glass beads of Anglo-Saxon England c. AD 400–700*, M Welsh (ed). Woodbridge: Boydell Press

Guilbert, G (ed), 1981 *Hillfort studies: essays for A H A Hogg*. Leicester: Leicester University Press

Gwynn, J (ed), 1906 *The Book of Armagh*. Dublin: Hodges Figgis & Co

Hamerow, H, 2006 'Special Deposits' in Anglo-Saxon settlements, *Medieval Archaeol*, **50**, 1–30

Handley, M, 2001 The origins of Christian commemoration in late antique Britain, *Early Medieval Europe*, **10**, 177–99

Hansen, L, 1982 Die skandinavischen Terra Sigillata-Funde zu ihrer Herkunft, Datierung und Relation zu den übrigen römischen Importen der jüngern Kaiserzeit, *Studien zur Sachsenforschung*, **3**, 75–99

Harden, D B, 1956a Glass vessels in Britain and Ireland, AD 400–1000, in D B Harden (ed) 1956b, 132–167

Harden, D B (ed), 1956b *Dark Age Britain*. London: Methuen & Co

Harden, D B, 1963 The glass, in L Alcock 1963a, 178–88

Harden, D B, 1972 Ancient glass, III: Post-Roman, *Archaeol J*, **128**, 78–117

Harden, D B, 1978 Anglo-Saxon and later medieval glass in Britain: some recent developments, *Medieval Archaeol*, **22**, 1–24

Harris, A, 2003 *Byzantium, Britain and the West: The archaeology of cultural identity AD 400–650*. Stroud: Tempus

Harry, R & Morris, C D, 1997 Excavations on the Lower Terrace, Site C, Tintagel Island 1990–94, *Antiq J*, **77**, 1–43

Hartgroves, S & Walker, R, 1988 Excavations in the Lower ward, Tintagel Castle, 1986, *Cornish Stud*, **16**, 9–30

Haseloff, G, 1987 Insular animal style with special reference to Irish art in the early medieval period, in Ryan (ed) 1987, 44–55

Hassall, M & Rhodes, J, 1974 Excavations at the New Market Hall, Gloucester, 1966–7, *Trans Bristol Glouc Archaeol Soc*, **93**, 15–100

Hawkes, S C, 1985 The early Saxon period evidence, in G Briggs, J Cook & T Rowley (eds) 1985, *The archaeology of the Oxford region*. Oxford, 64–108

Hayden, B & Cannon, A, 1983 Where the garbage goes: refuse disposal in the Maya highlands, *J Anthrop Archaeol*, **2**, 117–63

Hayes, J W, 1972 *Late Roman pottery*. London: British School at Rome

Hayes, J W, 1977 North African flanged bowls; a problem in fifth-century chronology, in Dore & Greene (eds) 1977, 279–87

Hayes, J W, 1980 *A supplement to Late Roman pottery*. London: British School at Rome

Heighway, C, 1984 Anglo-Saxon Gloucestershire, in A Saville (ed), *Archaeology in Gloucestershire*. Cheltenham, 225–47

Heighway, C & Parker, A J, 1972 The Roman tilery at St Oswald's Priory, Gloucester, *Britannia*, **13**, 25–78

Hencken, H, 1938 *Cahercommaun: a stone fort in County Clare*. Dublin: Royal Society of Antiquaries of Ireland

Hencken, H, 1950 Lagore Crannog: an Irish royal residence of the 7th to 10th centuries, *Proc Royal Irish Acad*, **53C**, 1–247

Henderson, J, 1989 The nature of the early Christian glass industry in Ireland: some evidence from Dunmisk fort, Co Tyrone, *Ulster J Archaeol*, **51**, 72–9

Henderson, J, 1993 Scientific analysis of the glass, in Campbell & Lane 1993a, 46–9

Henry, F, 1956 Irish enamels of the Dark Ages and their relations to the cloisonné techniques, in Harden (ed) 1956b, 71–88

Higgitt, J & Spearman, R M (eds), 1993 *The Age of Migrating Ideas: Early Medieval Art in Northern Britain and Ireland*. Edinburgh: National Museums of Scotland

Hill, P, 1997 *Whithorn and St Ninian: The excavations of a monastic town 1984–89*. Stroud: Sutton Publishing/Whithorn Trust

Hillier, B & Hanson, J, 1984 *The social logic of space*. Cambridge: Cambridge University Press

Hines, J, 2000 Welsh and English: mutual origins in Post-Roman Britain?, *Studia Celtica*, **34**, 81–104

Hines, J, 2003 Editor's note, *Medieval Archaeol*, **47**, 199–200

Hinton, D, 2000 *A smith in Lindsey: the Anglo-*

Saxon grave at Tatershall Thorpe, Lincolnshire. London: Society for Medieval Archaeology

Hodder, I, 1978a Some effects of distance on patterns of human interaction, in Hodder (ed) 1978b, 155–78

Hodder, I, (ed), 1978b *The spatial organisation of culture*. London

Hodder, I (ed), 1982 *Symbolic and structural archaeology*. Cambridge: Cambridge University Press

Hodges, R, 1977 Some early medieval French wares in the British Isles: an archaeological assessment of the early French wine trade with Britain, in Peacock (ed) 1977c, 239–56

Hodges, R, 1978 Early medieval ports of trade in northern Europe, *Norwegian Archaeol Review*, **11**, 97–101; 114–17

Hodges, R, 1981 *The Hamwih pottery: the local and imported wares from 30 years' excavation at Middle Saxon Southampton and their European context*, CBA Res Rep, **37**. London: Council for British Archaeology

Hodges, R, 1982 *Dark Age economics: the origins of towns and trade AD 600–1000*. London: Duckworth

Hodges, R, 1988 *Primitive and peasant markets*. Oxford: Blackwell

Hodges, R, 1989 *The Anglo-Saxon achievement*. London: Duckworth

Hodges, R, 2000 *Towns and trade in the age of Charlemagne*. London: Duckworth

Hodges, R & Whitehouse, D, 1983 *Mohammed, Charlemagne and the origins of Europe: archaeology and the Pirenne thesis*. London: Duckworth

Hodges, R & Hobley, B (eds), 1988 *The rebirth of the towns in the west AD 700–1050*, CBA Res Rep, **68**. London: Council for British Archaeology

Hollinrake, C & Hollinrake, N, forthcoming Excavations at Carhampton, Somerset

Hope-Taylor, B, 1977 *Yeavering: an Anglo-British centre of early Northumbria*. London: HMSO

Hübener, W, 1968 Eine studie zur spätrömischen Rädchensigillata, *Bonner Jahr*, **168**, 241–98

Huggett, J W, 1988 Imported grave goods and the early Anglo-Saxon economy, *Medieval Archaeol*, **32**, 63–96

Hunter, J, 1980 The glass, in P Holdsworth 1980, *Excavations at Melbourne Street, Southampton 1971–76*, CBA Res Rep, **33**. London: Council for British Archaeology

Hunter, J & Heyworth, M, 1998 *The Hamwic glass*, CBA Res Report, **116**. York: Council for British Archaeology

Hurst, H, 1976 Gloucester (Glevum): a colonia in the West Country, in K Branigan & P Fowler (eds) 1976, *The Roman West Country: classical culture and Celtic society*. Newton Abbot, 63–80

Hutchinson, G, 1979 The bar-lug pottery of Cornwall, *Cornish Archaeol*, **18**, 81–103

Ivens, R, 1984 Movilla Abbey, Newtonards, County Down: Excavations 1981, *Ulster J Archaeol*, **47**, 71–108

Jackson, K H, 1969 *The Gododdin*. Edinburgh: Edinburgh University Press

James, E, 1977 *The Merovingian archaeology of south-west Gaul*, BAR Internat Ser, **25**. Oxford: British Archaeological Reports

James, E, 1982 Ireland and western Gaul in the Merovingian period, in Whitelock *et al* (eds) 1982, 362–86

James, E, 1988 *The Franks*. Oxford: Blackwell

James, S, 1999 *The Atlantic Celts: Ancient people or modern invention?* London: British Museum Press

Jesson, M & Hill, D (eds), 1971 *The Iron Age and its hillforts*. Southampton: University of Southampton

Jope, E M (ed), 1966 *An archaeological survey of County Down*. Belfast: HMSO

Karagiorgou, O, 2001 LR2: a container for the military *annona* on the Danubian border?, in Kingsley & Decker (eds) 2001b, 129–66

Keay, S, 1984 *Late Roman amphorae in the western Mediterranean*, BAR Internat Ser, **S136**. Oxford: British Archaeological Reports

Kelly, F, 1988 *A guide to early Irish Law*, Early Irish Law Series, **3**. Dublin: Dublin Institute for Advanced Studies

Kelly, F, 2000 *Early Irish farming*. Dublin: Dublin Institute for Advanced Studies

Kilbride-Jones, H E, 1980 *Zoomorphic penannular brooches*. London: Society of Antiquaries

Kingsley, S, 2004 *Barbarian seas: Late Rome to Islam*. London: Periplus

Kingsley, S & Decker, M, 2001a New Rome, new theories on inter-regional exchange, in Kingsley & Decker (eds) 2001b, 1–27

Kingsley, S & Decker, M (eds), 2001b *Economy and exchange in the East Mediterranean during Late Antiquity*. Oxford: Oxbow Books

Kirkby, A & Kirkby M J, 1976 Geomorphic processes and the surface survey of archaeological sites in semi-arid areas, in D A Davidson & M L Shackley (eds) 1976, *Geoarchaeology: Earth Sciences and the past*. London, 229–54

Knight, J K, 1984 Glamorgan AD 400–1100: archaeology and history, in Savory (ed) 1984a, 315–64

Knight, J K, 1996 Seasoned with salt: insular-gallic contacts in the early memorial stones and cross-slabs, in Dark (ed) 1996, 109–20

Kopytoft, I, 1986 The cultural biography of things: commoditisation as process, in Appadurai (ed) 1986, 64–94

Lafaurie, J & Morrisson, C, 1987 La pénétration des monnaies Byzantines en Gaule mérovingienne et visigothique du VIe au VIIIe siècles, *Revue Numismatique* 6th series, **29**, 38–98

Laing, L, 1974 Cooking pots and the origins of the Scottish medieval pottery industry, *Archaeol J*, **130**, 183–216

Laing, L, 1975 *The archaeology of late Celtic Britain and Ireland c400–1200 AD*. London: Methuen

Laing, L & Longley, D, 2006 *The Mote of Mark: a*

Dark Age hillfort in south-west Scotland. Oxford: Oxbow Books

Lane, A, 1990 Hebridean pottery: problems of definition, chronology, presence and absence, in I Armit (ed) 1990, *Beyond the brochs*. Edinburgh: Edinburgh University Press, 108–30

Lane, A & Campbell, E, 2000 *Excavations at Dunadd: an early Dalriadic capital*. Oxford: Oxbow Books

Langlotz, E, 1969 Beobachtung in Phokaia, *Archäol Anzeiger,* **84**, 377–85

Lawlor, H C, 1925 *The monastery of Saint Mochaoi at Nendrum*. Belfast: Belfast Natural History & Philosophical Society

Lebecq, S, 1989 La Neustrie et la mer, in H Atsma (ed) 1989, *La Neustrie Les pays au nord de la Loire de 650 à 850*. Sigmaringen, 405–40

Lewis, A R, 1978 *The sea and medieval civilisations*. London: Variorum

Liversage, G D, 1968 Excavations at Dalkey Island, Co Dublin, *Proc Royal Irish Acad,* **66C**, 53–233

Lynn, C J, 1986 Lagore, County Meath and Ballinderry No 1, County Westmeath: some possible structural reinterpretations, *J Irish Archaeol,* **3**, 69–73

Mac Airt, S & Mac Niocaill, G, 1983 *The Annals of Ulster (to AD 1131)*. Dublin: Dublin Institute for Advanced Studies

McCormick, M, 2001 *Origins of the European Economy: Communications and Commerce AD 300–900*. Cambridge: Cambridge University Press

MacNeill, E, 1923 Ancient Irish Law: the law of status or franchise, *Proc Royal Irish Acad,* **36C**, 265–311

Mac Niocaill, G, 1972 *Ireland before the Vikings*. Dublin: Gill & Macmillan

Maddicott, J R, 2005, London and Droitwich, c. 650–750: trade, industry and the rise of Mercia, *Anglo-Saxon England*, **34**, 7–58

Maillé, Marquis de, 1960 *Recherches sur les origines chrétiennes de Bordeaux*. Paris

Mango, M, 2001Beyond the amphora: non-ceramic evidence for Late Antique industry and trade, in Kingsley & Decker (eds) 2001b, 87–106

Marsden, P, 1980 *Roman London*. London: Allen & Unwin

Mayet, F & Picon, M, 1986 Une sigillée phocéenne tardive (Late Roman C) et sa diffusion en Occident, *Figlina*, **7**, 129–42

Meaney, A L, 1964 *A gazetteer of early Anglo-Saxon burial sites*. London

Meehan, B, 1994 *The Book of Kells. An illustrated introduction to the manuscript in Trinity College Dublin*. London: Thames & Hudson

Megaw, A H S & Jones, R E, 1983 Byzantine and allied pottery: a contribution by chemical analysis to problems of origin and distribution, *Annual Brit School Athens,* **78**, 235–63

Metcalf, D M, 1988 The coins, in Andrews (ed) 1988, 17–59

Middleton, N, 2006 Early medieval port customs, tolls and controls on foreign trade, *Early Medieval Europe,* **13**, 313–58

Moore, H, 1982 The interpretation of spatial patterning in settlement residues, in Hodder (ed) 1982, 74–9

Moorhouse, S, 1986 Non-dating uses of medieval pottery, *Medieval Ceramics,* **10**, 85–124

Morrisson, C, 1999 La diffusion de la monnaie de Carthage hors d'Afrique du Ve au VIIe siècles, in S Lancel (ed) 1999, *Numismatique, langues, écrtitures et arts du livre*. Paris, 109–16

Munn, M L Z 1985 A Late Roman kiln site in the Hermionid, Greece, *American J Archaeol,* **89**, 342–3

Munro, R, 1882 *Ancient Scottish lake-dwellings or crannogs*. Edinburgh: David Douglas

Mytum, H, 1986 High status vessels in early historic Ireland: a reference in the *Bethu Brigte*, *Oxford J Archaeol,* **5**, 375–8

Nash-Williams, V E, 1950 *The early Christian monuments of Wales*. Cardiff: University of Wales Press

Näsman, U, 1984 Vendel period glass from Eketorp II, Öland, Sweden: On glass and trade from the late 6th to the late 8th centuries AD, *Acta Archaeologica,* **55**, 55–116

Naylor, J, 2004 *An archaeology of trade in Middle Saxon England*, BAR Brit Ser, **376**. Oxford: British Archaeological Reports

Nelson, B A, 1985 *Decoding prehistoric ceramics*. Carbondale

Nenquin, J, 1961 *Salt: a study in economic prehistory*. Brugge: De Tempel

Newby, M, 2005 Medieval glass lamps: the archaeological and iconographic evidence from central Italy, *Glass News,* **18**, 5–6

Newman, C, 1989 Fowler's type F3 early medieval penannular brooches, *Medieval Archaeol,* **33**, 7–20

Nieke, M R, 1993 Penannular and related brooches: secular ornament or symbol in action?, in Higgitt & Spearman (eds) 1993, 128–34

Nieke, M R & Duncan, H, 1988 Dalriada: the establishment and maintenance of an early historic kingdom in northern Britain, in Driscoll & Nieke (eds) 1988, 6–21

Nielson, A E, 1991 Trampling the archaeological record: an experimental study, *American Antiquity,* **56**, 483–503

Nowakowski, J A & Thomas C, 1990 *Excavations at Tintagel Parish Churchyard, Spring 1990, Interim Report*. Truro: Cornwall Archaeological Unit & Institute of Cornish Studies

Nowakowski, J A, Thomas C, 1992 *Grave News from Tintagel: An Account of a Second Season of Archaeological Excavation at Tintagel Churchyard, Cornwall, 1991*. Truro: Cornwall Archaeological Unit & Institute of Cornish Studies

Ó Chróinín, D, 1995 *Early medieval Ireland 400–1200*. London: Longman

Oddy, W A & Craddock, P, 1983 Scientific examination of the Coptic bowl and related Coptic metalwork found in Anglo-Saxon contexts, in Bruce-Mitford 1983, 753–7

O'Donnell, M, 1984 *An analysis of E ware in Ireland*. Unpublished MA dissertation, University College, Cork

O'Kelly, M J, 1962 Two ring-forts at Garryduff, Co Cork, *Proc Royal Irish Acad*, **63C**, 17–125

Olson, L, 1989 *Early monasteries in Cornwall*, Studies in Celtic Hist, **11**. Woodbridge: Boydell & Brewer

O'Mahany, T & Richey, A G, 1873 *Ancient Laws of Ireland*, vol 3. Dublin: HMSO

Ó Ríordáin, S P, 1942 The excavation of a large earthen ring-fort at Garranes, Co Cork, *Proc Royal Irish Acad*, **47C**, 77–150

Ó Ríordáin, S P, 1947 Roman material in Ireland, *Proc Royal Irish Acad*, **51C**, 35–82

Orton, C, 1975 Quantifying pottery studies: some progress, problems and prospects, *Sci Archaeol*, **16**, 30–5

Orton, C & Tyers, P, 1990 Slicing the pie – a framework for comparing ceramic assemblages, *Medieval Ceramics*, **14**, 55–6

Orton, C, Tyers, P & Vince, A, 1993 *Pottery in archaeology*. Cambridge: Cambridge University Press

O'Sullivan, A, 1998 *The archaeology of Lake settlement in Ireland*, Discovery Programme Monogr, **4**. Dublin: Royal Irish Academy

O'Sullivan, J, 1999 Iona: archaeological investigations, 1875–1996, in D Broun & T Clancy (eds) 1999, *Spes Scotorum: Hope of Scots*. Edinburgh: T & T Clark, 215–44

Parker, A J, 1984 Shipwrecks and trade in the Mediterranean, *Archaeol Review Cambridge*, **3**, 99–114

Parker, A J, 1992 *Ancient shipwrecks of the Mediterranean and Roman provinces*, BAR Internat Ser, **580**. Oxford: British Archaeological Reports

Parker Pearson, M, 2004 *South Uist*. Stroud: Tempus

Peacock, D P S, 1977a Late Roman amphorae from Chalk near Gravesend, Kent, in Dore & Green (eds) 1977, 295–300

Peacock, D P S, 1977b Roman amphorae, typology, fabric and origin, *Mélanges de l'École française à Rome*, **32**, 261–78

Peacock, D P S (ed), 1977c *Pottery and early commerce*. London: Academic Press

Peacock, D P S, 1982 *Pottery in the Roman world: an ethnoarchaeological approach*. London: Longman

Peacock, D P S & Thomas, C, 1967 Class E imported post-Roman pottery: a suggested origin, *Cornish Archaeol*, **6**, 35–46

Peacock, D P S & Williams, D, 1986 *Amphorae and the Roman Economy*. London: Longman

Pearce, S (ed), 1982 *The early church in western Britain and Ireland*, BAR, **102**. Oxford: British Archaeological Reports

Pearce, S 2004 *South-western Britain in the early Middle Ages*. London: Leicester University Press

Penhallurick, R D, 1986 *Tin in antiquity*. London

Pertz, G W (ed), 1874 *Monumenta Germaniae Historica, Diplomatum Imperii 1*. Hanover

Pestell, T & Ulmschneider, K (eds), 2003 *Markets in early medieval Europe: trading and 'productive' sites AD 650–850*. Macclesfield: Windgather Press

von Pfeffer, W, 1953 Zur typologie merowingerzeitlicher Gläser mit Fadenverzierung, *Festschrift des Römisch-Germanischen Zentralmuseums Mainz*, **3**, 147–60

Phillips, C W, 1934 The excavation of a hut-group at Pant-y-saer in the parish of Llanfair-Mathafon-Eithaf, *Archaeologia Cambrensis*, **89**, 1–36

Philpott, R A, 1998 Three Byzantine coins found near the north Wirral coast in Merseyside, *Trans Hist Soc Lancs and Ches*, **148**, 197–202

Plog, S, 1980 *Stylistic variation in prehistoric ceramics*. Cambridge: Cambridge University Press

Portnoy, A W, 1981 A microarchaeological view of human settlement space and function, in R Gould and M Schiffer, *Modern material culture: the archaeology of us*. New York, 213–24

Preston-Jones, A & Rose, P, 1986 Medieval Cornwall, *Cornish Archaeol*, **25**, 135–85

Price, J, 1992 Report on vessel and window glass, in Rahtz *et al* 1992, 132–5

Price, J, 1995 Glass tablewares with wheel-cut, engraved, and abraded decoration in Britain in the fourth century AD, in Foy (ed) 1995b, 25–34

Price, J, 2000a Late Roman glass vessels in Britain, from 350 to 410 and beyond, in Price (ed) 2000b, 1–32

Price, J (ed), 2000b *Glass in Britain and Ireland, AD 350–1100*, Brit Museum Occas Pap, **127**. London: British Museum Press

Price, J & Cottam, S, 1995 Late Roman and early post-Roman glass, in Alcock 1995, 99–103

Price, J & Cottam, S, 1999 *Romano-British glass vessels: a handbook*, Practical handbooks in archaeol, **14**. York: Council for British Archaeology

Prieto, F J N, 1984 Algunos datas sobre los importaciones de cerámica 'Phocaean Red Slip' en la peninsula Iberica, in T F C Blagg, R F Jones & S J Keay (eds) 1984, *Papers in Iberian archaeology*, BAR Internat Ser, **S193**. Oxford: British Archaeological Reports, 540–8

Quinnell, H, 1993 A sense of identity: distinctive Cornish stone artefacts in the Roman and Post-Roman periods, *Cornish Archaeol*, **32**, 29–46

Quinnell, H, 2004 *Trethurgy: excavations at Trethurgy round, St Austell: community and status in Roman and Post-Roman Cornwall*. Truro: Cornwall County Council

Rademacher, F, 1942 Fränkische Gläser aus dem Rheinland, *Bonner Jahrbücher*, **147**, 285–344

Radford, C A R, 1935 Tintagel: the castle and Celtic monastery, *Antiq J*, **15**, 401–19

Radford, C A R, 1956 Imported pottery found at Tintagel, Cornwall, in Harden (ed) 1956b, 59–70

Rahtz, P, 1970 Excavations on Glastonbury Tor, Somerset 1964–66, *Archaeol J,* **127**, 1–82

Rahtz, P, 1974 Pottery in Somerset, AD 400–1066, in V I Evison *et al* (eds) 1974, 95–124

Rahtz, P, 1979 *The Saxon and medieval palaces at Cheddar,* BAR, **65**. Oxford: British Archaeological Reports

Rahtz, P, 1982 The Dark Ages AD 400–700, in Aston & Burrow (eds) 1982, 99–108

Rahtz, P, 1988 Post Roman Avon, in M Aston & R Isles (eds) 1988, 73–82

Rahtz, P, 1993 *English Heritage Book of Glastonbury*. London: Batsford

Rahtz, P, Dickinson, T & Watts, L (eds), 1980 *Anglo-Saxon cemeteries 1979,* BAR, **82**. Oxford: British Archaeological Reports

Rahtz, P & Watts, L, 1989 Pagans Hill revisited, *Archaeol J,* **146**, 330–71

Rahtz, P, Woodward, A, Burrow, I, Everton, A, Watts, L, Leach, P, Hirst, S Fowler, P & Gardener, K, 1992 *Cadbury Congresbury 1968–73: a late/post-Roman hilltop settlement in Somerset*, Brit Archaeol Rep Brit Ser **223**. Oxford: Tempus Reparatum

Rahtz, P, Hirst, S, Wright, S M, 2000 *Cannington Cemetery: Excavations 1962–63 of prehistoric, Roman, Post-Roman and later features at Cannington Park Quarry, near Bridgewater, Somerset*, Britannia Monogr Ser, **17**. London: Society for the Promotion of Roman Studies

Randoin, B, 1981 Essai de classification chronologique de la céramique de Tours du IVe au IXe siècle, *Recherche sur Tours,* **1**, 103–14

RCAHMS, 1988 *Argyll: an inventory of the ancient monuments,* vol 6, *Mid-Argyll*. Edinburgh: HMSO

RCAHMW, 1991 *An inventory of the ancient monuments of Glamorgan* Vol 3(i): *Medieval secular defensive monuments.* Cardiff: HMSO

Reece, R, 1993 The coins, in Woodward & Leach 1993, 80–7

Renfrew, C, 1977 Alternative models for exchange and spatial distribution, in T Earle & J Ericson (eds), *Exchange systems in Prehistory*. London, 71–90

Reynolds, P, 1995 *Trade in the western Mediterranean AD 400–700: the ceramic evidence*. Oxford

Richey, A G (ed), 1879 *Ancient Laws of Ireland,* vol 4. Dublin

Rigoir, J, 1968 Les sigillées paléochretiénnes grises et oranges, *Gallia,* **26**, 177–244

Rigoir, J, Rigoir, Y & Meffre, J-F, 1973 Les dérivées paléochrétiennes du groupe atlantique, *Gallia*, **31**, 364–409

Rigold, S, 1975 The Sutton Hoo coins in the light of the contemporary background of coinage in England, in Bruce-Mitford 1975, 653–77

Riley, J A, 1975 Pottery from the first session of excavation in the Caesarea hippodrome, *Bull American School Oriental Res,* **218**, 25–63

Riley, J A, 1979 The coarse pottery from Berenice, in J A Lloyd (ed), *Excavations at Sidi Khrebish Benghazi (Berenice),* Supplements to Libya Antiqua, V, vol 2. Tripoli, 91–467

Riley, J A, 1981 The pottery from the cisterns, in J H Humphrey (ed), *Excavations at Carthage conducted by the University of Michigan VI*. Ann Arbor, 85–124

Riley, J A, Sidebotham, S, Hany, A, Hamroush, H A & Barakat, H N, 1989 Fieldwork on the Red Sea Coast: The 1987 season, *J American Research Centre in Egypt,* **26**, 127–66

Robinson, D, 1988 *Biglis, Llandough and Caldicot,* BAR Brit Ser, **188**. Oxford: British Archaeological Reports

Robinson, H S, 1959 *The Athenian Agora*, V: *Pottery of the Roman period*. Princeton: American School Classical Studies Athens

Rodziewicz, M, 1984 *Alexandrie III. Les Habitati romaines Tadives d'Alexandrie.* Warsaw

Roosen-Runge, H & Werner, A, 1960 The pictorial technique of the Lindisfarne Gospels, in T J Brown & R L S Bruce-Mitford (eds), *Evangeliorum Quattuor Codex Lindisfarnensis*, vol 2. Berne, 261–7

Rothschild-Boros, M C, 1981 The determination of amphora contents, in G Barker & R Hodges (eds) 1981, *Papers in Italian archaeology. 2, Archaeology and Italian Society: prehistoric, Roman and medieval studies*, BAR Internat Ser, **S102**. Oxford: British Archaeological Reports, 79–85

Ryan, J, 1942 Uí Echach Muman, in S P Ó Ríordáin 1942, 145–50

Ryan, M, 1973 Native pottery in early historic Ireland, *Proc Royal Irish Acad,* **73C**, 619–45

Ryan, M, 1981 Some archaeological comments on the occurrence and use of silver in pre-Viking Ireland, in Scott (ed) 1981b, 45–50

Ryan, M (ed), 1987 *Ireland and Insular Art AD 500–1200*. Dublin: Royal Irish Academy

Rye, O S, 1976 Keeping your temper under control, *Archaeol Physical Anthrop Oceania,* **11**, 106–37

de Saint Jores, J-X & Hincher, V, 2001 Les habitats mérovingien et carolingien de la 'Delle sur le Marais' a Giberville (Calvados), *Archéologie Medievale,* **30–1**, 1–38

Samson, R, 1999 Illusory emporia and mad economic theories, in M Anderton (ed), *Anglo-Saxon trading centres.* Glasgow, 76–90

Sanquer, R & Galliou, P, 1972 *Garum*, sel et salaisons en Armoriques romaine, *Gallia,* **30**, 199–223

Savory, H N (ed), 1984a *Glamorgan County History*, Vol 2. Cardiff: Glamorgan History Trust

Savory, H N, 1984b Early Iron Age Glamorgan, *c* 500 BC–100 AD, in Savory (ed) 1984a, 237–75

Schiffer, M B, 1972 Archaeological context and systemic context, *American Antiquity,* **37**, 156–65

Schiffer, M B, 1976 *Behavioural archaeology*. New York: Academic Press

Schlessinger, A & Walls, C, 1996 An early church and medieval farmstead site: excavations at Llanelen, Gower, *Archaeol J*, **153**, 104–47

Scott, B G, 1981a Some conflicts and correspondences of evidence in the study of Irish archaeology and language, in Scott (ed) 1981b, 115–19

Scott, B G (ed), 1981b *Studies in early Ireland.* Belfast

Scott, J, 1960 Loch Glashan, *Discovery and Excavation Scot*, 8–9

Sharpe, R (ed & trans), 1991 *Adomnan of Iona: Life of St Columba.* London

Shephard, A O, 1956 *Ceramics for the archaeologist.* Washington

Simms, K, 1978 Guesting and feasting in Gaelic Ireland, *J Royal Soc Antiq Ireland*, **108**, 67–100

Sims-Williams, P, 1990 *Religion and literature in western England, 600–800.* Cambridge

Smyth, A P, 1982 *Celtic Leinster.* Dublin: Irish Academic Press

Sode, T & Feveile, C, 2002 Segmented metal foil glass beads and hollow, blown glass beads with a coat of metal from the marketplace at Ribe, *By marsk og geest*, **14**, 5–14

Sommer, U, 1990 Dirt theory, or archaeological sites seen as rubbish heaps, *J Theoretical Archaeol*, **1**, 47–60

Soulas, S, 1996 Présentation et provenance de la céramique estampée à Bordeaux, *Aquitania*, **14**, 237–43

Sternini, M, 1995 Il vetro in Italia tra V–IX secoli, in Foy (ed) 1995b, 243–90

Story, J, 1999 Review of Wooding 1996b and Dark 1996, *Early medieval Europe*, **8**, 424–6

Stout, M, 1997 *The Irish ring-fort.* Dublin: Four Courts Press

Swift, C, 1998 Forts and fields: a study of 'monastic towns' in seventh and eighth century Ireland, *J Irish Archaeol*, **9**, 105–25

Tatton-Brown, V A, 1984 The glass, in H R Hurst & S P Roskams 1984, *Excavations at Carthage: the British mission, vol I, 1. The Avenue du president Habib Bourguiba, Salammbo: the site and finds other than pottery.* Sheffield: British Academy, 194–212

Taylor, J, 2000 Cultural deposition processes and post-depositional problems, in R Frankovitch & H Patterson (eds) 2000, 16–26

Theuws, F, 2004 Exchange, religion, identity and central places in the early Middle Ages, *Archaeological Dialogues*, **10**, 121–38, 149–59

Thomas, C, 1954 Excavation of a Dark Age site at Gwithian, Cornwall: interim report 1953–54, *Proc West Cornwall Field Club*, **1**, 59–72

Thomas, C, 1956 Excavations at Gwithian, Cornwall 1956, *Proc West Cornwall Field Club*, **1**, Appendix, 1–28

Thomas, C, 1957 Some imported post-Roman sherds in Cornwall and their origin, *Proc West Cornwall Field Club*, **2**, 15–22

Thomas, C, 1959 Imported pottery in dark-age western Britain, *Medieval Archaeol*, **3**, 89–111

Thomas, C, 1968 Grass-marked pottery in Cornwall, in J Coles & D Simpson (eds), *Studies in ancient Europe.* Leicester, 311–32

Thomas, C, 1971 *The early Christian archaeology of North Britain.* London: Oxford University Press

Thomas, C, 1976a The end of the Roman south-west, in K Branigan & P J Fowler (eds), *The Roman West Country.* Newton Abbot, 198–213

Thomas, C, 1976b Imported Late-Roman Mediterranean pottery in Ireland and western Britain: chronologies and implications, *Proc Royal Irish Acad*, **76C**, 245–55

Thomas, C, 1981 *A provisional list of imported pottery in post-Roman western Britain and Ireland*, Instit Cornish Studies Special Rep, **7**. Redruth

Thomas, C, 1982 East and West: Tintagel, Mediterranean imports and the early Insular Church, in Pearce (ed) 1982, 107–34

Thomas, C, 1985 *Exploration of a drowned landscape: archaeology and history of the Isles of Scilly.* London: Batsford

Thomas, C, 1987 The earliest Christian art in Ireland and Britain, in Ryan 1987, 7–11

Thomas, C, 1988a Tintagel Castle, *Antiquity*, **62**, 421–34

Thomas, C, 1988b The context of Tintagel: a new model for the diffusion of post-Roman Mediterranean imports, *Cornish Archaeol*, **27**, 7–25

Thomas, C, 1989 CAU excavations at Tintagel Island, 1988: the discoveries and their implications, *Cornish Stud*, **16**, 49–60

Thomas, C, 1990 'Gallici nautae de Galliarum provinciis' – a sixth/seventh trade with Gaul, reconsidered, *Medieval Archaeol*, **34**, 1–26

Thomas, C 1993 *English Heritage Book of Tintagel: Arthur and archaeology.* London: Batsford

Thomas, C & Fowler, P J, 1985 Tintagel: a new survey of the 'Island', *Annual Review RCAHME 1984–5*, 16–22

Thomas, C & Thorpe, C M, 1988 Catalogue of all non-medieval finds from Tintagel. Inst Cornish Stud unpublished report

Thomas, C & Thorpe, C M, 1993 Pottery, in Batey *et al* 1993, 55–60

Thorpe, C, 1988 The pottery, in S Hartgroves & R Walker 1988, 22–25

Thorpe, C, 1997 Ceramics, in Harry & Morris 1997, 74–82

Thorpe, W A, 1935 *English Glass.* London

Timby, J R, 1988 The middle Saxon pottery, in Andrews (ed) 1988, 73–124

Tomber, R & Williams, D F, 1986 Late Roman amphorae in Britain, *J Roman Pottery Stud*, **1**, 42–54

Tuffreau-Libre, M, 1980 *La céramique commune gallo-romaine dans le nord de la France (Nord, Pas-de-Calais).* Lille

Turner, S, 2006 *Making a Christian landscape: the countryside in early medieval Cornwall, Devon and Wessex.* Exeter: University of Exeter Press

Tyers, P, 1996 Roman amphoras in Britain, *Internet*

Archaeology, **1**, Available: http://intarchacuk/journal/issue1/tyers_tochtml. Accessed 22/08/2006

Tyler, A, 1982 *Prehistoric and Roman mining for metals in England and Wales*. Unpublished PhD thesis, University College, Cardiff, University of Wales

Valante, M, 1998 Reassessing the Irish 'monastic town', *Irish Hist Stud*, **31**, 1–18

Vroom, J, 2003 *After Antiquity: Ceramics and society in the Aegean from the 7th to the 20th century*. Leiden

Wailes, B, 1963 *Some imported pottery in western Britain, AD 400–800: Its connection with Frankish and Visigothic Gaul*. Unpublished PhD thesis, University of Cambridge

Walton Rogers, P, 2005 Dyestuff analysis on E ware pottery, in Crone & Campbell 2005, 61–2

Warner, R B, 1976 Some observations on the context and importation of exotic material in Ireland, from the first century BC to the second century AD, *Proc Royal Irish Acad*, **76C**, 267–89

Warner, R B, 1979 The Clogher yellow layer, *Medieval Ceramics*, **3**, 37–40

Warner, R B, 1988 The archaeology of Early Historic Irish kingship, in Driscoll & Nieke (eds) 1988, 47–68

Webster, L & Backhouse, J, 1991 *The making of England: Anglo-Saxon art and culture AD 600–900*, London: British Museum Press

Whitelock, D, McKetterick, R & Dumville, D (eds), 1982 *Ireland in early medieval Europe*. Cambridge: Cambridge University Press

Wickham, C, 2005 *Framing the early Middle Ages: Europe and the Mediterranean 400–800*. Oxford: Oxford University Press

Wilkinson, P F, 1995 Excavations at Hen Gastell, Briton ferry, West Glamorgan 1991–92, *Medieval Archaeol*, **39**, 1–50

Williams, J A, Shaw, M & Denham, V, 1985 *Middle Saxon palaces at Northampton*. Northampton: Northampton Development Corporation

Wilmott, T & Wilson, P (eds), 2000 *The Late Roman transition in the North*, BAR Brit Ser, **299**. Oxford: British Archaeological Reports

Wooding, J, 1983 *Class E pottery*. Unpublished undergraduate thesis, University of Sydney

Wooding, J, 1987 Some evidence for cargoes in trade on western coasts of Europe in the early Middle Ages, unpublished conference paper in *Sailing ships and sailing people*, Perth, Western Australia, January 1987

Wooding, J, 1988 What porridge had the Old Irish? E ware and early Irish history, *Australian Celtic J*, **1**, 12–17

Wooding, J, 1996a Cargoes in trade along the western seaboard, in Dark (ed) 1996, 67–82

Wooding, J, 1996b *Communication and Commerce along the western sea-lanes AD 400–800*, Brit Archaeol Rep Internat Ser **S654**. Oxford: Tempus Reparatum

Woodward, A & Leach, P, 1993 *The Uley shrines: excavation of a ritual complex on West hill, Uley, Gloucestershire, 1977–79*. London: English Heritage

Young, C J 1977 *The Roman pottery industry of the Oxford region*. BAR, **43**. Oxford: British Archaeological Reports

Youngs, S (ed), 1989 *The work of angels: masterpieces of Celtic metalwork, 6th–9th centuries AD*. London: British Museum Press

Youngs, S, forthcoming, Anglo-Saxon, Irish and British: hanging-bowls reconsidered, in J Graham-Campbell & M Ryan (eds), *Anglo-Saxon / Irish relations before the Vikings*. London: British Academy/Royal Irish Academy

Ypey, Y, 1963 Die funde aus dem frumittlelatlerlichen graberfeld Huinerveld bei Putten im Museum Nairac zu Barnveld, *Berichten R O B*, **12/13**, 99–152

Zeiss, H, 1941 Die Germanischen Grabfunde des frühen Mittelalters zwischen mittlerer Seine und Loiremündung, *Bericht der Römisch-Germanischen Kommission*, **31**, 5–173

Zimmer, H, 1909 Der Weinhandel Westgalliens nach Irland im I bis 7 Jahrhundert n Chr und sein Niederschlag in irischer Sage und Sprache, *Sitzungsberichte der Königlich Akademie der Wissenschaften, 1909*, 430–76

Index

Page numbers in *italics* denote illustrations.

Abbartez (France) 76
Abercorn (W Lothian) xvii, 4, 11, 116
Abu Mena (Egypt) 74
Adomnán 79, 96, 137
Airgialla 111, 113–14
Alcock, Leslie
   excavation archive 83, 96–7
   research by
      glass 54, 92–3
      pottery 4, 5, 6, 103
Alexandria (Egypt) 81, 128, 131
amphorae stoppers 23
ampullae 74, 75, Pl 38
Anastasius I 76
Anastius 130
Anazarbus (Turkey) 129
anchors 128
Anglo-Saxon Chronicle 118, 119
Annals of Ulster 132
annona 6
Antioch (Turkey) 19
Aquitaine
   E ware 5, 32, 46
   glass 58
   trade 13, 48, 133, 137, 140
Archaeology Data Service 2
Ardifuir (Argyll) xvii, Pl 45
   E ware *36*, *50*
   site characteristics 116
Argolid (Greece) 19
Armagh (Co Armagh) xvii
   glass/glass working *67*, 69, 92
   pottery 78
   site characteristics 113–14, 115, 116
Arnold, Chris 7
Athelney (Som) xvii, 118
Athens (Greece) 5
Atlantic Curtain 140
Austrasia 137, 140

Bacon Hole (W Glam) 118
Ballinderry No. 2 (Co Offaly) xvii
   brooch 46, 82
   E ware *40*, 46, *50*
   site characteristics 111, 114
Ballycatteen (Co Cork) xvii
   E ware *41*, *50*, 87
   site characteristics 110
Ballyfounder (Co Down) xvii
   E ware *41*, 134
   site characteristics 112
Bantham (Devon) xvii
   pottery 11, 26, 31, 103
   site characteristics 121
   tin 129
Bar Point (Scilly) xvii
   E ware 42, *45*, 51
Barille-la-Rivière (France), white gritty ware 38

Barking Abbey (Essex) 63, 64
barrels 79
barter exchange 134–5
Bath (Som) 118
beach markets 121
bead making 5, 54, 81, 92
beads 52, 81–2, Pl 40
Beaufay (France) 76
Belo (Spain) 16
Benalúa (Spain) 16, 23
Benghazi (Libya) 6
Bersu, Gerhard 4
Bethu Brigte 51
Biglis (Glam) 88
Birka (Sweden) 81
Birsay (Orkney) xvii
   glass 62, 63–4, Pls 26–8
   site characteristics 116
   tessera 78
   trade system 135
Blaenau Morgannwg 134
Book of Armagh 79
Book of Durrow 116
Book of Kells 72, 116
books 129
Boon, George 75
Bordeaux (France) xvii
   coins 75, 76
   glass 58, 62, 65, 69, 72, 138
   pottery 27, 28, 30–1, 32, 41, 138
   trade 7, 136, 138
Bourke, Edward 7
Boyne valley/estuary 112, 114
Bradford-on-Avon (Wilts) 118
Brandon (Suffolk) 64
Brega 110, 111, 114, 123
Brittany 76, 129, 131
Bro Morgannwg 134
brooches 46
Brough of Birsay *see* Birsay
Bruach an Druimein (Argyll) xvii
   unclassified pottery 77
Brude, King 96
Bryher (Scilly) xvii
Bueil (France) 37
Buiston (Ayrs) xvii
   coin 76
   dyes 80
   glass 62, 63, 64, 73
   metalwork 135
   organic produce 81
   pottery 4, *41*, *44*, 45, Pls 10, 12, 16, 19
   site characteristics 116
burials 99, 100, 104
Burrow, Ian 12
Byzantium
   coinage 74, 75–6, 129–30
   diplomatic initiatives 1, 10, 131–2
Byzantium (*cont.*)
   imports *see* Mediterranean imports

ships 120–1
trade routes and mechanisms 127–32

Cabinteely (Dublin) xvii, 14, 45
Cadbury Castle (Som) xvii
  Anglo-Saxon burials/metalwork 119
  glass 61, 73
  pottery 5, 14, *15*, *29*, 31, 87
  site characteristics 109, 118, 122, 138
  structured deposition 8
  taphonomic study 12, 87, *103*
Cadbury Congresbury (Som) xvii
  buildings 104
  glass 56, 58, 61, 95, 135
  pottery 5, 12, 18, 23, 78, 86, 87
  site characteristics 118, 119, 122, 138
  structured deposition 8, 97, 98
Cádiz (Spain) 58
Caerwent (Gwent) 75
Cahercommaun (Co Clare) 46
Caherlihillan (Co Kerry) xvii, 112, 116
Caldey Island (Pembs) xvii
  pottery 11, 12
  site characteristics 15, 117–18, 119
Camel, River 122
Camerton (Som) 118
Cannington cemetery (Som) xvii
  coins 75
  glass 61
  site characteristics 118, 122, 123
Carew Castle (Pembs) xvii
  E ware 11, *36*, *50*
  site characteristics 117
cargoes 128–30
Carhampton (Som) xvii, 118
Carlingford Lough 114
Cartagena (Spain) 23
Carthage
  glass 58
  lead 129
  mint 75, 76
  pottery
    African Red Slipware 6, 17, 18
    amphorae 6, 18, 19, 23
    Phocaean Red Slipware 16
  reconquest 132
  trade 127
Cashel (Co Tipperary) xvii
Casteljaloux (France) 76
Castle Hill, Dalry (Ayrs) xvii
  glass 64, *68*
  metalwork 135
  site characteristics 116
castles 124
Cathair Fionnurach (Co Kerry) xvii
cave site 123
Cefn Cwmwd (Anglesey) xvii
  DSPA *29*
  intaglio 78
  site characteristics 117
cemeteries 122, 123
censer 78
Chadenac (France) xvii
  E ware *47*, 48
chapel sites 119, 122
Charentes (France) 48
Charlemagne 7
Cheddar (Som) 55

Chester (Ches) 126
Chios (Greece) 19
Christianity
  E ware, association with 119, 122
  symbols 14–16, 27, *29*, 132
  see also Church; monastic sites
Chun Castle (Cornwall) xvii, 122, 129
Church
  secular powers, association with 115, 116
  trade, association with 4, 7, 9, 79, 132, 137
  see also Christianity; monastic sites
Cilicia (Turkey) 19
Cirencester (Glos) 118, 126
Clann Cholmáin 114
Clatchard Craig (Fife) xvii, 45, 73, 116, 135
Clogher (Co Tyrone) xvii
  glass 61, 62, 63
  pottery 5, 31, *41*, 78, 87, 134
  site characteristics 109–10, 111, 112, 113–14, 138
Clonmacnoise (Co Offaly) xvii
  E ware *42*, 45
  site characteristics 114, 115, 116, 117
coin-weight 78
coins/coinage 74–5, 82, 141
  Roman 75
  Byzantine 74, 75–6, 129–30
  Merovingian 48, 76
  Anglo-Saxon 76
Cold Knap (Cardiff) 118
Colossus of Rhodes 130
Colp West (Co Meath) xvii, 114
Columba, St, *Vita* 48, 96, 137
Compiegne (France), white gritty ware *38*, 41
Congresbury (Som) 122; *see also* Cadbury Congresbury
Conimbriga (Portugal) 16, 58
Connaught (*Connachta*) 112
Constantinople 75, 78
Continental imports
  coins 76
  date ranges *139*
  distribution *133*
  glass
    non-vessel 81–2
    vessels *see* Group B *under* glass
  miscellaneous 78–9
  organic produce 80–1
  pottery *see* Class E ware; DSPA; late white gritty wares *under* pottery
  trading system 132–9
Coombe (Kent) 60
copper 4, 116, 117, 121, 130, 138
Corbeilles (France) 39
Corbie (France), white gritty ware *38*
coriander 81
County Down Survey 113
Coygan Camp (Carmarth) xvii
  Phocaean Red Slipware *15*
  site characteristics 117
Craig Phadraig (Inverness) xvii, 116, 135
Craigs Quarry (E Lothian) xviii, 11, 116
crannogs 109, 110, 111, 116, 123, 124
Crickley Hill (Glos) 118
Críth Gablach 80, 111
Cruach Mhor (Islay) xviii, 116
cullet 54, 55, 92–3, 94–5, 96, 101
Cyprus 19

Dagobert II 48, 80
Dál Fiatach (*Muirthemne*) 111, 112, 113, 114, 115
Dál nAraide 113, 115
Dál Riata 113, 114, 115, 116, 141
Dalkey Island (Dublin) xviii
  burial 100
  glass *59*, 61, 62
  pottery
    E ware 31, *36*, *41*, *45*, 46, *84–5*, 87, 90
    Late Roman Amphorae 26
    unclassified 78
  site characteristics 7, 109, 114, 119, 124, 126, 138
  structured deposition 97
dates 80
decorative glass 81, Pl 41
Deer Park Farms (Co Antrim) 111, 112, 115
defences 110, 111, 122, 123, 138
Deganwy (Caernarfon) xviii, 117, 123, 124, Pl 53
Derrynaflan (Co Tipperary) xviii, 116
Dial Rocks (Scilly) xviii
Diarmait mac Cerbaill 114
Dieppe (France), pottery 28, *47*
dill 81
Dinas Emrys (Caernarfon) xviii
  pottery
    DSPA 27, *29*
    E ware 11
    Late Roman Amphorae 19, *20*
    vessel-to-sherd ratio 87
  site characteristics 117, 123, 124
Dinas Powys (Glam) xviii
  beads 81
  buildings 83, 87, *88*, 91–2, 99, 101, Pl 43
  glass 55, 56
    decorative 81, 82, 95
    Group B *59*, 60, 61, 62, 73, 135, Pl 23
    Group C *54*, 64, *66*–7, 69, Pl 31
    Group D *70*
  glass working 92, 95–6, 99, 101
  gold working 111
  metalwork 140
  pottery
    African Red Slipware *17*, 18
    DSPA 11, 27, 28, *29–30*, 31–2, 135, Pl 7
    E ware 31, 37, *40*, *42*, 45, 134
    Late Roman Amphorae 20, *22*, *23*
    Mediterranean coarsewares 25
    Phocaean Red Slipware 5, 14, *15*, 16, Pl 1
  site characteristics 62, 117, 122, 123, 124, 138
  structured deposition 8, 97–8
  taphonomic study
    background and discussion 12, 83, 101
    glass 92–3; discussion 96; fused glass *95*, 96; horizontal distributions *94*, 95; methodology 93; sherd size *93*; vessel-to-sherd ratios 93–4
    methodology 83; horizontal distribution plans 83; maximum sherd size curves 83, *84–6*; vessel-to-sherd ratio *86*, 87
    phasing reinterpreted 96, *97*, *98*, 101
    pottery 87; African Red Slipware 88–9; DSPA 89, *90*, *91*; E ware *90*–1, 92; inter-relationship of imports *91*, 92; Late Roman Amphorae 89, *91*; Phocaean Red Slipware 88, *91*; samian 87–8, *91*
    social interpretation 97–9; areas of activity *99*; child burial 100; disposal patterns, structuring of 100–1; rubbish disposal, processes of 99–100

dipinti 23, 24
diplomatic exchange 1, 124, 136
  glass 61, 73, 135
  pottery 135
Docco (Cornwall) 122
Doherty, Charles 9–10
Dolphin Town (Scilly) xviii
Dooey (Co Donegal) xviii
  glass 62, 63, 65
  site characteristics 111, 112
Dor shipwreck 24
dorkona 128, 129
Downpatrick (Co Down) xviii
  site characteristics 110, 111, 112–13, 114, 134
Doyle, Ian 7
Drim (Pembs) 118
Droitwich (Worcs) 80
dromos 128
Drumacritten (Co Fermanagh) xviii, 61, 114
Dry Drayton (Cambs) 61
Dublin Bay 112
Dumbarton Rock (Dunbarton) xviii, Pl 48
  E ware 42–3, *45*, 87
  glass 63, *68*, 73
  gold working 111
  site characteristics 112, 116, 123, 138
Dun Ardtreck (Skye) xviii, 8, 116
Dunadd (Argyll) xviii, Pl 44
  bead 81
  ceramic technology 51
  dyes 80, 116, 137
  enamelled disc 78
  glass 64, 73, 82, 135, Pl 29
  metalwork 79, 116, 140
  plant remains 120
  pottery
    DSPA 28, *30*, 31, Pl 8
    E ware 31, *37*, 39, *41–3*, 45, 49, *50*, *85*, Pls 9, 11, 13, 15, 17–18
    previous research 4
    unclassified 76, 77
  site characteristics 116–17, 123; agricultural land 109; trade 112, 133–4, 138, 139; weaponry 111
  tessera 78, 137, Pl 39
Dunamase (Co Laoise) 76
Dundalk (Co Louth) 114
Dundonald Castle (Ayrs) xviii, 116
  E ware *40*
Dundurn (Perths) xviii
  glass 63, 64, 73, 135
  pottery 78
  site characteristics 116
Duneight (Co Down) 111
Dungarvan Castle (Co Waterford) xviii
Dunmisk (Co Tyrone) 81, 82, 92
Dunnyneill Island (Co Down) xviii
  glass
    decorative 81
    Group A *57*, 136
    Group B *59*, 60–1, 63, Pl 25
  site characteristics 51, 109, 113, 114, 119, 124
Dunollie (Argyll) xviii, Pl 47
  E ware 5, *41*
  site characteristics 116
duns 116, 123
dyes 80, 82, 124, 137, 138; *see also* madder; orpiment
Dyrham, battle of 118, 119

Ederline (Argyll) xviii
Egypt 19, 25, 58; *see also* Alexandria
Eilne 113, 115
Eketorp (Sweden) 94, 96
Elie (Fife) xviii, 116
Ely villa (Cardiff) 100
emporia 7, 52, 119–20
enamelled disc 78
enclosures 123
Eóganacht kings 111
Eprave (France), white gritty ware *38*
Ergyng, kingdom of 100
Ethelbert, king of Kent 61
Evison, V 55
Evreux (France) 37
exchange *see* trade and exchange
Exeter (Devon) 22, 75, 125, 126, 138

Faversham (Kent) 61
feasting 114, 124, 134–5
   Cadbury Castle 103
   Dinas Powys 89, 91, 101
feathers 80, 129, 137
figs 81
Filibert, St, *Vita* 48, 136
Firth of Clyde 112
fish sauce (*garum*) 23
flooring material 99
forts 110, 111, 116, 123, 124, 134; *see also* hillforts
Frisian merchants 4
fruits 23, 80, 81
Fulford, Michael 6, 17, 19
furs 129, 137

Galicia 131
garnets 137
Garranes (Co Cork) xviii
   glass 61, 62, 81, 82
   pottery 26, *40*, *50*
   site characteristics 62, 109, 110, 111, 124, 138
Garryduff No. 1 (Co Cork) xviii
   glass working 92
   pottery 14, 31, *41*, *50*, 87
   site characteristics 109, 110
Gateholm (Pembs) 11
Gaza 19, 22, 24, 25, 127
gift exchange 134, 135, 136, 140
   Ireland 9, 110, 114–15, 124
   Scotland 116, 117, 124
Gironde (France) 76
glass
   classification 2–3, 54
   description
      Group A 56, *57*, 58, Pl 21
      Group B 56, *59*, 60
         blue globular beakers 61, Pl 23; blue vessels, other 61–2; claw beakers 60–1, Pls 22, 25; distribution *73*; Kempston-type beakers 61; late vessels in deep colours 63–4, Pls 26–9; palm cups/funnel beakers 62, Pl 30; phials and flasklets 62–3, Pl 24
      Group C 56, 64, Pl 36
         bichrome vessels 65, Pls 33–4; bowls 64–5; chronology 68–9; cone beakers *54*, 64, Pls 31–2; decoration of cones and bowls 65, *66–8*, Pls 31, 35; distribution *69*; taphonomy 69
      Group D 56, 69, *70*
      Group E *54*, 56, 69–70, *71*, 72, Pl 37

   discussion 54–6, 73
   distribution 54, *55*
   forms and function 72–3
   methodology 7–8, 11, 12
   previous research 4–5, 7
   trading system 135–8
   see also beads; decorative glass; glass making/working; taphonomic studies
glass making/working
   Dinas Powys 92–3, 95–6, 99, 101
   Dunadd 82
   Dunmisk 81, 82, 92
   Ireland 92
   Whithorn 69, 72, 73
   see also bead making; cullet
Glastonbury (Som) 78, 122
Glastonbury Mound (Som) xviii, 118
Glastonbury Tor (Som) xviii, 5, 104, 118, 122
Gloucester (Glos) xviii, 125, 126
Gododdin 52, 89, 96
gold/gold working 4, 111, 116, 117
Goodrich Castle (Herefs) xviii
Goodwick (Pembs) 118
Gracedieu (Dublin) xviii, 114
graffiti 20, 22, 23, 24, Pls 4–5
Grambla (Cornwall) xviii
   Phocaean Red Slipware *15*
   site characteristics 122
Gransha (Co Down) xviii
   E ware 46, *50*
   excavations 109
   glass 82
Gregory of Tours 136
Grotte de Villebois-Lavalette (France) 48
Guisseny (France) xviii
   E ware *47*, 48
Gwithian (Cornwall) xviii
   pottery 4, 5, 31, *40*, 87, 121
   site characteristics 121
   weight 121

Halliggye (Cornwall) xviii
Ham Hill (Som) xviii, 118, 123
Hamwic (Hants)
   coins 75–6
   emporium, interpretation as 7, 139
   glass 55–6, 92, 93, 96
      Group B 62
      Group C 64, 65
   pottery 39, 76–7, 136–7
Harden, D B 5, 55, 56
Harley Psalter 72
Hayes, John 5–6, 14
Helford estuary 122
Helgö (Sweden) 81
Hellesvean (Cornwall) xviii
Hen Gastell (Glamorgan) xviii, Pl 54
   glass 61, 62
   pottery 11, 27, *29–30*, 135
   site characteristics 62, 117, 123
Hencken, H 4
Herodotus 131
Herpes (France) xviii
   E ware *47*, 48
High Peak (Devon) xviii, 122
hillforts 110, 117, 118, 119, 121–2, 123
Hodges, Richard 6–7, 10
Holme Pierrepont (Notts) 58

holy water/oil 63, 74
honey 52, 80, 124
horns 80
hunting dogs 4
Hywel Dda 111

Ilchester (Som) 75, 119
industrial activity, associated with E ware 50, 51
Iniscealtra (Co Clare) xviii, 115, 116
inscriptions
    glass 56, Pl 21
    stone 78, 117, 138
intaglio 78
Iona (Argyll) xviii, Pl 49
    glass 63, 81
    manuscript production 117
    pottery
        African Red Slipware 26, 137
        E ware 40, 49, 50, 117, 137, Pl 14
    site characteristics 116, 117
Ipswich (Suffolk) 139
Ireland, patterns of distribution 9–10, 109–10
    discussion 115–16
    glass 63, 135
    historical context 114
    import site characteristics 110–11
    political geography 112, *113*, 114
    previous research 7
    Roman *126*, 138
    social factors 114–15
    trading routes *10*, 111, *112*
iron 80
Isle of Man 116
Islip (Northants) 60

Jarrow (S Tyne) 3
jewellery making 140
    Dunadd 116, 117
    Ireland 110, 111
    Wales and England 5, 122
John the Almsgiver, St, *Vita* 6, 76, 128, 131
Justin I 75
Justinian 6, 75, 76, 130, 131, 132

Karanis (Egypt) 58
Kaupang (Norway) 81
Keay, Simon 6
Kedrah (Co Tipperary) xviii
The Kelsies (Cornwall) xviii, 121
Kenfig (Glam) 118
Kent, kingdom of 61, 135
Kilbride (Co Cavan) xviii
Kildalloig Dun (Argyll) xviii
    E ware 50, 134
    rubbish disposal 108
    site characteristics 116
Killederdadrum (Co Tipperary) xix
Killibury (Cornwall) xix, 122
Killucan (Co Westmeath) xix, 45, 114
kingdoms and regions *1*, 13
    England 118–19, 131
    Ireland 112, *113*, 114, 132, 134
    Scotland 116
    Wales 122, 132, 134
Kiondroghad (Isle of Man) xix, 116
Knowth (Co Meath) xix, 110, 111, 114, 123
Kos (Greece) 19

Lagore (Co Meath) xix
    barrels 79
    E ware 31, *41*, *42*, 45, *50*
    glass
        Group B *59*, 62, 63, 79
        millefiori rods 81, 82
    glass working 92
    metalwork 78–9
    site characteristics 109–10, 111, 114, 123, 124, 138
Laing, L 6, 52
Lament for Cynddlan 99
lamps 49, 73
Langford Lodge (Co Antrim) xix, 112
lapis lazuli 80
Lavret (France) xix
Le Mans (France) 76
Le Yaudet (France) xix, 48
lead 118, 129, 130, 138
leather 4, 80, 117, 124, 129, 137; *see also* shoes
Leinster (*Laigin*) 111, 112, 114
Les Cléons (France) xix
    E ware *47*, 48
Lesser Garth (Mid Glam) xix
    E ware *37*, 134
    site characteristics 117
Lezoux (France) 28
Linney Burrows (Pembs) xix, 118
Lisdoo (Co Fermanagh) xix, 114
Lisduggan North No. 1 (Co Cork) xix
Lisleagh 1 (Co Cork) xix, 109
literacy 117
Little Dunagoil (Bute) xix, Pl 50
    glass 61–2
    late white gritty ware 52, *53*
    site characteristics 116, 123
Little Hoyle Cave (Pembs) 104
Llancarfan (Vale of Glam) 11
Llandaff charters 100
Llandough (Glam) xix, 117, 122
Llanelen (W Glam) xix, 63, 117
Llangorse (Powys) 12
Llantwit Major (Vale of Glam) 11
Loch Ederline (Argyll) 116
Loch Gara crannog (Co Sligo) 96
Loch Glashan (Argyll) xix, Pl 46
    bead 81, 117, Pl 40
    book satchel 117
    dyes 116, 134
    E ware 31, 39, *40*, 46, 49, *50*, 53, Pl 20
        sherd size curve *85*
        vessel-to-sherd ratio 87
    site characteristics 116, 117
    taphonomic study 12, *85*, 87, 105, 140
Lochlee (Ayrs) xix
    pottery *41*, 52, *53*
    site characteristics 116
Loígis, kings of 76
London 19, 125, 139
Longbury Bank (Pembs) xix
    buildings 104
    excavation 12
    glass 63, 64–5, *67–8*
    pottery *15*, *29*, 31, *37*, 87
    silver offcut 78
    site characteristics 117, 124
    taphonomic study 12, 103–4
Looe Island (Cornwall) xix, 122
Lough Faughan (Co Down) xix, 79, 109, 112

Lough Foyle 110, 112, 114
Loughshinny (Dublin) xix, 26, 114
Luce Sands (Dum & Gall) xix, 11, 81, 116
Lusk (Dublin) xix, 114
Lydford (Devon) xix, 122

madder 48, 49, 80, 116, 134, 137
malachite 80
Málaga (Spain) 58
Mane-Geren (France), E ware 47
Marculf's *Formulatory* 80–1
Margam (W Glam) xix, 11, 12, 117
Marseille (France) 14, 23, 62
Marshes Upper No. 3 (Co Louth) xix
Maurice Tiberius 75
Mawgan Porth (Cornwall) xix, 122
May's Hill (Scilly) xix
    pottery 28, *37*
    site characteristics 119
Meath (*Mide*) 112, 114
medicines 129
Mediterranean imports
    ampullae 74, 75, Pl 38
    coins 75–6
    date ranges *139*
    distribution *133*
    glass
        non-vessel 81
        vessels *see* glass, Group A
    miscellaneous 78
    pottery *see* African Red Slipware; Late Roman Amphorae; Mediterranean coarsewares; Mediterranean 'packages'; Phocaean Red Slipware *under* pottery
    trading system 126–32, 138
Menas, St 74
Mendips 118, 119, 130, 138
Meols (Wirral) xix
    ampulla 74, 75, Pl 38
    coins 74, 75, 76
    trade 74, 112
merchants 131–2, 134, 136, 138
Mercia, kingdom of 73
Merey (France), pottery 37, *38*
Merida (Spain) 131
Merovingian imports 48, 76, 79
Merovingian pottery *see under* pottery
middens 104, 108, 121, 122
millefiori rods 81–2, 95
Minchin Hole (W Glam) 118
monastic sites 123, 124, 132
    England and Wales 117–18, 120, 122
    Ireland 9, 111, 115–16
    Scotland 116, 117
Moreton (Wirral) 75, 76
mosaics 78
Mote of Mark (Dum & Gall) xix, Pl 51
    glass 56, 96
        Group B *59*, 62, 63, 73
        Group C 64, 65, *66–7*, Pls 32, 35
        plaque 81, Pls 41–2
    industrial activity 50
    metalwork 140
    pottery 4
        DSPA *30*, 31
        E ware 31, *41*, *42*, *43*, *45*, 50
        unclassified *77*
    site characteristics 116, 123

tessera 78
Mothecombe (Devon) xix, 121, 129
Movilla Abbey (Co Down) 81
Moylough belt-shrine 79
Moynagh Lough (Co Meath) xix
    glass *59*, 62, 96
    site characteristics 109, 111, 114
Muids (France) 37
Muirbretha 79, 80, 81, 115
Mull of Kintyre 112
Mullaroe (Co Sligo) xix
    glass *59*, 62, 63, 96, Pl 24
Munster 111

Nantes (France) 30, 31, 48
Nendrum (Co Down) xix, 115–16
Neustria 137, 140
New Pieces (Montgom) xix
    DSPA *29*
    site characteristics 109, 117
Newgrange (Co Meath) 75, 126
Newtonlow Crannog (Co Westmeath) xix
Noirmoutier (France) 31, 48, 136
Northampton (Northants) 55
Northumbria, kingdom of 73, 76
nuts 23, 52, 80, 81, 124

object cultural biographies 9
O'Donnell, Mary 7
oenach 9, 115
olive oil 4, 19, 23, 24, 128
olives 23, 81
organic produce 80–1
Orléans (France) 30, 76
orpiment 80, 116–17, 137

Padstow (Cornwall) xix, 122
Pagans Hill (Som) xix, 61, 63, 73, 119
Palestinian amphorae 6, 19, 22, 25, 127
Pant-y-Saer (Anglesey) 46, 118
Paris (France), St-Denis 48, 65, 80, 117
Paris basin 32
Parrett, River 118
Patrick, St 4, 126
Peacock, David 5, 17, 32
pearls 137
Penmachno (Gwynedd) 78
Penselwood (Som) 118
perfume 63
Perran Sands (Cornwall) xix, 122
petrological studies 6, 25, 28, 32
pewter 118, 126
Phillack (Cornwall) xix, 14, 122
Phocaea 5, 14, 19
Picts 116
pilgrims 26, 76, 82, 137; *see also ampullae*
plague 132
plaque, glass 81, Pls 41–2
Poitiers (France) 28, 48, 49, 52–3
Poitou (France) 48
political geography *see* kingdoms and regions
porridge 7
Port y Candas (Isle of Man) xix
    E ware *41*, 49
    site characteristics 116
Porthellick (Scilly) 76
Portlaoise (Co Laois) xix, 76
Portmahomack (Ross) 117

pottery
  African Red Slipware
    associations 25
    distribution *18*
    trading system 127–8, 137, 138
    typology 16, *17*, 18, Pl 2
  DSPA
    chronology 27–8
    distribution *27*, 31–2, 135
    provenance 28–31
    trading system 133, 135, 138
    typology 27, *29–30*, Pls 7–8
  E ware 32
    chronology 44–6
    distribution 44, *46*, 133, *134*, 135
      Ulster *113*, 115
    function 49–52
    production 32–4
    provenance 46–9
    trading system 132–3, *134*, 135, 136–9
    typology *33*, 34–5, *36–8*, 39, *40–4*, *45*, *47*, Pls 9–20
  Late Roman Amphorae
    associations 25–6
    contents 23–4
    distribution *22*
    trading system 127–9, 130–1, 132, 138
    typology 18–19, *20–3*, 24, Pls 3–6
  late white gritty wares 52, *53*
  Mediterranean coarsewares 24–5
    distribution *25*
  Mediterranean 'packages' 25–6
  Merovingian 32, 34, 36–7, *38*, 39, 41, 43, 48
  methodology 7–8, 11–12
  Phocaean Red Slipware
    associations 25–6
    distribution *16*
    trading system 127–8, 131, 132, 138
    typology 14, *15*, 16, Pl 1
  previous research 4, 5–6, 7
  Roman 125–6
  Saintonge ware 48, 79, 138
  souterrain ware *113*, 115
  unclassified 76, 77, 78, 82
  see also petrological studies; taphonomic studies
Poundbury (Dorset) 3
Praa sands (Cornwall) 129
Preston on the Hill (Ches) 74
Princetown (Devon) 75
Prittlewell (Essex) 61
Procopius 131
prunes 138

quartz 137
Quentovic (France) 80

Radford, C A R 4, 102, 120
raisins 81
Raith Airthir (Oristown) 114
Raithliu 111
Randalstown (Co Meath) xx, 114
Rathgureen (Co Galway) xx, 112
Rathintaun crannog 61 (Co Sligo) xx, 62, 63
Rathlin Island 112
Rathmullan (Co Down) xx, 112
raths 109, 113, 115
Ravenna (Italy) 78
Reask (Co Kerry) xx, 116
Reawla (Cornwall) xx

research project
  aims 1–3
  data, approaches to 7–10
  methodology and structure 11–13
  previous research 4–7
  scope and terminology 3–4
resin linings 24
reticella rods 63, 65, 82, Pl 26
Rhenen (Neths), white gritty ware *38*
Rhineland 46, 61, 62
Rhodes (Greece) 19
Ribe (Denmark) 81, 94
Rigoir, J and Y 5
Rijnsburg (Neths), white gritty ware *38*
Riley, John 6, 18–19
ring-ornament 79
Rome (Italy) 23
Rouen (France) 32, 48, 80
Rouillé (France) 49
royal sites 62, 96, 140
  Cornwall 120, 122, 124, 138
  Ireland 110–11, 112, 113, 114, 123, 124, 138
  Scotland 116–17, 124, 138
  Somerset 118, 122, 124, 138
  Wales 117, 122, 124, 138
rubbish disposal 8–9
  Cadbury Castle 103
  Dinas Powys 98, 99–101, 108
    glass 96
    pottery 88, 89, 91, 92
  Kildalloig Dun 108
  Loch Glashan 105
  Longbury Bank 104
  Tintagel 102–3
  Trethurgy 104, 108
  Whithorn 106, 108

St Albans (Herts) 140
St Gervais B wreck 128
St Merryn (Cornwall) xx
St Michael Caerhays (Cornwall) xx, 122
St Michael's Mount (Cornwall) xx, 122
St Pierre-du-Vauvray (France), white gritty ware 37, *38*
Saint-Laurent-des-Combes (France) xx
Saintes (France) 48
salt 80, 82, 136, 138
Samson (Scilly) xx
  E ware 31, *36*, 37, *41*, *42*, 43, *45*
  site characteristics 119
Samson of Dol, St, *Vita* 122
Sardis (Turkey) 19
Sarthe (France) 48
Schiffer, M B 8
Scilly
  site chacteristics 119–20
  trading function 51, 111, 121, 124, 128, 134
Scotland, patterns of distribution 116–17
Scots 116
Scotti 3
Scrabo Hill (Co Down) xx
  E ware *44*, 45
  site characteristics 110, 112, 134
scramasax 78–9
Shannon estuary 112
shield-bosses 79
shipping 10
ships 120–1, 128
shoes 136

Síl nAedo Sláine 114
silk 129
silver
   England 118, 121, 130, 138
   Ireland 111, 141
   Scotland 116, 117
   Wales 141
silver offcut 78
sites
   characteristics 109, 123–4
     Cornwall and Devon 119–22
     Ireland 109–16
     Scotland 116–17
     Somerset 118–19
     Wales and the Marches 117–18, 122
   listed xvii–xx
   locations *2*, *3*
slaves 4, 13, 100, 124, 129, 131, 137
Slievegrane Lower (Co Down) xx
Smithstown (Co Meath) xx, 114
Soissons (France), white gritty ware *38*
Sommer, Ülrike 8
Sommery (France), white gritty ware *38*
sooting, E ware 49, 51, 134, Pl 16
South Cadbury *see* Cadbury Castle
south Glamorgan, kingdom 122, 134
spices 80, 81, 124, 129
spindle whorls 87, 101
Spittal Ballee (Co Down) xx, 112, 134
Strabo 4
Straits of Gibraltar 127
Strangford Lough 112, 136
Stranraer (Dum & Gall) 52
structured deposition 8, 97–8, 100
studs, glass 92
Sudbrook (Mon) 11
Sutton Hoo (Suffolk) 78, 81
Swords (Dublin) xx
Syria 131, 136

taphonomic studies 8–9, 12, 102, 108
   Cadbury Castle *103*
   Dinas Powys, *see under* Dinas Powys
   Loch Glashan 105, 140
   Longbury Bank 103–4
   Tintagel *102*, 103
   Trethurgy 104–5
   Whithorn 106–8
Taplow (Bucks) 61
Tarbat (Easter Ross) xx, 135
Tattershall Thorpe (Lincs) 96
Taunton (Som) xx, 78
Tean (Scilly) xx
   belt-fitting 79
   E ware 31, *42*, 45
   site characteristics 119
Teeshan (Co Antrim) xx
   dye 80
   E ware *36*
   site characteristics 113
tesserae 78, 94, 137, Pl 39
Therouanne (France), white gritty ware *38*
Thomas, Charles 4, 5, 19, 24, 32, 34, 119
Thorpe, C 24
tin
   extraction 76, 126, 129–30, 131
   ingots 121, 129
   smelting 122

trade 4, 122, 129, 131, 132, 138
use of, Dunadd 116
Tintagel (Cornwall) xx, Pl 55
   glass
     Group A 56, *57*, 58
     Group B 63, 135–6
   harbour 120–1, 128, Pl 56
   metalwork 79
   plant remains 120
   pottery 26
     African Red Slipware *17*, 18
     amphorae stoppers 23
     classification 4, 32
     DSPA *29–30*, 31
     Late Roman Amphorae 19, *20*, 22–3, 24
     Mediterranean coarsewares 24–5
     Phocaean Red Slipware 14, *15*, 16
     site characteristics 120–1, 122, 124, 132, 138
   taphonomic study 12, *102*, 103
Tours (France) xx
   pottery 28, *47*, 48, 52
Tourville-la-Rivière (France), white gritty ware *38*
trade and exchange
   discussion by region
     Cornwall and Devon 119–20, 121–2
     Ireland: historical context 114; routes 111, *112*;
       social factors 114–15
     Scotland 116–17
     Somerset 118
     Wales 117–18
   mechanisms of 125
     changing systems 138–9
     Continental trading system 132–3; distribution of
       E ware *133–4*, 135; distribution mechanisms
       136–8; DSPA 135; glass 135–6
     Mediterranean trading system 126–7; cargoes
       128–30; distribution of goods *133*; Mediterra-
       nean 'packages' 25–6; new model 132; routes
       127–8; scale of trade 130–1; ships 128; traders
       131–2
   previous research 4, 6–7, 9, 10
   Roman background *125*, 126
   routes *10*, 127–8
     glass 64, *73*
     to Ireland 111, *112*
     pottery *125*
   trading sites
     defined 51–2, 123–4, 138
     Ireland 51, 109, 114
     Scilly 51, 119–20, 121, 122, 134
     Wales 117–18
     Whithorn 117, 124, 134
   see also merchants
tramping voyages 10, 128, 137
Trethurgy (Cornwall) xx
   glass 56, 58
   pottery 22, 26, *41*
   site characteristics 121, 122, 129
   structured deposition 8, 97, 98
   taphonomic study 104–5, 108
   tin 121, 129
   weight 121
tribute 9, 117
Trim (Co Meath) xx, 76
Ty Mawr (Powys) 118

Uí Eachach 111
Uí Echach Cobo 113, 115

Uí Néill 114
Uisneach 114
Ulaid 111, 113
Uley (Glos) 118
Ulster 112, *113*, 114, 115, 126
Upper Marshes (Co Louth) 113
urbanism 1, 9

Valencia (Co Kerry) 112
Vandals 6, 75
Vendée (France) 48
Vendel (Sweden) 61
Vesuvius (Italy) 80
Vienne (France) 138
Villebois-Lavalette (France) xx
vinegar 138

Wailes, Bernard 5, 32
Wales 117–18
Warner, Richard 5
weaponry 110, 111, 138
Wenlock Priory (Shrops) xx, 117
Wheeler, Sir R E M 4
Whithorn (Dum & Gall) xx, Pl 52
   Anglo-Saxon control 3
   glass 2–3, 56, 73, 95, 135
      Group A 56, *57*, 58, 136, Pl 21
      Group B *59*, 60, 61, 62, 63, 73, Pl 30
      Group C 65, *66–8*, 69, 73, Pls 33–4, 36
      Group D 69, *70*, 73
      Group E *54*, 65, 69–70, *71*, 72, 73, Pl 37
   glass working 69, 72, 73
   metalwork 135

metalworking 117
organic produce 81
pottery
   African Red Slipware 18, 26, Pl 2
   DSPA *29*, 31
   E ware 31, 39, 41, *42*, 45, 46, *50*, 134
   Late Roman Amphorae 23, Pls 4–6
   methodology 12
   unclassified 77–8
tesserae 78
site characteristics 116, 117, 124, 134, 138, 140
taphonomic study 12, 106–8
Williams, David 6
window glass 63
wine trade 124, 136
   Bordeaux 7
   church, association with 4, 7, 9, 122, 132
   containers 4, 23, 24, 79, 129, 132
   E ware, association with 52, 79, 80, 138
Winklebury Camp (Hants) 85–6
Wooding, Jonathan 7, 10
Wroxeter (Shrops) 81, 102

Yassi Ada
   amphorae 6, 19, 24, 26, 128, 131
   cargo value 129
   graffiti 22
   Phocaean Red Slipware 16, 128
Yeavering (Northumb) 54
Yeo, River 118
York (Yorks) 19, 63, 64, 125, 126

Zimmer, H 7, 10, 79